UNVEILING DESIRE

UNVEILING DESIRE

Fallen Women in Literature, Culture, and Films of the East

EDITED BY
DEVALEENA DAS AND COLETTE MORROW

RUTGERS UNIVERSITY PRESS
New Brunswick, Camden, and Newark, New Jersey, and London

Library of Congress Cataloging-in-Publication Data

Names: Das, Devaleena. | Morrow, Colette.
Title: Unveiling desire : fallen women in literature, culture, and films of the east / edited by Devaleena Das, Colette Morrow ; foreword by Nawal El-Saadawi ; contributions by Devaleena Das ; contributions by Colette Morrow ; contributions by Firdous Azim ; contributions by Paramita Halder ; contributions by Hafiza Nilofar Khan ; contributions by Amrit Gangar ; contributions by Naina Dey ; contributions by Louis Betty ; contributions by Lavinia Benedetti ; contributions by Tomoko Kuribayashi ; contributions by Meenakshi Malhotra ; contributions by Chandrani Biswas ; contributions by Radha Chakravarty ; contributions by Feroza Jussawalla ; contributions by Kuhu Sharma Chanana.
Description: New Brunswick, Camden : Rutgers University Press, 2018. | Includes bibliographical references and index.
Identifiers: LCCN 2017012773 (print) | LCCN 2017050281 (ebook) | ISBN 9780813587868 (E-pub) | ISBN 9780813587875 (Web PDF) | ISBN 9780813587851 (hardback) | ISBN 9780813587844 (paperback)
Subjects: LCSH: Women—Sexual behavior—Orient. | Femmes fatale—Orient. | Symbolism—Orient. | BISAC: SOCIAL SCIENCE / Women's Studies. | PERFORMING ARTS / Film & Video / History & Criticism. | LITERARY CRITICISM / Asian / General. | LITERARY CRITICISM / Middle Eastern.
Classification: LCC HQ29 (ebook) | LCC HQ29 .U58 2018 (print) | DDC 306.7082095—dc23
LC record available at https://lccn.loc.gov/2017012773

A British Cataloging-in-Publication record for this book is available from the British Library.

∞ The paper used in this publication meets the requirements of the American National Standard for Information Sciences—Permanence of Paper for Printed Library Materials, ANSI Z39.48-1992.

www.rutgersuniversitypress.org

Manufactured in the United States of America

We dedicate this book to the transgressive women—past and present—who made it possible and the feminist men who supported its creation, development, and publication.

CONTENTS

FOREWORD

Unveiling Desire: Fallen Women in Literature, Culture, and Films of the East offers new perspectives of different characters of women and various female professions imposed on them by the patriarchal, classist, religious, racist system. This system is universal, not Eastern or Western, not Islamic or Christian or other. It is inherited from the old slave period in history and survives until today, the neopostmodern slave capitalist patriarchal system. Women and slaves were and are used by their masters: physically, spiritually, sexually, economically, socially, morally, and religiously.

Women and slaves never submitted to this multiple oppression and exploitation. The so-called sexual prostitution was and is a profession created by the system to satisfy the sexual needs of the hypersexual male. But only women are punished or condemned like their Mother Eve; the hypersexuality of men is accepted or even praised.

The book offers a new discourse to undo these injustices and double standards, to liberate the so-called hypersexually erotic, hysterical, rebellious woman from the prison of patriarchy, religion, and politics. To undo the major taboos inherited since slavery, to show the power of women in their struggle and resistance, this book offers a model for transnational feminist research that promotes equality, justice, freedom, and dignity for all and encourages women to resist old-slave-colonial and neocolonial sexual and cultural constructs.

It is an illuminating book, and I hope many women and men read it in the East and in the West as well.

Nawal El-Saadawi
Cairo, Egypt
July 26, 2015

UNVEILING DESIRE

INTRODUCTION

DEVALEENA DAS AND COLETTE MORROW

> We Were Artists . . . Not *Gandi Kanjri* [dirty entertainers]
>
> —Louise Brown, *The Dancing Girls of Lahore*

> She was no longer as beautiful as she'd once been. Her skin was waxy looking, and her features puffy. Or perhaps I was only seeing her that way. A tree may look as beautiful as ever; but when you notice the insects infesting it, and the tips of the branches that are brown from disease, even the trunk seems to lose some of its magnificence.
>
> —Arthur Golden, *Memoirs of a Geisha*

> I now knew that all of us were prostitutes who sold themselves at varying prices, and that an expensive prostitute was better than a cheap one.
>
> —Nawal El-Saadawi, *Woman at Point Zero*

When women's performance of sexuality crosses normative boundaries, it is the object of patriarchal fear and fascination. The trope of female fallenness puts women back "in their place": they are virgins and chaste wives and mothers if they obey the rules, but whores and outcasts if they transgress. Of course, local contexts determine specific expressions of this binary not only with respect to fixed conditions, such as received traditions and histories, but also in relation to dynamic processes in which individuals and social institutions employ the virgin/whore opposition to warrant and pursue diverse agendas. *Unveiling Desire* explores the fallen woman trope and the virgin/whore dichotomy in cultural and artistic production of the East, looking for commonalities and differences that enhance our understanding of how it maintains and changes sexual politics, the principles and processes that structure gender relations and distribute power among these formations, locally and globally. This exploration is undertaken with a mindfulness that, in addition to the trope's intracultural functions and meanings, the West has utilized and continues to deploy female fallenness to colonize the East, particularly in the Orientalist construction of the West as a superior male Self in relation to an Eastern Other figured as female, fecund, irrational, emasculated, and sexually transgressive, with all these labels signifying "uncivilized," "inferior," and in need of rescue and governance. *Unveiling Desire* deconstructs this cluster of colonizing oppositions, whether their focus is the female body and women's sexuality or they are manifest as Orientalism. In so doing, the book counters Orientalism in Western feminism—stereotyping and objectifying Eastern women's oppression and imposing foreign solutions to it—which is ongoing despite some Western practitioners' recognition of the problem and their attempts to resist it. Thus *Unveiling Desire* contributes to developing feminist transnational, anti-imperialist conversations about literature, film, cultural production, and critical theory that are mediated not by imperialist asymmetries but, as scholars such as Lila Abu-Lughod, Joan Scott, Sara Mills, Ella Shohat, and Robert Stam advocate, by acknowledging women's common suffering and embracing our sexuality in order to fashion mutually beneficial, equitable partnerships, alliances, coalitions, and collaborations.

ORIENTALISM AND SEXUALITY

Claiming and transvaluing misogynist epithets that vilify feminine sexuality has proven an effective strategy for empowering women and fostering feminist social change in the late twentieth and early twenty-first centuries, as terms such as *randi* (slut), bitch, *daayan* (witch), dyke, queer, *churel* (hag), and tranny have become badges of honor for many, signifying resistance to patriarchal regulation of women's sexuality. This tactic of recuperating unruly feminine sexuality has led, in practical application, to legislation that, for instance, criminalizes so-called date and marital rape and sets definitions of consensual sex that demand full, mutual, uncoerced, continuing assent among partners ("yes-means-yes"), as well as unprecedented mass protests against women's sexual abuse and secondary victimization of survivors, such as demonstrations following the death of a young woman (identified only as Nirbhaya, or "fearless") who was gang raped in Delhi in 2012, which drew thousands of men and women.

But for many Western feminists and in a great deal of scholarship, the process of recovering women's sexuality stops far short of the global, too often leaving intact views of Eastern women that are as inaccurate, monolithic, dismissive, colonizing, and patriarchal as the "homegrown" sexism that they face. One of these stereotypes comes directly from colonial-era Orientalism that depicts Eastern women as mysterious, tantalizingly veiled, erotic figures whose life purpose is pleasuring men in the sexual free-for-all of the harem. Another stereotype, often imbricated in Islamophobia, has become more prominent in the post-9/11 era. It stipulates that Eastern women are docile, submit passively to their extraordinarily authoritarian, male "masters," and need to be rescued from this oppression, an Orientalist commonplace that has accrued a troubling (anti)feminist bent as it is cited to justify all sorts of Western interventions ranging from the Iraq War (President George W. Bush said it would liberate women) to Code Pink's implicit endorsement of Imran Khan's 2012 run for the presidency of Pakistan when the group's members joined his country-wide march against US drone bombings.

Orientalism, Edward Said argues in his 1978 book of the same name, is a Western construction of the East that congealed during and served Europe's colonial expansion. Said's claim that the Western sense of superiority and the doctrine that Easterners are the "white man's burden" gave birth to polarities or stereotypes that misrepresent both East and West, but he writes scantily and ambiguously about the effects of Orientalism on women because he is preoccupied with developing a critique of the East's "feminization," constructions of the East as an emasculated entity that needs saving from its own inferiority and weakness. Notably, in objecting to such feminization as irrational, Said ignores how it plays out in relation to Eastern women, although colonialists routinely appropriated women's issues to configure and maintain the power imbalance between them and colonized populations.

Since *Orientalism*'s publication, numerous postcolonial, feminist-transnational scholars have interrogated these scholars' silences about gender. As Gayatri Chakravorty Spivak's 1993 essay "Can the Subaltern Speak?" famously observed in her discussion of *sati*, "The abolition of this rite by the British has been generally understood as a case of 'White men saving brown women from brown men.' White women—from the nineteenth century British Missionary Registers to Mary Daly—have not produced an alternative understanding. Against this is the Indian nativist argument, a parody of the nostalgia for the lost origins: 'The women actually wanted to die.' The two sentences go a long way to legitimize each other. One never encounters the testimony of the women's voice-consciousness" (*Colonial Discourse* 93). In this critique, Spivak underscores that Eastern "women's voice consciousness" was missing from discussions of Orientalism—whether their focus was European imperialism, resistance to it, or other nodes of inquiry.

In a similar vein, Islamic feminist and Egyptian-American writer Leila Ahmed tackled a parallel exclusion of Eastern women from US discourses, ranging from feminist scholarship to international studies, including the "vernacular" of the public sphere. By her own account, in 1980, early in her sojourn in the United States, Ahmed protested the assertions of a panel of Arab women at the National Women's Studies Association who presented a "rosy pictures of women in Islam," but by 1982, in her essay "Western Ethnocentrism and Perception of the Harem," she explains that after two years in the United States, she understood the women's stance: "American women 'know' that Muslim women are overwhelmingly oppressed without being able to define the specific content of that oppression, in the same way that they 'know' that Muslims—Arabs, Iranians, or whatever—are ignorant, backward, irrational, and uncivilized. These are 'facts' manufactured in Western culture, by the same men who have also littered the culture with 'facts' about Western women and how inferior and irrational they are" (523). What stands out here, at least with respect to "feminist" scholarship, is that it replicates patriarchalism by failing or refusing to admit Eastern women's voices into discussion.

Joyce Zonana was the first to name this phenomenon "feminist Orientalism" in her 1993 essay "The Sultan and the Slave: Feminist Orientalism and the Structure of *Jane Eyre*." In it, Zonana explains that feminist Orientalism is a strategy that British women writers used during the colonial period to displace "the source of patriarchal oppression onto an 'Oriental,' 'Mahometan' society, enabling British readers to contemplate local problems without questioning their self-definition as Westerners and Christians." She calls this "a literary strategy of using the Orient as a means" for "Western self-redemption . . . transforming the Orient and Oriental Muslims into a vehicle" for "criticism of the West itself" (4). For instance, writes Zonana, in Charlotte Bronte's *Jane Eyre*, Bronte allows Jane to think of Rochester as a "Sultan" and herself a "slave," thereby providing the readers "a culturally acceptable simile by which to understand and combat the patriarchal 'despotism'" (593). Indeed, Mary Wollstonecraft, Elizabeth Barret Browning, and nineteenth-century European women's travel narratives habitually use Eastern societies to critique women's position in the West.

Fatemeh Keshavarz identifies additional traits of feminist Orientalism in *Jasmine and Stars: Reading More Than Lolita in Tehran* (2003), although she uses the nomenclature "new Orientalism." Her book is important because it registers the post-9/11 shift in Orientalism that conflates Islam and the East, which of course has been accompanied by a surge in Islamophobia in the West. Thus Keshavarz and many others have addressed this specific manifestation of Orientalism, feminist and otherwise. Keshavarz notes that feminist Orientalism offers a totalizing narrative of Islam in which (1) men are brutes who incessantly abuse women; (2) women submit to these men passively and, in some versions of this narrative, take pleasure in their oppression; and (3) women are intellectual lightweights who can parrot information but cannot analyze or create works, whether scholarly or artistic, and they are incapable of developing or carrying out activism (without the West). She also contends that a conspicuous inattention to class difference is a prominent feature of new Orientalism. Keshavarz is particularly concerned that feminist Orientalism conceives of feminism and Islam as antithetical. In Keshavarz's words, feminist Orientalism "erases feminist identity. . . . It refuses to acknowledge their [Muslim feminists'] commitment to gender equality on the basis of their Muslim faith" (34). Keshavarz writes that as a result feminist Orientalism is silencing, reductive, absolutist, authoritarian, and arrogant. Feminist Orientalism is, she says, a failure to listen and, of course, facilitates a Western agenda of political and cultural appropriation, militarily and economically. While Keshavarz focuses on representations of Islam and Muslim by so-called hyphenated Americans and Europeans such as Azar Nafisi, author of *Reading Lolita in Tehran: A Memoir in Books,* the characteristics that she attributes to feminist Orientalism are certainly deployed by other Western feminists.

Since Spivak, Ahmed, Zonana, and Nafisi articulated these critiques, some Western feminist paradigms have emerged that attempt to remedy these problems. For example, in 1994, Ella Shohat and Robert Stam, in *Unthinking Eurocentrism, Multiculturalism and the Media,* proposed polycentric multiculturalism, which is designed to resist epistemological privileging of "a single community or part of the world, whatever its economic or political power" (87). Shohat and Stam explain that polycentrism restructures communal relations "within and beyond the nation-state according to the internal imperatives of diverse communities" using a "systematic principle of differentiation, relationality and linkage" (48). It ensures that power relations are guided by a sympathetic perspective toward "underrepresented, marginalized, and oppressed" communities, envisioning dynamic transformation from within rather than imposed from without (87). It values the double consciousness engendered by a social location that straddles both the margins and centers of power. Moving beyond essentialism, it rejects so-called identity politics, conceptualizing "identities as multiple, unstable, historically situated, the products of ongoing differentiation and polymorphous identifications" (87). Finally, polycentrism seeks to effect change through dialogue and reciprocal exchanges that recognize conditions and institutions are permeable and mutable (88).

Sara Mills proposes a materialist, feminist postcolonial method that is designed to resist feminist Orientalist errors. Her essay "Gender and Colonial Space" (published in *Feminist Postcolonial Theory: A Reader,* 2003) and her book *Gender and Colonial Space* argue that feminist materialism's advantage is that it resists erasure of colonized subjects, regardless of their geographic location, by examining the practical mechanisms and effects, no matter how quotidian, of colonialisms. Additionally, this approach, with its focus on material realities, facilitates developing remedies for the continuing consequences of colonialism and offers concrete means of resisting ongoing Orientalism, albeit in new forms that we identify as feminist Orientalism, neoimperialism, and market globalization. Mills adds that this method considers colonialism in terms of local contingencies in colonized territories as well as in the imperial "homeland," including, for example, political leaders' desire to satisfy constituents in order to maintain elective positions. Mills, following theorist Mary Louise Pratt, also advocates for conceptualizing colonial encounters, particularly studies of sexualities, as zones of contact that collide, overlap, and butt up against each other, but without assuming that any of the entities involved are homogeneous. Rather, she reminds us that the colonizer-colonized relationship is mediated by class and race as well as gender, so that colonial discourses are multivocal and heterogeneous and that such heterogeneity suggests no actor is wholly powerless or omnipotent in the colonial system. Mills goes on to recommend that scholars attend to diverse voices and consider artifacts contested sites whose study can lend insight into colonialism's power structures.

These maneuvers, combined with an anti-imperialist consciousness on the part of scholars whose social location aligns with a position of dominance (as does hers as a British scholar studying colonization), can resist replicating colonial stratifications of power and, in our words, create spaces for Eastern women's voices in Western scholarship.

Joan Wallach Scott demonstrates just how difficult, thorny, and polarizing creating such spaces can be when she addresses the specific issue of Orientalist and feminist Orientalist attacks on *hijab* in her book *The Politics of the Veil* (2007), which looks at French attempts to ban "veiling" in order to maintain a secular public sphere. We should note that her work highlights the slippery nature of Orientalist binaries, for in this context, the Eastern Other is conflated with "Muslim," whether recent immigrants or first-, second-, and third-generation French who are perceived as unassimilated by ethnic French. In other words, Scott discusses the internal Other, the insider-outsider, who is constructed by the racialized nature of the debate about wearing "religious"—that is, Muslim—accessories and clothing styles (a discourse that has only heated up in the intervening years as bans on full body "veils" and face coverings went into effect in 2010 and, as of this writing, prohibitions against burquinis have proliferated in France in 2015–16). Scott points out that the first steps in ending such Orientalist hysteria, so to speak, are to attend to the specificities and complexities of current and historical contexts and, importantly, to recognize rather than repress difference. She argues that such recognition is imperative, even when differences seem irreconcilable. Meaningful discussions, she says, are facilitated by refusing to objectify Others and rejecting the notion that cultures are singular, unchanging, homogeneous, and exempt from interrogation. And referring to the French debate, when such conversations dichotomize secularism and religion, she advises Western secularists to keep in mind that so-called fundamentalism (a misnomer when applied to Islam, by the way, because of its strong tradition of interpretation in pursuit of enlightenment) does not threaten "a secular way of life" (24). Scott's emphasis on embracing difference is crucial to her suggestions outlining how Westerners can participate in these difficult exchanges without silencing Other voices. She points out that "communion" (meaning complete agreement and cultural uniformity) is not an element of community and, in fact, that it is neither possible nor ideal. As she writes, "The issue is not common being, but being-in-common" (200). What Scott means is that democracy does not hinge on perfect consent (or the radical secularism that we have seen in France) but hinges on continued disagreement that incorporates multiple diverse voices.

Do Muslim Women Need Saving? (2013) by Lila Abu-Lughod also looks at the specific experiences of Muslim women post-9/11. Abu-Lughod, a sociologist, opens her book by recounting a conversation with an acquaintance, Zaynab, in Egypt on the eve of the so-called Arab Spring in 2010. Zaynab is shocked to learn the topic of Abu-Lughod's new research project, which is "how many women in the West believe that Muslim women are oppressed" (7). Zaynab protests:

"But many women are oppressed! They don't get their rights in so many ways—in work, in schooling, in.... It's the government. The government oppresses women. The government doesn't care about the people. It doesn't care that they don't have work or jobs, that prices are so high that no one can afford anything. Poverty is hard. Men suffer from this, too" (7). Zaynab's point that women's oppression originates in the state rather than religion is underscored in Abu-Lughod's focus on the problematics of the Western propensity to frame women's suffering as a matter of rights, choices, and freedoms. Significantly, Abu-Lughod does not reject these principles; rather, she recommends listening to Muslim women, instead of imposing these principles in a one-size-fits-all approach, and, second, redefining what rights, choices, and freedoms mean according to such testimony. In fact, she suggests that the "universal rights" approach is reductive in that it can iconize women into unidimensional representations of abjection (our language). For example, with respect to consent to marriage, Abu-Lughod recounts strategies that Egyptian Muslim women are using to insert themselves into decision-making processes, such as invoking the Qur'an's prohibitions against forced matches, while insisting that through prayer the woman herself can determine whether the marriage is consistent with God's will—surrendering to God's will being a central principle of Islam ("Muslim," literally means "one who submits their will to God") (146). Abu-Lughod says that, rather than asking if Muslim women have rights (hence the title of her book), the questions should be "what the concepts of 'Muslim women's rights' or 'the oppressed Muslim woman' are doing in the world and who is making use of these concepts" (151). Abu-Lughod offers four strategies that enable listening to Muslim women. The first is to realize that oppression has multiple causes, and when gender is used to analyze them, attention must be paid to "opportunities" and "possibilities" specific to local conditions. Similarly, Abu-Lughod argues that suffering should not be blamed solely on Islam and that Westerners should recognize that we all share the experience of suffering—it is our common lot. She cites the example of war, which has negative consequences worldwide regardless of religion, nation of origin, and other social locations. Abu-Lughod also says that power differentials must be acknowledged in initiatives addressing oppression and that Westerners should look to and be led by local women and honor their solutions to oppression. Finally, Abu-Lughod urges Western women to engage in honest self-reflection aimed at developing an anti-imperialist consciousness.

AIMS

We are conscious that, in titling our book *Unveiling Desire: Fallen Women in Literature, Culture, and Films of East*, we risk invoking Orientalism and sensationalizing Eastern women's sexuality. Do we intend to play the voyeur, prick desire, and penetrate what has been apotheosized as Oriental? No, our overarching aim is to enable attentive listening to Eastern women's voices by creating a venue for them among Western audiences, and we have chosen the trope of the "fallen" woman to achieve this goal because it is a site of common ground between Eastern and Western women as well as a stage for the performance of a wealth of local contingencies. To use Scott's language, it is an experience of "being-in-common" but not "common being," for, without essentializing, both East and West have scorned feminine sexual sovereignty and self-determination. Thus the trope of female fallenness facilitates dialogues that seek to answer questions about women's sexuality, such as the nature of social and historical ideologies that promote gendered norms underwriting women's vilification and, second, whether transgressive women, such as lesbians, as Kuhu Sharma Chanana argues in this volume, are a "clarion call" against patriarchy. Do fallen women merely warn of the drastic consequences of resisting patriarchal models of womanhood, such as the "feminine conformist ideal"? Or do subversive, resisting women anticipate a world beyond despotic chauvinism? How do historical Orientalism and feminist Orientalism today sustain misogynist, colonizing uses of the fallen woman trope to distribute power to some and deny it to others—and most importantly, how can Eastern and Western women "be in common" in order to resist perpetuating such imperialism?

Obviously, there are no perfect or complete answers, and in fact, the scope of these questions is staggering; nevertheless, *Unveiling Desire* tackles them by conceptualizing commonality and difference as "two sides of one coin," as imbricated in each other rather than as discrete constructs. The value in this approach is that it diverts the tendency of each of these "ways of knowing" to move toward a polarizing feminist Orientalism. By this we mean, on one hand, that looking only for undifferentiated commonality ultimately leads to the flaccid notion that women throughout the world have a homogeneous experience of gender oppression unmediated, for example, by class-caste status, sexuality, and innumerable local contingencies. This erasure of difference fuels, among many Westerners, numerous fallacies, including but not limited to the idea that sexism has been cured in the West, that Western remedies for sexism are a fix-all, and along a different tack, that all it takes to end sexism anywhere is for women to congregate to celebrate an essentialized, idealized version of womanhood. Likewise, envisioning commonality and difference as coterminus circumvents the Orientalist propensity to see only alterity, to view Other as so "different" as to be inhuman.

Thus, as Abu-Lughod recommends, *Unveiling Desire* acknowledges that suffering is perhaps the most common experience that women have and that it is inextricably linked to a remarkably durable, cross-cultural, though particularized, misogyny that is evident in specific attempts to regulate—contain and control—women's sexuality. From this perspective, differentiated commonality is the shared ground among the chapters in this volume. Specifically, of course, the book is concerned with the trope of fallenness as a means of restricting female sexuality. Hence *Unveiling Desire*'s chapters formulate analyses of "fallen" women that invoke and interrogate notions of sexuality at play in Eastern women's lives, women's writing, and representations of women in literature and film, all of which examine how the trope and its correlate, the virgin/whore dichotomy (in its multiple iterations), have been used, modified, and resisted according to local social norms, which themselves are contingent, heterogeneous, and prone to shifting.

NOTES ON FALLENNESS AND THE VIRGIN/WHORE DICHOTOMY

One of the challenges with deconstructing binaries is that we must invoke them in order to subvert them, which, of course, risks reifying them. Nevertheless, we would be remiss not to acknowledge the different trajectories that the fallen woman trope and the virgin/whore dichotomy have taken in the East and West even as we point out commonalities among Eastern and Western women's experiences of it. Needless to say, the East is not a monolithic space with a single history; hence, the performance of the virgin/whore dichotomy varies throughout the region. It is obviously impossible to catalogue all of the trope's permutations, but *Unveiling Desire*'s chapters offer a starting point for discussion. For instance, as Chandrani Biswas points out in her chapter, "Desire and Dharma: A Study of the Representation of Fallen Women in the Novels of Bankim Chandra," the virgin/whore dichotomy was inscribed in the region's legal and religious discourses by way of the Code of Manu, perhaps in the second century BCE, the earliest date scholars associate with the code's composition (the latest is 300 CE). Addressing a male audience only, as do many texts regulating women, the code mandates women's subordination to men in marriage: "Obedience to her husband is the beginning, and the middle and the end of female duty" (qtd. in Sangari and Vaid 43). This precept, Biswas demonstrates, threads through Indian mythology, scripture, fairy tales, classical romantic tales, and other genres to shape audiences' notions of conjugal love, and it becomes an important element of female virtue.

The Code of Manu also stipulates that a virtuous wife refrains from earthly pleasure after her husband's death (Manu IX: 14–18), and two contributors to this volume in addition to Biswas examine how this belief plays out in representations of women in nineteenth-century Bengali fiction by men. Meenakshi Malhotra's "Dark Goddess for a Fallen World: Mapping Apocalypse in Some of Bankim Chandra Chatterjee's Novels" examines Bankim Chandra's treatment of female characters in *Bishabriksha* (*The Poison Tree*) and *Krishnakanter Will* (*Krishnakanta's Will*) and these women's defiance of the rigidly enforced convention that widows must mourn their late husbands in isolation and austerity for the rest of their lives. Radha Chakravarty executes a similar maneuver in her analysis of Tagore's *Chokher Bali* in "The Fallen Woman in Bengali Literature: Binodini Dasi and Tagore's *Chokher Bali*."

In addition to detailing the model of virtuous womanhood, the Code of Manu warns that women are inherently seductive and should be avoided. Centuries later, during the partition of the Indian subcontinent in 1947, which is examined in several chapters in *Unveiling Desire*, this and other patriarchal ideas about women, especially the view that attacking them is the most effective (if not easiest) means of humiliating the enemy Other, triggered "gender genocide" (our term). Women were raped—sometimes in the presence of male family members—paraded naked in public, and pressed into service as sex slaves. Frequently, their families and communities of origin blamed survivors for their own victimization and refused to allow them to return home. Thus we see that deeply rooted beliefs emanating from the virgin/whore binary—that women embody seductiveness and invite their own violation—influenced the shape that interstate conflict took during the partition and how communities recovered from it.

The longevity of the virgin/whore opposition is also evident in Tomoko Kuribayashi's chapter on Moto Hagio's "Iguana Girl." In Japan during the second half of the twentieth century, career-oriented women began delaying marriage or remained single as they pursued employment outside the home. Such women soon were stereotyped as self-indulgent narcissists obsessed with worldliness. In essence, they were labelled fallen because they resisted marriage and motherhood. Kuribayashi's analysis of "Iguana Girl," a manga narrative featuring a conflicted mother-daughter relationship, demonstrates that the pressure to live up to such an extreme ideal of motherhood has extremely negative consequences for women and their families.

Nonetheless, Japan also provides an example of the fluidity of sexual mores and how they are mediated by multiple factors, such as class. During Japan's Tokugawa *shogunate* (1603–1867), which was the country's last feudal government, contemporary Confucian tracts promoted women's chastity and devotees of some minor religions considered heterosexual sex polluting, but in actuality women were not condemned for engaging in sex work or premarital sex (including cohabitation), having multiple sex partners, or divorcing their husbands. Rather, as Amy Stanley explains in *Selling Women: Prostitution, Markets, and the Household in Early Modern Japan*, "the location and timing of intercourse . . . marked certain sex acts as transgressive" (4). Accordingly, sex near a sacred site and "tempting" a celibate monk were immoral. One exception was women from aristocratic and wealthier peasant families. They were expected to abstain from premarital sex, an example of how class status mediates sexual norms (4). Thus, in early modern Tokugawa, standards measuring women's fallenness contrasted significantly with those in other areas of the world during the same era except in cases determined by family wealth. In most of East Asia, for example, the same sexual behaviors tolerated in Tokugawa were condemned because they violated the Confucian mandate that women obey their husbands, a point that Lavinia Benedetti makes in "Representing Bad Women in *Wu Zetian Si Da Qi'An*: Political Criticism in Late Qing Crime Fiction." Writing about Chinese detective fiction in the Tang Dynasty, *gong'an xiaoshuo* (公案小说; *gong'an* for "court case" and *xiaoshuo* for "fiction"), she argues that regardless of class status, fallen women—whether Empress Wu Zetian or Mrs. Zhou, a commoner—serve as foils to showcase the investigator hero's righteousness. Readers know that the women are corrupt and malevolent because the Empress Wu and Mrs. Zhou do not conform to rules of filial piety, which, in the Confucian paradigm, are essential for maintaining not just family order but the order of the state and the cosmos.

One thing that becomes apparent in this all too brief survey of the virgin/whore dichotomy in the East is that this binary coexists with a tradition of privileging communal welfare over the needs and desires of the self. For instance, in Confucianism and Daoism,[1] maintaining communal order is a duty that trumps self-realization. Likewise, Buddhism stipulates that the self should be abandoned and sublimated because it is the source of evil; hence, a selfless existence is the ideal. Hinduism takes a similar view while also embracing a gendered construct of self. In the *Bhagavad Gītā*, Lord Krishna states that the body is a "Field," or a temporary garb that is *Prakriti* (feminine primal nature) while the soul is *Purusha* (masculine pure consciousness). The "Field," made of ego, senses, and the four elements, is a representation of the "I," an incessant source of earthly pleasure and pain and an oxymoronic space of absence and presence. These histories and concepts show that material particularities and philosophical commonalities conjoin to create the variegated landscape in which the trope of female fallenness operates in the East, while also forging intersections and divergences from its performance in the West.

The virgin/whore dichotomy's history in the West is as deeply rooted as it is in the East. It is often associated with the Victorian period in England, but it can be traced back to Judaic influences on Christian cultures transmitted through the Hebrew Scriptures. The book of Genesis recounts how Adam and Eve were expelled from paradise and sin was introduced to the world through Eve's seduction of Adam, convincing him to disobey God's command to abstain from the fruit of the tree of knowledge of good and evil. According to Roman Catholic doctrine, Mary, considered the mother of God's human-divine incarnation, Jesus Christ, later embodied a sanitized version of Eve. Mary, as the *virgin* mother, "sanctified" motherhood by synthesizing the "good mother" and virgin. Despite this recuperation of Eve, since the early medieval period in Europe, patriarchs of the Roman Catholic Church, deeply suspicious that the "original sin" was sexual—perhaps because they, at least in the cases of St. Augustine and St. Jerome, had numerous relationships with fallen women in their youth, later blaming these women for separating them from God—infused in Christianity the idea that carnal sin is the worst of all transgressions. Women, responsible for man's fall from God's grace, are by their nature temptresses whose wiles should be avoided at all costs except for the purpose of reproduction under the auspices of marriage, which was considered a flawed alternative to the priesthood. While later ages cast marriage in a kinder light, the virgin/whore topos permeates Western literary, artistic, and intellectual production from Chaucer to Freud (who used it to name men's attraction to sexually uninhibited women and concomitant impotence with chaste wives)—and beyond.

In the mid-twentieth century, US feminists challenged the virgin/whore binary as they grappled to articulate the tenets of what would rapidly become a new area of scholarship. Kate Millett, in *Sexual Politics,* argues, "The large quantity of guilt attached to sexuality in patriarchy is overwhelmingly placed upon the female, who is, culturally speaking, held to be the culpable or the more culpable party in nearly any sexual liaison, whatever the extenuating circumstances. A tendency toward the reification of the female makes her more often a sexual object than a person. This is particularly so when she is denied human rights through chattel status. . . . *Woman is still denied sexual freedom and the biological control over her body through the cult of virginity,* the double standard" (emphasis added; 76). While Millett, writing in 1969, notes that equating morality with virginity objectifies women, liberal feminists of the same era argued that patriarchal valorization of women's role as mother restricted them from the public sphere where they could access the economic and political power they needed to counter their oppression. Furthermore, although radical feminists did not share liberal feminists' hope that entering the public sphere and reforming it from within would be successful, they shared the view that women's oppression was determined in part by "structures of reproduction and sexuality" (Putnam Tong 11). In aggregate, these US critiques of the virgin/whore dichotomy reject the validity of externally imposed regulation of women's bodies by adapting the dominant society's rhetoric of rights and choice to their cause of liberating women. This emphasis on rights can be traced to the influences of the Greek philosophies that undergird Western cultural traditions, the early modern European notion of the person as "self," and the Enlightenment contention that the self is a citizen with agency and political and property rights. Then there is the recurring theme of the "I" in Romanticism and, in the nineteenth century, the Freudian idea of ego—the mediator between the conscious and the unconscious that lends the individual a sense of personal identity—that has become, along with reason, a preeminent designation of humanness in the modern era in the West. Thus the language of women's rights and choice permeates US feminisms, and liberal feminism, which is the most mainstream, recognizable Western feminism, continues to advocate for rights-based remedies that primarily relate to women's exclusion from public-sphere leadership, including workplace equity, entrepreneurship, seeking public office, complete control of reproductive decisions, and the resources to implement these choices.

Consequently, for all its misogyny, the virgin/whore dichotomy offers feminists around the world an opportune "meeting place" for staging resistance to patriarchal regulation of their bodies and sexuality. Indeed, one point where Eastern and Western feminisms intersect—where we "are-in-common"—is in our embrace and celebration of unruly female sexuality. Contesting rather than submitting to patriarchal injunctions against "fallenness," feminists worldwide claim and transvalue the virgin/whore dichotomy not only to assert sexual autonomy individually but also as a praxis facilitating society-wide gender justice whether the goal is as specific as ending rape culture or the broader aim of replacing cis- and heteronormativity. Thus feminists represent women's sexuality and sexual agency as pleasurable and empowering rather than threatening, sinful, or warranting punishment and control, and we wish to emphasize, this is not merely a rhetorical gesture or a personal choice. It is a principle on which feminist social change rests and should be called on more often in this capacity, for it is as valid and effective as the women's rights approach, and more so depending on the contexts.

French feminist Helene Cixous, for example, argues that women's sexuality can be a source of inspiration, resourcefulness, vision, and ingenuity. She accepts the contention that perceptions of women's sexuality contribute to determining their social status and political power for better and worse, but she goes further, arguing for an expanded notion of female sexuality as creative principle along the lines, we argue, of the Hindu concept of Shakti, a dynamic, liberating force, when she suggests that female orgasm melds together the physical, intellectual, psychological, and spiritual in an experience of *jouissance*, an "explosion, diffusion, effervescence, abundance... [that] takes pleasure (*jouit*) in being limitless" (qtd. in Ermarth 160). Thus quashing *jouissance*, says Cixous, disables women from forging unique, empowered voices and silences them.

Cixous's notion of *jouissance* is similar to Eastern feminists' celebration of their sexual energy, a force that they consider a source of knowledge and creativity, a means of subject constitution, and a strategy for resisting patriarchal control. Poets like Toru Dutt[2] in India, for instance, often located female body and *jouissance* at the core of sylvan locales and natural wilderness. Later in the twentieth century, an upsurge of like-minded feminist writers and artists from different parts of Asia and the Middle East followed suit, along with border-crossing feminists such as Maxine Hong Kingston and Chitra Banerjee Divakaruni,[3] whose works are set in the East or feature so-called hyphenated subjectivities and communities. Kamala Das,[4] Taslima Nasreen, and Nawal El Saadawi, who graciously wrote the foreword to *Unveiling Desire*, are also among just a few of the illustrious, daring souls whose compositions declaim the joy of female desire. Another is the twentieth-century poet Gauri Deshpande, a Marathi-Indian novelist, short story author, and poet, who celebrates amaranthine female sexuality and the female body in poems such as "On a Lost Love": "I am the earth / Vast deep and black / and I receive / the first rain / sweet, generous, / lashing, throbbing; / its smell forever in my blood / its imprint deep / within my / quick. / Yellow daisies burst out / on my breast and thigh at its very touch" (10). Not surprisingly, many of these women are labelled "fallen," and some have paid a high price for their feminism.

For instance, Nasreen, a Bangladeshi poet and novelist who was born Muslim and now practices feminist secular humanism, lives in exile and has not been permitted to enter Bangladesh since 1994. She has also faced on-and-off difficulties traveling to India, all triggered by the publication of her 1993 novel, *Lajja* (*Shame*), which relates the story of a Hindu family living in Bangladesh when widespread violence breaks out in South Asia after Hindu radicals demolished the Babri Masjid, a mosque, in Ayodhya in 1992. Additionally, religious radicals have issued several *fatwas* (religious judgments) calling for her death, the latest as of this writing issued by the Islamic State in Iraq and al-Sham (ISIS) in June

2016. Her alleged crimes include blasphemy and violating moral and cultural values. Indeed, Hanifa Deen calls Nasreen "the female Rushdie" because of similarities between reactions to her novel and the *fatwa* that Ayatollah Khomeini issued against Salmon Rushdie's *Satanic Verses*, a novel that satirizes Islam ("The 'Female Rushdie': Fallen Prose of a 'Fallen Woman'").[5] Significantly, Nasreen's work models the transnational approach that *Unveiling Desire* proposes, for in addition to proudly self-identifying as a lesbian, she urges women to claim and deploy sexual pleasure and energy as a matter of rights. For example, Nasreen protests a plan to open a sex shop in Mecca by questioning whether women will be able to patronize it:

> I . . . want to know, whether in this sex shop, a woman would be able to shop alone for her personal needs. In a country where women don't have minimum personal liberty, and have no other identity beyond being sex slaves to men, there cannot be any doubt that the sex shop being opened there will be exclusively for the sexual pleasure of men. If there is indeed any pleasure to be gained out of those shops, they would be exclusively for the men. The women are not to partake in any such thing. Those who do not have basic human rights must never aspire to sexual rights either. And those that do not have sexual freedom or rights, have no sexual pleasure. Sex slaves take no pleasure in sex—they need to be freed of their slavery first. ("Will Saudi Sex Slavery Ever End?")

Taking Nasreen and feminists like her as an inspiration, *Unveiling Desire* eschews Western research models that homogenize and stereotype the East and limit advocacy for women to a rights-based approach. Thus the book presents a diverse yet balanced canvas of arguments and perspectives in an array of chapters that offer provocative, insightful explorations of the trope of fallenness and the virgin/whore dichotomy, attending carefully to women's sexuality and its representation in literary and filmic artifacts by women and men.

SECTIONS

Unveiling Desire presents a pageant of fallen women in literature, film, theater, and religion in the East, and in the process, it also sheds light on how female sexuality is conceived in different parts of the Eastern world. As twenty-first-century scholars, the authors of these fifteen chapters problematize the concept of the fallen woman as it appears in particular epochs, geographies, and social contexts, therefore complicating the trope of women's "fallenness" and the virgin/whore dichotomy.

Part I: Chastity, Fidelity, and Women's Cross-Cultural Encounters

This section of *Unveiling Desire* deals with the topos of fallenness in literature's relation to women's displacement during social crises. Essays on the 1947 partition of the Indian subcontinent, Bangladesh's 1971 War of Liberation, and

Marjane Satrapi's graphic novel *Persepolis: The Story of a Childhood* (2000) about the Islamic Revolution in Iran suggest that the female body becomes a contested site during periods of unrest as competing factions angle for power by regulating, violating, and appropriating women's sexuality. These analyses also argue that female characters in the texts in question counter these maneuvers by claiming existential spaces for themselves. Thus Colette Morrow, in "Feminist Neoimperialism in Marjane Satrapi's *Persepolis*," asserts that *Persepolis*'s depiction of an Iranian girl's rite of passage during the 1979 revolution is complicated by contradictions between public and familial values about gender and women's role in society, although the book is flawed by conspicuous feminist Orientalism. The second chapter, Firdous Azim's "The Forgotten Women of 1971: Bangladesh's Failure to Remember Rape Victims of the Liberation War," examines two narratives that explore the plight of the women who were raped during Bangladesh's struggle for independence, Shaheen Akhtar's *Talaash* (Dhaka: Mowla Brothers, 2005), translated into English as *The Search* (New Delhi: Zubaan, 2011), and the second a short documentary film, *Shadhinota*, or *A Certain Freedom*, directed by Yasmine Kabir (2003). The last two chapters in part 1 are based on Indian subcontinent partition literature. Paramita Halder, in her chapter, "Fragmented State, Fragmented Women: Reading Gender, Reading History in Partition Fiction," analyzes the works of Jamila Hasmi, Rajinder Singh Bedi, Amrita Pritam, Sadat Hasan Manto, and Lalithambika Antharjanam, focusing on how the female characters' status as icons of community honor and conservators of the Indian nation's future made women vulnerable to the pervasive violence that accompanied public chaos during the partition. Hafiza Nilofar Khan's chapter, "The Trope of the 'Fallen Women' in the Fiction of Bangladeshi Women Writers," scrutinizes representations of the *biranganas* (war heroines) of the 1971 war in the fiction and short stories of Bangladeshi writers Selina Hossain and Niaz Zaman. These chapters have a common focus, which is how the literature features female characters' subject constitution processes unyoked from historical, normative definitions of female fallenness.

Part II: Forbidden Desires and Misogynist Enculturation

Chapters in part 2 consider misogynistic representations of patriarchally proscribed forms of women's desire ranging from polyandrous longing to a yearning for material power in polygamous family structures. These analyses of Indian literature, film, and children's tales delve into how Western colonial influences complicate such misogyny and how Eastern women have challenged their enculturation into patriarchal values. Devaleena Das's "Polyamorous Draupadi: *Adharma* or Emancipation?" recasts Draupadi, the female character from the Indian epic, the *Mahābhārata*, as a model not of fallenness but of a feminist who claims her sexuality, celebrates it, and employs it to break down barriers to her exercise of agency. Amrit Gangar's chapter, "Damaged Goods! Managed Gods! Indian Cinema's Virtuous Hierarchies," takes a different tack, tracing representations of women in

Indian film back to their prototypes in Hindu scripture and mythology, concluding that Indian cinema is a warehouse of movable goods, objectifying images of fallen women that attract mass audiences and perpetuate old misogynies. Third, "*Roop Taraashi*: Sex, Culture, Violence, Impersonation and the Politics of the Inner Sanctum" by Naina Dey examines a collection of folk tales, *Thakumar Jhuli* (*Grandmother's Bag*), that Dakshinaranjan Mitra Majumder collected and published in nineteenth-century Bengal. Dey argues that the tales resist Anglicization of Bengali children during British rule, express patriarchal fears of women, and socialize audiences into an ideal of girl- and womanhood that is passive and submissive.

Part III: Political Economy and Questioning Tradition in the Far East

Part 3 focuses on literature of, or set in, the Far East, offering sociological and psychoanalytic readings of gender or sexuality in three genres: ancient Chinese detective stories, Japanese manga, and Western male sex fantasy. A common theme in these chapters is the tension between tradition and change. The piece written by Louis Betty, "More Than Just an Exchange of Fluids: Southeast Asian Prostitutes and the Western Sexual Economy," challenges stigmas attached to sex workers in the Far East. Grounding his analysis in the work of Enlightenment-era thinkers such as Restif de la Bretonne, the Marquis de Sade, and Charles Fourier, and also the fiction of contemporary novelist Michel Houellebecq, Betty offers a conservative analysis that suggests sex tourism is a product of sexual alienation in the era following the so-called sexual revolution. Benedetti in "Representing Bad Women in *Wu Zetian Si Da Qi'An*: Political Criticism in Late Qing Crime Fiction" identifies the literary and political uses of the fallen woman figure in, as noted previously, Chinese detective fiction of the Tang Dynasty, *gong'an xiaoshuo* 公案小说, *gong'an*. Kuribayashi, in her chapter, "The Problematic Maternal in Moto Hagio's Graphic Fiction: An Analysis of 'Iguana Girl,'" follows with a look at "unnatural" mothering in "Iguana Girl," a graphic narrative by Moto Hagio. Here Kuribayashi argues that the mother character's self-disgust at her inability to fulfill the Japanese ideal of motherhood causes conflict with her daughter, who later fears that she will not love her own girl child.

Part IV: Unchaste Goddesses and Transgressive Women in a Turbulent Nation

The late colonial period and early postcolonial eras in India are fraught with complex intersections of national and sexual politics. The chapters in this section examine nineteenth-century Bengali literature against the backdrop of fissures between different nationalist movements, proponents of Hindu orthodoxy on one hand and progressive reformers on the other. In this process, divergent factions constructed an opposition between the "New Woman" (*nabeena*) and the "traditional woman" (*pracheena*) and deified the feminine to attract followers and consolidate support. However, as the chapters in part 4 suggest, such categorization of feminine principle—"Shakti"—can be slippery. Malhotra opens this section with the chapter "A Dark Goddess for a Fallen World: Mapping Apocalypse in Some of Bankim Chandra Chatterjee's Novels," which examines fallen women in Bankim Chandra's novels in light of his attempts to engender a shared, nationwide sensibility capable of unifying the putative Indian state. Biswas, in "Desire and Dharma: A Study of the Representation of Fallen Women in the Novels of Bankim Chandra," also explores the fallen woman trope in Bankim Chandra's novels, concluding that the transgressive women featured in them are strong people conscious of the injustices they face because of sexism and classism and that these figures develop idiosyncratic strategies for overcoming obstacles. Next, Radha Chakravarty in "Binodini Dasi and Tagore's *Chokher Bali*" compares the autobiographies of Binodini Devi, a famed nineteenth-century actor whose attempts to move from marginality to a central position in mainstream society were constantly rebuffed because she was a sex worker, to representations of a fictional Binodini (not based on the actor's life) in Tagore's novel *Chokher Bali* (*A Grain of Sand*). Chakravarty concludes that the actor Binodini's experiences reveal patriarchal hypocrisies, whereas in the book, Binodini is a new type of female character in Indian fiction in that she exhibits a remarkably well-developed subjectivity and innovation.

Part V: The Moral Frontiers of Lesbianism in the East

Part 5 addresses the transgressiveness of same-sex desire and the fallenness of sexual "outsiders," particularly lesbians and transgender people. Feroza Jassawalla's chapter, "Shaking the Throne of God: Muslim Women Writers Who Dared," advocates for a reassessment of the widespread belief that homosexuality is antithetical to Islam. She argues that historical artifacts, early Muslim scholarship, and the Qur'an's teachings on homosexuality do not support or justify homophobia and, further, that recent South Asian Muslim fiction by women offers evidence that homosexuality is integral to and accepted within Muslim communities. The other chapter in this section is entitled "Homoeroticism and Reaccessing the Idea of 'Fallen Woman' in Keval Sood's *Murgikhana* (*Henhouse*)." Contributed by Kuhu Sharma Chanana, this chapter argues that while the book appears to take a progressive approach to lesbianism, it undermines this position by employing the lesbian protagonist to normalize heterosexual women's transgressions of traditional sexual mores.

Collectively, the chapters that comprise *Unveiling Desire* place the fallen woman in historical and ideological contexts in order to foster cross-cultural understandings of the epithet "fallen" and to unpack and interrogate the web of ideologies that define women's fallenness. These chapters look at unconventional heroines (who may not be given this status in the original texts) and their power to diminish and reduce the withering gaze of patriarchal judgment. In so doing, *Unveiling Desire*'s chapters present nuanced, critical analyses that acknowledge women suffer also from imbalances of power and inequitable distributions of resources caused by intersections of sexism and Orientalism locally and globally. While emphasizing that misogyny is differentiated—differently performed—and complicated by local politics of racism, caste-classism, and colonization, *Unveiling Desire* also identifies common ground in both Eastern and Western patriarchies' attempts to deprive women of sexual sovereignty. Paradoxically, this may provide feminists a shared space that enables women to reclaim their sexuality and deploy it to empower themselves and reconstruct society in a feminist mode.

NOTES

1 Confucianism is an ethical and philosophical system developed from the teachings of the Chinese philosopher Confucius (551–479 BCE). It believed that "the secular is the sacred" and supported family and social harmony rather than the otherworldly spiritual world. "Daoism," also known as Taoism, is one of the two great indigenous philosophical traditions of China. It suggests that thought and practice that are sometimes viewed as "philosophical" can be "religious," or a combination of both.

2 Tora Dutt (b. 1856–77) was an Indian poet and novelist who wrote in French and English. Her poem "Our Casuarina Tree" is a favorite today. Her longer pieces were discovered and published posthumously.

3 Chitra Banerjee Divakaruni is a prolific Indian-American novelist, screenwriter, playwright, and poet. She authored *Palace of Illusions: A Novel*, which revises the *Mahābhārata* from the perspective of its female protagonist, Draupadi. See Devaleena Das's chapter "Polyamorous Draupadi: *Adharma* or Emancipation?" in this volume.

4 Kamala Das is the author of the autofictional *My Story*, in which she traces her path to self-realization through racism and a difficult marriage by taking control of her sexuality.

5 In this volume, see "Shaking the Throne of God: Muslim Women Writers Who Dared" by Feroza Jussawalla for more on the injunction against Salmon Rushdie.

WORKS CITED

Abu-Lughod, Lila. *Do Muslim Women Need Saving?* Harvard UP, 2013.

Ahmed, Leila. "Western Ethnocentrism and Perceptions of the Harem." *Feminist Studies*, vol. 8, no. 3, 1982, pp. 521–34.

Araújo, Marta, and Silvia Maeso. "Introduction." *Eurocentrism, Racism and Knowledge: Debates on History and Power in Europe and the Americas*, Palgrave Macmillan, 2015, pp. 1–22.

Arthurs, Jane, and Jean Grimshaw. *Women's Bodies Discipline and Transgression*. Cassell, 1997.

Brown, Louise. *The Dancing Girls of Lahore*. Harper Collins, 2009.

Chong Chong, Kim, and Yuli Liu. *Conceptions of Virtue: East and West*. Marshall Cavendish Academic, 2006.

Chow, Rey. *The Protestant Ethic and the Spirit of Capitalism*. Columbia UP, 2002.

Cracium, Adriana. *Fatal Women of Romanticism*. Cambridge UP, 2002.

Deen, Hanifa. "The 'Female Rushdie': Fallen Prose of a 'Fallen Woman.'" The Australian National University Gender Institute, 12 Aug. 2013, Australian National University, Canberra, Australia. Lecture.

Deshpande, Gauri. *Lost Love*. Writer's Workshop, 1970.

El-Saadawi, Nawal. *Woman at Point Zero*. Zed Books, 2007.

Ermarth, Elizabeth Deeds. *Sequel to History: Postmodernism and the Crisis of Representational Time*. Princeton UP, 1991.

Feng, Menglong. *The Chinese Femme Fatale: Stories from the Ming Period*, translated by Anne E. Melaren, Wild Peony, 1994.

Golden, Arthur. *Memoirs of a Geisha*. Knopf Doubleday, 1999.
Gray, Thomas, and Gilbert Wakefield. *The Poems of Mr. Gray*. G. Kearsley, 1786.
Harman, Gilbert, and Judith Thomson. *Moral Relativism and Moral Objectivity*. Wiley-Blackwell, 1996.
Houghton, Rev. Ross C. *Women of the Orient: An Account of the Religious, Intellectual and Social Condition of Women in Japan, China, India, Egypt, Syria and Turkey*. Hitchcock and Walden, 1877.
Karim, Lamia. "Transnational Politics of the Reading and (Un)making of Taslima Nasreen." *South Asian Feminisms*, edited by Ania Loomba and Ritty A. Lukose, Duke UP, 2012, pp. 205–20.
Keshavarz, Fatemeh. *Jasmine and Stars: Reading More Than Lolita in Tehran*. U of North Carolina P, 2007.
Kittredge, Katherine. *Lewd and Notorious*. U of Michigan P, 2003.
Manu, Patrick Olivelle, and Suman Olivelle. *Manu's Code of Law*. Edited by Patrick and Suman Olivelle, Oxford UP, 2005.
Menon, Ritu, editor. *No Woman's Land: Women from Pakistan, India and Bangladesh Write on the Partition of India*. Women Unlimited, 2004.
Millett, Kate. *Sexual Politics*. U of Illinois P, 2000.
Mills, Sara. "Gender and Colonial Space." *Feminist Postcolonial Theory: A Reader*, edited by Reina Lewis and Sara Mills, Routledge, 2003, pp. 692–719.
Nasreen, Taslima. "Will Saudi Sex Slavery Ever End?" *No Country for Women*, Free Thought Blogs, 7 Sept. 2015, freethoughtblogs.com/taslima/2015/10/07/will-saudi-sex-slavery-ever-end-2/.
Plato, John M. Cooper, and D. S. Hutchinson. *Plato: Complete Works*. Edited by John M. Cooper and D. S. Hutchinson, Hackett, 1997.
Putnam Tong, Rosemarie. *Feminist Thought: A More Comprehensive Introduction*. Westview, 1998.
Sangari, Kumkum, and Sudesh Vaid, editors. *Recasting Women: Essays in Colonial History*. Kali for Women, 1989.
Scott, Joan Wallach. *The Politics of the Veil*. Princeton UP, 2009.
Shohat, Ella, and Robert Stam. *Unthinking Eurocentrism: Multiculturalism and the Media*. Routledge, 2014.
Sjoberg, Laura, and Caron E. Gentry. *Mothers, Monsters, Whores: Women's Violence in Global Politics*. Zed Books, 2007.
Spivak, Gayatri Chakravorty. "Can the Subaltern Speak?" *Colonial Discourse and Post-Colonial Theory: A Reader*, edited by Patrick Williams and Laura Chrisman, Harvester Wheatsheaf, 1994.
Stanley, Amy. *Selling Women: Prostitution, Markets, and the Household in Early Modern Japan*. U of California P, 2012.
Winnifrith, Tom. *Fallen Women in the Nineteenth-Century Novel*. Macmillan, 1994.
Woolf, Naomi. *Promiscuities: An Opinionated History of Female Desire*. Random House, 2011.
Zonana, Joyce. "The Sultan and the Slave: Feminist Orientalism and the Structure of *Jane Eyre*." *Signs*, vol. 18, no. 3, 1993, pp. 592–617.

PART I CHASTITY, FIDELITY, AND WOMEN'S CROSS-CULTURAL ENCOUNTERS

1 ⑥ FEMINIST NEOIMPERIALISM IN MARJANE SATRAPI'S *PERSEPOLIS*

COLETTE MORROW

This chapter analyzes *Persepolis*, a coming-of-age story about Marji, an Iranian girl growing up in Iran during the Islamic Revolution and the Iran-Iraq War. Written by Marjane Satrapi, the graphic novel was published after 9/11 when President George W. Bush infamously included Iran on the "Axis of Evil" because of the country's alleged support for terrorist groups and its nuclear power program. Morrow examines how, in these politically charged contexts, *Persepolis* achieves Satrapi's oft-stated goal of "humanizing" Iran and Iranians for Western audiences by foregrounding Marji's passage into adulthood in a series of vignettes that use feminist Orientalist stereotypes that demonize Muslims, a strategy that US audiences, including feminist scholars, generally fail to recognize. Countering conventional wisdom in US scholarship on the book, Morrow concludes that Marji's fallenness is her failure to develop a mature sense of self that would have enabled her to safely negotiate sharply contrasting gender codes in her family culture and Iran's public sphere. Unceasingly rebellious and resistant, she is sent to Austria to finish secondary school because she cannot cultivate and deploy a self-protective borderland (*mestiza*, in Gloria Anzaldua's words) consciousness.

INTRODUCTION

In 2003, Pantheon Books published an English translation (from French) of Marjane Satrapi's graphic novel, *Persepolis: The Story of a Childhood,* in the United States. Set in Iran against the backdrop of the 1979 Revolution when Mohammad

Reza Shah Pahlavi was deposed and the Islamic Republic of Iran established, this coming-of-age story featuring Marji Satrapi, its charismatic, precocious protagonist and narrator who constantly rebels against the country's new cultural hegemony, was an instant hit.[1] *Story of a Childhood*'s extraordinary success in the United States coincided with President George W. Bush's so-called War on Terror, during which his administration twice considered taking military action against Iran (soon after 9/11 and again from 2005 through 2007). Although the United States did not launch an attack on Iran, Bush infamously included Iran on the "Axis of Evil" because of the country's alleged support for terrorist groups and its nuclear power program, which, according to Western governments and the United Nations, could have been converted to produce nuclear weapons ("State of the Union Address"). During this period, Iranian-American diasporic fiction and prose, most notably Azar Nafisi's *Reading Lolita in Tehran: A Memoir in Books* (2003), which transnational feminists and postcolonial scholars in Iran and the United States decried as neo-Orientalist because its diatribes against the Islamic Republic promoted the case for US military intervention in Iran, garnered huge audiences (Rowe 254 and 271; Dabashi; Bahramitash 234).[2] In these politically charged contexts, Satrapi's goal in writing *Story of a Childhood* was, as she often stated, to "humanize" Iran and Iranians. Educators and activists, including feminists, who were working to foster respect for populations perceived as "suspect" in the post-9/11 hate-fest, quickly introduced *Story of a Childhood* to secondary schools and universities, while other enthusiastic fans flocked to Satrapi's book signings, lectures, and later, film showings. Scholarly essays subsequently lauded its ability to "provide a productive avenue for beginning the process of critical thinking necessary in order for Western students to reconsider their [false, negative] beliefs about Iran, gender, and war" (Botshon and Plastas 2).

Story of a Childhood does prompt US audiences to reconsider stereotypes about Iran and Iranians, but at the expense of fostering Islamophobia. On one hand, Marji's character effectively counters depictions of Iranians and Iran as "evil." She is a charismatic character whose antics evoke empathy among readers who can see themselves in the jeans-wearing, heavy metal-loving, back-talking youngster with spunk because she is like them, an "ordinary" girl made "different" only by the extraordinary circumstances of her life. However, in addition to calling attention to commonalities between US readers and Iranians like the Satrapi family in such representations of Marji, the book also argues that Islam is responsible for Iran's misdeeds at home and abroad. In effect, it recuperates Iran's image by blaming Islam for all that demarcates Iran as the West's antithesis, including the country's suspected support of terrorism, human rights violations, oppression of women, and totalitarianism.

In so doing, *Story of a Childhood* does not distinguish between Islam as a whole and Khomeinism, which was a unique phenomenon in the Muslim world when Grand Ayatollah Sayyid Ruhollah Mūsavi Khomeini, its architect, designed the Islamic Republic on the basis of his radical reinterpretation of the Qur'anic notion of *velayat-e faqih* (clerical authority). According to Khomeini, theocentrism is the only legitimate form of government, a tenet inconsistent with 1,500 years of Islamic theology. Thus Khomeinism is a politicized form of Islam that, as such, Ervand Abrahamian argues, "broke sharply with Shia traditions" (3) by establishing, as Adib-Moghaddam writes, a never-before-seen form of government (5). Khomeinism also departed from the Sunni institution of the caliphate, which for most of its history distributed rule between religious leaders and hereditary, lay monarchs.[3] Khomeinism was also innovative in its synthesis of disparate Muslim and non-Muslim ideologies, fusing, for example, Marxist ideas (though Khomeini rejected Marxism and persecuted socialists during his reign), nationalism, and Islamic precepts to fashion populist remedies for Iranians' "economic, social, and political grievances" (Abrahamian 3, 17, 30). These problems, held Khomeinism (and the vast majority of Iranians agreed regardless of their political affiliation), were the result of Mohammad Reza Shah's totalitarianism, US exploitation of the country's resources and control of the government (evidenced by the CIA-engineered overthrow of democratically elected Prime Minister Mossadegh in 1953), and *gharbzadegi* (Westoxication or Occidentosis),[4] Western-driven market globalization and cultural imperialism. *Gharbzadegi,* according to Khomeinism, led to secularism and a concomitant decrease in religion's importance, erasure of Iranian culture, immorality, and social injustice in the form of increasing poverty and intensifying class stratification. In addition to this populism, Khomeinism was socially conservative, invoking legal and other materials that had dubious connections to the Qur'an to develop idiosyncratic interpretations of scripture to justify imposing draconian regulations on private and public spaces. Violations and dissent were punished with execution (at least seven thousand from 1979 through 1985), detention without trial, rigged trials, torture, and rape. Clerics and lay people who opposed Khomeinism (especially Khomeini's radical notion of *velayat-e faqih*) on the basis conventional Islamic perspectives and other theocentric models of government that did not align with Khomeinism were targeted for persecution,[5] which is an incontrovertible indicator of Khomeinism's unorthodoxy.

FEMINIST NEOIMPERIALISM

Because *Story of a Childhood* does not clarify that Khomeinism's theology, extreme social conservatism, and political despotism deviate significantly from orthodox Islam—and, in fact, continues to be considered illegitimate by even conservative Muslim scholars and clerics—it humanizes Iran but only by scapegoating a synecdochic version of Islam. This maneuver clearly imbibes feminist neoimperialism,[6] a pseudo or convoluted feminism that, among its other traits, characterizes Islam as a uniquely oppressive form of patriarchalism in order to justify Western interventions in Muslim societies under the auspices of women's liberation. Fatimeh Keshavarz, in *Jasmine and Stars: Reading More Than Lolita in Tehran,* identifies feminist neoimperialism's Islamophobic strategies and features, which include (1) essentializing the nature of Islam and Muslims, (2) focusing excessively on veiling, (3) depicting Islam as a monolithic belief system mired in religiosity, (4) characterizing Muslim men as misogynistic bullies and terrorists, (5) representing individual experiences as totalizing explanations of Muslim culture, and (6) portraying middle-class status as universal while erasing experiences of the working classes and poor (26–45). In short, feminist neoimperialism genders the false dichotomy between West and East that, as Edward Said famously argues in *Orientalism*, depicts the East as the inferior Other in relation to the "superior" Western Self.

The performance of feminist neoimperialism in *Story of a Childhood* resonated well with audiences, including feminist readers (especially those who, ironically, worked to resist Islamophobia in the post-9/11 era) because it sublimates Islamophobia into a desire to rescue Marji (and, symbolically, all Muslim women) from Islam vis-à-vis dramatic confrontations that she has with Muslim characters who are represented as ignorant, stupid bullies. While Marji "wins" these conflicts (at least until the end of the book) because, as her autonarrative insists, she is cleverer than her tormentors, these episodes make the point that she is contained within a milieu that is repressive and hostile and from which she needs liberating. The book thus appeals to the Western, feminist savior complex[7] (Spivak 48–50; Abu-Lughod 122–23; Cole), a self-edifying desire to impose an ethnocentric form of feminism on Other women—a topic explored by Lila Abu-Lughod in *Do Muslim Women Need Saving?* and Chandra Talpade Mohanty in *Feminism without Borders: Decolonizing Theory, Practicing Solidarity*. Just as colonial-era European men sanitized Orientalism as ennobling of themselves, making it a matter of saving "brown women from brown men," in the words of Gayatri Spivak (296), the history of US feminisms is littered with salvific sentiments, which not only are imperialist on their face but also justify colonizing agendas, feminist or otherwise. For example, the Feminist Majority Foundation, after almost a decade-long initiative aimed at ending gender apartheid in Afghanistan, welcomed the US invasion of Afghanistan in 2001 as an opportunity to reinstate women's rights, a position that, as Ann Russo argues in "The Feminist Majority Foundation's Campaign to Stop Gender Apartheid: The Intersections of Feminism and Imperialism in the United States," enabled Bush to argue that the war would liberate women (559). The feminist savior complex, therefore, is a matter of Western feminism colluding with the patriarchal, neoimperialist, neo-Orientalist agenda, but in a manner that appears to take the moral high ground. In *Story of a Childhood*, this tactic, of course, makes Marji even more sympathetic to readers while shrewdly, deftly reifying Islamophobia and feminist neoimperialism rather than resisting them.

But most US scholarship on the book, instead of bringing critical attention to this Islamophobia and neoimperialism, celebrates *Story of a Childhood* as a "borderlands" text that deconstructs the East/West binary, with some analyses going so far as to suggest that *Story of a Childhood* counters Islamophobia. Nima Naguibi and Andrew O'Malley argue in "Estranging the Familiar: 'East' and 'West' in Satrapi's *Story of a Childhood*" that the book "upsets the easy categories and distinctions . . . between the secular West and the threatening religious East" (245). Amy Malek makes a similar point in "Memoir as Iran Exile Cultural Production" when she states that *Story of a Childhood* synthesizes "traditionally Western genres with Iranian history, culture and storytelling, producing a particularly constructive opportunity to create . . . a third space from which to question dominant notions in Western society regarding Iran and Iranian culture and history" (359).

In "Crossing Cultures/Crossing Genres: The Re-invention of the Graphic Memoir in *Story of a Childhood* and *Story of a Childhood 2*," Lopamudra Basu likewise asserts, "Satrapi's reworking of autobiography as graphic memoir disrupts the categorization of Iranian female identity as one in direct opposition to modern Western female identity, positing one as complete suppression by religious authority and the other as the apotheosis of freedom and individualism" (1). Manuela Constantin asserts in "Marji: Popular Commix Heroine Breathing Life into the Writing of History" that Satrapi "questions cultural assumptions and . . . deconstructs the role of stereotyping in the articulation of ideologies" (438).

Monica Chiu opines, "By capitalizing on standard images of veiled Iranian women, Satrapi ironically individualizes her protagonist Marji, collapsing the terrain between accepted impression (or stereotype) and personal, lived experience" (101). Chiu subsequently concludes that Satrapi's use of space and images "offers a corrective to the notion of mutually exclusive divisions between colonizer and colonized, modernity and tradition, secular and religious, the institution and the private individual" (108). Furthermore, claims Stacey Weber-Feve, *Story of a Childhood* "mobilizes in both word and image stereotypes and generalizations of the Islamic Republic and clichés of Western ideology in manners that contest traditional ways of both being and seeing and their methods or processes of constructing meaning and identity" (324). Joseph Darda adds that as an autographic text, *Story of a Childhood* is a transnational account that "falls outside U.S. frames of understanding and thus works to unsettle them" (38).

This consensus that *Story of a Childhood* contests "U.S. frames" and encourages Westerners to reconsider negative stereotypes largely rests on the argument that as Marji matures and completes her rite of passage from child- to adulthood, she selects elements of both Western and Eastern cultures to develop a hybrid sense of self that is empowering and enables her to function proficiently in both milieus. However, these analyses overlook that Marji's task is to develop a sense of self that enables her to enter Iranian, not Western or US, society and that the borders that she must cross lie between Iran's new cultural hegemony and her family's now marginalized ethos. Furthermore, the book's conclusion does not support the claim that she acquires social skills that serve her well in Iran, for *Story of a Childhood* ends with Marji leaving the country to go to school in Austria because her evolving sense of self ill prepares her for adulthood in Iran. In fact, the antics that the scholarship calls empowering actually endanger Marji, for even minor rebellions can lead to imprisonment, torture, rape, and death. Third, rather than suggesting that she is learning to negotiate disparate private and public values, *Story of a Childhood* consistently represents Marji's rite of passage as a binarized choice between her freethinking, secular family culture and the oppressive Khomeinist order, though, as noted previously, without distinguishing between it and Islam as a whole.[8] That the contrast between the two spheres is built by excessively focusing on veiling, characterizing all Khomeinists as Muslim bullies and Khomeinist men as misogynistic, monstrous Muslims, and often does not acknowledge how class status differentiated Iranians' experiences and cultivates an insidious feminist neoimperialism that dilutes or sanitizes Islamophobia, reconstituting it for Western audiences as a principled antioppression stance—readers' prejudices about Iran are challenged with humor, but the structure of Islamophobia is left intact, including the "righteousness-endowing" desire to rescue women from Islam.

VEILING AS SPECTACLE AND MYOPIC VISION

In fairness, Iran's 1979 revolution creates a particularly challenging social landscape for Marji's journey into adulthood. Initially, a broad coalition of activists across the political spectrum—left to right, secular to theocratic, liberal to conservative, and poor, working- and middle-class—united to depose US-backed Mohammad Reza Shah Pahlavi from the throne, and Marji's parents, as did most everyone in Iran, supported a change in government. In fact, as members of the Qajar Dynasty that the Pahlavis had ousted in 1925, Marji's family long had chafed against the Shah's totalitarian reign. As elites—members of the upper class (though some scholars identify them as middle class) who are secular, left-leaning, and appreciative of both Western and Eastern cultural values—Marji's parents look forward to a more open, democratic society. But when Khomeinist supporters of the revolution begin to consolidate power after the Shah flees the country, the Satrapis are increasingly alienated from the public sphere, even more so during the second phase of the revolution, when Khomeini bested competing clerics and politicos to become Iran's supreme leader.

In these contexts, Marji's challenge is not to integrate into the dominant society but, like others whose rites of passage are marked by a fissure between familial and public values, to negotiate contrary beliefs effectively. She must develop a hybridized consciousness that enables her to move back and forth across ideological boundaries (in Iran) successfully rather than follow the traditional trajectory of individuation and separation leading to full incorporation into the dominant society. However, as the following discussion demonstrates, the many confrontations that Marji has with civil and school authorities running up to *Story of a Childhood*'s dramatic ending strongly argue that she fails to develop a sense of self that enables her to internalize her family's values and navigate public mores, which is critical because flouting the Khomeinist hegemony puts her in danger. These episodes demonstrate that Marji is entrapped in the liminal space between child- and adulthood as the book concludes. She is, in this sense, fallen, not morally, but because she does not forge an adult sense of self appropriate for the circumstances or acquire the psychosocial skills that she needs to protect herself.

As the story unfolds, vignettes track Marji's maturation processes, and from the start, *Story of a Childhood* employs *hijab* (privacy, modesty, often mistranslated as "veil") to demarcate the boundaries between the Satrapis and public values.[9] *Story of a Childhood*'s opening chapter is entitled "The Veil," and the book's first panel features Marji, who is seated at a table or desk wearing a *chador* (a body-length piece of dark fabric that constitutes the traditional *hijab* style in Iran). In this iconic graphic frequently used to market *Story of a Childhood*, Marji's facial expression is unhappy, angry, and bored. In a word, she is sullen because she must wear a *chador* to school. The second panel depicts four of Marji's female classmates in the same pose wearing identical black chadors. Their expressions vary somewhat, evidence that Chiu invokes to argue that *Story of a Childhood* counters feminist neoimperialism by showing that even in postrevolutionary Iran's totalitarian theocracy, the girls' different countenances signify their ability and freedom to assert individuality (102). However, the minor differences etched on the girls' faces do not erase signs of their common resentment of forced veiling. As Lila Barzegar points out, to readers for whom *hijab* already signifies Muslim misogyny, the girls' obvious discontent incites Islamophobia (30), and of course, Chiu's critique of *hijab*, which is correct when it is mandated, assumes that *hijab* extinguishes individualism per se, which itself is feminist neoimperialism.

After this opening manifesto, Marji relates that schools were segregated by gender soon after the revolution (the beginning of the 1979–80 school year, approximately six months after the Shah fled the country on January 16, 1979), and this revelation leads into a flashback about massive women's demonstrations for and against mandatory *hijab* that occurred in 1979 (Jaynes 1).[10] On the top panel of page five, *chadori* (meaning *chador*-wearing women) cluster on the left shouting, "The veil, the veil, the veil," and a group of "uncovered" women, one of them Marji's mother, who is named Taji, are on the right countering with "Freedom, freedom, freedom" (5). This depiction of women's revolutionary-era political activism as a face-off rather than a serious debate over women's status and concerns trivializes the female electorate by reducing them to opponents or supporters of *hijab*. It implies that regardless of Iranian women's political positions and the serious nature of their objectives, the women are engaged in an absurdist, misdirected, futile shouting match about *hijab*. This is problematic for two reasons. The first is that it misrepresents the complex, varying significations of *hijab* during the revolutionary period, and second, it belittles women's key role in the revolution.

In the first phase of the revolution until the Khomeinist mandate to veil in 1980, the *chador* could connote protest of the Shah's government, anger at *gharbzadegi*—US dominion in Iran—personal piety, a heightened sense of political efficacy, support for Khomeinism, or a combination of these positions. Valentine Moghadam explains in "Women in the Islamic Republic of Iran: Legal Status, Social Positions, and Collective Action," "Huge contingents of middle-class and working-class women . . . [wore] the veil as a symbol of opposition to Pahlavi bourgeois or Westernized decadence" (1). Mahnaz Afkhami, in her account of the feminist Women's Organization of Iran's march against the Shah, adds that women took a pragmatic approach to *hijab*: "The secretary of the Kerman branch at a prerevolutionary meeting. . . . When queried about the identities of the veiled women who had led demonstrations in her city the week before . . . responded, 'They are our own members. We kept saying, "Mobilize the women." Now they're mobilized, and they shout, 'Down with the regime!'" (131). Ann H. Betteridge's "To Veil or Not to Veil: A Matter of Protest or Policy" shows that women also donned *hijab* in order to express their heightened sense of political agency: "Some women who had previously gone bareheaded expressed their new appreciation of their role [in direct political processes]" (109). However, none of this emerges in *Story of a Childhood.* Rather, the book simplifies the matter by focusing exclusively on the Khomeinist position on *hijab* and even then misses the import of the moment for the Khomeinist movement, which the women's demonstrations proved was too weak to seize power at the time. In February 1979, a month after the Shah left, Khomeini was reported saying that he preferred women to dress modestly, and this triggered the protests featured in *Story of a Childhood.* After the marches, which attracted some fifteen thousand people, Khomeini did not return to the issue until 1980. Superficial consideration admittedly suggests that the protests were about dress code, but the more important story here is that Iranian women were politically mobilizing in unprecedented numbers, and if we see Khomeini's comments as a litmus test of their political commitments and his relative power at the time, the inevitable conclusion is that Khomeini did not have sufficient support to consolidate power (because the protests forced him to defer action on *hijab* for a year) and, further, that women were a constituency he needed to cultivate in order to do so.

Women were "major participants in the revolution," suggests Moghadam (1) both prior to the Shah's departure and throughout the period that new governance structures were established in Iran, and Mary E. Hegland explains further in "Aliabad Women: Revolution as Religious Activity" (171). Not only that, but many women's entrée to the revolutionary process, Afkhami writes, was through Iran's twenty-year-old women's movement, which, importantly, had a history of working with rather than against religious sensibilities (130). These scholars' research affirms that women had a well-developed political consciousness and understood the efficacy of collective power. In this context, the 1979 protests for and against veiling must be understood as women's bid to shape the future of Iran's government. Iranian women were insisting that they have a hand in determining the best way forward for them. Moreover, they were an important demographic group, particularly right after the Shah's government and the opposition coalition collapsed and no one party was strong enough to assert control.

During this critical period, women emerged as a key group who, like men, had been concerned with the Shah's corruption and brutality, the economic effects of US interventionism, and as Moghadam writes, "Westernized decadence" prior to the revolution (1). At the same time, women experienced these phenomena differently than men, viewing *gharbzadegi* through particularities arising from the intersection of class and gender. While the general definition of decadence in the years leading up to the revolution often focused on objectification and sexualization of the female body, which proliferated in public spaces through marketing, film, Western clothing styles, and in urban areas with an influx of Westerners insensitive to and often contemptuous of local gender and sexual norms, poor and working-class women also felt Westernization as a devastating attack on the institution of motherhood. As US influence in Iran increased, these women experienced a steep decline in their standard of living, while Western corporations, Westerners, and Pahlavi cronies grew wealthy off Iran's natural resources and the government racked up debts to the Western military-industrial complex. The ground for this state of affairs had been set when in 1941 Mohammad Reza Shah Pahlavi assumed the throne after his father, Reza Shah Pahlavi, abdicated in the face of the Anglo-Soviet Invasion. Mohammad Reza Shah consistently furthered Western European and US interests in the region and ensured the West had steady access to Iran's oil by ceding profitable drilling and production rights to first British and later US corporations. In 1953, after Prime Minister Mohammad Mosaddegh attempted to nationalize Iran's oil industry, the United States and England engineered a coup—Operation Ajax—overthrowing him and centralizing power in the Shah. After that, the United States propped up Mohammad Reza Shah's regime so that international corporations could extract Iran's resources, especially oil, 40 percent of which was controlled by US firms by 1979, and Mohammad Reza Shah adopted policies that promoted modern capitalism and industrialized the economy. His economic programs, euphemized as "land reform" at the time, entailed dismantling the agricultural estates of the previous dynasty's elite class, such as Marji's family, which terminated ancient patronage arrangements between landowners and their laborers, dispossessing the latter. Many workers and their families thus migrated from rural to urban areas seeking employment; however, industrialization did not generate sufficient jobs to sustain this population.

Economic hardship forced lower-class women into the workplace, which they viewed as robbing them of their honored status as mothers, a role that lent many women satisfaction, a sense of dignity, and feelings of self-worth and was critical to their spirituality, for as Zahra Kamalkhani explains, "Motherhood, rather than other structural role relations such as wife, is the dominant idiom in the Islamic discourse on morality" (*Women's Islam: Religious Practice among Women in Iran Today*). Thus women in this demographic deeply resented the constraints that working outside the home placed on their ability to fulfill their maternal responsibilities. To use the organizing theme of *Unveiling Desire*, they saw themselves involuntarily thrown into a state of fallenness by economic structures the United States imposed on Iran with the Shah's consent. They were, as a result, receptive to Khomeini's claims that the Shah's Western-influenced policies had created economic injustice and demeaned women by displacing them from their revered place in the family, a position promised in the Qur'an. His pledge to both restore economic stability and return women to "a loftier ground for appreciation," as the new Republic's Constitution eventually framed the issue, resonated well among disenfranchised poor and working-class women. As Deniz Kandiyoti argues, "It is significant that Khomeini's exhortations to keep women at home found enthusiastic support among many Iranian women despite the obvious elements of repression. The implicit promise of increased male responsibility was attractive," especially to women who had suffered disproportionately under the Pahlavis (283). Notably, other political factions, from moderate to left, failed to appeal to women during this period and, in fact, urged them to put aside their concerns and focus on the bigger picture ("On the Question of *Hijab*" 126). Consequently, one interpretation of Khomeini's subsequent ascent to power is that sufficient numbers of Iranian women preferred economic security and the benefits of adhering to patriarchal moral codes—the respect accorded to and spirituality associated with motherhood—over rights and freedoms and that his attention to these concerns gave him an advantage over parties that ignored women and their issues. But none of this evident in *Story of a Childhood,* and the image of two groups of women shouting each other down would be completely ludicrous if not for the ominous footnote that Marji's mother fears for her life because a photograph of her and other anti*hijab* demonstrators was published in European newspapers. Though *hijab* was not irrelevant, the book's reduction of women's concerns to the *chador* clearly manifests feminist neoimperialism's obsession with veiling.

SPLIT SUBJECTIVITY

The next frame in "The Veil" that explores *hijab* is a drawing of Marji that splits her figure in two halves. This crucial yet often overlooked image shows Marji's right side garbed in a *chador* against a background of leaved vines evocative of paisley design. The other side of the panel features a hammer, ruler, gears, and cogs in the background and the left portion of Marji's body is clothed *sans chador*. Each side of the panel reverses the other's negative space: on the left, the negative space is black, and on the right, it is the traditional white. The caption reads: "I didn't really know what to think about the veil. Deep down I was very religious but we were very modern and *avant-garde*" (6). This conditions readers to accept the graphic's contention that religion and modernity are mutually exclusive and, further, adversarial or competing ideologies. One cannot be both modern and religious the caption suggests, and in the context of *Story of a Childhood,* readers understand religion to mean Islam.

Providing the background for Marji's *chador*-clad image, the right panel's paisley-like design symbolically conflates Islam and Khomeinism, for highly stylized flora is one of two most important design elements in Islamic art (calligraphy being the other). Vegetative design has embellished mosques, *madrassas* (religious schools), and minarets (the mosque tower[s] from which the *muezzin,* or "crier," calls the faithful to prayer) from the time these edifices emerged in Islam, and by the ninth century, these patterns had evolved into arabesques that, because they repeat flawlessly and as often as wished, signify divine infinity. Melding such a prominent element of Islamic sacred art with the *chador* would not be remarkable in many contexts, but following so closely on frames showing Marji's antipathy toward the *chador* and her mother's participation in protests against *hijab,* there is no doubt that here the vegetation builds the synecdochic confusion between Islam and Khomeinism. The contrast between the nature of the objects featured in the left side of the panel and the right side reinforce this slippage. The hammer,[11] ruler, and gears are, of course, the tools of science and technology and, when combined with the figure of Marji unadorned by a *chador,* bespeak progress and enlightenment—the "modern" and "avant garde" qualities that she associates with her family. This frame leaves no doubt that "modern" is the reverse of "Islam" and that female agency, symbolized by Marji's decision not to wear a *chador* is "not Islamic" according to *Story of a Childhood*'s logic. Thus this panel not only deploys feminist neoimperialist mainstays—preoccupation with veiling and misrepresentation of one manifestation of Islam as constitutive of its whole—but also frames Marji's opportunities for forging a mature adult self as a starkly delineated choice between her forward-looking family culture and Khomeinism albeit represented as Islam.[12]

MISOGYNY

Story of a Childhood further develops the topos of *hijab* in chapter 10, "The Trip." This time it also takes a swipe at Muslim men. One page into this chapter, the Satrapis learn that the government is closing Iranian universities and will revise the "decadent" curriculum so that "children are not led astray from the true path of Islam" and do not become imperialists (73). Marji's mother exclaims, "Soon you'll have to trade your car for a camel. God, what a backward policy!" This conversation occurs around June 12, 1980, the date that the universities shut down, and it shows that Khomeini's power has expanded considerably in the year that elapsed since the Shah fled Iran, for the Ayatollah had been calling for this closure since April largely because the universities were the site of leftist (and some pro-Western) opposition to theocentric governance. Of course, Taji's analogy, that camels are to Khomeinists what cars are to her class and ideological cohorts, reveals her elitism and shows that by this point, the divide between the Satrapis' views and the public climate has widened significantly.

The growing gap between the family's private values and public "morality" is even more evident when, not long after, Marji's mother's car breaks down and two "bearded guys" who Taji identifies as "fundamentalist bastards" tell her that women like her, meaning women who do not wear a *chador* in public, "should be pushed up against a wall and fucked, and then thrown in the garbage" and that if she doesn't "want that to happen, she should wear a veil" (74). The final frame in this series shows the family watching television. A heavily bearded television announcer who is not wearing a tie, a style that indicates he is devout, is shown with his left arm raised, forefinger pointing upward says, "Women's hairs emanates rays that excite men. That's why women should cover their hair! If in fact it is really more civilized to go without the veil, we are more civilized than animals" (74). The caption reads, "And so to protect women from all the potential rapists, they decreed that wearing the veil was obligatory" (74). The satire, of course, is savagely brilliant and exposes grotesque hypocrisy—as vigilantes roam the streets threatening to rape women who do not conform to the *hijabi* dress code, the government mandates *hijab* to protect women from rapists. Moreover, this episode's juxtaposition of sexual harassment and threats of sexual assault against blaming-the-victim "protectionism," the idea that women's bodies and behaviors must be regulated to protect them from harm that men can wreak, highlights the oppressive illogic of misogyny. But once again this deserved critique of Khomeinism is mired in feminist neoimperialism not only because it recycles the totalizing Islamophobic cliché that Muslim men are misogynists but because it confuses Khomeinism and Islam, perpetuating negative stereotypes of Islam. That Taji commits this fallacy suggests that she is implicated in neo-Orientalism and occupies a state of fallenness, if not morally, at least politically and intellectually, which in turn raises the possibility that she embodies the persona whose feminist neoimperialism concerns Keshavarz the most—the Iranian (or Easterner) who gives Western powers an excuse to colonize the Other.

REBELLION

Not surprisingly, conflict over *hijab* becomes one site of Marji's rebellion against the new regime as the differences between her family culture and the public sphere continues to increase. In a chapter entitled "Kim Wilde," Marji encounters two overzealous members of the women's branch of the Guardians of the Revolution, a volunteer "army" composed mostly of poor, low-skilled, undereducated volunteers tasked with enforcing Khomeinist mores in the public arena that primarily targets violations relating to gender-related behaviors. As Marji explains, their duties include ensuring that women conform to the Khomeinist uniform: "Their job was to put us back on the straight and narrow by explaining the duties of *Muslim* women" (133; emphasis added). Illustrations in this passage underscore that the women are hostile, angry, controlling, judgmental, ill-educated, and provincial. They threaten to detain Marji for letting a bit of her hair show under a headscarf, wearing tight jeans, "punk" shoes, and a Michael Jackson button (132–34). Bullies who use intimidation to repress dissent, the women verbally abuse Marji with a hysterical, irrational ferocity rooted in an intersection of religiosity and anti-Western hatred. Nevertheless, their anger is not as illogical or unfounded as *Story of a Childhood* portrays, for it stems from their oppression in Iran's recently overturned, US-created, morally Westoxified culture and economy. From the *chadoris'* perspective, Marji's apparel signifies their economic disenfranchisement (they could never have afforded her outfit even if they wanted it) and the moral degradation of *gharbzadegi*. Yet *Story of a Childhood* registers none of these considerations as it suggests that the *chadoris* are enraged because as Muslims they are, by definition, monstrously fanatic. Nothing of the class struggle or deep concerns about how Pahlavi-style Westernization affected women is revealed here or in the book's other denunciations of Islam. And as in other episodes that feature *hijab*, the book does not acknowledge the substantial differences between Islam and Khomeinism, which misrepresents Islam as an absolutist religion that insists on undifferentiated, society-wide compliance with its particular codification of moral behavior, particularly with regard to gender, and tolerates no dissent.

School is another setting where Marji resists the new hegemony, and in fact, one of her first acts of public rebellion occurs at school, albeit accidentally. Marji is sitting in a classroom soon after schools, which had been closed during the worst violence of the revolution, reopened in the early postrevolutionary period. The teacher instructs students to tear out pictures of the Shah from their textbooks. Marji turns to another girl and says, "But she is the one who told us that the Shah was chosen by God." Immediately the girl reports Marji to the teacher: "Teacher, she says that the Shah was chosen by God!!!" The teacher reprimands Marji, saying, "Satrapi, you shouldn't say things like that. Stand in the corner!" (44). Marji is shocked that her classmate would mischaracterize the comment as support for the Shah rather than an expression of confusion about the teacher's sudden shift from pro- to anti-Pahlavi propaganda. This reveals that Marji is too naïve to realize that before the revolution the teacher feared being punished if she did not support Pahlavi propaganda that the Shah was Iran's divinely appointed ruler and that in the new climate would face a similar fate if she did not conform to the new order. As in Marji's encounter with the *chadoris,* the narrative highlights these ironies while suggesting that the teacher, and by implication other accomodationists, is a mindless crowd-follower and fails to acknowledge that the teacher's inconsistency and hypocrisy are reasonable given her vulnerability in two authoritarian regimes that relied heavily on informants to flush out opponents. Nor does *Story of a Childhood* concede that Marji's elite class status and sense of privilege, even at this point in the revolution, make a difference in the ease with which she can enact rebellion, at least relative to the teacher who, as a well-educated professional, was among those who suffered in the Pahlavi economy and, later, was highly suspect in the Khomeinist regime. Again, the book simply characterizes a rational response to oppression as duplicity and illogic if not stupidity.

CONCLUSION

Approximately a year later, sometime shortly after Iraq, exploiting the instability and international isolation of its long-term enemy and with the support of the United States, invaded Iran in September 1980, a less naïve and more insubordinate Marji incites her classmates to mock the cult of martyrdom that the government promoted to foster support for its war of attrition against Iraq. Here, *Story of a Childhood* offers strong evidence that Marji is not developing the consciousness required to move back and forth between her family and public cultures, for she completely fails to understand the country's highly charged, nationalist, emotional, and psychological climate during wartime. As battlefield casualties rise astronomically, the state stages public displays of grief honoring the dead, and in schools, students twice a day beat their breasts to mourn and show support for the troops. The caption for the first of an eight-frame sequence explains that Marji couldn't resist ridiculing these rituals: "After a little while, no one took the torture sessions seriously anymore. As for me, I immediately started making fun of them." The graphic in that frame places Marji center and frontstage with laughing classmates upstage on her left and right. Marji's arms are raised above her head, and bug-eyed, she says, "The martyrs! The martyrs!" In the next frame, she is lying with her back on the floor with her arms and legs raised toward the ceiling, gyrating back and forth. The classmates hover above her, one on the right and one on the left. Marji exclaims, "Kill me!" The third frame shows her lying on her stomach slyly peeking up at the teacher, who asks, "Satrapi! What are you doing on the ground?" As three classmates, upstage and left, look on and giggle at the show, Marji replies, "I'm suffering, can't you see?" (97).

The fourth frame recalls a day when the girls are given the task of knitting winter hoods for the troops. The caption reads, "Every situation offered an opportunity for laughs: Like when we had to knit winter hoods." Marji and two girls are standing behind a table. A fourth is sitting beside them. Marji is leaning into the table looking at the other girls who are wearing oversized misshapen hoods that cover their heads and most of their faces. She is inciting them to laughter by sticking her tongue out at them. The teacher says, "Stop that! Or I'll call the principal!!" (97).

The final three frames on the page recount the school's celebration of the revolution's anniversary. Marji and her classmates decorate a classroom with toilet paper and the teacher reproaches the class, saying, "What are those garlands? Toilet paper? You are as worthless as your decorations! You're worthless!! You hear me?! Worthless!!" Marji retorts, "poopoo," and because no one will betray her, the entire group is suspended (97). At this point, Marji's parents support her emphatically, joining other parents in protesting the suspension but to no avail. In a parting shot, the teacher instructs them to ensure that the girls wear their *chadors* properly. Marji's father retorts, "If hair is as stimulating as you say, then you need to shave your moustache" (98). Once again the book offers readers an interpretation of the situation that elides all but the most facile explanations of Marji's conflicts with authority figures. In this case, her father makes this encounter a matter of dress code rather than Marji's failure to navigate boundaries between public mores and family beliefs in a manner that is effective or even safe. Instead, the focus is on the ridiculousness of forced veiling, which is not illegitimate, but it continues *Story of a Childhood*'s pattern of blaming everything from unreasonability to repression, including Marji's poor judgment in this episode, on veiling.

Marji's rebelliousness intensifies as time passes, and in 1984 after an Iraqi bomb hits a neighbor's home and kills one of her friends, her public behavior becomes increasingly risky. The book's last chapter, "The Dowry," opens with an explanation: "After the death of Neda Baba-Levy, My life took a new turn . . . I was fourteen and a rebel. Nothing scared me" (143). In this sequence, readers learn that Marji defies school rules prohibiting girls from wearing jewelry and jeans. When the principal tries to take a bracelet away from her, Marji clasps her hand around it and resists. The conflict continues a second day, and when the principal again demands the bracelet, Marji accuses her of stealing students' jewelry and selling it. As Marji and the principal tussle over the bracelet, the principal falls down. Marji is expelled.

At her next school, Marji immediately tangles with the religion teacher. During the lesson, the teacher says, "Since the Islamic Republic was founded, we no longer have political prisoners." Marji publicly contradicts her declaring, "My uncle [Anoosh] was imprisoned by the Shah's regime, but it was the Islamic Republic that ordered his execution. You say that we don't have political prisoners anymore. But we've gone from 3000 prisoners under the Shah to 300,000 under your regime. How dare you lie to us like that?" (144). Her classmates applaud vigorously. When her father learns about this episode, he praises Marji, comparing her to Uncle Anoosh. The expression on his face is proud as he puts his arm around her shoulder. But Marji's mother is deeply shaken and castigates both Marji and her father: "Maybe you'd like her to end up like him [Anoosh], too? Executed? You know what they do to the young girls they arrest? . . . You know what that it's against the law to kill a virgin? So a guardian of the revolution marries her . . . and takes her virginity before executing her. Do you understand what that means??? If someone so much as touches a hair on your head, I'll kill him!" (145). That clinches it for Marji. Soon thereafter, her parents send Marji to Austria for her own protection, which is where *Story of a Childhood* ends.

Thus in the book's final frame, Marji remains in the liminal state between child- and adulthood. She has never displayed or deployed a hybridized subjectivity that would have enabled her to negotiate what has admittedly become a chasm between private and public values. Instead, she resists the social hegemony rashly and recklessly, demonstrating that her moral development is arrested, a consideration that undercuts scholars' claims that Marji is a "typical" Iranian girl who deconstructs the Orientalist East/West binary. In this sense, Marji is a fallen character, and significantly, *Persepolis* also fails. It commits all the errors of feminist neoimperialism, thereby perpetuating Islamophobia. It puts an exaggerated focus on *hijab* without distinguishing between Khomeinism and Islam while remaining silent about the critical role that economic suffering played in the appeal that Khomeinism held for many Iranian women. Consequently, it depicts Muslim women as monstrous figures afflicted by irrational religiosity and Muslim men as bullies. Clearly, the Khomeini regime's *hijab* mandate and so many of its gender policies were misogynist and oppressive, but the problem in *Story of a Childhood* is that it essentializes the nature of Islam and Muslims as cruel and irrational, to say the least. The book's popularity in the United States, especially among activists working to offset the Bush government's characterization of Iran as "evil," shows that *Story of a Childhood* successfully humanized Iran but at the cost of reinforcing and perpetuating Islamophobia. Moreover, *Story of a Childhood* offers an extratextual tale of US failure, one that begins with the United States' first excursion into the Middle East where its neoimperialist colonization of Iran not only caused countless numbers of people to suffer under the Shah's regime but also fostered Khomeinism, the antecedent of later extremist theocentrism embraced by the Islamic State in Iraq and al-Sham (ISIS), the Taliban, Al Qaeda, and more. This neoimperialist journey ultimately led the United States into two wars against Iraq perhaps in pursuit of oil although that motive is still contested by the wars' supporters, but certainly out of a desire to control a region on whose resources the global economy and order rest—a project that failed miserably in light of postwar, post-Arab Spring tyranny and genocide and the endeavor's intrinsic moral fallenness as measured by the human suffering it has caused.

NOTES

1 Henceforth, this volume will be referred to as *Story of a Childhood* to distinguish it from the second of the two-part graphic novel, *Persepolis 2: The Story of a Return*, which this chapter does not consider, as it was published separately in 2004. *Story of a Childhood*'s popularity prompted *Time* magazine to declare it one of the best "comix" of the year, and the *New York Times* dubbed it a "Notable Book." In 2007, the film version, which combined both books, debuted at the

Cannes Film Festival, winning the Jury Prize, and Pantheon then released *The Complete Story of a Childhood* in the United States. By 2010, *Newsweek* anointed *Story of a Childhood* the fifth best fiction book of the decade. In 2013, the paperback version of the book topped the *New York Times* best-seller list in the graphic novels category.

2 Transnationalist feminists Fatemeh Keshavarz and Nawal Ammar took the position that *Reading Lolita in Tehran* is neoimperialist, and they were joined by a host of postcolonialist scholars, such as Hamid Dabashi, John Carlos Rowe, Negar Mottahedeh, and Seyed Mohammad Marandi.

3 Despite the use of the word *caliphate* by Islamic State in Iraq and al-Sham (ISIS) to describe its aim of establishing theocratic governance in Syria and Iraq, historically caliphates were only nominally theocratic, for after Muhammad's death, all but two Arab heads of state were dynastic heirs who practiced de facto separation of state and religion by relegating spiritual leadership to the clergy and retaining control of government. Only the first and second caliphs, Abu Bakr and Umar, headed both state and religious hierarchies, though Shi'as do not consider either leader legitimate, backing Ali, Muhammad's son-in-law and cousin. This dispute over succession, of course, caused the rift between Sunnism and Shi'ism.

4 The term *gharbzadegi* is variously attributed to Ahmad Fardid (1940s) and Jalal Al-e-Ahmad, who used it to describe the West's influence in Iran in his 1962 book *Occidentosis: A Plague from the West.*

5 See Feroza Jassawalla's chapter, "Shaking the Throne of God: Muslim Women Writers Who Dared," in this volume.

6 Note that feminist neoimperialism, feminist Orientalism, and New Orientalism refer to roughly the same behaviors and ideology. I use "feminist neoimperialism," this volume's introduction offers an overview of feminist Orientalism, and Keshavarz prefers the term New Orientalism. Keshavarz is specifically concerned with so-called hyphenated Americans (and Europeans) like Azar Nafisi who deploy feminist neoimperialism/Orientalism to encourage US intervention in their countries of origin. Readers familiar with the development of feminism no doubt will recognize feminist neoimperialism's antecedents in two variants of mid-twentieth-century feminisms in the United States, liberal and radical feminism, whose racism, classism, and universalizing tendencies gave rise to a discourse of blame and rescue. Although few feminist scholars consciously perpetuate these values and the women's, gender, and sexuality studies curriculum teaches against them, feminist neoimperialism stubbornly persists in mainstream feminisms in the United States and among some activists and academics (who should know better).

7 *Mainstream* is a catchall word referring to the assortment of feminist principles held by a US public sympathetic to the women's movement project of attaining equal economic rights. Mainstream feminism, also referred to as Second and Third Wave feminism, capitalist feminism, white feminism, access feminism, and pop culture feminism, is akin to but not identical with liberal feminism as a philosophy.

8 The idea of identity defined by multiplicity connotes a strength derived from the flexibility of numerous possibilities rather than the restrictions resulting from the rigidity of an externally imposed, often subordinate, social status (Castillo 12–19). Identified with Gloria Anzaldúa's notion of *mestiza* (hybridized) consciousness, this theory of individual and collective self-empowerment employs concepts and realities of border cultures, such as the multiplicity of "identity" and experience, to reconcile the conflicting values and modes of subjectivity associated with the different social locations through which subjectivity is constituted.

9 One of Anzaldúa's purposes is to define *mestiza* consciousness against a history of Western thought based on binaries in which one term is privileged over the other.

10 The *New York Times* reported that fifteen thousand women participated in this event (Jaynes 1).

11 Interestingly, the hammer is also a symbol of Christianity in that it is the tool used to nail Jesus Christ to the cross. It appears in Blake's "The Tyger": "What the hammer? what the chain, / In what furnace was thy brain? / What the anvil? what dread grasp, / Dare its deadly terrors clasp!" Here is one of the tools wielded by the smith, who figures God as creator.

12 To understand Satrapi family culture, it is important to remember that they are members of the Qajar Dynasty that preceded the Pahlavis. For as long as the Qajars governed Iran, they

clashed with the *ulama*, Islamic scholars whose authority theoretically superseded the monarchy, and the dynasty is known for resisting religious rule (Algar 15), which in part accounts for their secularism. In addition to being fiercely nationalistic, an important theme in *Story of a Childhood*, the family's embrace of Western ideals such as democracy, choice, and individual freedoms, which they associate with modernization, is consistent with the Qajar's complex relationship with the West, as Afsaneh Najmabadi explains in *Women with Mustaches and Men without Beards: Gender and Sexual Anxieties of Iranian Modernity*. She notes that the Qajars' 136-year exchanges with the West were mutually beneficial and, in part because Iran was never fully colonized, not deagentizing. During the Iranian Constitutional Revolution (1905–11), for instance, the Qajars allied with the British against parliamentarians, though later the Qajars were unseated by Mohammad Reza Shah Pahlavi in a coup facilitated by Britain in the early 1920s (5).

WORKS CITED

Abrahamian, Ervand. *Khomeinism: Essays on the Islamic Republic.* U of California P, 1993.

Abu-Lughod, Lila. *Do Muslim Women Need Saving?* Harvard UP, 2013.

Adib-Moghaddam, Arshin. "Introduction." *A Critical Introduction to Khomeini*, edited by Arshin Adib-Moghaddam, Cambridge UP, 2014, pp. 1–18.

Afkhami, Mahnaz. "The Women's Organization of Iran: Evolutionary Politics and Revolutionary Change." *Women in Iran: From 1800 to the Islamic Republic*, edited by Lois Beck and Guity Nashat, U of Illinois P, 2004, pp. 107–35.

Al-e-Ahmad, Jalal. *Occidentosis: A Plague from the West.* Edited by Hamid Algar, Islamic Publications International, 1984.

Algar, Hamid. *Mīrzā Malkum Khān: A Study in the History of Iranian Modernism.* U of California P, 1973.

Bahramitash, Roksana. "The War on Terror, Feminist Orientalism, and Orientalist Feminism: Case Studies of Two North American Bestsellers." *Critique: Journal of Critical Studies of Iran and the Middle East*, vol. 14, no. 2, 2005, pp. 223–37.

Barzegar, Lila. *Story of a Childhood and Orientalism: A Critique of the Reception History of Satrapi's Memoir.* MA Thesis, Colorado State U, 2012.

Basu, Lopamudra. "Crossing Cultures/Crossing Genres: The Re-invention of the Graphic Memoir in *Story of a Childhood* and *Story of a Childhood 2*." *Nebula*, vol. 4, no. 3, 2007, pp. 1–19.

Betteridge, Ann H. "To Veil or Not to Veil: A Matter of Protest or Policy." *Women and the Revolution in Iran*, edited by Guity Nashat, Westview, 1983, pp. 109–28.

Blake, William. "The Tyger." *Poetry Foundation.* https://www.poetryfoundation.org/poems-and-poets/poems/detail/43687.

Botshon, Lisa, and Melinda Plastas. "Homeland In/Security: A Discussion and Workshop on Teaching Marjane Satrapi's *Story of a Childhood*." *Feminist Teacher*, vol. 20, no. 1, 2009, pp. 1–14.

Bush, George W. "State of the Union Address." 2000 State of the Union. Capitol Building. Washington, DC. 27 Jan. 2000.

Chiu, Monica. "Sequencing and Contingent Individualism in the Graphic, Postcolonial Spaces of Satrapi's *Story of a Childhood* and Okubo's *Citizen 13660*." *English Language Notes*, vol. 46, no. 2, 2008, pp. 99–114.

Chute, Hillary. "The Texture of Retracing in Marjane Satrapi's *Story of a Childhood*." *Women's Studies Quarterly*, vol. 36, no. 1 and 2, 2008, pp. 93–110.

Cole, Teju. "The White Savior Industrial Complex." *The Atlantic*, 21 Mar. 2012, http://www.theatlantic.com/international/archive/2012/03/the-white-savior-industrial-complex/254843/.

Constantine, Manuela. "Marji: Popular Commix Heroine Breathing Life into the Writing of History." *Canadian Review of American Studies/Revue Canadienne D'etudes Americaines*, vol. 38, no. 3, 2008, 430–47.

Dabashi, Hamid. "Native Informers and the Making of the American Empire." *Campus Watch: Monitoring Middle East Studies on Campus*. 1 June 2006. http://www.campus-watch.org/article/id/2802/.

Darda, Joseph. "Graphic Ethics: Theorizing the Face in Marjane Satrapi's *Story of a Childhood*." *College Literature*, vol. 40, no. 2, 2013, pp. 31–51.

Hegland, Mary E. "Aliabad Women: Revolution as Religious Activity." *Women and Revolution in Iran*, edited by Guity Nashat, Westview, 1983, pp. 171–94.

Jaynes, Gregory. "Iran Women March against Restraints on Dress and Rights." *New York Times*, p. 1, 11 Mar. 1979. http://www.nytimes.com/1979/03/11/archives/iran-women-march-against-restraints-on-dress-and-rights-15000.html?_r=0. Accessed 16 Aug. 2016.

Kamalkhani, Zahra. *Women's Islam: Religious Practice among Women in Iran Today*. Routledge, 1998.

Kandiyoti, Deniz. "Bargaining with Patriarchy." *Gender and Society*, vol. 2, no. 3, 1988, pp. 274–90.

Keshavarz, Fatemah. *Jasmine and Stars: Reading More Than Lolita in Tehran*, 1st ed., Islamic Civilization and Muslim Networks, U of North Carolina P, 2007.

Malek, Amy. "Memoir as Iranian Exile Cultural Production: A Case Study of Marjane Satrapi's *Story of a Childhood* Series." *Iranian Studies*, vol. 39, no. 3, 2006, pp. 353–80.

Marandi, Seyed Mohammed. "Reading Azar Nafisi in Tehran." *Comparative American Studies*, vol. 6, no. 2, 2008, pp. 179–89.

Moghadam, Valentine. "Women in the Islamic Republic of Iran: Legal Status, Social Positions, and Collective Action." *Iran after 25 Years of Revolution: A Retrospective and a Look Ahead*, Woodrow Wilson International Center for Scholars, 16–17 Nov. 2004. *Wilson Center*, Nov. 2003. Lecture. https://www.wilsoncenter.org/sites/default/files/ValentineMoghadamFinal.pdf.

Mohanty, Chandra Talpade. *Feminism without Borders: Decolonizing Theory, Practicing Solidarity*. Duke UP, 2003.

Mujahidin-e-Khalq. "On the Question of Hejab." *In the Shadow of Islam: The Women's Movement in Iran*, compiled by Azar Tabari and Nahid Yehaneh, Zed, 1982, pp. 126–27.

Nafisy, Azar. *Reading Lolita in Tehran: A Memoir in Books*. Random House, 2008.

Naghibi, Nima, and Andrew O'Malley. "Estranging the Familiar: 'East' and 'West' in Satrapi's *Story of a Childhood*." *English Studies in Canada*, vol. 31, no. 2–3, 2005, pp. 223–48.

Najmabadi, Afsaneh. *Women with Mustaches and Men without Beards: Gender and Sexual Anxieties of Iranian Modernity*. U of California P, 2005.

Pohl, Reynaldo Galindo. "Report on the Human Rights Situation in the Islamic Republic of Iran by the Special Representative of the Commission, Mr. Reynaldo Galindo Pohl, Appointed Pursuant to Resolution 1986/41." *Iran Human Rights Documentation Center*. United Nations Economic and Social Council. Commission on Human Rights 43rd Session. 28 Jan. 1986. http://iranhrdc.org/files/pdf_en/UN_Reports/Reynaldo%20Galindo%20Pohl/E.CN.4.1987.23-1986%20Pohl%20Report.pdf.

Rowe, John Carlos. "Reading *Lolita in Tehran* in Idaho." *American Quarterly*, vol. 59, no. 2, 2007, pp. 253–75.

Russo, Ann. "The Feminist Majority Foundation's Campaign to Stop Gender Apartheid: The Intersection of Feminism and Imperialism in the United States." *International Feminist Journal of Politics*, vol. 8, no. 4, 2006, pp. 557–80.

Satrapi, Marjane. *Persepolis: The Story of a Childhood*. Random House, 2003.

Spivak, Gayatri. "Can the Subaltern Speak?" *Marxism and the Interpretation of Culture*, edited by Carrie Nelson, reprint ed., U of Illinois P, 1988.

Weber-Feve, Stacey. "Framing the 'Minor' in Marjane Satrapi and Vincent Paronnaud's *Story of a Childhood*." *Contemporary French and Francophone Studies*, vol. 15, no. 3, 2011, 321–28.

2 THE FORGOTTEN WOMEN OF 1971

Bangladesh's Failure to Remember Rape Victims of the Liberation War

FIRDOUS AZIM

> Can one explain all this? Is there a language to describe this experience? What language shall I use?
>
> —Shaheen Akhtar, *The Search*

This chapter by Firdous Azim examines two narratives that explore the plight of women who were raped during the Bangladesh Liberation War in 1971. The first is a novel, Shaheen Akhtar's *Talaash* (Dhaka: Mowla Brothers, 2005), translated into English as *The Search* (New Delhi: Zubaan, 2011), and the second a short documentary film, *Shadhinota*, or *A Certain Liberation*, directed by Yasmine Kabir (2003). Both the novel and the film trace the experiences of a woman/women raped in the war and, in their own ways, show the limits of speech and representation. The chapter juxtaposes the difficulties of fictional representations of wartime rape against the difficulties that a historical recounting entails. It also looks at how the Bangladesh feminist movement attempts to bring these women into public purview to honor and celebrate them. The chapter emphasizes challenges involved in such initiatives and how feminist endeavors delve into forgotten abuses, bring back memories, and create new places for women in artistic representation and the national imaginary.

History writing and nation making are interrelated, and in much of the world, the political nature of historical narration is a contested terrain. These debates are marked by the complexity and the difficulty of delineating the role of women in nation formation. In the case of Bangladesh, disputes about the national narrative center around the 1971 War of Liberation, and the roles ascribed to different individuals and forces delineate the nation's fractured contemporary political positions.[1] Women figure in this history either as participants in the conflict or as victims of violence. Forty-four years after the independence of Bangladesh, we have yet to see a history that concentrates on the role of women during the liberation war of 1971. In Bangladesh and elsewhere, war narratives need to take on rape and sexual oppression, as well as the participation of women in armed and violent struggle. In the mainstream representation, women are seen either as victims or as survivors of atrocities, and we witness a tendency to elide over their active participation: the plight of women is expressed through emotive language such as "loss of honor" or the national "shame" associated with war rape, which is interjected into and interrupts the "glorious" annals of the War of Liberation. The inclusion of women's role in the war would thus add a twofold, if not a manifold, dimension to the history of the liberation struggle. A gendered history of war and liberation complicates the linear narrative of victory and independence and helps focus on the problems of women's positioning in war and victory.

Texts about women in 1971 tend to be divided between looking at women as participants and viewing women as victims. The scale of the rapes meant that great efforts had to be made toward the rehabilitation of victims of war rape in the early years of Bangladesh from 1972 to 1974.[2] In numerous shelter homes across the country, pregnant women were helped to either give birth to their babies, give them up for adoption, or undergo abortions. Active measures were taken to return women to their families, and in a valiant effort to honor them, Sheikh Mujibur Rahman, the then prime minister, bestowed the title of *birangona*, or "war heroine" on them.[3] It is this question of honor and its loss that has riddled rehabilitation efforts and needs to be seen as part of the discourse of honor and shame that pertains to notions of women's sexuality. As early rehabilitation efforts faded or were wound up, the notion of honor led to the destruction of many records in the mistaken idea that these would leave a litany of shame and attach opprobrium to the women involved. Women from the centers dispersed, and their destinations were not documented. Some women were taken in by their families, some left the country, and others could perhaps hide their identities in new locations. The vast majority were left in conditions of dire poverty, eking out a living working as domestics, begging, or in sex work. Lack of documentation has also made it very difficult to gather information on these women—they are truly the forgotten women of 1971.

It is from fragments of first-person interviews, from memories of the war, that a history of women can be excavated. This chapter will look at a novel, a piece of historical/anthropological research, and a film in order to make this excavation. All are based on first-person interviews with *birangonas* and can be related to an effort to integrate the women's voices into the national imaginary. The first is a novel by Shaheen Akhtar entitled *Talaash*, which has subsequently been translated into English by Ella Dutta as *The Search*. This novel emerged from a research project on women's experiences in 1971, which the author undertook as part of a team put together by a women's human rights group, Ain-o-Salish Kendra (ASK). Some of the people interviewed in the monograph resulting from the ASK research are featured in the second piece. Yasmin Saikia's *Women, War and the Making of Bangladesh: Remembering 1971* goes further than solely focusing on the atrocities committed by Pakistani soldiers in 1971 and draws in women of other communities, specifically Bihari women, to show that sexual violence against women was prevalent during the war and how the vulnerabilities of a community were exploited through the bodies of its women.[4] This discussion will be followed by an examination of Yasmine Kabir's 2003 film *A Certain Liberation*, which draws on the life of Gurudashi Modol, a woman who lost her entire family during the war. The thirty-seven-minute-long footage offers a picture of courage and fortitude but also questions the notion of liberation at both the personal and national levels.

COLONIAL AND POSTCOLONIAL NARRATIVES OF RAPE

Whether novel, film, or research, these artifacts' representations of violence against women bring us face to face with the limits of representability. Each document talks about silence, showing how speech stops. One of the ways of understanding this silence—the inability to speak horror—can perhaps be gleaned from Julia Kristeva's "Powers of Horror: An Essay on Abjection." Kristeva sees the horror and the abjection of the body in terms of the uncanny—even as something that goes beyond the uncanny and that lies on the borderline between the conscious and the unconscious: "The in-between, the ambiguous, the composite. The traitor, the liar, the criminal with a good conscience, the shameless rapist, the killer who claims he is the savior" (4).

There is a strange seepage of the bodies—of the rapist and the raped—and the division of the horror into its agent and victim is blurred as societies try to take stock of the violence that has been unleashed. Another attempt to look at representations of torture is Judith Butler's *The Frames of War: When Is Life Grievable?* (2009). Here Butler examines representations of violated bodies, especially the images of the Iraq War's Abu Ghraib torture incidents. The circulation of these pictorial representations, the need to share information, provides Butler a space from which to analyze the ways torture and cruelty are brought into discourse, as images or representations make their presence felt, and hidden, silent acts surface in the conscious realm. The framing of the tortured body takes precedence in her analysis, transforming the tortured frames into bodies that matter. Torture and horror are written on the body itself, reminiscent of the tree of life that is imprinted onto Sethe's back in Toni Morrison's *Beloved* (1987), which then delineates a map of violation.

The violated body can be seen as a part of a colonial semiotics, upheld in the phrase "unspeakable horrors," which encapsulates the stereotypes that had been brought into being by the colonial venture. The "dark" barbarity and savagery of "other" races were cloaked in an envelope of silence, which then allowed the proliferation of the imagination, further distancing the "savage other" from the "civilized self."

It is in this light that Joseph Conrad's *Heart of Darkness* (1899) becomes a landmark delineation of the European subject going native. Here the European Kurtz himself participates in "unspeakable acts," and the unspeakability of the acts occupies a liminal space between the European and the African. This process belies efforts to keep divisions between the civilized and the barbarous in neat categories, and the meeting of the "civilized" and the "Other" blurs the differences between the two. Furthering this trope into delineations of rape, the colonial literary canon is marked by another silence, as seen in E. M. Forster's *A Passage to India* (1924), for example. This silence is an ambiguous one, as the reader is left to wonder whether Adela really was attacked in the Marabar caves. Whether hallucination or attack, the inscrutability and incomprehensibility that marks the incident in the caves is the main hinge on which the plot of the novel rests, using this space to redefine the colonizer-colonized divide.

These canonical colonial novels thus formulate the space between the colonizer and the colonized in different ways. *Heart of Darkness* blurs the boundaries by drawing the African and the European together into the execution of unspeakable acts, while *A Passage to India* delineates a realm of incomprehensibility that solidifies the gaps between the two. Pictorial representations of these "horrors" have been attempted through the films based on these novels: Francis Ford Coppola's *Apocalypse Now* (1979) and David Lean's *A Passage to India* (1984). The hints and the silences in the written texts are transposed to symbolic representations in the films. In *Apocalypse Now*, the film takes us up the river Mekong, with US soldiers firing into the villages nestled in the forests that surround the banks, plumes of smoke bespeaking the destruction unleashed by the occupying forces. As the boat approaches Kurtz's outpost, the Kurtz figure, played by Marlon Brando, is portrayed as so grotesquely obese that he is hardly able to move. The outpost is infested with monkeys, and the breakdown of order is portrayed through this grotesque representation. In the film version of *A Passage to India*, the approach to the caves is lined with erotic statuary, and a hint of repressed desire and sexuality in the novel is represented through an Orientalist stereotyping of Indian sexual worship. These slippages and differences between literary and visual representation are worthwhile to follow, as they engender a wonderful discourse between modes of representation and the limits of representability.

For the moment, though, let us trace the colonial representation to its postcolonial phase, where the same kind of silence prevails. For instance, rape and bodily violence pervade the partition literature about the division of British India into the states of India and Pakistan. Bapsi Sidhwa's *The Ice-Candy Man* (1991), published in India and the United States under the title *Cracking India*, uses the narrative voice of a little girl, Lenny, to describe the horrors unleashed in Lahore during the time of partition. Familiar scenes and sights are transformed by the violence that lurks in and around, and the innocent flirtation that the Ayah (Nanny) enjoys is marred when she is kidnapped by a Muslim admirer, the Ice Candy Man, and later found in the red-light district. We are not made to witness the rape, but the change in the Ayah's personality—her subjectivity—is part of the uncanniness of the situation that is described. Lenny and the Ayah had dwelt in a prelapsarian world of communal harmony: the Hindu Ayah with her Parsi ward, surrounded by Ayah's admirers, who were Muslim, Hindu, and Sikh. In Lenny's eyes, there is no difference of class or religion. This innocence is completely shattered by the kidnapping of the Ayah, for which the little girl is responsible. The familiar is transformed into the horrible, and Lenny's next meeting with her beloved Ayah is with a stranger whose smile doesn't reach her eyes, whose voice has become brazen, and who, though she draws Lenny into her lap, is changed beyond recognition. The Ice Candy Man also appears in this scene, and the charming young man with whom Lenny had been half in love herself now seems to be a stranger, shifting between a strange, violence-concealing unctuousness and a hitherto unperceived blatancy.

This novel has been rendered into a film entitled *Earth* by Deepa Mehta (1998). Echoing the element of earth, the film is shot in sepia tones, bringing out the before and after of the violence. Narrated in the little girl's voice, the film tries to encapsulate the enormity of the partition violence in the kidnapping incident. At this point, it would be useful to bring in another rendition of the partition violence. Research into partition violence has only gained a greater focus since the beginning of this century, as though it took a period of half a century to address the horrors unleashed at that moment of nation-making. Urvashi Butalia's historical study *The Other Side of Silence: Voices from the Partition of India*, for instance, is very conscious of unlocking a silence by using first-person interviews to probe what hitherto remained unspoken. It is interesting to see the nature of the interviews—how many are with women who were actually raped and how many with rescuers, family members, and so on. While creating a record of first-person accounts previously missing from the public discourse, the book's use of these categories reifies the convention that rape and assault on the body need to be cloaked and framed within a national narrative or a feminist critique. Readers are left wondering whether the unspeakable can be spoken or if it always remains on the other side of silence.

This long detour into the colonial and postcolonial narratives of violence and rape is meant to frame the analysis that follows. It is a way of delving into the silence that shrouds the narratives of the raped women of 1971. It is also an effort to understand the feminist critiques of national historiography, following from Butalia's earlier analysis. Each of the texts that I will be examining is by a woman, and the women authors are very conscious about the sensitivity and difficulty of representing raped and violated bodies.

PARABLE OF A NATION

Let us begin with *The Search*, which recounts the story of Mariam, a *birangona* who is also known by her nickname of Mary, vis-à-vis an interview conducted by a young female researcher, Mukti, who was born the night that the Pakistani army unleashed its horror on the people of Bangladesh.[5] When the novel opens in 1971, Mary is living in Dhaka as a student with her brother and is in love with

Abed, a University of Dhaka student leader. As the movement for Bangladesh's autonomy and independence rages outside, Mary discovers she is pregnant. All efforts to make Abed take responsibility for the coming baby are thwarted as the young student activist has no time for such matters while the movement gathers heat and momentum. Mukti, whose name means freedom, is a researcher who is trying to unravel Mary's story and those of other *birangonas*. Mukti was born on the night of March 25, 1971, as Operation Searchlight, the Pakistani term for its campaign of mass violence in Bangladesh, begins. Like Saleem Sinai in Salman Rushdie's 1981 novel, *Midnight's Children*, Mukti is a child whose life embodies the life of the nation itself. By making her a woman, and someone in search of the voices of raped women, the national narrative is made to undergo a feminist sifting. What emerges from this process is ambivalence and complexity. Mary, for example, is a *birangona* but, in her own telling, was a young woman in love, who had in a way been violated prior to her rape by Pakistani invaders, or at least was in the process of being abandoned by her lover. Mary's pregnant body is already a symbol of female vulnerability much before the rapes that are perpetrated on her.

The Search is a picaresque novel as the narrative follows Mary through her many mis/adventures. Bodily inscriptions become important. The motif of blood pervades through the novel, which after all is set during the War of Liberation. We come across the motif of blood for the first time on the night of March 25, as the Pakistani army attacks sleeping citizens and as Mukti, alias freedom, is born amid the bloody carnage. This is also the night that Mary miscarries, and as the blood seeps out of her body, it mingles with the blood that is being spilled all over. The blood of the martyr, the blood of childbirth, and the blood of an aborted birth meld and become harbingers of the nation as it comes into being. The woman's body stands at the center of this narrative of birth, independence, and nationhood—but the picture is an ambiguous and uncertain one. Uncertainty runs through the narrative as in the description of Sundari's swamp, which is the landmark that Mary and her brother Montu follow on their journey back to their village home where their parents reside. It is an ambiguous landmark, reassuring brother and sister that they have come close to home, and at the same time, legend has it that a tree in the swamp composed of the blood of murdered and tragic women lures the hapless to their deaths in the dangerous marsh. Thus fleeing Dhaka on the fateful night of March 25, for Mary and Montu, safety, like Sundari's marsh, remains a mirage that seems to be welcoming them home, even as they are inexorably lost.

The central portion of the novel is associated with Mary's sojourn in a Pakistani mass rape camp. Juxtaposed with our knowledge of what happened in the camps is the uncertainty that marks Mary's recounting. "Did she have a *dupatta* [long scarf that is a symbol of modesty], or was she wearing a sari? Was there a fan in the room?" asks Mukti, as she seeks details of Mary's internment twenty-eight years after the fact. Mary's answers are unsure and hesitant, saying that she may have had a *dupatta*, and yes, there was a fan, as they were in a schoolroom. "Then why did she not hang herself?" wonders Mukti. Mary's inability to give definite responses to the questions posed to her delineates the limits of representability, both in artistic renderings as well as in historical recounting. While she is unable to recount clearly now, Mary and her companions had been completely aware that they would be asked to bear testimony and, even as prisoners in the camp, had hoped that strands of hair or pieces of cloth would bear witness to their situation in the future. The inability to express is accompanied by an inability to comprehend. Twenty-eight years later, the researchers are as befuddled as social workers had been earlier when, immediately after the war, some of the women opted to leave with the Pakistani army to prisoner of war camps in India. The novel refers to Nilima Ibrahim's *Ami Birangona Bolchi* (*I, the Heroine Speaks*; 1978). On hearing that women preferred to be with their rapists rather than remain in Bangladesh, Nilima Ibrahim had rushed to them in order to understand the nature of their choice. Puzzled at the explanations offered to her, Ibrahim waited for four years before she could publish the interviews: women said they were leaving as an act of revenge, and the befuddled researcher/social worker was left to wonder about who the revenge was against. Mukti's research also brings her face-to-face with attitudes and emotions that are completely beyond her ken.

The motif of blood—the splashes of red—through which Mary's story began is echoed in this central portion of the novel but in a totally incomprehensible way, framing the narrative through red blots. This story of violation, violence, and torture is suddenly interrupted with a scene of desire, embellished with snow-white sheets on which roses are strewn and red wine is drunk. Mary paints a scene of love with a Major Ishtiaque, picturing him as proffering her sympathy and understanding. This extravagant scene strikes an incongruous note and belies belief, as the story of torture and rape that we have been acquainted with provides no space for love and desire. This then can be read as a moment of fantasy, where the mind transcends physical boundaries to find plenitude and fulfillment. But in this episode, Mary's fantasy of love and romance is broken, and she is brought back to reality through an accidental glimpse of a photograph of Major Ishtiaque's wife that slips out of his pocket. The photograph provides the mirror image through which a recognition of self can take place. As Mary dreams of a life with her Pakistani lover, of walks in the Shalimar gardens of Lahore, this chance glimpse brings her back to a harsh reality. The photograph is accompanied by a letter in which the major's wife writes that she hopes that he is being faithful to her and not falling into the snares of long-tressed Bengali women, and it startles Mary back to the reality of her situation. This is a strange moment of identification. Staring at this photograph, Mary merges into that other woman in the georgette *dupatta*. The moment of recognition in the mirror also separates the two women, and Mary is brought back to the realization that Major Ishtiaque is indeed her enemy and that there can never be love between them. The binaries—Pakistani/Bengali, friend/enemy, lover/rapist—establish themselves in a moment of recognition, as the woman in the photograph and Mary blend into each other, even while they are completely separated into irreconcilable positions.

The Search is a story of a woman's desire for a firm social and sexual position. The continuous violence and violations make this an impossible aim for the woman. Slipping in blood and excreta, stripped of all clothing, the national narrative does not know how to contain these experiences and incorporate them into the annals of glory and victory. When the story of rape slips into that of love and desire, the divisions between the collaborator and the patriot—the willing mistress of the Pakistani major and the violated *birangona* or war heroine—that the national discourse tries to establish, are blurred. This ambiguity of position becomes more pronounced after independence as Mary slips and slides between conflicting roles—wife or prostitute, when every sexual act feels like rape—and husband, rapist, and sexual customer blur into each other. Mary's figure becomes that of Kristeva's "in-between, the ambiguous, the composite" (4).

FORGOTTEN MEMORIES AND BLURRED BOUNDARIES

While attempting to foreground the voices of the raped women of 1971, *The Search* becomes a parable of the nation itself and of the limitations of the efforts of national history writing, which has had to struggle with the question of wartime violence against women. Historical research on the issue of war rape has remained incomplete and unsatisfactory, simply because of the difficulties associated with recovering the voices of these women. With this in mind, let us turn to Yasmin Saikia's work. Entitled *Women, War and the Making of Bangladesh: Remembering 1971*, this book broadens the canvas against which a history of violence and rape against women in the 1971 War of Liberation may be read.[6] Her search as a researcher takes her to many sites, first to the women raped and violated by the Pakistani army, as well as to Bihari women who were raped by Bengali nationalists, and to the daughters of women who suffered wartime rape. She frames these memories and acts of recalling with voices of other women who had participated in the war as either social workers, rescuers of violated women after the war, or women who had been trained in armed combat. Finally and most dramatically, she includes interviews with people who had been perpetrators and who had performed many unspeakable acts themselves.

The operative word in Saikia's work is amnesia, echoing the trope of forgetting, along with the inability to express or comprehend the effects of acts of mass violations. The amnesia that Saikia identifies is both at the national political level as well as in personal lives. Beginning with the personal level, we see how women associate the act of rape with becoming unconscious. The first interview in the chapter entitled "Victims' Memories" begins with Nur Begum's story. She says that her body is scarred by the violence in 1971, and she still bears the bite marks on her body. She goes on to say, "When I was first captured, the Pakistani military kept me naked. I was unconscious when it happened" (115). Similarly, Taslima's mother reports having fainted for four or five hours (143).[7] She becomes pregnant, and her journey through life makes her realize that she shares her suffering with other women. She directly refers to the public obliteration of such memories, with the destruction of the records of the rehabilitation centers. The loss her own diary is equated with the obliteration of public memory: "I wrote all this down in a diary, but it got lost; it was stolen. I wish I could give it to you now" (145). The child is aborted, the diary is lost, later records are obliterated—it seems that there has been a concerted effort to wipe out the memory of the atrocities. Just as the mind freezes at the moment of torture, so do subsequent events function to eradicate the memory. This amnesia is a shared one, thus making it difficult to bring back to discourse the past horrors. The glorious annals of war and victory concentrate on the clear-cut division between enemy and ally, making it difficult to incorporate these confused and half-articulated stories. However, these stories do not end with the destruction of records and memories. Daughters are present at the interviews, so that the intergenerational or the continuous level of atrocity and suffering can be gleaned. The scars are not carried on the body of the woman alone but part of the legacy that she bequeaths to her daughters.

Set against these stories of unconsciousness and amnesia is the interview with Ferdousi Priyabhashini, who is one of the few women who has publicly shared her story of rape and violation. Priyabhashini is a well-known figure and admired for the courage with which she speaks about her experiences in 1971. The interview with her that occurs in the book is open and frank, talking in detail about how her "private parts" had been lubricated to ease the rape. Interspersed within this story of violation is a love story as she talks about a major with whom she was in love. Even during this horrific ordeal, she claims to have experienced the love of one man: "I became his lover, and believe me it was true love," she says (134). She feels that this Pakistani army officer, Altaf Kareem, had offered her true love. We are jolted into attention as a story of love and affection and care is interspersed within a tale of multiple rapes and untold violence. Priyabhashini takes care to separate her own experience of love from her sister's, whom she blames as being a willing sexual participant with the Pakistanis. "I had another sister; she was shameless. She went to the Pakistani army officers of her own will. No one raped her forcibly" (134). Priyabhashini's testimony is indeed slippery and leaves us wondering about the distinctions between the willing collaborator and the forced victim. How is agency or will determined in such a situation? Don't her own feelings of love for Altaf Kareem make her situation a consensual one? Priyabhashini's story blurs the lines between complicity and force, and the admission of love makes it difficult to draw clear boundaries between the *birangona* and the Pakistani collaborator, rapist and lover, enemy and friend. These well-defined positions slip and slide into each other during the course of Priyabhashini's interview as it is reported in the book. Acts of horror seem to beget their own ways of coping, and one wonders how to read these stories of rape, how to identify points of slippage, and how to realize what has been forgotten or occluded in the retelling.

The chapter ends with an interview with a group of Bihari women. The fate and status of Biharis is perhaps the most overlooked in Bangladesh, as they continue to reside in a gray area between acceptance and rejection, with as many as 160,000 to 200,000 still living in desperate conditions in refugee camps in Bangladesh.[8] Thus the cacophony of voices that can be heard in this interview, which is subtitled "The Story of Nurjahan Begum and a Group of Bihari Women," is a result of a long silence and neglect. Women talk of homelessness, but also of the ways in which they find themselves in Bangladesh. "I came to this country with my husband," says Nurjahan. "Nobody asked me if I wanted to come here. I came here from India" (154). The stories of migration and movement across borders narrated here refer to the 1947 partition, and the horrors of partition reoccurred as new territories were drawn and new borders delineated. If territory is the determinant of nationality, these women should have been considered Bangladeshis at the time of their interviews, but in the national discourse, they have been identified as the enemy. How is this position to be reconciled within the nation-state as defined by the boundaries of Bangladesh? We are here presented with the problems of territorialization and nation making, and a debate about ethnicity and place is needed before we can place these women into any firm position. "We came from Kolkata in a goods train," says Khairun. But before that she lived in Lucknow, where her parents still are. "We came and made our homes here," she continues. "But they destroyed it; and now they tell us we don't belong here. Where will we go? We have no home?" (Saikia 154). Movement, migration, homelessness—all these are states of being that no redrawing of national boundaries has solved for these people.

Drawing the canvas wider and casting further afield to understand the process and effects of rape victims' reintegration into society, Saikia seeks out social workers who played a major role in the rescue and rehabilitation efforts after the war. Talking to Suhasini in the Sylhet district of Bangladesh, Saikia is again faced with the narrowness of the national discourse, which remains limited to the victims of Pakistani rape and that, even while it purports to save and rescue violated women, can only speak of them in terms of a bourgeois morality. A gallant and brave woman, imbued with Gandhian ideals, Suhasini had protected women who had been raped and were pregnant and had given birth. Her main effort seems to have been in concealing the knowledge of rape and ensuing childbirth from those around the women: "But it is better not to talk about them. It will open up too many disturbing wounds and cause problems for the families" (Saikia 162). This has been the national impulse: to hide and to forget, in order to go on living after unspeakable horrors.

A chapter on women warriors leads to a reflection on women's participation in armed conflict, of how women take up the role of the soldier. There is a feeling that history has an even more difficult time in reconciling with the figure of the armed female militant. So far, the image of women as victim or rescuer, though forgotten and not talked about, is in a way more acceptable than women in the role of combatant. Women's war even during liberation seems to have been fought on two fronts—against the perceived enemy but also against the patriarchy. The women interviewed in this section talk about the protective zeal of their male compatriots, who would not allow them into the battlefield. Mumtaz, for example, had participated in the war by carrying arms across the border, but even this was a subject of much debate, as it was feared that Pakistani soldiers could easily ambush and capture her, thus jeopardizing future operations. The difficult imbrications of the figure of woman into the annals of war are echoed even when women want to volunteer as freedom fighters to play a glorious role in the liberation of the country.

Amnesia pertaining to 1971 is even more pronounced in the case of Pakistanis recalling their experiences. The act of recall is marked by denial, shirking of responsibility, and shifting of blame. Saikia ends her book by including interviews with perpetrators. Leaving aside the ethical considerations that are always brought to bear on such kinds of endeavors, let us pause a moment to read a mother's story that is narrated in the book. Malik was a soldier on duty in East Pakistan during 1971. He would write to his mother who, unable to read, would go to the local schoolmaster, who would read out the letters in a gathering of women. The mother recounts her feelings as the letters were read aloud. She was the proud mother of a heroic soldier, but within the tales of victory and glory, there lurked a subterranean horror. Denial was the mother's first reaction; it was felt that the cruelties being described had been inaugurated by the Bengalis. Further, the mother felt that her son could not possibly take part in such acts. She suddenly stops in her recounting, asking God for forgiveness. In her moment of repentance, she prays that her son be saved "from committing violence and to save the women and children of East Pakistan because no women should suffer the loss of a child or be dishonoured in war" (231). Redemption and atonement are not to be had, except by a mutual recognition of culpability and perhaps confession. If there is a hint of speaking truth for reconciliation in this survey of the 1971 scenario, it is disavowed as the scale of horror and violence are perhaps too difficult to enunciate. There are references to Colonel Nadir Ali, who completely lost his sanity under the burden of the guilt that he carried with him—had been rendered unconscious in his own way perhaps. The final redemption for him comes through poetry, in an artistic pursuit through figurative speech.[9]

These interviews are the most controversial, treading close to the ground covered in another book Sarmila Bose's *Dead Reckoning: Memories of the 1971 War* (2011), which is often read as an apologia for Pakistani generals. As a genre, of course, interviews of perpetrators of violence attract suspicion, as they are seen to provide an opportunity for justification for horrible crimes. This tendency is evident, for example, in the controversy surrounding the recent documentary *India's Daughter* (2015). The maker of the documentary, Leslee Udwin, has had to justify the interview with the convicted criminals, as many viewers have felt that the film provides an opportunity to exonerate the rapists. Saikia's interviews with Pakistani army personnel can be put through the same kind of questioning, especially as she juxtaposes these interviews with Bangladeshi perpetrators of war crimes, as witnessed in the interview with Kader Siddiki. Kader Siddiki is a famous *muktijoddha*, or "freedom fighter," a sector commander and, as the only civilian sector commander, is one of the heroes of the liberation war. However, he gained worldwide notoriety through the publication of a photograph in the international press as he bayoneted Bihari "collaborators" openly in a stadium in 1972. On being asked about this, Siddiki confesses that though at that time his act had been applauded as one of revenge and justice, he feels contrite and ashamed as he thinks back on this act of instinctual retribution (238). An interesting addition to his story has been the adoption of a baby girl, who had been found by a rickshaw puller, abandoned and injured. Kader Siddiki adopted this little girl and welcomed her into his family. He had no idea who she was and whether she was Hindu, Muslim, Bihari, or Bengali. This act of adoption had become for the family an act of atonement, and there was a search for a humane and benevolent part of themselves as they spread their arms of affection to this stranger in their midst.

The search for a common humanity—of *monushotta* in Bengali or *insaniyat* in Urdu—may prompt researchers to look for moments of benevolence and kindness. But the concept of shared humanity also involves an equal culpability or a collective sinking into abysses of evil and horror. In *Heart of Darkness*, Kurtz's last words—"The horror, the horror"—have echoed through the years as a comment on the human condition. There is an effort in all these representations to find the horrors that are unleashed by all actors in moments of conflict and strife and to bring out some elements of benevolence and forgiveness through mutual recognition and acknowledgement.

In many ways, Saikia's historical/anthropological account is reminiscent of Butalia's account of the horrors of partition. Both writers are conscious of the limitations of the first-person voice, especially the act of recall and remembering, and assiduously frame their narratives by bringing in evidence from various sources, thus exposing the breadth and enormity of the horror and the complexity involved in the act of remembering. Significantly, both begin their research journey through their own lives, as each foregrounds her motivation in embarking on the act of bringing back to discourse that which has been forgotten. On the other hand, the fictional/artistic renderings—the novel and the film—seem to eschew the authorial voice and instead concentrate on the twists and turns in the narratives of the women being portrayed to reveal the difficulty of the task.

Saikia allies her search for a common space of humanity to the wider history of South Asia, where independence in 1947 had been accompanied by a bloody partition, and people had undergone gruesome experiences of atrocities and violence. The violence enacted on women's bodies has already been referred to. The colonial rendering attempted to justify the horrors it unleashed through a system of binaries, by which the colonizer and the colonized were divided into separate categories. The postcolonial moment in South Asia seems to be marked and marred by a similar system of bifurcation, dividing Hindu and Muslim, Bihari and Bengali, Bengali and Pakistani into implacable and irreconcilable positions. The works we have been looking at try to bridge these divisions, and the moments in which these boundaries are blurred are also moments of spontaneous articulation, and in the burdens of guilt and suffering, there may lurk a common thread of reconciliation.

MADDENING AMBIGUITY

We have followed the forgotten women of 1971 through a fictional rendering and a piece of historical/anthropological research. A representation through film will form the final part of the triptych of images that this chapter has been tracing. Yasmine Kabir's *A Certain Liberation* is an important document, as it seeks not to reveal the horrors of war and the violations committed but to celebrate the life of a woman who has lived through such experiences. In the process, the film plays on the word *liberation* and, by adding the adjective *certain*, seeks to qualify and question the very notion of freedom.[10] The word liberation refers to both national liberation and the freedom of the individual woman. Our heroine is Gurudasi Mondol, whose husband and children had been killed in front of her eyes by Pakistani soldiers during the war and who herself had been left for dead after being raped.

The film begins with a boat trip, as Gurudasi guides the film crew to the spot where the atrocities had taken place. As she is unable to describe the act in words, the camera dwells on her facial expressions in an effort to decipher the courage and fortitude it takes to survive such an incident. The film then follows Gurudasi to Kopilmoni, the town in North Bengal where she now resides, with the camera trailing her as she freely roams its streets. A well-known figure, Gurudasi has indeed been welcomed and incorporated into the fabric of the community and has carved out a space for herself. After the silence that we encountered in our previous texts, the film is full of dialogue; in fact it is quite garrulous. Gurudasi feels that the nation—the government—owes her, and she seeks recognition and recompense for her suffering. In her search for reparation, she feels that she deserves an audience with the prime minister. In fact, it is her picture in a newspaper with a cap on her head and stick in hand, as she waits outside the stadium where she is denied entry on Independence Day celebrations, that brought her to the attention of the filmmaker and inspired Kabir to explore Gurudasi's story.

Communal harmony is part of the story that Gurudasi engenders. Hindu herself, she lives in a Muslim household, which has eschewed the consumption of beef in her honor, and whose members have made space even in their very cramped quarters for her prayer room. She has more or less adopted the little boy in the family, and the unconditional love that she showers on him has the effect of making him a thoroughly spoiled child. Though her presence and story garners respect, people do not hesitate to label her a mad woman, and it seems it is her insanity—being unconscious—that allows the community to tolerate her. Gurudasi's "madness" works in many ways. Her freedom from all kinds of patriarchal and social control is possible because of her state of mind, but at the same time, it is a commentary on the limitations of that freedom. The adjective in the title is illustrated through the dual status that she has, both revered and tolerated as a war heroine. She is free to castigate one and all for the situation of the country and to comment on the limited nature of the liberation. Her familiar figure represents for the community the sufferings of the war, as well as a woman who has lost her moorings.

Gurudasi sees herself as the mother of the community, not just of the boy whom she has so lovingly adopted. She insists on being addressed as mother, and her jaunts through the streets of the town take her to the local government headquarters, where she demands her rights and recognition of her position. She walks into tea stalls, making others pay for her food. She extracts her dues from the community, who seem to be proud of having her in their midst. But this acceptance, as mentioned earlier, is part of a tolerance for the somewhat mad, the mildly insane. This play with the notion of liberation brings together both national and personal dimensions. The ability to walk freely through the streets is a part of a feminist agenda, and Gurudasi's freedom is indeed the fulfillment of a feminist ideal. As Gurudasi wanders freely through the streets, she spreads her hands out in a gesture of dance, accompanied by the boys who follow her. The camera slows down to capture the dancing figure and leaves the viewer to puzzle over its significance. This dancing figure is not easily reconcilable with all the other meanings that have been associated with Gurudasi—symbol of the suffering induced by the 1971 war or the mother figure that she insists on representing. The accepted meanings are turned upside down, and the choreography of the dance brings forth many new interpretations. The significance of the dancing figure can be made to elicit many meanings and, read metonymically, hovers between the madness and maternal affection that she is associated with and the unity that her presence wields in the community.

The dancing Gurudasi thus evokes a prelingual state of being, which feminist theory has associated with the feminine, the preconscious state of being evokes a *jouissance* that is precluded as language enters the realm of symbolic speech.[11] Let us try to see how this figure can be reconciled with the figure of the mother, which is the role that we (and the national discourse of liberation) can easily identify with Gurudasi. In Bengali iconography, motherhood is invested with a near divine status. This iconography has been translated into national discourse, especially in literature. The mid-nineteenth-century novelist, Bankim Chandra Chatterjee, for example, is seen to have laid the foundations for the anticolonial nationalist struggle by invoking the nation as goddess and mother. His novel *Anandamath*, written in 1882, addresses the nation as mother, and the young men and women—the warriors—devote themselves to the liberation of the mother as nation. The trope of mother worship is related to goddess worship, which is a part of Hinduism as practiced in Bengal. In the religious iconography, goddesses take on contrasting forms. In her avatar as Durga, the goddess brings fertility and prosperity but also represents the daughter who can only pay an annual visit to her parental home. In her incarnation as Kali, the goddess becomes a slayer of evil and is a destructive force to be feared. Due to its complexities, this dual nature of goddess worship was difficult to incorporate into the national imaginary, which transposed these meanings to view the mother as a captive woman and her children as young and brave warriors who would liberate her from the shackles of foreign or British rule.

However, the limitations of this nationalized discourse soon became visible, as the Muslim majority in Bengal could not respond to the worship of the mother-goddess. As the century progressed, it was again through literary writings that this mother-goddess motif was transposed into that of the mother-nation. In Rabindranath Tagore's writing, for example, the nation as mother is a symbol of the soil and water of Bangladesh, and she is envisioned as a unifying figure endowed with a natural benevolence, drawing all her children together. The struggle for Bangladeshi nationhood encompasses all these aspects of the mother figure, to which the primacy of the mother tongue or the Bengali language has been added. To wit, a linear and mainstream history of Bangladesh traces the beginnings of the search for Bangladeshi nationalism in the language movement of 1952. That movement had been for the incorporation of Bengali as one of the state languages of Pakistan. As the struggle for the establishment of Bengali as state language gained momentum, the differences between the two wings of Pakistan were revealed starkly. In this process, Pakistan, or West Pakistan, emerged as the enemy, and the process of self and othering was transposed from colonial binaries into the nationalist struggle.

Julia Kristeva's 1975 article entitled "Motherhood According to Giovanni Bellini" is a reflection on the representation of the mother-child image in Renaissance paintings, and it offers a useful frame for looking at motherhood as a national construct in Bangladesh.[12] With the advent of the Madonna and child paintings, the earlier paintings that had concentrated on the figure of the baby Jesus were transformed into an image of mother and child. Child and mother painted as locked into an embrace and a gaze as their eyes focus on each other in representations of the Madonna. While these paintings are part of a deification of the mother as Mary, motherhood is at the same time drawn into the framework of the bourgeois family. The iconic and central status that these mother and child paintings have acquired in Western art renders every other image of the mother transgressive, and only these mother and child images can be invested with a divine or holy status. Similarly, the dancing Gurudasi, the Gurudasi who walks the streets, or the woman who suckles a child years after she has given birth, transgresses the role of mother even while she insists on her status as the mother of the community. Just as the sense of liberation or freedom is qualified by that very uncertain word "certain," all other images and tropes that symbolize the nation are similarly qualified and put to question in this film.

BIRANGONA TO FREEDOM FIGHTER

Film, novel, or research: each representation is an act of memorializing, looking for, remembering, documenting. Bringing back to memory—to discourse—involves a recapitulation of the horrors and violations that the war of 1971 had entailed. It is in this effort that the texts encounter moments of silence, of evasion, of unconsciousness, of amnesia. Factual recapitulation or artistic rendering, the readers/viewers are alerted to moments of slippage, of discord, which nevertheless gesture toward a deeper understanding, even of arenas that lie beyond conscious utterance.

The three texts that we have been looking at are by women and indeed embody a feminist effort to uncover and decipher what has been hidden and veiled. Patriarchal notions have constructed the lives and sufferings of these women as a loss of honor, equating the restitution of their honor with the honor of the country. When we go beyond that nationalist discourse, to look at the individual woman, notions of honor and shame become muddled. There are moments of complicity, even a sharing in the enactment of unspeakable acts, where the loss and the honor are completely befuddled. The enemy and the self merge and blend, and the binaries that the national history would like to keep intact are belied—Pakistani, Bangladeshi, Muslim, Hindu, Bengali, or Bihari.

However, after decades of amnesia, there has been a revival of interest in the *birangonas* in Bangladesh. After years of struggle by women's groups, the government of Bangladesh has recently recognized the raped women of Bangladesh as freedom fighters. They have been honored as *muktijoddhas*, or "freedom fighters," with all privileges and status. There had been, among various groups, a debate regarding recognizing *birangonas* as freedom fighters. As stated earlier, the title of *birangona* or brave woman had been awarded by Sheikh Mujibur Rahman as a title of honor for raped and violated women. In the ensuing years, this nomenclature had led to further dishonoring of the women, who have been ostracized as Pakistani whores, and who therefore hesitated to use the title for themselves. Most *birangonas* wanted to be addressed as freedom fighters. Freedom fighter groups, on the other hand, opposed this inclusion as joining the freedom struggle was seen as a voluntary and brave act, and not one of passive suffering at the hands of the enemy. Feminist groups such as Naripokkho had preferred the term *birangona* and felt that the titled needed to be reinvested with the honor and dignity that it was meant to convey.[13] The recent declaration has been welcomed, as this means that a process of reparation and restitution of status will be set in motion, and perhaps in old age, violated and raped women will enjoy a modicum of comfort and dignity. However, the debate over the nomenclature can be seen to reveal another kind of discomfort. The affected women would like to erase the opprobrium of rape, freedom fighters want to ensure that nothing tarnishes their glorious fight, whereas feminists were involved in an effort to acknowledge *birangonas'* struggles and dignify the lives of women who had been raped and ensure that reparations would be made. The recognition of *birangonas* as freedom fighters does make the reparation and rehabilitation effort easier, but the question that remains is whether another occlusion—another act of forgetting, another inability to look at the horror in the face—is happening. This further elision is an example of our collective inability to confront the nature of suffering and sexual violations. There is a danger that the personal experiences of these women will still elude historical accounts, and the unspeakability of their sufferings keep the women unrepresented.

A feminist historiography seeks to give voice to women, to unearth buried histories. Such an excavation is always interesting as it redraws the contours of memory, adding new dimensions to established stories and narratives. Our reading of these representations of the founding moment of Bangladesh unsettles the glorious history of a successful struggle and, by blurring the boundaries between the enemy and the patriot, questions the nature of all struggles and causes.

NOTES

I would like to dedicate this chapter to Naripokkho, whose work on the *birangonas* has led me to think deeply about the subject of war violence and women.

1 When India achieved independence from Great Britain in 1947, the region was divided into the Dominion of Pakistan and the Union of India, with boundaries drawn largely on the basis of religious affiliation—majority-Muslim regions constituted Pakistan, while India was predominantly Hindu. Consequently, Pakistan consisted of two distant, noncontiguous areas—present-day Pakistan and Bangladesh—with numerous cultural, regional, and economic differences. Discrimination and deprivation led to a growing rift between the two wings of Pakistan, and the liberation war of 1971 was the founding moment of Bangladesh, which gained independence on December 16 after a bloody war marked by genocide and mass rape. The war divided the nation into forces that were deemed to be collaborators of Pakistan and the nationalists fighting for Bangladesh's independence.
2 The most commonly cited estimates put the number of rapes at two hundred thousand to four hundred thousand. Although not a legally recognized category at the time, these rapes were war crimes systematically conducted by Pakistan (Totten 49). Susan Brownmiller, who in 1975 conducted one of the first studies of this campaign, reported that women were raped "on the spot" and then held "in military barracks for nightly use" (82). Women were also imprisoned in "mass rape camps" (Malik 154–55). A postwar pregnancy crisis emerged with estimates ranging between twenty-five thousand and seventy thousand (Totten 49).
3 *Birangona* is the feminine version of the word *bir*, or "hero." Hence the title was awarded to mark these women as brave but, as the article will go on to show, it acquired negative connotations in colloquial use.
4 Biharis are residents of the eastern state of India called Bihar, which shares a border with Bangladesh and its neighboring state, Jharkhand. While Biharis are often represented as a homogeneous group based on their geographic origins, they can be Muslim or Hindu, their caste-class status varies, and as an Indo-Aryan ethno-linguistic group, the majority speak Bhojpuri, but there are also Biharis who speak Maithili, Urdu, and Nepali. Intra-Bihari conflicts are deep-seated, as conservative, orthodox Biharis self-identify primarily along the lines of religion or caste-class status rather than ethnicity or place of origin. Tension and discrimination are thus common between Muslim and Hindu Biharis and between Brahams and non-Brahams.

During the partition of India in 1947, many Muslim Biharis migrated to East Pakistan (present-day Bangladesh). Those who moved to Pakistan are known as Muhajirs, or Muslim immigrants. After Bangladesh's liberation in 1971, the Biharis were left behind when the Pakistani army and civilians evacuated. The Bihari population in Bangladesh found itself unwelcome and, for a long period, was stripped of citizenship in both countries. Pakistan feared a mass influx of Biharis could destabilize a fragile and culturally mixed population, and Bangladeshis scorned the Biharis for having supported and sided with Pakistan during the war. These Muslim Biharis were called "stranded Pakistanis" and remained stateless for thirty-three years. In May 2008, a Bangladeshi court ruled that Biharis who were either minors in 1971 or born after 1971 are Bangladeshi citizens and have the right to vote. Three hundred thousand Biharis now live in Bangladesh, although a significant number remain in the refugee camps to which they were relegated after the war, while others have assimilated.
5 All references to the novel are from the English translation.
6 The book will henceforth be referred to as *Remembering 1971*.
7 Victims are identified only by their first names in *Remembering 1971*.
8 Biharis, unlike ethnic Bengalis, did not gain citizenship when Bangladesh was constituted as an independent nation. Until 2008, Biharis in Bangladesh who were born prior to the War of Liberation were stateless and denied citizenship by the governments of Pakistan and Bangladesh, which resulted in their decades-long sequestration in refugee camps.
9 By his own account, Colonel Nadir Ali, who as a Pakistani officer during the genocide was aware of it but denies ordering or participating in it, experienced an episode of paranoid schizophrenia when ordered to return to Pakistan for a promotion in recognition of his heroism: "I was a mental patient for two years, was hospitalized for six months and lost my memory in the process of treatment. I was retired as a disabled person in 1973" (par 35). Ali subsequently reconstructed himself as a poet and writer.

10 It is interesting to note the differences in the titles. The Bengali film is entitled *Shadhinata*, or *Liberation*, whereas in the English translation, the freedom or liberation has been qualified with the word *certain*.

11 Luce Irigaray, *This Sex Which Is Not One* (1985), or Julia Kristeva, *Desire in Language* (1980), use psychoanalytical theory to locate the origins of feminine speech as being anterior to the entry into the symbolic order. This also provides a way of looking at states of the "unconscious," which then becomes the locus of feminine desire.

12 Anthologized in *Desire in Language*, pp. 237–70.

13 Naripokkho is a leading woman's activist group in Bangladesh. It has been working with *birangonas* since 2012, and as a member of the group, the author has personally participated in many of these discussions.

WORKS CITED

Akhtar, Shaheen. *The Search*. Translated by Ella Dutta, Zubaan, 2011.

Ali, Nadir. "Liberation War: Historicizing a Personal Narrative." *Uddari Weblog*, Punjabi maaNboli Literature, Creators and Publishers, 30 Mar. 2011, http://www.uddari.wordpress.com/2011/03/30/liberation-war-historicizing-a-personal-narrative-by-col-nadir-ali/. Accessed 6 July 2016.

Apocalypse Now. Directed by Francis Ford Coppola, performances by Marlon Brando, Robert Duvall, Martin Sheen, Frederic Forrest, Albert Hall, Sam Bottoms, Larry Fishburne, and Dennis Hopper, United Artists, 1979.

Bose, Sarmila. *Dead Reckoning: Memories of the 1971 War*. C. Hurst, 2011.

Brownmiller, Susan. *Against Our Will: Men, Women and Rape*. Bantam, 1976.

Butalia, Urvashi. *The Other Side of Silence: Voices from the Partition of India*. 1998. Penguin, 2000.

Butler, Judith. *The Frames of War: When Is Life Grievable?* Verso, 2009.

A Certain Liberation. Directed by Yasmine Kabir. 2003.

Chatterjee Chandra, Bankim. *Anandamath, or the Sacred Brotherhood*. Translated by Julius Lipner, Oxford UP, 2005.

Conrad, Joseph. *Heart of Darkness*. 1899. Penguin, 2000.

Earth. Directed by Deepa Mehta, performances by Aamir Khan, Maia Sethna, and Nandita Das, Cracking the Earth Films, 1999.

Forster, E. M. *A Passage to India*. 1924. Penguin, 2000.

Ibrahim, Nilima. *Ami Birangona Bolchi (The War Heroine Speaks)*. UP Limited, 1994.

India's Daughter. Directed by Leslee Udwin, Berta Film, 2015.

Irigaray, Luce. *This Sex Which Is Not One*. 1977. Translated by Catherine Porter and Carolyn Burke, Cornell UP, 1985.

Kristeva, Julia. *Desire in Language: A Semiotic Approach to Literature and Art*. Edited by Leon S. Roudiez, translated by Alice Jardine and Thomas Gora, Columbia UP, 1980.

———. *Powers of Horror: An Essay on Abjection*. 1980. Translated by Leon Samuel Roudiez, Columbia UP, 1982.

Malik, Amita. *The Year of the Vulture*. Orient Longman, 1972.

Morrison, Toni. *Beloved*. Knopf, 1987.

A Passage to India. Directed by David Lean, performances by Peggy Ashcroft, Judy Davis, Victor Banerjee, James Fox, Alec Guinness, and James Wilson, Thorn EMI Screen Entertainment, 1984.

Rushdie, Salman. *Midnight's Children*. Penguin, 1981.

Saikia, Yasmin. *Women, War and the Making of Bangladesh: Remembering 1971*. Duke UP, 2011.

Sidhwa, Bapsi. *The Ice-Candy Man*. 1988. Penguin, 1991.

Totten, Samuel, editor. *Plight and Fate of Women Following Genocide. Genocide: A Critical Bibliographical Review* Vol. 7. Transaction, 2012.

3 ⑥ FRAGMENTED STATE, FRAGMENTED WOMEN

Reading Gender, Reading History in Partition Fiction

PARAMITA HALDER

Paramita Halder, in this chapter, discusses how women as icons of community honor and conservators of the cultural and biological future of the nation became vulnerable during the partition, losing nearly all control of their bodies due to the pervasive violence that marked its inception. Analyzing the works of Jamila Hasmi, Rajinder Singh Bedi, Amrita Pritam, Sadat Hasan Manto, Lalithambika Antharjanam, and Jyotirmoyee Devi, this chapter considers how women's social effacement, their rejection by natal kin and community after sexual assault and rape, was a common response to attacks on women. It concludes by examining how these fallen female protagonists attempt to restore the community's sanity, protract human life, and maintain the continuity of the very society that marks them as fallen and denies them kinship structures and moral support.

In 1947, as the Indian subcontinent was severed in two, with the present-day states of India and Pakistan eventually emerging from the divide, women were the primary targets of the communal strife that broke out across the region as a result of this reapportionment of the Indian subcontinent.[1] Their physical vulnerability was exploited, and often those who were sexually violated were rejected by their natal kin and larger communities. These women, whose individual choice was otherwise customarily ignored, were ostracized, and their agency, already low, declined precipitously. Considered "fallen" and "dishonored," their sagas reveal how patriarchal concepts of woman- and nationhood were used to marginalize them and, in fact, women in general. Whether documentary or fictional, partition narratives, as they are called, offer a cipher revealing the hidden forces that shaped partition survivors' predicament. *The Ice-Candy Man*, by Bapsi Sidhwa; the short story "Exile," by Jamila Hasmi; *The Skeleton*,[2] a novel by Amrita Pritam; *The River Churning*, a novel by Jyotirmoyee Devi; and Lalithambika Antharjanam's "The Mother of Dhirendu Mazumdar" interrogate violated women's fates during and after the partition. In addition to examining the extreme psychological damage these women suffered as a result of their initial violation and subsequent revictimization by family members, purported rescuers, and their home communities, these tales argue that longstanding patriarchal beliefs and discourses about womanhood, even those that appear to honor women, created the cultural conditions that made women particularly vulnerable to the violence.[3]

During the partition of the subcontinent, lines were drawn on two frontiers, east and west across the states of Punjab[4] and Bengal,[5] respectively. In both regions, women, already trapped by age-old patriarchal norms, were abducted, raped, and murdered, and upon survivors' return home, they were frequently ostracized by their families and communities.[6] Sidhwa's *Ice-Candy Man*[7] is a representative text that provides insight about this phenomenon. Lenny, the protagonist of the novel, is a young Parsee girl who lives with her family in Lahore, which, with a Muslim-majority population, was located in Pakistan after the partition.[8] This decision catalyzed rioting that targeted Hindus and Sikh minorities. Lenny lost her favorite *ayah* (nanny) during the riots. In the disturbing months following the violence, Lenny spends her time scrutinizing happenings around her. From the terrace of her house, she observes that the abandoned house of a Hindu neighbor has been converted into a camp where a number of female riot victims are kept. Lenny cannot understand why the women are in the camp because nobody broaches this tabooed topic in front of the children: "The servants evade questions as if there is something shameful going on" (189). Lenny imagines that the camp is a women's prison where female convicts are kept, but in reality, of course, the women have nowhere else to live because the outside world shuns them. They are considered less than human, which Lenny's reference to them as "night animals" makes clear: "We still don't know anything about them. Who they are, where they are from. They keep to themselves unobtrusively conducting their lives lurking like night animals in the twilight interiors of their layers, still afraid of being evicted from property they have somehow managed to occupy" (190). One camp resident, Hamida, appeals for a position as household help for Lenny's family, and her anxiety and embarrassment indicate the acute tragedy of the women's situation: "'I am not frightened of work brother,' says the woman in thickly accented, village Punjabi. 'I will sweep, clean, milk the buffalo, churn the butter, wash clothes, clean out latrines, make *chappaties* [round, unleavened bread]. . . . After all, I've been a housewife.' She stops speaking abruptly and looks unaccountably guilty and even bashful. Suddenly, folding her knees, she hunkers down on the bedroom floor and draws her *chuddar* forward over her face" (191). After Hamida describes herself as a "fallen woman," Lenny asks her godmother what that means and gets the answer:

"'Hamida was kidnapped by the Sikhs,' says Godmother seriously . . . 'She was taken away to Amritsar. Once that happens, sometimes the husband—or his family—won't take her back'" (215). The iniquity of denouncing wives and daughters who have been abducted or sexually violated becomes obvious even to Lenny, a child.

Patriarchy rigidly specifies the extent of women's sphere, and in the normative structure of patriarchal society, women's identity typically is constructed within the four walls of her home. When women who have established a sense of self rooted in a patriarchally defined domestic space are violently ousted from their homes, they are denied a basic marker of their sense of self. Ananya Jahanara Kabir observes that for these fallen women, not only their bodies, but also their very existence becomes a source of pain: "The combination of physical violence with physical dislocation during partition means that not just the body, but also the body's place in the world becomes a site of trauma" (179). This is evident when Hamida's inner agitation and mental turmoil are translated into body language. To fill up her inner void and to escape the demons of that stalk her, she perpetually seeks some physical activity and is never in a tranquil state:

> Hamida has to be restrained from latching on to Mother and massaging and pummeling her limbs whenever she finds mother sitting, sewing or reading in bed. Hamida does not know what to do with her hands in mother's presence. And when idle, in fluttering panic they reach out and massage whoever is at hand. Adi [Lenny's younger brother] wiggles and slips away from her grasp. Or, if she is too insistent kicks out. I let her hands have their will with me and tolerate her irksome caress. She is a starved and grounded bird and I can't bear to hurt her. Sometimes her eyes fill and the tears roll down her cheeks. Once, when I smoothed her hair back, she suddenly started to weep, and noticing my consternation explained: "When the eye is wounded, even a scented breeze hurts." (193)

The text thus indicates how these women are marked as outcasts and kept within closely guarded boundaries, invisible to the outer world. But, ironically, they are easy prey for their rescuers. Lenny's account of the nighttime sounds emanating from the women's activities hints at their revictimization in rehabilitation camps: "The mystery of the women in the courtyard deepens. At night we hear them wailing, their cries verging on the inhuman. Sometimes I can't tell where the cries are coming from. From the women—or from the house next door infiltrated by our invisible neighbors" (212).

In response to partition violence, in December 1947, the Inter-Dominion Conference convened in Lahore, and India and Pakistan agreed on steps to be taken for recovering and restoring the abducted women. Direct evidence of this abuse is provided by Ritu Menon and Kamla Bhasin's documentation of the camps' conditions. One of their interviews with a social worker named Kamlaben Patel who was stationed in Lahore from 1947 to 1952 and actively involved in repatriating camp residents illustrates the women's plight. She recounts interviews with about six hundred women that she conducted from February through March 1948 during the recovery process. They hint that the women had been raped by camp guards:

> We asked them, what did you eat? Who was responsible for this miserable condition you find yourself in? How did you come to the camp? More than that they could not have answered as they were in a daze and so mentally disturbed. They had just been dumped. But this much they themselves told us, that they had been supplied to the army. Those who were older did not say anything but the young ones sometimes talked to us. I asked one of them whether they got food and she answered yes, we got very good food, but ever since we have come to this camp, our food has been stopped. I asked, what kind of delicious food were you given and she answered, "The meals of the men were very good." Then we understood what she meant. We had no definite proof of course. (82–83)

Thus partition fiction as well as the oral narratives such as those collected by Melon and Bhasin unravel stories of the abuse that female victims of partisan violence endured not only at the hands of their abductors but also by society at large, their kin, and those who were supposed to be their saviors.

In Amrita Pritam's *Skeleton*, which is set in the Punjab region of present-day Pakistan, the protagonist is a Hindu girl, Pooro, who is abducted and raped by a local Muslim lad named Rashida, and who is rejected by her parents when she returns home because they worry about the shame and disgrace she brings the family: "Daughter, this fate was ordained for you, we are helpless. . . . Who will marry you now? You have lost your religion and your birthright" (9–10). When Pooro is rejected by her father, her mother's explains that if they let Pooro stay, they risk losing the family's honor: "Daughter, it would have been better if you had died at birth! If the *Shaikhs* [community elders] find you here they will kill your father and your brothers. They will kill all of us" (10). Pooro is completely traumatized by her parents' lack of concern for her and her future. She is, as Jenny Edkins's definition of trauma suggests, devastated by her family's betrayal. As Edkins explains, trauma arises from such a sense of betrayal—a shattering of certainty about the set order of things: "It seems that to be called traumatic—to produce what are seen as symptoms of trauma—an event has to be more than just a situation of utter powerlessness. In an important sense, it has to entail something else. It has to involve a betrayal of trust as well" (4). Pooro, who had been convinced that her parents would protect her and give her security, is traumatized when they break this trust and become her tormentors, transforming her family from a source of refuge into a site of condemnation and rejection. Her trauma is compounded when the community in which she is a member turns against her. She is spared homelessness when eventually Rashida takes her back, marries her, and treats her well, but she cannot escape the psychological trauma of her abuse and subsequent rejection by her family.

Pooro's trauma is exacerbated even more by her lack of autonomy in Rashida's home where she is renamed Hamida after the marriage. Her transformation from Pooro to Hamida, from a young Hindu girl to Rashida's wife, and then to the mother of Rashida's son, follows, the narrative suggests, as if preordained by destiny. She has absolutely no command or choice over the course of her life. She is not even sure who she is—Hamida or Pooro. She suffers an acute existential dilemma, and her sense of self is blurred: "In her dreams, when she met her old friends and played in her parent's home, everyone still called her Pooro. At other times she was Hamida. It was a double life: Hamida by day, Pooro by night. In reality, she was neither one nor the other; she was just a skeleton without a shape or a name" (1).

This crisis of identity is perhaps the most common feature of accounts of female victims of partition violence. For example, Hamida, the new *ayah* in *Ice-Candy Man*, does not want to disclose her previous identity, but she can never forget her past—that she was a simple housewife with family and children. Nevertheless, this information surfaces in her unconscious verbal slips. Her body language, nervous movements, fluttering hands—all are indicators of the extreme psychological agony that she unsuccessfully tries to repress. Essentially, the fallen women of the partition become eternal fugitives, a displaced people from their own families and society, shown in the figure of Pooro, who becomes Hamida, whose sense of self is distorted by these multiple rejections. Thus, when Pooro describes herself, she says that she has become a "skeleton" without a soul, without a shape or a name (even though her new name is tattooed on her arm!).

In addition to exploring the effects of multiple rejections and displacement on subject constitution—the subject-in-process, as Julia Kristeva terms it—partition narratives depict the consequences for creation of the subject when women's bodies are sites of trauma, thus indicting society for mass violence against women. Antjie Krog, writing on the subject of gender and conflict in the context of South Africa, explains the connection between physical trauma and subject formation: "The body is the one reality we can possess, igniting the sense of self. The allegiance of body is the first ally of the self. Therefore, during instability, in anger and frustration, in ethnic frenzy and hysterical nationalism, the bodies of women become a particular kind of battlefield. . . . And when the body becomes the site of torture and severe trauma, an important channel for experiencing reality is affected" (203). In the context of the partition, this trauma is multifaceted, for it involves both physical wounding, as in the original meaning of the term "trauma," and uprooting the body from its original place in the world, which, of course, wounds the mind. In Pritam's narrative, the agonizing experience of having to marry her rapist, foregrounded in misogynist ideas that her victimization makes Pooro a fallen woman, drives her to hate her own body, which becomes especially evinced when she realizes she is pregnant:

> Pooro sat on her haunches with a sack spread beneath her feet. She was shelling peas. She pressed open a pod and pushed out the row of peas with her finger. A slimy, little slug stuck to her thumb. She felt as if she had stepped into a cesspool; she clenched her teeth, flicked off the slug and rubbed her hands between her knees. Pooro stared at the three heaps in front of her: the empty husks, the pods, and the peas she had shelled. She put her hand on her heart and continued to look vacantly into space. She felt as if her body was a pea-pod inside which she carried a slimy, white caterpillar. Her body was unclean. If only she could take the worm out of her womb and fling it away. (1)

Pooro considers her body unclean and imagines that the fetus is an abhorrent worm that she wants to cast away. Her scarred psyche, which bears witness to similar suffering among innumerable women, exhibits signs of abjection, as defined by Julia Kristeva in *Powers of Horror: An Essay on Abjection*. Kristeva suggests that the abject is an element of selfhood that is has been rejected by hegemonic beliefs that order society. Such rejection splits off that part of the self from the subject but does not wholly eliminate it. Therefore, the "abject" is an unintegrated piece of the self that provokes disgust, and confronting it is often necessary for subject formation, according to Kristeva: "There looms, within abjection, one of those violent, dark revolts of being, directed against a threat that seems to emanate from an exorbitant outside or inside, ejected beyond the scope of the possible, the tolerable, the thinkable. It lies there, quite close, but it cannot be assimilated" (1). Pooro's pregnancy triggers her to confront the abject, for the unborn child is an outward sign and embodiment of her humiliation. Indeed, the pregnancy literalizes the concept of abjection by occupying an in-between space: it is a neither-nor, an outside-inside entity that the mother cannot totally assimilate or totally reject. Moreover, because Pooro's already vitiated body bears the fetus within, the abjectification is doubled, and she, along with the fetus, is situated between the boundary of nature and culture, between human and nonhuman. Such ambiguity, says Kristeva, emerges from abjection: "Abjection is, above all, ambiguity" (9). Importantly, Kristeva's analysis argues that abjection is engendered by oppressive moral and ideological codes, and stories like *The Skeleton* and the *Ice-Candy Man* demonstrate that the violence unleashed against women during the partition was driven by society-wide misogyny as much as by individual actors.

An episode in *The Skeleton* that further underscores the predicament of female victims of partition violence involves a mad woman. As Pooro tries to cope with her own trauma, she feels strangely drawn toward this woman, who has totally lost her senses and runs half-dressed through the village. Keeping in mind the social scenario at the time, it can be assumed that this figure is also a victim of the atrocities. Some rascal, taking advantage of the mad woman's vulnerable condition, impregnates her. The situation becomes even more humiliating as community leaders try to hush up the affair instead of providing the woman with medical attention. Local officials try to render her invisible by running her out of town: "One evening the elders of the *Panchayat* (a local elected government unit similar to a city council)[9] took the mad woman by the hand and left her in the dark at some distance from Sakkar. 'Out of sight, out of mind!' they assured one another. 'Let some other village take care of her now'" (21–22). The mad woman is a symbol of social disgrace, and Pooro realizes that she could be in a similar condition if her husband, Rashida, had abandoned her after abducting and raping her. The mad woman becomes Pooro's external double, her alter-ego, and Pooro's deeply buried anguish and terror emerge in nightmares that she, too, will become mad: "Hamida dozed off to sleep beside the cot. She dreamt of Rashida galloping away with her lying across his saddle; she dreamt of his keeping her in a gardener's hut for three nights and days and then throwing her out; she dreamt of her turning insane and running about the village lanes with a life quickening in her womb . . . and then giving birth to a child under the shade of a tree" (23). This dream is an obvious key to her scarred psyche and, as Freud suggests, reveals Pooro's psychological processes: "The study of dreams may be considered the most trustworthy method of investigating deep mental processes" (7). In fact, it shows that Pooro suffers from what Freud called "traumatic neuroses" (now, of course, known as Post-Traumatic Stress Syndrome), which he observed among soldiers returning from battlefields who relive their traumatic experiences in nightmares: "Now dreams occurring in traumatic neuroses have the characteristic of repeatedly bringing the patient back into the situation of his accident, a situation from which he wakes up in another fright" (7). Furthermore, as Pooro's alter ego, the woman reinforces the theme that the violated women of the partition are the bare bones of their former selves, psychologically disembodied, so to speak. Earlier in the text, Pooro described herself as "a skeleton, without a shape or a name" (11). When the mad woman first appears, the narrator depicts her similarly: "She is neither young nor attractive; she is just a lump of flesh without a mind to go with it . . . living skeleton . . . lunatic skeleton . . . a skeleton picked to its bones by kites and vultures" (22). The image of the "skeleton" thus recurs in the novel. This portrayal—the women are soulless frames—of the consequences of their victimization by abductors, families, communities, and patriarchal values underscores the fact that their psychological agony totally drains them of emotion, rendering them empty cages, so to speak. This evacuation of selfhood is a process that Krog asserts is grounded on the connection between physical trauma and subject constitution: "The body is the one reality we can possess, igniting the sense of self. The allegiance of body is the first ally of the self. Therefore, during instability, in anger and frustration, in ethnic frenzy and hysterical nationalism, the bodies of women become a particular kind of battlefield. . . . And when the body becomes the site of torture and severe trauma, an important channel for experiencing reality is affected" (203). Thus *The Skeleton* suggests that both Pooro and the mad woman suffer from a denial of self caused by their abuse.

This routine, society-wide denigration of women is rooted in patriarchal ideologies that shape cultures, systematically deprive women of their moral leadership, and prevent them from establishing social and economic partnerships with men, which, in turn disempowers them, renders them economically dependent, and excludes them from public—especially political—leadership. Moreover, it leads to their repeated victimization. During the unnatural circumstances of the partition, such routine denigration provided the foundation for and fueled the violence against women. Furthermore, men's irregular, frenzied behavior was validated by longstanding patriarchal mores defining femininities and masculinities and that delegated subordinate roles to women. Thus attacks on them were not an aberration but a natural consequence of the patriarchal "normalcy" perpetuated by cultural mores and expressed in sociopolitical discourses. Significantly, then, partition narratives not only call attention to the atrocities against female victims but also highlight the reasons women were targeted for violence during the partition.

One of the tropes that appears in Hindu Indian discourses that sets the stage for the violence women experienced during the partition is woman as goddess. Not surprisingly, this trope is reworked in partition literature where "fallen" women are almost inevitably associated with goddess figures at some point or another, most often to expose the negative consequences of this patriarchal metaphor. Typically, partition narratives tap into longstanding depictions of women as icons who bear in their bodies the honor and purity of their family, community, and nation. This notion prompts men from rival communities to equate defiling women with championing and confirming the "inherent" superiority of their group affiliations, whether such associations are rooted in religion, ethnicity, or nationalism. One nuanced passage in Sidhwa's *Ice-Candy Man* that addresses this phenomenon demonstrates that only a faint line differentiates woman as an object to be abused from woman as a goddess: "The covetous glances Ayah [Lenny's nanny] draws educate me. Up and down, they look at her. Stub handed twisted beggars and dusty old beggars on crutches drop their poses and stare at her with hard alert eyes. Holy men, masked in piety, shove aside their pretenses to ogle her at lust. Hawkers, cart drivers, cooks, coolies and cyclists turn their heads as she passes, pushing my pram with the unconcern of the Hindu goddess she worships" (3). This episode occurs early in the novel before the partition riots when Ayah is introduced as a wonderful, unearthly creature worshipped by her numerous male admirers. Importantly, at this juncture, she holds an advantageous position compared to her beaus, who woo her fervently, and it is up to her to decide which one she prefers. However, over the course of the narrative, the partition crisis inverts this power structure as mass violence renders Ayah increasingly vulnerable. Previously a goddess worshipped by her suitors, she devolves, in their eyes, to an object to possess, to violate. In fact, her devotee, the Ice-Candy Man, who is instrumental in her abduction, becomes the predator and she the prey. The narrative thus foregrounds the way that a woman, whether she is revered as a goddess or considered a fallen woman, is ultimately victimized by patriarchal codes.

Notably, this imposition of the goddess image on victimized women underscores the manner in which the goddess trope entraps women between two dichotomizing representations of femininity. Women are celestial beings in whose chastity the purity of her family and community resides, which makes them prime "conquests" of members of rival communities and, when they are violated, renders them fallen in the same societies that they supposedly embodied. This pattern is evident in Jamila Hashmi's short story "Exile," which deals with a Muslim woman's postpartition trauma after a Sikh youth abducts her and forces her into marriage. Though Bibi, the protagonist, is relentlessly haunted by nostalgia and a sense of alienation from her family and surroundings, she has to rebuild her life by playing the role of a dutiful wife and mother in her new family in the village of Sangraon in northern India. Her struggles reveal the ambiguity embedded in the goddess/fallen woman dichotomy. Once, years after her marriage, when Bibi comments that she has grown old, her daughter Munni says: "You aren't old. You are like the image of a goddess. Even Bari Ma says so" (56). This praise from her abductors and tormentors, who call her a Devi, "the Lakshmi"[10] of the household, causes Bibi to reflect: "How could Munni have understood the distances I had traveled? The spaces that separate one life from the next are immense. When human beings lose hope, their bodies become hard and brittle. Then they look like gods ready to be worshipped. I have waited for long on the roads of Sangraon for those who had been separated from me, that my eyes have turned to stone. My heart has become empty. I have become Laksmi" (56).

Paradoxically, Bibi, who has waited in vain for her natal kin to rescue her, nevertheless strives to appease her in-laws, and as she describes herself as a stonehearted goddess, she drives home the point that she has been deprived of her feelings and lost control over her body. Her voice is ignored, and her wishes are never considered. She has become the "Laksmi," the bearer of the family's sanctity and prosperity but, through this transformation, has been made into an empty-hearted idol. In sum, she is deprived of her most basic human right, the right to determine her own destiny. Patricia Uberoi addresses this double-edged phenomenon of women's deification in patriarchy: "That women should be so manifestly objects of worship seems to be something of an explanatory embarrassment in an intellectual environment in which the actual and symbolic denigration of women (essentially their victimization) is seen as the primary truth of gender relation" (325). "Exile" thus deconstructs the false opposition of goddess/violated woman, showing that women's deification, instead of being a solace or honor, is an insidious imposition of patriarchal constraint and, in the context of the partition, is inextricably linked to women's abuse.

Hindu India, like many other societies, long has been obsessed with female chastity. In previous eras, this obsession was manifest in customs like *sati* and *jauhar brata*. In *sati*, the wife of the deceased sacrifices her life in the funeral pyre of her husband to preserve her chastity and to prove her undying devotion to her husband. In turn, she is deified, sometimes even worshipped with fervor at a temple erected in her name. *Jauhar* was usually carried out by Rajput women when they feared being violated in an impending invasion. This ritual culminates in a mass suicide whose purpose is to safeguard their purity. Even in the mid-nineteenth century when the Indian renaissance reached its peak and nationalism was promoted as a tool against British colonialism, women could not break free of their age-old image as vanguards of their community's honor and decency or the idea that women had a duty to preserve their own and the community's honor even at the cost of self-destruction. During this period, proponents of India's independence conflated nationalism and women's status. Thus nationalist leaders counteracted women's oppression by traditional practices by projecting women in an idealized and glorified light. As Maithreyi Krishnaraj explains, "Stung by British (and Christian) condemnation of practices such as *purdah, sati*, child marriage and prohibition of widow remarriage, nationalists responded diversely by justifying these customs in the light of the Hindu religion, by claiming that in an earlier purer age women had enjoyed a much higher status, by calling for reforms, by holding up to ridicule the behavior of western women, and by elevating virtues attributed to Indian women into a key symbol of the struggle for independence" (1).

Paradoxically, this maneuver embedded a traditional patriarchal ethos in Indian nationalism, representing woman as a life giver and life preserver—the lifeline of the future nation. Nationalist iconography also reinforced the enduring idea that women are or should be passive sufferers—for their families, communities, and nation—another example of patriarchal cooptation of women's individual strivings, failures, triumphs, and realizations. This, of course, robs women and their activities of any relevance and meaning per se, reducing their value to how well they serve this trinity. Indeed, the independence movement sacralized and feminized the state-in-the-making as the Motherland, *Deshamatrika*. Frieda Hauswirth describes this phenomenon: "Serve the mother, free the mother, *Vande Mataram*—it was a cry to appeal as could no other to all the mother—complexed youth of India, and to all the women whose only hope and consolation lies in motherhood. 'Serve the Great Mother!' That cry supplanted the old call to the worship of ancient goddess with a vital flaming of immediacy and directness" (231). Clearly then, the tropes of female citizen as goddess and the nation as suffering mother, although they use gynocentric language and iconography, serve the patriarchal, masculinist state rather than women themselves.

The "fall" of the nation becomes so akin to the "fall" of thousands of women of the nation, many writers on the social history and of fiction based on it could not escape the obvious trope of this woman-nation paradigm. In 1947, the partition line was etched in the two sides of the country. The stories discussed in this chapter so far are based on the western part of the country. It would be imperative to draw on a tale from the eastern part of the nation where the partition occurred. Lalithambika Antharjanam's "The Mother of Dhirendu Mazumdar" offers a nuanced interrogation of how the construct of the nation as a helpless mother crying out for freedom from the shackles of foreign rule that were initially deployed in support of the Indian independence movement rendered women potential victims of the mid-twentieth-century partition riots. In this story, which spans both the period of the independence movement and the subsequent partition, in a dialogue between the protagonist, a mother named Shanti Devi and her son, Dhirendu, the mother implores him not to pursue the dangerous path of the struggle for freedom and the end of colonial rule: "I broke down, 'My son, a mother is more important than one's motherland. A mother has a heart which can be broken. A country is mere rock and earth.' Dhiren kissed my forehead, 'No, my mother. This country is composed of the hearts of *crores* and *crores* [millions and millions][11] of mothers like you. All of them feel pain; all of them are anxious and in tears. If I am to die for this grief-stricken motherland, my mother should smile and sing *Vande Mataram*.[12] Promise me mother that you will smile'" (516).

Dhiren's fervent speech demonstrates that the nexus between women and nationalism is based on the view that women are symbols of a pure, inviolate country crying out for preservation of its sanctity and safety, and the image of the nation as a female form, the motherland, recurs throughout Antharjanam's story. Despite his mother's fears, Dhirendu joins the nationalists under the tutelage of Surya Sen, more popularly known as Master-Da, one of the eminent leaders of Bengal's freedom movement. During this turbulent period, Surya Sen, disguised as a *Sanyasin* (a female sage), takes refuge in the family's mansion. As he leaves, he discloses his true identity to Dhirendu's mother and implores: "Forgive me mother, I am Surya Sen. Also known as Master-Da. We worship our motherland as Maha Kali. Swords in a hundred hands! *Chakras* [disks][13] in a hundred hands! The blood smeared head of the enemy. Intestines for garlands. But now for the first time I have seen the goddess as Annapurna;[14] I have seen her as the compassionate one. I want this image to remain in my heart forever. Bless me" (514).

These words, uttered by a revolutionary freedom fighter, reflect the nationalists' use of woman as goddess, a *devi*, to legitimate their goals. Dhirendu later voices a similar sentiment in his defense of the nationalist movement: "Mother, do you know that in olden times, the mothers in Greece used to sacrifice their sons to the Goddess of war. Dying for one's motherland is salvation. Isn't my mother a goddess?" (515). Tanika Sarkar observes that such deification is an underhanded means of fetishizing the putative state: "As is usual with nationalist discourses, the country is not a piece of land with actual people living on it. It is abstracted from the people and is then personified as the Mother Goddess, the most recent and the most sacred deity in the Hindu pantheon. The people then are not the '*desh*' ['country'] itself, but are sons of the mother, detached from the imagined entity and put in a subordinate relation to it" (160). Thus as we take into account the nationalist discourses of late nineteenth- and early twentieth-century India, it is easy to reach the conclusion that the relationship between women and nationalism turns on patriarchally crafted conceptions of nation and national identity. Rick Wilford explains that with the emergence of statehood, women remain trapped in the vicious grip of ethnic nationalism while men are free, active agents: "Women, that is, are commonly constructed as the symbolic form of the nation whereas men are invariably represented as its chief agents and, with statehood achieved, emerge as its major beneficiaries" (xi). This, of course, is not a unique occurrence. Women bear this burden of representation in diverse locations across the globe and during different historic epochs. Nira Yuval Davis puts this problematic use of women in nationalist disquisition in global contexts:

> Women are often required to carry the "burden of representation" as they are constructed as the symbolic bearers of the collectivity's identity and honor, both personally and collectively. Claudia Koontz (1986:196) quotes the different mottoes which were given to girls and boys in the Hitler youth movement. For girls it was "be faithful; be pure; be German." For boys, "live faithfully; fight bravely; die laughingly." The national duties of the boys were to live and die for the nation; girls did not need to act. They had to become the national embodiment. A figure of a woman, often a mother, symbolizes in many cultures the spirit of the collectivity, whether it is Mother Ireland, Mother Russia or Mother India. (29)

In "The Mother of Dhirendu Mazumdar," Shanti Devi is placed in the "woman as nation" paradigm, and although she is not sexually desecrated, she is violated when, after the partition, she is ousted out of her Bangladeshi home and relocated in a new, truncated India, where she becomes a beggar on the streets of Calcutta.

With partition, the thousands of years old legacy of India as a country accommodating millions of people belonging to different religious groups, having diverse cultural and linguistic identities, and yet upholding a unity and cohesiveness was shattered with an apparent finality. Three new nations emerged—all three withstanding the sharp pangs of desecration, struggling to find new identities separate from the others and yet with inseparable bonds with each other. First, the age-old patriarchal social norms and then the nationalist discourse founded on the same ideologies have paralleled the identity of a pure, inviolate country with the identity of the pure, inviolate women of the country. The resulting persecution of women becomes multidimensional. Yet in the grand historiography of the nation, a marked omission of the history of these victimized women of the nation can be noted.

Jyotirmoyee Devi's novella *Epar Ganga, opar Ganga,* translated as *The River Churning,* is a notable narrative that highlights this lapse in history. The narration begins with the protagonist, Sutara, reflecting on the omission of the history of pain and loss, of the privation of common people in general and the plight of women in particular in the grand narratives of the nation. In her authorial preface, Jyotirmoyee Devi mentions that she had initially titled the novel *Itihashe Stree Parva,* or *The Woman Chapter in History,* which she changed on her editor's request. True to the initial title, the novel studies the unwritten history of the nature of persecution of woman during the partition and goes deep into the question of the victimized woman's subsequent losses—loss of family, homeland, identity, social agency, and the right of choice.

The novel is set against the backdrop of the partition holocaust—the communal strife, mass killing, abduction, and migration in the eastern part of the country—and moves onto allusions of parallel events in the western part, as Sutara also moves accordingly. The narrative unfolds with Sutara losing her kin in the riots of the Noakhali district of East Bengal in the autumn of 1946. Her parents are killed and her sister is abducted. Sutara loses consciousness in the course of the carnage and escapes corporeal harm miraculously. She recuperates in the care of family friend and neighbor Tamizzudin and his family. Her kin, her brothers and their family who migrated on the other side, do not make any effort to bring her back. After six months, with the initiative of Tamizzudin Shaheb, she finally crosses the border to be reunited with them. As she crosses the river flowing by her village, she looks onto the surrounding landscapes, the embankments, the trees, the hamlets, and the receding horizon and remembers her parents, sister, and old life. The all-too-familiar landscape transforms into a site of trauma and, instead of giving solace, evokes only pain and nostalgia. The desperation of the adolescent girl gets hope only in the fact that she is going to the refuge of her relatives in Calcutta. But as she finally reaches Calcutta and arrives in her brother's in-law's house, where her brother and sister-in-law Bibha have taken refuge to escape the communal strife raging across the area, Sutara's sense of relief is brutally shattered. She immediately faces antagonism from the householders. Bibha's mother and aunt strongly disapprove of Sutara's presence as her prolonged contact with a Muslim family has already branded her as "polluted." In view of these staunch upholders of community's purity and honor, Sutara has already lost her lineage and birthright. The fact that the elderly women of the household are most vocal in their disapproval corroborates the fact that women, being products of patriarchy, with time move from the disadvantaged group to agents as they are fully integrated in the patriarchal system and, as Nira Yuval Davis and Floya Anthias surmise, "actively participate in the process of reproducing and modifying their roles as well as being actively involved in controlling other women" (11). The most noteworthy point is that the unsullied nature of Sutara's sexual purity does not guarantee the integrity of her total self as mere presence with the alien community ensures an alterity from the others of her social group; her presence is a possible threat to the controlling set of dictums of Hindu community and an untrustworthiness that makes her reintegration into it impossible. The much sought after refuge for Sutara thus becomes a new site of denial and exile. Her terrifying loneliness and powerlessness is manifested mostly in her silence. She is routinely shunned from social events. She mutely endures harassments as she is eschewed from auspicious ceremonies like marriages and is seated for dinner alone in a separate room so as to save others from her polluting presence. Sutara, a source of constant awkwardness and embarrassment to her relatives, ultimately escapes the multiple instances of persecution as she is admitted to a boarding school run by Christian missionaries.

In this somewhat neutral space, she gets refuge, completes her education, and becomes a professor of history in a Delhi college. As she moves from Noakhali to Calcutta, from her relatives' house to the boarding school and then to Delhi, Sutara remains a fragmented and fugitive figure disdained by family and society. In the boarding school, she meets girls having similar shared history of violence, although any discussion on the taboo subject is prohibited. At Delhi, Sutara forms a sort of association with some Punjabi refugee girls who migrated from the western part of the border to settle in and around the capital. Sutara's tattered psyche is manifested in her inability to form an evocative discourse with them. Sutara wants to ask about their side of the story and about their quandary during the partition but cannot begin any coherent dialogue on the shared tale of pain and loss. In Jyotirmoyee Devi's tale, the protagonist at first does not get to vent about her traumatic experience. Nobody asks about what she faced in the past months. Every effort is made to make her invisible, to amputate her and her realities from the family history. Her silence speaks not only of her repressed trauma but also of the historical silence compounded by familial silence, a silence founded on the nexus of community honor and collective shame around the incidents. Veena Das writes about the silences of women victims of the partition holocaust and how this silence is integrated into cultural narrative. Das speaks of the world being divided into "that in which speech is possible and that in which it becomes a taboo" (70). Women are denied the chance to resist and heal trauma through narrative. While Das mainly speaks of the women victims who were married to their abductors and their silences in their husbands' houses where any "carelessly uttered words can disrupt her whole world," here Sutara cannot and is not allowed to narrate her experience to her natal kin, in the family she is rightfully a part of, and in the newly formed nation of which she is a rightful citizen. In her authorial preface, Jyotirmoyee Devi writes that not only are the sagas of the women of the nation eluded in history but also the language in which the plight of the women can be narrated has not been discovered as yet (94). Inger Agger writes in her seminal work detailing her journey through the narratives of forty refugee women telling of their political persecution in the Mideast and Latin America: "In this space they begin to experience the necessary turning point between the wordless nothing dominated by chaotic anxiety and the wordless fellowship given form and expression in the symbol of the circle and its healing ritual" (126).

This "wordless nothing" also forms the partition reality of most of the female victims of riot. Social historians trying to retrieve personal traumatic experiences through documentation of oral narratives write of the healing power of narrating personal memories whereby mourning and reconciliation become possible. Maybe Sutara moves from wordless nothing to wordless fellowship, as she joins in worship and rituals in the house of her colleague Kaushlyabati and hears some tales of pain and loss from the womenfolk who have come to take part in the *puja*, but she cannot share her personal experience. Time and again, the narrator portrays Sutara as a mute figure, continuously pondering and reminiscing. In the course of the narrative, as Cathy Caruth says, "Psychic trauma involves intense personal suffering, but it also involves the recognition of realities that most of us have not begun to face" (vii). Sutara becomes extremely aware of the dynamics of a prejudice-ridden society and transforms from a naïve girl to an economically empowered and independent individual. But her fragmented self-identity, lack of trust in others, and shattered self-confidence bar her from forming friends or getting into any deep and meaningful relationships. She has correspondence with her relatives in Calcutta but does not go back there. She has connections with Tamizzudin's family especially with his daughter Sakina, Sutara's childhood friend, but is speechless when the latter suggests that she marry her brother Ajij. She cannot forget the past. The prospect of marriage to the same community who ravaged her family seems to be a betrayal of her parents' and sister's death and of her personal tragedy. Sutara is all too aware of the bigotry of her community. But to be assimilated into Tamizzudin Saheb's family who protected and sheltered her is also not possible. Her inability to be integrated in either of the two rival communities, one who bore her and the other who sustained her, constructs Sutara's fragmented social identity. The narrative expands from a hamlet of east Bengal to Calcutta and then to Delhi, with allusions to Karachi in Pakistan and to London. But Sutara fails to find root anywhere. She strives to be economically independent and becomes self-sufficient, but to be able to totally come out of the trauma is impossible. Though the novel ends with the possibility of her accepting a marriage proposal, the narrative largely brings out the fragmented and fugitive reality of Sutara's existence. Jyotirmoyee Devi's writing thus remains exemplary in its vivid portrayal of dislocation, sense of loss and betrayal, the utter feeling of alienation, and the consequential fracturing of identities of the female victims of the riots and is a pointer to the silences around these realities.

All five narratives—*The Ice-Candy Man*, "Exile," *The Skeleton*, *Epar Ganga, opar Ganga*, and "The Mother of Dhirendu Mazumdar"—have different stories to tell, yet each individual story demonstrates how communal values about womanhood teamed up with nationalist sentiment to focus partition violence against women. As icons of goodness and protectors of communal morality and sanctity, with responsibility for reproducing the cultural and biological future of their society, women were especially vulnerable to rival factions. For eons, the woman's sexuality has been a metaphor for the unviolated, chaste, and pure. This obsession with women's purity fostered the belief that the invasion of the "sacred" space of women's bodies is the ultimate degradation of "the enemy," and, for the woman, a sacrilege worse than death, not because it violates her, but because it undermines the honor, sanctity, and integrity of her entire community. This fetishization of the purity of the female body facilitates easy renunciation of these so-called fallen women. Thus partition texts reveal how women's bodies become sites of large-scale conflict on one hand and, on the other, how mass violence that tears apart the fabric of normal life deprives them of home and hearth. This multifaceted assault on women is the tragic dialectic of the "fallen" woman and nationhood thematized in partition literature.

NOTES

1 The Partition of India occurred in August 1947, as the nation attained freedom from two hundred years of British rule. The British Indian Empire was split into Dominion of Pakistan (it later split into Pakistan and Bangladesh) and the Union of India. The decision was followed by the largest mass migration in human history. The United Nations High Commissioner for Refugees (UNHCR) estimates fourteen million Hindus, Sikhs, and Muslims were displaced during the time. Riots broke out in all parts of the two newly formed countries. History has rarely witnessed a fratricidal war of such magnitude. The estimates of how many people died vary hovering in the 500,000 to 1.5 million range, thousands of children were lost and abandoned, and between 75,000 to 100, 000 women were raped and abducted.

2 When Khushwnat Singh translated the novel into English, it and another novel by Amrita Pritam were published in one volume entitled *Pinjar*.

3 Of course, women's victimization during the partition of Indian subcontinent is not a singular or exclusive occurrence. Women are typically among the first victims of mass violence and social crisis. Inger Skjelsbæk's and Dan Smith's research on gender roles in peace and politics write, for example, that during war rape is used as a deliberate weapon repeatedly. In particular, they note that "rape piles vulnerability on vulnerability" on women (4) and that a rape attack "exploits not only the physical vulnerability of the woman, but also her subsequent sense of shame and defilement, and all too often [results in] . . . rejection by her partner, family and community" (5).

4 Today the region of Punjab is divided between northern India and Pakistan.

5 Bengal is located in the southern portion of the Indian subcontinent in present-day India and Bangladesh.

6 Many women committed suicide to thwart the genocide and mass sexual assaults.
7 Published in the United States as *Cracking India.*
8 Similarly, Muslims were attacked in areas with a majority population of Sikhs and Hindus.
9 A *Panchayat* is the cornerstone of local self-governance in villages and small towns with an elected head called a *sarpanch.*
10 Devi is the Hindu goddess, and Lakshmimi is the *devi* of wealth, fortune, and prosperity (both material and spiritual). She is the consort and active energy of the god Vishnu.
11 One crore denotes ten million in the Indian numbering system.
12 *Vande Mataram* literally means, "I praise thee, Mother" or "Hail to the Mother(land)!" and is a poem from Bankim Chandra Chatterjee's 1882 novel *Anandamath.* During the Indian independence movement, it became a hymn to the Motherland, and "*Vande Mataram*" became a national cry for freedom from British rule.
13 In Sanskrit, *chakra* means "wheel" or "disk." In yoga meditation, it refers to a center of consciousness, and in Ayurveda medicine, this term refers to wheels of energy throughout the body. The character Surya Sen uses *chakra* to mean a weapon.
14 Hindu goddess of food.

WORKS CITED

Agger, Inger. *The Blue Room: Trauma and Testimony among Refugee Women; A Psycho-Social Exploration,* Zed Books, 1994.
Antharjanam, Lalithambika. "The Mother of Dhirendu Mazumdar." *Stories about the Partition of India,* edited by Alok Bhalla, Harper Collins, 1999.
Caruth, Cathy. *Trauma: Explorations of Memory.* Johns Hopkins UP, 1995.
Das, Veena. "Composition of the Personal Voice: Violence and Migration," *Studies in History,* vol. 7, 1991, pp. 65–77.
Davis, Nira Yuval, and Floya Anthias, editors. *Woman-Nation-State.* Macmillan, 1989.
Devi, Jyotirmoyee. *Epar Ganga, opar Ganga.* Translated by Enakshi Chatterjee as *The River Churning: A Partition Novel,* Kali for Women, 1995.
Edkins, Jenny. *Trauma and the Memory of Politics.* Cambridge UP, 2003.
Freud, Sigmund. *Beyond the Pleasure Principle.* Translated and edited by John Strachey, Norton, 1961.
Hashmi, Jamila. "Exile." Translated by Alok Bhalla. *Stories about the Partition of India,* edited by Alok Bhalla, Harper Collins, 1999.
Hauswirth, Frieda. *Purdah: The Status of Indian Women.* Butler and Tanner, 1981.
Kabir, Ananya Jahanara. "Gender, Memory, Trauma: Women's Novel on the Partition of India." *Comparative Studies of South Asia Africa and the Middle East,* vol. 25, no. 1, 2005, pp. 177–90.
Krishnaraj, Maithreyi. "Permeable Boundaries." *Ideals, Images and Real Lives: Women in Literature and History,* edited by Alice Thorner and Maithreyi Krishnaraj, Orient Longman, 2000, pp. 1–36.
Kristeva, Julia. *Powers of Horror: An Essay on Abjection.* Translated by Leon S. Roudiez, Colombia UP, 1992.
Krog, Antjie. "Locked into Loss and Silence: Testimonies of Gender and Violence at the South African Truth Commission." *Victims, Perpetrators or Actors? Gender, Armed Conflict and Political Violence,* edited by Caroline O. N. Moser and Fiona C. Clark, Zubaan, 2005, pp. 203–16.
Menon, Ritu, and Kamla Bhasin. *Borders and Boundaries.* Kali for Women, 1998.
Pritam, Amrita. "The Skeleton." *The Skeleton and That Man,* translated by Khuswant Singh, Sterling Publishers, 1992.

Sarkar, Tanika. "Nationalist Iconography: Image of Women in 19th century Bengali Literature." *Ideals, Images, and Real Lives: Women in Literature and History*, edited by Alice Thorner and Maithreyi Krishnaraj, Orient Longman, 2000, pp. 159–75.

Sidhwa, Bapsi. *The Ice-Candy Man*. Penguin, 1989.

Skjelsbaek, Inger, and Dan Smith. *Gender, Peace and Conflict*. Sage, 2001.

Uberoi, Patricia. "Feminine Identity and National Ethos in Indian Calendar Art." *Ideals, Images, and Real Lives: Women in Literature and History*, edited by Alice Thorner and Maithreyi Krishnaraj, Orient Longman, 2000, pp. 322–46.

Wilford, Rick. "Women, Ethnicity and Nationalism: Surveying the Ground." *Women, Ethnicity and Nationalism: The Politics of Transition*, edited by Rick Wilford and Robert L. Miller, Routledge, 1998, pp. 1–22.

Yuval-Davis, Nira. "Gender and Nation." *Women, Ethnicity and Nationalism: The Politics of Transition*, edited by Rick Wilford and Robert L. Miller, Routledge, 1998, pp. 23–35.

4 THE TROPE OF THE "FALLEN WOMEN" IN THE FICTION OF BANGLADESHI WOMEN WRITERS

HAFIZA NILOFAR KHAN

In this chapter, Hafiza Nilofar Khan scrutinizes the *biranganas* (war heroines) of the 1971 war in the fiction and short stories of Bangladeshi writers Selina Hossain and Niaz Zaman, who are often labelled as "pariahs" or "fallen women" by their communities. In contemporary Bangladeshi literature (written in English or translated from Bangla to English), typically bold, nontraditional pictures of female protagonists reclaim their bodies and sexuality. These fictional Bangladeshi women transgress the boundaries of social norms and revolutionize the way readers look at women's bodies. In this chapter, Khan examines how this process plays out in Hossain's and Zaman's works and redefines the trope of the fallen woman in Bangladeshi literature.

Bangladeshi women generally have two major identity components: they are South Asian Muslims on the one hand and Bengalis on the other. In fact, because of their "Bengaliness," which they share with the Hindus of West Bengal (Kolkata) in India and express through common language, festivities, music, food habits, and dress code, among other things, their "Muslimness" has acquired a distinct characteristic even within the Muslims of South Asia. These religious and cultural identity markers coexist in most Bangladeshis in various degrees. Interestingly enough, although they seem irreconcilable, the opposing political ideologies of the two women leaders of Bangladesh—Khalida Zia, prime minister from 1991 to

1996 and 2001 to 2006 and leader of the Bangladesh National Party (BNP), and Sheikh Hasina, head of the rival Awami League, who has served as prime minister from 1996 to 2001 and 2009 through the time of this writing—also reflect these two major streams of national identity formation, "Muslimness" and "Bengaliness," respectively.[1]

However, whether Bangladeshi women consider themselves to be Muslims first and foremost or define themselves primarily by their Bengali cultural identity, owing to the stronghold of patriarchal beliefs and practices well rooted in both religion and culture, they often become victims of gender discrimination and oppression. The patriarchal mind-set of Bangladesh highly values concepts of honor and purity, particularly with regard to women, and has a very rigid notion of the feminine ideal. It demands virginity and chastity from unmarried as well as married women for the sake of family honor and to safeguard primogeniture—that is, to ensure that men's rightful heirs are not deprived of their inheritance. In order to regulate female sexuality, young girls are encouraged to follow social decorum that discourages free mixing with the opposite sex, and early marriage is often their fate. Despite the advancements that Bangladeshi women have made in the fields of education and economics, the gender-based patriarchal constructions of ideal Bangladeshi womanhood demand domesticity, docility, and asexuality from them. In an environment where polygamy is legal, but marital rape makes no case, and where son-preference is often the practice, institutions of marriage and motherhood prove to be limiting in terms of women's bodily and sexual rights. Any deviation from the patriarchal norms leads to women's stigmatization, often lending them the label "fallen woman." Though generally the term is assigned to a woman guilty of sexual misconduct, a raped woman or a woman associated with any kind of criminal act can also be deemed a fallen woman. A fallen woman is considered beyond hope of redemption, and society is eager to get rid of her.

As in English Victorian fiction, the trope of the "fallen woman" is all pervasive in Bangladeshi fiction. In the writings of contemporary Bangladeshi women such as Selina Hossain and Niaz Zaman, however, the female characters who transgress the prescribed boundary for the "angel in the house" are not ostracized or relegated to the margins of society. Characters like Motijan in Hossain's short story "Motijan's Daughters," Parul in "Parul Becomes Mother," and Proshanti in her novel *Atomic Darkness* are all wives who have extramarital affairs and, in some cases, children out of wedlock. Shabina in Zaman's novel *A Different Sita* sleeps with multiple men, including her husband's friend and a Pakistani general. She also has a child out of wedlock with her lover. By general standards of Bangladeshi religio-cultural morality, these women should be considered "fallen women" and treated as outcasts for violating social norms. Indeed, at times some of these women characters momentarily question their own morality; however, they are not depicted as inherently detestable or pitiable. They do not attempt to discretely sweep their radical beliefs and acts under the social rug of "decency"; nor are they declared mad, or terminally ill, or institutionalized. They are not banished or killed by the end of the story. Instead, the writers celebrate their characters' bodily emancipation and evoke sympathy for these women's bold and nontraditional sexual drive and reproductive powers. In this chapter, I focus on the authors' problematization of certain religiocultural and political practices as justifications or rationale for the wives' transgressions. My chapter argues that these authors assert that certain Islamic and Bengali cultural practices and political history are greatly responsible for goading the women into so-called moral transgression. It is my contention that because of the oppressive discourse surrounding marriage—motherhood and nationhood in particular—the authors exonerate their women protagonists and perceive them in an agentially positive light rather than as "fallen women."

In order to contextualize the wives' transgression in Hossain's fiction, it is necessary to elaborate on the nature of the institutions of marriage and motherhood as they exist in Bangladesh. Hossain holds patriarchal practices of early marriage, dowry, domestic violence, marital rape, son preference, and polygamy responsible to a great extent for the oppression and tarnished image of married women in Bangladeshi society. Because of anxiety over female sexuality and at times poverty, in both the Islamic and Bengali cultures, early marriage for girls, especially in rural villages, is often projected as the norm in her fiction. In her book *Ethics in Social Practice,* Hasna Begum opines that "the most important code regarding marriage in Bengali society is to marry daughters when they are still girls" (66). The author gives examples from history of medieval Bengal and folklore to prove that marriage before attaining puberty has been the norm in Bangladesh for centuries. Parvez Babul, in his article "Early Marriage, Inequalities and Violence Against Women," holds that "more than 70% of brides in Bangladesh are less than eighteen years, and over 26% of those girls are between the ages of eight to thirteen" (3). Much of Hossain's fiction, including *The Shark, the River and the Grenades,* "The World of Love and Labour," and "Motijan's Daughters," depicts child brides as victims. In her article "Security of the Marginalized Women," she regrets, "Though a law against child marriage was passed in 1929, such marriages continue down till today. . . . This was amended in 1984 and men and women could marry at the age of 21 and 18 respectively, or older. It was said that if anyone married a girl under 18, this would be considered a punishable crime. The person conducting the marriage would also be liable to punishment. Even so, child marriage continues in the villages. Even the law can't safeguard women. The family and society has marginalized them" (20). Though Hossain blames the weakness of Bangladeshi law for not being able to end child marriage, she does not regard poverty as the sole reason for it. In her words, "If this happens, this happens not because of poverty, but because of a low level of culture. It is, in the final analysis, a question of values. And values must change" ("Culture" 17–18). The author believes that parents often render their girl child's body disenfranchised on account of their own greed and lack of knowledge about their daughter's rights.

Though it is more in tune with Hindu practices than Islamic, the system of dowry, or paying the groom's side money or gifts, is yet another source of oppression for the Bangladeshi wives that is highlighted in Hossain's fiction. In her dissertation, *The Cultural Picture of Dowry System and Its Reflection in Bangla Literature*, Maleka Begum argues that dowry in its contemporary shape did not exist among subcontinental Muslims before the twentieth century. She traces the origin of dowry to the caste system prevalent among Indian Hindus. Nusrat Ameen similarly holds that the concept of dowry in Bangladesh originated from ancient Hindu custom. Both these scholars argue that while the practice originally entailed a father's voluntary and unconditional giving away of a small amount of his assets to help his daughter and son-in-law to start a new life, over time it has become a mandatory obligation. In her book *Wife Abuse in Bangladesh: An Unrecognized Offence*, Ameen provides the new definition of dowry: "Whatever is presented, whether before or after marriage under demand, compulsion or social pressure as consideration for the marriage can be said to be dowry" (40). With this evolved version of dowry, which is often tied to a father's reputation and his daughter's well-being in her new home, dowry-related crimes are escalating. As Babul reports, "More than 70% of domestic violence occurs for dowry related reasons, and that mostly upon thirteen-eighteen-year-old wives" in Bangladesh (5). Through her fiction, Hossain insists that Bangladeshi parents stop viewing dowry as a form of gratitude payment to the groom and his family for accepting a daughter and helping shed their unwanted burden.

On top of being victims of early marriage and dowry, the wives in the fiction of Hossain are also thrust into a marital system where husbands are given the upper hand with regard to material, physical, and sexual rights over them. According to the Islamic narrative on marriage, a wife's heaven lies under her husband's feet. In the introduction to my dissertation, *Treatment of a Wife's Body in the Fiction of Indian Sub-Continental Muslim Women Writers*, I hold that "the concept of marriage in the Islamic subconscious as a contract of ownership/authority of a man over a woman further reinforces the idea of a wife's body as a commodity for domination and sexual enjoyment by the husband" (2008, vi). The Bengali marital discourse also propounds that the husband is the final authority of the house, and a wife ought to please her husband under all circumstances. Thus, as my dissertation proposes, Bangladeshi wives ideally should embody sacrifice, devotion, and purity as the result of the influence of feminine archetypes such as Sita and Yashoda in the Hindu myths that play a prominent role in shaping historical and current Bangladeshi cultural beliefs.[2]

Indeed, the Islamic and Bengali traditions also emphasize the fact that a wife is her husband's responsibility, and it is his moral and legal duty to provide for her and to protect her. Unfortunately, however, most husbands in Hossain's fiction get away with breaching these marital contracts because of gender discrimination, sexual double standards, and laws steeped in patriarchy in Bangladesh. Husbands in the fiction of Hossain also often take advantage of the facts that there is no legal punishment for marital rape, it is easier for them to get a divorce, and polygamy is still legally permissible.

Hossain's fiction also depicts son preference as yet another social practice rooted both in Islamic religion and Bengali culture that turns marital life and motherhood into an oppressive social role for Bangladeshi women. Since a son carries his family name, is legally bound to take care of his parents, and according to the Islamic system, inherits more than his sister, he is preferred over a daughter. Again, daughters are considered to be liabilities because they require a dowry to be married and eventually become part of their husbands' family. They are also not legally bound to support their natal family. For all these reasons, there is often pressure on mothers to produce only sons, and they carry a sense of powerlessness if they don't. In her book *Whither Women's Studies in Bangladesh?*, Mahmuda Islam shows her concern over the practice of son preference in these words: "It is true that women are getting education and entering job market, but is son preference modified by these developments? Hardly any critical analysis has been made on the viability of the son preference syndrome, its present status and its effect on future development of women's situation" (36). Though this trend is changing in Bangladesh's middle and upper classes, as Hossain elaborates in her short stories, "The World of Love and Labour," "Mohini's Marriage," "The Stream," and "Motijan's Daughters," among the majority of the lower classes, son preference is still a glaring reality. Moreover, Hossain underpins in polygamy the fate of mothers in rural Bangladesh who live under the threat of their husbands bringing in a new wife if they fail to produce sons.

Motijan in "Motijan's Daughters" is a young village bride who finds herself trapped in a traditional Bangladeshi marriage. Her husband, Abul, has a mistress with whom he spends days, without returning home. Her mother-in-law, Gulnoor, is aware of her son's extramarital affair, yet she ignores it because she considers it his privilege as a man. Gulnoor also makes it a habit to torment her daughter-in-law for the dowry that her father failed to deliver. As time passes and Motijan does not conceive, the abuse intensifies. Motijan is often denied food, tied up with rope, and forced to eat grass despite the fact that she does all the domestic chores without complaint. Abul is a witness to all of Motijan's woes but decides to stay silent and condone his mother's cruel acts since he is a jobless *ganja* (hemp resin) addict himself. Such negligence and torture isolate Motijan, plunge her into depression, and raise her desire for a soulmate. The narrator provides justification for her subversive aspirations: "At this moment of ultimate silence she felt the need of a companion, someone very close to her, someone to whom she could open her heart" (157). Abul, however, is too careless to notice his wife's emotional needs. All he knows is that he has sexual rights over her. So when he returns from his mistress's house, he tries to thrust himself upon Motijan. This prompts her rebellious mind to fantasize that she is being comforted by another man, Lokman, her husband's oft-visiting village friend: "She wanted to kick Abul off the top of her body. But she restrained herself. . . . When the stench of *ganja* hardened inside her chest, she could feel Lokman's tall and slender figure coming within her reach. She stretched her hand trying to touch him, and his body seemed to curl into her fist" (162). Dejected, made a victim of marital rape, but with no one in the family to turn to, Motijan develops an illegitimate relationship with Lokman. Hossain paints the romantic scene between the two with a few quick but approving strokes: "The rains came just at the moment, falling in torrents. Inside the room, Lokman pressed Motijan to his chest in a tight embrace. For the first time in her life, Motijan truly experienced the intense sensation of a man's touch on her body" (163).

Motijan's dreams of motherhood are also fulfilled by her lover, Lokman. However, when Motijan gives birth to her first daughter, Abul callously mocks her for not being able to produce a son and continue the family line. Because of the practice of son preference, Gulnoor refuses to look at the child's face. Nevertheless, Motijan presses her daughter to her chest and showers endless love on her. The child empowers Motijan to stand up for herself. For example, when Gulnoor warns her against producing any more daughters, Motijan boldly declares, "If I could I would give birth to a hundred daughters" (159). In a rural environment where selective abortion of female fetuses and gross neglect of daughters after birth are rampant, Motijan declares that daughters' lives are as important as those of sons. Soon she gives birth to another daughter with her lover.

The birth of this second daughter only adds to the abuse that Gulnoor heaps on Motijan. The mother-in-law berates Motijan for not being able to continue the family line and threatens that she will find Abul a second wife in order to produce male progeny; Motijan suddenly breaks into a mocking laughter and declares, "If I had left it to your son, I wouldn't have got these girls even" (165). Challenging the patriarchal system of son preference, Motijan reclaims daughters as a source of strength and pride rather than a shameful burden. Motijan's bold acknowledgment of her extramarital relationship and her embrace of motherhood outside wedlock come across as subversive and justified actions in the face of the religio-social environment that Hossain's protagonist finds herself thrust into. As Afsana Begum Orthy comments in "Gender Analysis: Motijan's Daughters," Motijan is quick to assert her decision-making agency through the birth of her two daughters whom she had out of wedlock. By deciding to raise her daughters from Lokman, her lover as her future economic supports instead of waiting for her philanderer husband to impregnate her, Motijan makes a radical move towards her own liberation and happiness. Motijan's decision to openly acknowledge the illegitimacy of her children and claim her right over them defies not only her husband's and mother-in-law's authority but also questions the morality of the institution of marriage. (6). As the story ends, Motijan, daughters in her arms, stands boldly before her mother-in-law in the middle of her husband's house and resolutely declares that the girls are her best support system. She values the bodily and psychological connection she feels with her daughters even as she understands that her own significance and power within the marital family is contingent on the birth of sons. Indeed, by allowing Motijan fulfillment and empowerment outside of the typical institutions of marriage and motherhood in Bangladesh, Hossain sheds fresh light on the trope of the "fallen woman" in Bangladeshi literature. Thus in Hossain's telling, Motijan's transgressions—her illicit affair and her failure to bear sons—are depicted as resistance to oppression even though her marital family and the larger community consider them stigmatizing. Hossain's transformation of Motijan from a victim of family violence and the sexual double standard into a self-empowered figure whose agency grows over the course of the story subverts patriarchal mores that depict women like Motijan as fallen.

Parul in "Parul Becomes Mother" is yet another example of a wife character in Hossain's fiction who easily falls into the category of a "fallen woman" but who breaks out of the dominant patterns of gender and marital ideologies embedded within the Islamic and Bengali cultures of Bangladesh. Like Motijan, Parul is a lower-class village wife who dares to seek physical satisfaction outside of marriage when her husband deserts her for another woman. Parul is embittered and humiliated when she learns that her husband not only disappeared without a word but is happily remarried and living with his new wife elsewhere. A question that keeps nagging her is, "When does a husband stop needing his wife?" Her reply is inevitably, "When she cannot give him her body" (162). Parul, however, knows that she did and could sexually satisfy her husband. She also contributed toward her household by working as a part-time domestic for her neighbors. When memories of scrounging whatever food and clothing she could manage for herself and her husband arise, she reflects that "a happy go lucky, carefree, society's ass kicking type life is the only life worth living" (163). She fears, however, that since her husband left without a proper divorce, he might return any time and claim his legal position in her life. Hence she quickly plans her revenge. She decides to pursue sexual pleasure by indulging in several relationships. "I have whosoever I wish and whenever I wish," she brags, challenging the sexual prowess that male privilege in Bangladeshi Muslim societies valorizes (165). Since she lives by herself in the village and is not answerable to any in-laws, she easily devises this unconventional means of thwarting the status quo. Soon, however, she finds herself pregnant, and her sexual urges begin to diminish. She starts refusing male company. When the men she has been sleeping with find out about her pregnancy, they become anxious to learn the paternity of her child. As further revenge against the patriarchal society, Parul decides to keep the identity of her child's father a secret from them. In my article "South Asian Fiction and Marital Agency of Muslim Wives," I argue, "Parul proclaims that the mother's womb that holds a baby is its ultimate identity component, irrespective of the father, or any cultural or institutional sanction" (22). Though her "lovers" start hovering around her hut and hope that this implied threat will prompt Parul to divulge her secret, she remains strong and grudgingly decisive in reclaiming her reproductive rights. Like Motijan, Hossain provides Parul sufficient justification to rebel against the status quo and rejoice in her subversive actions, despite having become a "fallen woman" according to patriarchal social norms. Importantly, as this story concludes, readers learn that instead of condemning Parul, dejected village women secretly wish that they had Parul's courage. This ending suggests that it is possible for communal values to change when an individual dares breech patriarchal rule.

Proshanti, the protagonist of *Atomic Darkness,* is yet another wife in Hossain's fiction who can fall into the category of a "fallen woman" because of having an extramarital affair and who is treated sympathetically by the author. Unlike Motijan and Parul, Proshanti belongs to the upper strata of Bangladeshi society. She is a married freelance journalist and has two children. Like her literary counterparts, however, she never feels entrenched in her marriage owing to her husband's promiscuous nature. Her husband, Onupom, has casual affairs with all sorts of women, including his secretary. He is careless regarding his flings, since he believes that those are his male prerogative. His behavior creates a huge schism in his marital relationship, yet he chooses to ignore his wife's needs and pain. Proshanti also feels emotionally betrayed by her husband because he holds her responsible for giving birth to an autistic child. Though Proshanti had nothing to do with the medical emergency during her delivery, and later she proves to be the best caregiver for her son, she is held responsible for her son's disabilities.

Embittered by her failed marriage and false charges of being a bad mother, Proshanti wishes for a passionate companion with whom she can share her life's burdens and joys. Her dreams come true when she takes a fifteen-day vacation to Bali and meets Tatian, a handsome and caring artist from Jakarta. A friendship quickly develops between the two. As they happily roam around the island, Onupom becomes jealous and arrives at the island. His double standard regarding marital commitments seems pathetic to Proshanti, but she remains determined not to allow him to ruin her vacation. Since she is financially independent, she manages to change her flight and spend more time with Tatian. Before leaving, however, Proshanti makes it clear to him that once they part, she will not keep in touch through any means, whether calls or e-mails. Indeed, Proshanti's affair is short-lived, and unlike Motijan and Parul, she has no offspring from it. Yet she does not keep this experience a strictly guarded secret from her husband. Like Motijan and Parul, Hossain furbishes this wife with sufficient, genuine reasons to defeat her husband in his own game and challenge the patriarchal status quo.

Although Proshanti's decision to prioritize her children over her lover may seem to be an instance of internalization of the Bangladeshi cultural requirement that mothers should be totally selfless, it can also be traced to her Buddhist beliefs. From Buddha's teachings, Proshanti had learned to shun temporary pleasures of earth and find a stoic peace within. Her decision to immortalize the moments with Tatian only in her memory, rather than materializing them in an ongoing relationship, not only frees her of the stigma of being self-centered like Onupom but also absolves her from charges of marital transgression. This deviation from the pattern of resolution that marks women's bids for self-empowerment in Hossain's short stories might initially appear anomalous, but it is not. Significantly, all three mothers—Motijan, Parul, and Proshanti—have in common their commitment to their children, and more important, they also realize that conforming to patriarchal constructions of womanhood does not serve them or their children well. In other words, in one way or another, all three of these characters suggest that nonpatriarchal models of womanhood—including one that privileges female sexual agency—constitute good mothering. Thus Hussain turns the fallen woman trope on its head, so that the novel essentially argues for the integrated nature of physical and spiritual empowerment: Hossain makes the radical assertion that so-called sexual transgression can be a means of women's spiritual fulfillment and even edification, which completely transvalues the construct of female fallenness.

Like Hossain's wives, Shabina, the protagonist of Niaz Zamin's *A Different Sita,* which is set during the 1971 War of Liberation, can also be regarded as a "fallen woman" because of her extramarital affair, which results in a pregnancy, and her "complicity," as she considers it, in her own rape.[3] But in contrast to the women in Hossain's fiction, Shabina is not a victim of the typical patriarchal practices surrounding marriage and motherhood, for her circumstances are controlled by the patriarchal institutions of war, racism, and nationalism rather than individual characters alone—husbands, in-laws, and children. Thus Zaman problematizes the trope of the fallen women in Bangladeshi literature by providing justifications for her protagonist's transgressive actions in the light of the political atmosphere during the 1971 Bangladeshi War of Liberation and her character's religiocultural identity.

On a personal level, Shabina doubly betrays her husband, Haider, by falling in love with Saeed, his old friend and schoolmate who is a Pakistani Army major stationed in Dhaka during the war. Saeed enters Shabina's life when the 1971 war is raging between the two wings of Pakistan and Haider is abducted by the Pakistani Army on charges of having assisted Bangladeshi freedom fighters. Despite threats to his own life, Saeed assists Shabina in her search for her husband. He also frequents her house in order to help her with the day-to-day hurdles of running a household with small children during chaotic moments of war. Most importantly, he is successful in saving Shabina from the clutches of Pakistanis like Mr. Rizvi and Brigadier Gul who try to exploit her sexually. Hence a close intimacy develops between him and Shabina.

It is significant that Shabina's infidelity occurs in the context of a war that dramatically redefined individual and group relationships along the lines of socially constructed identities such as nationality, religion, and ethnicity. Haider, in contrast to the husbands featured in Hossain's works, is neither promiscuous nor abusive. Rather, structural violence rooted in and triggered by patriarchal institutions of dominion create the conditions in which he fails to fulfill his spousal responsibilities, no matter how unwillingly, and his prolonged absence during a time of crisis leads to Shabina's transgressions. In her article "*A Different Sita*: A Novel by Niaz Zaman," Sutapa Chaudhuri highlights the role of the 1971 war in revealing and reconfiguring interpersonal and communal relationships. It was, she explains, "a time when family allegiances, kinship and affinities are inverted, tested and called into question" (90). Furthermore, according to Chaudhuri, the peculiar nature of this turbulent war-riddled time transforms Shabina into a different Sita than the mythological figure—one who betrays her husband, has untold secrets, and is stigmatized. It is, however, not just the unpredictably challenging times of political upheaval that bring Shabina close to Saeed. Both of them share Urdu language and culture as common identity components. Though married to Haider, a Bengali man, Shabina is an Urdu-speaking Bihari settled in Bangladesh.[4] Additionally, the fact that both are Muslims makes it easier for them to bond on a personal level despite animosity between their nations. Consequently, *A Different Sita* highlights the impact of macrolevel patriarchal institutions on women's lives, arguing that, as in the case of the 1971 war, affective bonds and affiliations—family, marriage, friendship—break down and are replaced by associations based on binarized constructions of ethnicity, national origin, and religion, social locations that are designed to categorize previously heterogeneous communities into homogenous groups of Self/Other.

The differences between this context and the circumstances faced by Hossain's characters, especially Motijan and Parul, evokes feelings of confusion and guilt in Shabina although, like them, she seeks comfort in the arms of her lover during her husband's long absence. In her words, "I was violating the bond of marriage, violating every legal and moral code that bound husband and wife" (160–61). This quote shows that Shabina's transgressive act is made not impulsively or in a fit of passion but with the full consciousness that she is breaking the stereotype that Muslim women are passive and exercise no individual consent/choice in their sexual relationships. One feels sympathetic toward Shabina when she reminisces that until then there had been no secrets between her and Haider, but after Saeed there was one that she could "never tell"—by pursuing the affair, Shabina has created for herself an individual space that she does not have to justify to anyone (163). This has the effect of shifting conventional definitions of "women's morality" away from sexual fidelity and reframing it as a matter of self-realization. The implicit claim is that denying women agency is far more immoral than sexual "fallenness."

Despite the various justifications behind Shabina's marital transgressions and the pricks of conscience that Shabina feels from time to time, the fact that she, a Bangladeshi housewife, has an affair with an enemy officer can also be seen as a scandalous and treasonous act from the Bangladeshi nationalistic standpoint. She is unfaithful to both Haider and her country as she pursues the relationship with Saeed. Moreover, Shabina might also be seen as betraying her country when she "consents," as she considers it, to rape, "willingly" sleeping with a Pakistani general for three nights, though this sexual transgression is committed only in order to free her husband from the enemy's custody, and she bravely manages to kill the general in the end. In his review of the novel, Shahid Alam comments on Haider's disappearance and its impact on Shabina as treason against the nation as well as a moral transgression: "This time she despairs and promises to herself to go to any length to rescue him. Again, for a second time, she succeeds, but has to pay, as well as extract, a heavy price to do that." Essentially, Shabina offers her body to the general in order to release her husband but is unable to recognize that her lack of other options—her decreased agency during the occupation by Pakistan—and the inequitable distribution of power between her and the general render their sex coercive. Consequently, she blames herself, and because of the fear of being stigmatized, she does not reveal the incident to anyone, including Haider. She views herself an accomplice in the Pakistani general's crime and fears that she cannot dare to claim the title of a *birangana* (war heroine), the honorific that the Bangladesh Army conferred on women raped by Pakistani troops during the 1971 war.[5] Shabina is doubtful that anyone would approve of her method of saving her husband and deem her heroic.

Regardless of her qualms and self-reproval, Shabina is successful in her mission of reuniting with her husband, but her ordeals are not easily over, which only increases her sense of guilt particularly over her affair with Saeed. Haider and her eldest son, Hammad, are killed in crossfire right after Bangladesh is declared independent. Shabina holds herself accountable for these deaths: "Was it a punishment for Saeed?" (255). She is, however, quick to brush the thought aside as her lover was long dead. Shabina's old maid is not that quick to absolve her mistress of all blame. Seeing the dead bodies, she starts wailing: "The *petni* [evil spirit] has devoured Dulha Bhai [Haider]. She has eaten up Hammad." By calling Shabina a *petni* who has eaten up her husband and son, the maid pronounces judgment on behalf of all those Bangladeshi women who internalize patriarchy's strict moral standards for wives. Despite her own doubts, Shabina retorts by saying, "There is no *petni* Sakinar Ma. It is our tragedy," and moves on with the proceedings for the funerals, but the maid is resentful. She refuses to consider the utter helplessness, insecurity, uncertainty, frustration, and anxiety of the war period that compel Shabina to act the way she did. Throughout the many ordeals caused at the personal and state level, Shabina manages to keep silent and composed throughout. The reasons she provides for her stoic tolerance, "I had to protect myself, my remaining son, and the child growing within me," bespeak not only her secret pregnancy but also her strength in singlehandedly raising her children (257).

Bad times finally recede in Shabina's life after her two remaining sons are grown up, and she gathers courage to reveal the dark secrets of her life to them in writing. In the prologue of her story, she promises her children a candid record of her life in these words: "I write it down for you two so that you know what happened during those months of the war. And why one of you has brown eyes and the other grey" (preface). Shabina wishes that her sons love each other despite their different races and fathers. By sharing her secret with her children, she is finally able to bury her ignominiously bitter past and also voice her resistance against patriarchal insistence on purity of roots and lineage. Like Hossain's characters, she challenges the conditions that oppress women, albeit with more reservations and self-recrimination than they did.

The trope of the "fallen woman" in Bangladeshi fiction is complicated in the hands of Hossain and Zaman. Though their protagonists such as Motijan, Parul, Proshanti, and Shabina violate many patriarchal proscriptions government for wifehood, motherhood, and nationhood, their actions are depicted sympathetically as resistance to oppressive religiosocial and political provocation. Hence despite challenging the sexual double standards of their Muslim and Bengali cultural constructions, and embracing illegitimate children, the wives in Hossain's fiction are empowered rather than castigated. In particular, Zaman's *A Different Sita* shows that national, ethnic, and religious divisions can be rendered meaningless and questions the rhetoric of war by allowing her protagonist a peaceful ending and the chance to broaden the hybrid identity frontiers of Bangladeshi women.

NOTES

1 The Bangladesh National Party's platform generally aligns with Muslim-identified objectives, while the Awami League espouses secular-left positions. Both Khalida Zia and Sheikh Hasina are members of powerful families who have dominated Bangladesh's rocky political history since the nation was established in the 1970s, a period marked by high levels of instability, corruption, strong-arm partisanship, incessant strikes and demonstrations, two presidents' assassinations, nineteen failed coups, and most recently, terrorist attacks apparently inspired by external agents and executed by young male Bangladeshis. Neither woman is associated with women's and/or feminist initiatives in Bangladesh.

2 Sita is the major female character in the Hindu epic *Ramayana*. Wife of Prince Rama, a god who is the story's male protagonist, Sita joins Rama in exile in the Dandaka forest when rivals for the throne threaten his life. Later she is kidnapped by Ravana, King of Lanka, and the *Ramayana*'s demonic antagonist. Rama twice punishes Sita harshly for alleged sexual infidelity, but on both occasions, she proves chaste and pure. Sita is considered the feminine ideal. Yashoda is featured as the god Krishna's foster-mother in the Hindu Puranas, an extensive collection of ancient Hindu stories composed in Sanskrit thought to be compiled by Vyasa, narrator of the *Mahābhārata*. Yashoda traded her daughter for Krishna when they were newborns in order to save him from his uncle, Kamsa, king of Mathura, who previously had murdered six of Krisha's seven older brothers. Yashoda subsequently raised Krishna, who, despite being a god, needed maternal guidance in childhood. Yashoda's wise mothering, and her absolute devotion to Krishna, traditionally is upheld as the model all mothers should emulate.

3 When India achieved independence from Great Britain's colonial rule in 1947, the region was divided into the Dominion of Pakistan and the Union of India, with boundaries drawn largely on the basis of religious affiliation—majority-Muslim regions constituted Pakistan while India was predominantly Hindu. Consequently, Pakistan consisted of two distant, noncontiguous areas, present-day Pakistan and Bangladesh with numerous cultural, regional, and economic differences. Discrimination and deprivation had led to a growing rift between the two wings of Pakistan, and the liberation war of 1971 was the founding moment of Bangladesh, which gained independence on December 16 after a bloody war marked by genocide and mass rape. The war divided the nation into forces that were deemed to be collaborators of Pakistan and the nationalists fighting for the independence of Bangladesh.

4 See Firdous Azim's chapter in this volume.

5 Estimates put the numbers of rapes of Bangladeshi women by Pakistan's military at two hundred thousand to four hundred thousand during the War of Liberation. These rapes were systematically conducted by Pakistani troops to demoralize the population of Bangladesh and its army (Totten 49). Susan Brownmiller, who in 1975 conducted one of the first studies of this campaign, which would now be recognized as a war crime in international law, reported that women were raped "on the spot" and then held "in military barracks for nightly use" (82). Women were also imprisoned in "mass rape camps" (Malik 154–55). A postwar pregnancy crisis emerged with estimates ranging that between twenty-five thousand to seventy thousand

(Totten 49). See Firdous Azim's article "The Forgotten Women of 1971," in this volume for analysis of the postwar rhetoric used to both honor *biranganas* and obscure the complex nature of the mass rapes and their consequences from Bangladesh's nationalist discourses.

WORKS CITED

Alam, Shahid. "Tale Told by an Unusual Heroine." *The Daily Star,* 14 Jan. 2012, http://www.thedailystar.net/news-detail-218235. Accessed 28 Feb. 2014.

Ameen, Nusrat. *Wife Abuse in Bangladesh: An Unrecognized Offence.* Dhaka UP, 2005.

Babul, Parvez. "Early Marriage, Inequalities and Violence against Women." *Observer Magazine,* 5 Sept. 2003, pp. 3–8.

Begum, Afsana. "Gender Analysis: Motijan's Daughters." Academia.edu, http://www.academia.edu/978674/Gender_analysis_Motijans_Daughters_by_Selina_Hossain. Accessed 28 Feb. 2014.

Begum, Maleka. "The Cultural Picture of Dowry System and Its Reflection in Bangladesh." Dissertation, U of Dhaka, 2004.

Brownmiller, Susan. *Against Our Will: Men, Women and Rape.* Bantam, 1976.

Chaudhuri, Sutapa. "*A Different Sita*: A Novel by Niaz Zaman." *CHAOS,* vol. 2, no. 1, 2014.

Hossain, Selina. *Atomic Darkness.* Anyaprokash, 2003.

———. "Culture and the Child: The Bangladesh Perspective." *Bangladesher Meye Shishu.* Mowla Brothers, 2002, pp. 14–18.

———. "Motijan's Daughters." *Selected Short Stories of Selina Hossain.* Bangla Academy, 2007, pp. 17–29.

———. "Parul Becomes Mother." *Selected Short Stories of Selina Hossain.* Bangla Academy, 2007, pp. 161–67.

———. *Security of the Marginalized Women: The Bangladesh Context.* Forum on Women in Security and International Affairs (FOWSIA) Bangladesh Freedom Foundation, 2002.

———. *Selected Short Stories of Selina Hossain.* Bangla Academy, 2007.

Islam, Mahmuda. *Whither Women's Studies in Bangladesh?* Women for Women, 1994.

Johri, Rachana. "From Parayi to Apni: Mother's Love as Resistance." *South Asian Mothering: Negotiating Culture, Family and Selfhood,* edited by Jasjit K. Sangha and Tahira Gonsalves, Demeter, 2013.

Khan, Hafiza Nilofar. "South Asian Fiction and Marital Agency of Muslim Wives." *Journal of International Women's Studies,* vol. 14, no. 3, 2013, pp. 174–93, vc.bridgew.edu/jiws/vol14/iss3/13/.

———. "Treatment of a Wife's Body in the Fiction of Indian Sub-Continental Muslim Women Writers." Dissertation, U of Southern Mississippi, 2008.

Malik, Amita. *The Year of the Vulture.* Orient Longman, 1972.

Totten, Samuel, editor. *Plight and Fate of Women Following Genocide. Genocide: A Critical Bibliographical Review,* vol. 7. 2008. Transaction, 2012.

Vance, Carole S. "Pleasure and Danger: Towards a Politics of Sexuality." *Pleasure and Danger: Exploring Female Sexuality.* Routledge & Kegan Paul, 1984.

Zaman, Niaz. *A Different Sita.* Writers Ink, 2011.

PART II FORBIDDEN DESIRES AND MISOGYNIST ENCULTURATION

5 POLYAMOROUS DRAUPADI

Adharma or Emancipation?

DEVALEENA DAS

> Draupadi's black body comes even closer. Draupadi shakes with an indomitable laughter that *Senanayak*[1] simply cannot understand. Her ravaged lips bleed as she begins laughing. Draupadi wipes the blood on her palm and says in a voice that is as terrifying, sky splitting, and sharp as her ululation, "What's the use of clothes? You can strip me, but how can you clothe me again? Are you a man?"
>
> —Mahasweta Devi, "Draupadi"

In this chapter, Devaleena Das looks at female sexual desire outside the moral and religious codes of marriage. Reflecting on the ambiguous representation of Draupadi, who was simultaneously married to five brothers called Pandavas in the *Mahābhārata*, as both whorish and chaste, Das's chapter tackles a rare and important exception to the virgin/whore dichotomy. Thus Das critiques the patriarchal politics of monogamy, polygamy, and polygyny and then goes on to cull feminist revisions of these concepts from Draupadi's story. An important strategy that she uses in this project is pointing out that claims that Draupadi is whorish are rooted in the *Mahābhārata*'s chauvinist misappropriation of the Hindu philosophical theory of *dharma* (the moral code of conduct). At the same time, Das's chapter warns that to regard Draupadi as an exceptional woman is a manifestation of patriarchalism. Rather, she sees Draupadi as a contemporary Everywoman who mocks patriarchal shaming of women's bodies and sexuality and is bold enough to openly condemn and resist misogynist uses of dharma to control women. Das concludes that Draupadi, whom she considers an early feminist voice, offers a model of empowered feminist empowered for Indian women today.

INTRODUCTION

From Eve in the Garden of Eden to the goddess Kali in ancient Hindu mythology to Queen Scheherazade of *One Thousand and One Nights* or Spider Grandmother of Native American folklore, mythological representations across the world offer complex views of womanhood as transgressive, benevolent, wise, ingenious, seductive, munificent, and independent. Draupadi, the princess in the Sanskrit epic the *Mahābhārata,* which is attributed to Vyasa, is an ancient feminist voice, ever challenging and questioning the patriarchal agenda of controlling women's desire and expressing how in a "man's world" that desire comes at a heavy price. To me, she is an evolutionary figure forever contemporary, forever new.[2] By delving into the character of Draupadi and her critique of *dharma,* a major element in Hindu moral philosophy that entails far more than "fate" or "just desserts" as it is understood in colloquial use in the West, in this chapter, I will analyze how Draupadi's ocean of desire and sexual potency problematizes her position in the virgin/whore binary *between* fallenness and virtue (rather than on one side or the other).[3] Anxiety regarding Draupadi's uncontrollable desire, an androcentric psychosis, is pervasive, found in the Buddhist Jataka[4] stories that represent Draupadi having an illicit sexual relationship with a hump-backed servant, the folk tale "Bheel Bharata" of the Bheel tribes of Rajasthan[5] that feature passion between her and Vasuka Naga, a "snake" king, and in *Devi Bhagavata Puraana,*[6] in which Kichaka, a distant brother-in-law, rapes her as punishment for her transgressive nature. I will assert that the future of India promises to yield many rebellious Draupadis and fewer Sitas or Radhas, the latter who are female figures embodying the patriarchal ideal of femininity.[7] Finally, looking at Draupadi's story in feminist revisionist mythologies, I argue that she wields a polyamorous subjectivity that future women of India will embrace.

EPIC BACKGROUND: WHO IS DRAUPADI?

Before I reflect on Draupadi and her rebellious attempts to revolutionize the sexual politics of Hindu moral philosophy, a brief overview of her character and role in the two-thousand-year-old *Mahābhārata* is necessary. In the original Sanskrit text, Draupadi was born out of fire when King Draupad (from whom Draupadi derives her name) of the Panchal region performed a sacrificial rite in hopes of siring a son who would kill his enemy.[8] Fully grown and in the bloom of her youth, Draupadi emerged from the sacrificial fire-altar like the Greek Athena springing from Zeus's head or the Hindu goddess Durga[9] emerging from the combined fury of the great gods. When Draupadi participates in a *Swyamvar* (a ceremony in which a woman publicly chose her life partner) to identify a worthy, heroic king to be her husband, by fluke she ends up marrying five brothers called the Pandavas.[10] Although the ceremony is called *Swyamvar* (where *swyam* emphasizes the "self"—i.e., the choice of the bride), in reality Draupadi's father devises a test that gives the advantage to a particular warrior who is a strong political ally. Accordingly, the contestants must shoot the eye of a revolving fish while they look at the reflection the fish casts in water. All the great warriors fail, including the villainous antagonist, Duryodhan. Karna, a man of unknown parentage, is almost successful, but Draupadi prevents him from participating in the competition after Krishna subtly warns her that Karna could win.[11] Ultimately Arjuna, a champion in archery and the third of the Pandavas, wins Draupadi, angering Duryodhan, who is the cousin to the Pandavas.

After the *Swyamvar*, Arjun tells his mother, Kunti,[12] who does not realize that he is referring to Draupadi, that as a Brahmin, he has been given the most precious alms of the day, and Kunti in her ignorance commands that the alms should be equally distributed among and enjoyed by her five sons, the Pandavas. Thus Draupadi marries all five brothers, and in this polyandric union, she gives birth to five sons, each fathered by a different husband. Throughout the marriage(s), Draupadi is faithful to her husbands, but they do not reciprocate: most of the Pandavas marry innumerable princesses as part of various political strategies or out of sexual passion and all have multiple lovers.

Aside from suffering this double standard, Draupadi endures her husbands' fortunes along with them, including the aftermath of Duryodhan's retaliation against the Pandavas for his loss of the *Swyamvar* competition. Seeking revenge, Duryodhan and his four brothers, known as the Kauravas, pit themselves against the Pandavas in a game of dice held at the royal Kuru court.[13] Duryodhan, his brothers, and Karna are near to defeating the Pandavas when Yudhisthira, the eldest of Draupadi's husbands, uses her as his last stake and loses. Duryodhan immediately takes possession of Draupadi, who was menstruating, and drags, molests, and strips her in view of the full court. Enraged, Draupadi exhorts her husbands to seek revenge against Duryodhan. This triggers the Kurukshetra War between the Pandavas and the Kauravas. All the warriors except the Pandavas and Lord Krishna die in battle, bringing chaos, decadence, and death to the kingdom.

DRAUPADI'S *ADHARMA* VERSUS YUDHISTHIRA'S *DHARMA*/PRACTICALITY VERSUS IDEALISM

Draupadi's polyandrous marriage flies in the face of the Hindu belief that non-monogamous women are fallen, but none of the witnesses object, including the Pandava brothers; Kunti; her own brother, Dhrishtadyumna; her father, Draupad; and Sage Vyasa, the author of the *Mahābhārata*. Her enemies forever call her a whore because of it. Yet Draupadi is silent! She does not protest. Why? Because Yudhisthira, the eldest of Draupadi's five husbands, resolves the issue by citing *dharma* before Draupadi has a chance to protest the marriage. For this reason and other occasions when Yudhisthira adjudicates "wisely" in the *Mahābhārata*, Hindus revere him for his righteousness and impartiality, and he is called *Dharamraj* or the king of *dharma*.

The Hindu concept of *dharma*[14] is complex, but the nearest translation is "morality," "virtue," and "law and order." Etymologically, *dharma* originates from the word *dhy*, which means "to establish"; hence, *dharma* is synonymous with the "order" that keeps individuals, society, divinities, and natural or cosmic forces from reeling out of control. One important aspect of *dharma* is its opposite yet imbricated construct, *adharma*, which is "immorality," "vice," "unlawfulness," and "chaos." Significantly, *dharma* is generally considered universal and eternal, but it can be relative when there is a question of choosing the better of two bad options. Thus *dharma* is not a systematic set of guidelines, and this complicates how it is used to adjudicate problems, for moral decision making is, of course, inextricable from social contexts—beliefs, for example, about gender, class, caste, and other social locations. Hence the "better good" is idiosyncratic, which infuses *dharma* with internal contradiction. In any event, when Yudhisthira argues that obeying a mother's edict is the greatest *dharma*, he is making a relative choice, which in the traditional, patriarchal, Hindu paradigm is a choice between chaos and the social harmony that sustains civilization.

In contrast to her silence about her marriage or Yudhisthira's use of *dharma* to justify violating prohibitions against polyandry, after the ill-fated dice game where she is lost to Yudhisthira, her demands that the Pandavas seek vengeance on the Kauravas include a critique of *dharma* that is one of the earliest feminist interventions against the androcentrism embedded in it. If we look carefully at Draupadi's interrogation of *dharma*, we see that it is an impressive feminist intervention in Hindu teleology, for she asserts that *dharma* is a patriarchal device, subverts *dharmic* logic, and exposes Yudhishtri as oppressive rather than just.

In the episode featuring her disrobing just after the defeat of her husbands in the dice game, Draupadi, the only woman present in the court, exposes *dharma* as a patriarchal mandate that allows men to control women sexually, emotionally, and psychologically:

> What prince is there who playeth staking his wife? . . . Morality, however, it hath been said, is the one highest object in the world. . . . Let not that morality abandon the Kauravas. . . . In this assembly are persons conversant with all the branches of learning devoted to the performance of sacrifice and other rites . . . persons some of whom are really my superiors and others who deserve to be respected as such. . . . The illustrious son of *Dharma* is now bound by the obligations of morality. Morality, however, is subtle. Those only that are possessed of great clearness of vision can ascertain it. Thou draggest me who am in my season before these Kuru heroes. This is truly an unworthy act. But no one here rebuketh thee. Assuredly all these are of the same mind with thee. O fie! Truly has the virtue of the Bharata gone! . . . Else, these Kurus in this assembly would never have looked silently on this act

> that transgresseth the limits of their practices. . . . Else, why these foremost of the Kuru elders look silently on this great crime? (129)

But stupefied and mindless, Yudhishtri is silent in the face of Duryodhan's assault on Draupadi, because he has already decided to follow his *dharma* as Duryodhan's slave; thus, in his mind, Yudhishtri has no right to protest against his new master: "Yudhishthira sat there unmoved, like one who has lost his senses. He did not reply, in words that were either good or bad" (182). Here, Yudhishtri's silence communicates that it is his *dharma* to submit to Duryodhan's authority. But Draupadi responds with a brilliance that paralyzes the male arbiters of *dharma* when she demands to know why Yudhishtri has the right to use her as his last stake when he had already lost himself in the game, and she commands the messenger who is supposed to deliver her to the Kauravas to "Go back to the assembly hall and ask that gambler from the Bharata lineage [Yudhishtri] whether he first lost himself or me. . . . The foremost among the elders of the Kuru lineage have chosen to ignore this terrible transgression of *dharma* by the king" (182–83). However, her question remains unanswered, and the third husband, Arjuna, merely defends Yudhishtri and his concept of *dharma*: "Observe the supreme *dharma*. According to *dharma*, one should never cross one's elder brother. The king was challenged and he followed the *dharma* of the *Kshatriyas* [warriors]. He gambled because of the desires of the enemy. That is our great deed" (184). In return, Draupadi points out the internal contradiction embedded in the concept of *dharma* and demands answers from the Pandavas' grandfather, Vishma, a man who is admired for his greatness and had a special power to desire death for himself only when he wishes: "Where is the *dharma* of the lords of the earth? According to *dharma*, it has earlier been heard that wives are not brought into an assembly hall. That earlier eternal *dharma* has been lost" (188). Vishma tries to answer tactfully but must admit that Draupadi's argument is undeniable: "I have already said that the course of *dharma* is supreme. Even the great-souled *brahmanas* in this world are incapable of comprehending its course. When a powerful man uses force, that is perceived as *dharma* by the world. But if a feeble one speaks about *dharma*, that is not regarded as *dharma* by others. I am incapable of answering your question certainly. The issue is subtle, deep, complicated and important. . . . It is my view that Yudhishthira is the supreme authority on the question. He should himself say whether you have been won or have not been won" (188–89). Alas! Yudhishtri maintains his silence, his best weapon for protecting his concept of *dharma*, and the king, Duryodhan's father, praises him: "O Yudhishthira! O son! You know the subtle path of *dharma*. You are humble, immensely wise and serve your superiors. O descendant of the Bharata lineage! Where there is intelligence, there is peace. Therefore, tread the path of serenity. . . . Supreme men do not indulge in hostilities. They do not know enmity and see good qualities, leaving out bad qualities. O Yudhishthira! It is only the worst among men who use harsh words in a quarrel. Those who are average reply to such words, but the supreme among men never respond" (193).

But this does not deter Draupadi, whose challenge employs the feminist tactic of casting the female gaze on the moral impuissance of her husbands and the assembled Kurus, arguing that *dharma* is as ineffectual as they are. With an incisive tongue, Draupadi reminds her husbands that vengeance is the cure for her misery. She rejects the patriarchal bluffing in Yudhisthira's use of *dharma* to justify her violation and the Pandavas' passive assent to it. The practical logic that guides Draupadi is that if someone is inhuman enough to participate in molestation, he is capable of bearing its consequences; therefore, revenge is not *adhamra* (immoral). With Amazonian spirit, she argues that the greatest *dharma* for a warrior is to restore honor: "O king! *Dharma* that causes affliction to our friends and our own selves is vice. It is not *dharma*. It is bad *dharma*. A man who always resorts to *dharma* follows weak *dharma*. . . . One who suffers *dharma*'s afflictions for the sake of *dharma* alone is not learned. He does not know the true purpose of *dharma*" (270–71). But privileging his commitment to reconciliation and forgiveness above maintaining her honor, Yudhishtri persists in rejecting Draupadi's stance, which is that the choice between forgiveness and violence should be determined relative to her violation—the harm inflicted on her—so that that the value of forgiveness is not diminished. In essence, she argues that forgiving Duryodhan is a weakness rather than a salutary dedication to *dharma* because disregarding her suffering dehumanizes her. Despite this appeal, Yudhishtri never embraces this recalibration of *dharma* because, mired chauvinism, the desire to control and regulate the symbolic order lies at the heart of his concept of *dharma*. Thus Draupadi takes every chance she can to jeer at her husbands, reminding them that time and again their pretense of upholding *dharma* has failed to protect them.

In this sense, Draupadi is almost every Hindu wife who struggles with the impositions of patriarchalism. She is the guilty girl and the rebellious woman who refuses to accept that marriage is an institution that should confine her body and mind. She is the raped and molested victim in every corner of India who waits for justice for centuries. Above all, Draupadi redefines *dharma* as a dizzying patriarchal set of social, historical, cultural, and religious institutions that oppress women but euphemize this domination in lofty principles such as "reconciliation," "responsibility," "preservation of order," and "justice."

DRAUPADI IN INDIA TODAY

The reason that Draupadi is an Indian Everywoman, so to speak, is that Yudhisthira's understanding of *dharma* continues to shape Hindu orthodoxy today. For example, Mohandas K. Gandhi's principle of nonviolence, *Satyagraha* (persistence in truth), is based on Yudhisthira's definition of *dharma* in the *Mahābhārata* even though *dharma* is a violent principle, according to Romila Thapar's *The Past before Us: Historical Traditions of Early North India*: "Violence is evil but evil is so defined as to apply to those who do not follow the *Dharmaśāstra*" (220). In other words, *dharma* endorses punishing or killing nonbelievers.

Perhaps this is why, despite Gandhi's association with nonviolence, *Satyagraha* is widely considered an eminently effective *weapon* against powerful enemies, obstacles, and oppressions. Its core component, according to Gandhi, involves a soul force or love that is a form of passive resistance, or *ahimsa* (nonviolence)—again the paradox! The literal translation of the root word, *satya*, is "truth"; therefore, in this case, "soul force" means the force or power of truth. However, in Hindu philosophy, "truth" is *nirguna*, meaning "beyond human intellect." Consequently, the concept of the *Satyagraha*, the "power of truth," is not only more complex than nonviolence but also abstract, slippery, and doesn't inevitably connote lofty ideals. Just as Yudhishtri used *dharma* to excuse his implicit consent to—if not psychological participation in—Duryodhan's assault on Draupadi, *Satyagraha* can be deployed to regulate and degrade women.

The work of scholars like Géraldine Forbes (28), Madhu Kishwar (1691–1702), Radha Kumar (53–73) and Sujata Patel (377–87) on Gandhi's support for women's liberty and his stance on women's roles is helpful in understanding how the *dharmic* principle of *Satyagraha* can, in application, perpetuate their oppression. For instance, Gandhi believed that death was preferable to sexual violation, to women's "fallenness." During the 1946–47 Hindu-Muslim conflicts in the Indian subcontinent, for instance, he advised Hindu women who had been raped by Muslim men in the Noakhali[15] riots "to commit suicide by poison or some other means to avoid dishonor . . . to suffocate themselves or to bite their tongues to end their lives" and claimed that "women must learn how to die before a hair of their head could be injured" (355). This stance is consistent with Gandhi's view that the ultimate political hero was Ram, a hero in the epic *Ramayana* who, married to the idealized Sita, is both divine and mortal. Worshipped for his discipline and steadfastness, Ram was Gandhi's guiding figure. An aggressive woman like Draupadi—contrasted with Ram's idealized wife, Sita, who epitomizes compassion and submission to her husband's decisions—could never become a female role model among the likes of Gandhi, Ram, or Yudhisthira. Given the continuing sway of the *Mahābhārata* in Indian cultures and Gandhi's influence on the mores and institutions of the modern Indian state, Yudhishtri's concept of *dharma* maintains a hold over Indian society, which necessitates an alternative for women.

DRAUPADI AND DESIRE

Returning to the analysis of the text, it's important to recall that when Draupadi was forced into polyandry with the Pandavas, Vyasa, a character in the *Mahābhārata* who is also thought to be its author, enters the text as a sage and narrates that Draupadi is destined to marry five brothers because of her unquenchable and unnatural desire in a previous life. He states that Draupadi's inordinate passion had prompted her to pray to Shiva for a husband with five heroic qualities, and this is why she must marry the Pandavas. Notably, this contention camouflages the fact that all five brothers desire Draupadi and compete against each other for her. It strategically, manipulatively misrepresents the brothers' sexual rivalry not only as *dharma* but as caused by the female characters' shortcomings—Kunti's ignorance of the *Swyamvar*'s terms and conditions and Draupadi's purportedly excessive desire. Another tactic that the narrative uses to frame the Pandavas' lust as virtue is Yudhisthira's mandate that Draupadi will live with each husband in one-year rotations. If any of the brothers breaks this rule, that brother will voluntarily punish himself by committing to twelve years of celibacy. Yudhisthira, of course, never bothers to ask Draupadi about her views, and her eternal silence about the arrangement constitutes an aporia in the text that is replicated in the lack of attention to Draupadi's revolving-door conjugal relations in the scholarship on the *Mahābhārata*.

This troubling aporia in the criticism is an example of how ideas about the sanctity of divine revelation deny women agency, choice, and desire; although, of course, nothing is left unsaid when it comes to chaos and deviation from normative monogamy, which the *Mahābhārata* and other versions of the story blame on Draupadi's passion. In the Jataka version, for example, Draupadi is portrayed as a nymphomaniac, and her sexuality is seen as the seed of destruction. Yet the scholarship does not address the many questions this raises about the intersection of power, gender, and ideology in Hindu mythology or why the weight of the patriarchy falls on the shoulders of women, denying them rights in order to sustain itself and its privileges. More specifically, what are alternative interpretations of Draupadi's excess of desire, emotion, and rage? What lies between idealization of womanhood as *sati*, pious and holy in Hinduism, and woman as whore? And what realities does the virgin/whore binary engender in women's lives? Finally, why is women's sexuality politicized? To respond to these questions, we must delve into the political dimensions of desire and gender.

The subject of desire in Eastern philosophy, particularly in Hinduism, is treated distinctly differently than in western philosophy. In western philosophy, desire primarily has been understood as the bodily "Other" that is in a dichotomous relationship—with a privileged, usually immaterial principle—the mind/body dualism—and this opposition organizes much of the West's cultural and intellectual production. Thus, for example, in the story of creation in the Hebrew Scriptures, Eve's consumption of the forbidden fruit, her satiation of bodily desire (understood as carnality from at least the early medieval period in Europe) separates humanity from God. In contrast, Hinduism does not construct desire as a completely uncontrollable force that diverts us from more edifying thoughts and pursuits. In fact, throughout Vedic literature, desire is variously represented as the soul's wish to unite with God, as *Kamadeva*,[16] the god of human love, or as the fuel driving the engine of creation in the universe. In the *Rig Veda*, for instance, desire is seen as the first seed of the mind in which "poets seeking in their heart with wisdom found the bond of existence in nonexistence" (Doniger O'Flaherty 25). Accordingly, we must view Vyasa's condemnation of Draupadi's desire in the *Swyamvar* scene as anomalous to Hindu philosophy and inconsistent with other passages in the *Mahābhārata*, including those that valorize Draupadi's displays of excessive desire and enable her to articulate a comprehensive revision of Yudhishtri's patriarchal, rule-bound ideas about *dharma* and desire.

Thus aside from Vyasa's comments during the *Swyamvar*, the *Mahābhārata* reveals, albeit in bits and pieces, numerous examples of Draupadi's unruly desire, particularly in its representation of her relationship with Krishna, who, as an avatar of the god Vishnu, appears in human form as Kunti's nephew.[17] Krishna is a friend of Draupadi's father, and she admires him and his philosophy from the moment she first meets him. Significantly, Draupadi is attracted to Krishna because he is master of *lila*, or the divine play that disrupts and overturns the social order with unrestrained exuberance. In their unique friendship, Draupadi addresses Krishna as *sakha* (male companion or confidant) while Krishna addresses Draupadi as *sakhi* (female companion or confidant). The *sakha-sakhi*[18] relationship is constituted on unqualified love and trust without limit. It is selfless even when it includes flirtatious romance. Interestingly, the word *sakha* is phonetically linked to the word *śākhā*, which literally means "branch" or "limb," but in this context, can be understood as a sexual entendre referring to a body part. This connection to the corporeal perhaps also hints that *sakha-sakhi* relationship sublimates intense erotic and romantic attraction into divine love. As a result of maintaining this intimate trust, the *sakha* and *sakhi* are able to understand each other spontaneously and intuitively, without words or the slightest gesture. An example of this unspoken communication occurs during the *Swyamvar* when, as mentioned previously, in an unspoken hint, Krishna warns Draupadi that Karna is not a suitable husband. Another is when Draupadi beseeches Krishna, in his incarnation as the god Vishnu, to save her from being publicly stripped after the infamous dice game between the Kauravas and Pandavas.

Draupadi's desire for Krishna is also apparent in a scene in which he is injured. Krishna's *chakra* (the body's vital energy) beheads his cousin, King Sisupala,[19] for insulting him and the Pandavas, but in so doing, Krishna injures his finger and writhes in pain as it bleeds profusely. In the presence of her husbands and other great kings, Draupadi tears a piece of cloth from her saree's hem and uses it to staunch Krishna's blood. Draupadi's spontaneous reaction and her failure to stay calm in the face of Krishna's suffering are transgressive, especially since they occur in the setting of the royal court. Her yearning to relieve Krishna's pain is not constrained by courtly codes of behavior that prohibit women's public display of emotion for a man who is not her husband. Furthermore, as Draupadi's desire for Krishna is reflected in her tears as she pines to transfer Krishna's pain into her body—she feels his injury as if it were her own—and in this respect, she also flouts the social convention that a Hindu wife should not give consideration to any man other than her husband. In fact, Draupadi's desire is so compelling that it persuades Krishna to vow, in the presence of the court, to love and protect her across space and time.

Another version of Krishna and Draupadi's story that illustrates her passion for him is found in the *Devi Bhagavata Puraana*. Krishna is swimming with the Pandavas and loses his loincloth. Seeing his embarrassment, Draupadi tears off the portion of her saree that covers her breasts and gives it to Krishna. The sexual innuendo is remarkable as Krishna's body, undulating in the water, excites Draupadi. Here, they symbolically consummate their desire, and notably, Draupadi's passion for Krishna only increases because her mystic relationship with Krishna defies social boundaries, always transcendental, always new. The *lila* of separation and the desire to be united is the ultimate expression of attraction and spontaneous reciprocity. This desire is creative and erotic and, in Draupadi, acts as the life force that sustain her even in the face of polyandric oppression.

Another place where the *Mahābhārata* reveals Draupadi's desire is in the subtexts of her relationship with Karna, who is Kunti's illegitimate son and thus a half-brother to the Pandavas. Little is said about Draupadi's feelings about Karna, but he is attracted to her throughout the *Mahābhārata*. Karna desires Draupadi from the day of the *Swyamvar* where he almost won her, but of course, she deflected his advances and ultimately chose Arjun. At that point, Karna's desire is inflamed by the insult, so perhaps he thought that he was entitled to a "share" of Draupadi based on Kunti's inadvertent directive that the brothers should share her. At one point, Karna even calls Draupadi a whore, but this is a case of love disguised as contempt because Karna also praises Draupadi for her intelligence. Later, for example, he is impressed that she manages to recoup the wealth and power her husbands lost in the dice game with the Kauravas: "Draupadi became unto the sons of Pandu as their salvation. Indeed, the princess of Panchala, becoming as a boat unto the sons of Pandu who were sinking in an ocean of distress, hath brought them in safety to the shore" (80).

FEMINIST REVISION OF DRAUPADI'S DESIRE

Chitra Banerjee Divakaruni is among contemporary feminist writers whose fiction has given voice to Draupadi's desire as part of a larger movement to empower Indian women to resist patriarchal strictures that deny women control of their bodies and disallow their sexual pleasure. Her *Palace of Illusions* retells the *Mahābhārata* from Draupadi's point of view, and the plot centers on Draupadi's love not only for Krishna but also for Karna.

Palace of Illusions opens just before the *Swyamvar*. In Divakaruni's retelling, interactions between Draupadi and Karna are uncomfortable after Draupadi marries the five Pandava brothers. In her version of their relationship, Draupadi and Karna look for opportunities for eye contact, Draupadi sometimes regrets that she resisted Karna, Draupadi enjoys Karna's flame for her even both are married and never unite, and Draupadi believes that she would have been much happier with Karna than with the five brothers. In Divakaruni's hands, Draupadi, who cannot forgive her father for treating her like "a worm dangled at the end of a fishing pole" (57), is transformed from Vyasa's misogynistic trope of female fallenness into a flesh-and-blood woman. This Draupadi celebrates her sexuality and lovemaking, reveling in "how to send out a lightning-glance," "how to bite the swollen lower lip," how to walk with a swaying back or—depending on the lord's mood—how to bring variety in bed, from that of "a lioness" to a "trembling dove" (62). In *Palace of Illusions,* Draupadi also negotiates her love with Karna and Krishna openly and with agency: "If what I felt for Karna was a singeing fire, Krishna's love was a balm, moonlight over a parched landscape" (356), which reinforces her desirability. In Divakaruni's version, Draupadi, Krishna, and Karna hold hands as they enter the palace of love and equality together (whereas Yudhishtri is the only Pandava to reach heaven), which shows that rather than being fallen, Draupadi is sanctified by the suffering and pain of her polyandric marriage and her polyandrous desire for Krishna and Karna.

Thus Divakaruni's (re)vision of the myth of Draupadi's desire runs the gamut from the sexual to the actual to the imagined, and as such, it is an attempt to catalyze social change by recasting the ancient myth. Myth, of course, is a narrative of ideology that expresses, transmits, and forms social values and, importantly, regulates society. As Adrienne Rich writes in "When We Dead Awaken," an essay published in 1971, "Re-vision—the act of looking back, of seeing with fresh eyes, of entering an old text from a new critical direction—is for women more than a chapter in cultural history: it is an act of survival" (18). This is precisely the project that Divakaruni undertakes in *The Palace of Illusions,* for the novel unleashes Draupadi's desire and, in the process of depicting it as liberating, invests Draupadi with a sense of pride, power, and prowess. In so doing, Divakaruni shows how sexual subjectivity is integrally linked to authoritative power and, as she defines Draupadi's desire outside rigidly controlled norms, reminds us of the concept of *sankalpa* (ritualistic intention) that gives purpose to all actions. Women are generally believed to be incapable of *sankalpa* as it relates to solemn determination and then putting one's decision to effect, but Draupadi's *sankalpa* is stronger than her five husbands' as she cautiously restores their lost powers, directs them to defeat Duryodhan's empire, and finally becomes the queen of that empire.

The philosopher and poet Aurobindo Ghosh's[20] interpretation of desire in the *Bhagavad Gītā* is relevant here. In his analysis, Ghosh explains that to be desireless is impossible: "Desire is the impulse of the Force of Being individualised in Life to affirm progressively in the terms of succession in Time and of self-extension in Space, in the framework of the finite, it's infinite Bliss" (*The Life Divine* 208). Ghosh goes on to quote the *Bhagavad Gītā* to make his cases, "I am in beings the desire which is not contrary to their *Dharma,*" pointing out that desire can be divine and achieve "*ananda* [bliss]" (274). Draupadi achieves *ananda* when she sublimates into Krishna's female form, which is called Krishnaa. Krishnaa is the feminine version of Krishna, and Draupadi is known by that name in all versions of the *Mahābhārata.* She shares Krishna's thought, *lilas,* and flirtations and also realizes what Krishna feels about her. The holistic philosophy of Vaishnavism[21] can also be related to Divakaruni's portrayal of Draupadi. Vaishnavism celebrates romantic and erotic desires as a means of achieving spiritual and religious fulfillment. While Vaishnavism is not directly mentioned in *The Palace of Illusions* because Vaishnavism is a philosophy or theory, Divakaruni seems to admire Krishna and his philosophy of love and life, which establishes a connection between Vaishnavism to the novel. At the beginning, Draupadi explains how "Krishna, whose complexion was ever darker than mine, didn't consider his colour a drawback. I'd heard his stories about how he'd charmed his way into the hearts of the women of his hometown of Vrindavan—all 16,000 of them. And then there was the affair of princess Rukmini. . . . She'd sent him a most indecorous love letter asking him to marry her (to which he'd promptly and chivalrously responded by carrying her off in his chariot). He had other wives, too—over a hundred, at least count" (8). Her admiration at Krishna's "enigmatic smile that forced me to do my own thinking" (8–9) is at the end seen not as transgressive but divinely when Draupadi after her fall from heaven sees Krishna's "serene, affectionate" face and says "I hesitate, wondering what my husbands would think, then realize it doesn't matter. . . . I can take his arm in view of everyone. If I wish, I can embrace him with all of myself," but she asks Krishna, "*Are you truly divine?*" to which Krishna answers, "Yes, I am. You are, too, you know!" (359).

Additionally, Vaishnavism considers gender fluid and believes that the ultimate reality is personal, which is reflected in the novel's ending when all three characters, Draupadi, Krishna, and Karna, ascend into heaven. Thus in the light of Aurobindo Ghosh's philosophy of desire and Vaishnavism's principle of true human love as a path to divinity, *The Palace of Illusions* ends when Draupadi's much desired touch of Krishna breaks "a chain that was tied to the woman-shape," and Draupadi exclaims, "I am buoyant and expansive and uncontainable. . . . I am beyond name and gender and the imprisoning patterns of ego" while with her other hand, she reaches out for Karna, and she affirms, "We rise" (360). This eternal rendering of love beyond all regulations is infinite bliss and divinity, which was perhaps Draupadi's *sankalpa* of her life from the beginning.

Although Divakaruni's mission of re-visioning the ancient myth of Draupadi and viewing it from fresh perspectives offers readers enticing perspectives of her character, scholars such as US Indologist Wendy Doniger O'Flaherty argue that Draupadi's hypersexuality is an idealized representation in the *Mahābhārata*. She suggests that it is out of reach of ordinary women because when the *Mahābhārata* was composed, "there is no other evidence that women at this time actually had multiple husbands," and polyandry is reflective of men's fears of what might happen were women to have that freedom (296). First, Doniger O'Flaherty's claim that there is no evidence of women having multiple husbands during the Vedic period (c. 1500–500 BCE) is inaccurate, as exemplified in the stories of Surya,[22] the daughter of the sun god in the *Rig Veda* who is married to twin gods, and of the *Ramayana*'s Bali and Sugriv, who share a common wife.[23] Furthermore, in the eleventh century, the Muslim scholar Alberuni reported that polyandry and cicisbeism were practiced widely in the region.[24] Second, although Doniger O'Flaherty's historicization of Draupadi's sexuality is a worthy endeavor, assessing her character vis-à-vis polyandry is a mistake because in the original epic, Draupadi never consents to marrying the Pandavas. Therefore, it is far more relevant to look at Draupadi's extramarital desire than the forced marriage and the intensity and multifocality of her passion show that Draupadi unapologetically is hypersexual in the *Mahābhārata*. Divakaruni's *Palace of Illusion* underscores this analysis (rather than concocting it) when, shifting narrative authority from Vyasa to Draupadi, Draupadi becomes the agent in her construction of a sexual and political self through "self-storying as activism." Of course, polyandry does not ensure women's freedom, and it can be, as in the *Mahābhārata*, a patriarchal tool used to oppress women, such as when the narrator castigates Draupadi because she is the unconscious whose overflowing desire challenges, disrupts, breaks down, and threatens the masculine *dharmic* and symbolic order.

That polyandry can oppress women is demonstrated by the fact that in the *Mahābhārata* Draupadi's desire is "fallen"—both excessive and transgressive—in order to give definition to the Pandavas' desire. Consequently, Draupadi inhabits the space—borderlands—between an androcentric version of womanhood defined by compliance and subordination that accommodates the interests and desires of men like the Pandavas and an alternative, noncompliant form of femininity that resists patriarchalism. In contrast, men like Arjun, the third of Draupadi's five husbands; Vim, the second Pandava husband; and Krishna have multiple lovers and wives and enjoy broad sexual access to a large variety of women, but they are not labelled as hypersexual or transgressive. For instance, Arjun fell in love with Krishna's sister, Suvandra, and after kidnapping her, married her. Arjun also married Chitrangada, the daughter of the king of Manipura and Ulupi/Uloopi, who is, in some versions of the story, a tribal woman and, in other tales, a *nagini* (half serpent and half human). Vim or Bhim married Hidimbi, a female monster, and Valandhara, the daughter of the king of Kasi. Both Arjun and Bhim had sons with each of their wives. Krishna, of course, had many lovers such as Radha and the *gopinis* (female cowherds/female admirers) as well as many wives. His first wife is Rukmini, the princess of Vidarbha, who is considered an avatar of Lakshmi, the goddess of wealth, and he also had eight principle queen-consorts called the Ashtabharya(s) or Ashta-bharya(s).

This contrast between the *Mahābhārata*'s treatment of Draupadi's polyandry and the polygyny of the male characters shows that Draupadi is designed to silence women's desires. For example, in the epic, Karna and Duryodhan, when their desire for her is frustrated by the Pandavas, do not hesitate to label her as a deceptive harlot: "That whore cavorts daily with those five Pandavas shamelessly touching them all" (Hiltebeitel 268). Nevertheless, the text undermines itself in this respect because in the process of Draupadi's silencing, an alternative expression of women's sexual subjectivity emerges in the *Mahābhārata*, one that deconstructs the virgin/whore dichotomy by occupying the space between these patriarchally created oppositions. Another phenomenon occurs in *The Palace of Illusion* in which Draupadi becomes more self-conscious and aware of her desires in her polyamorous relations. Hence Draupadi is not fully viewed as "fallen" in Divakaruni's novel although other fictional female figures' unconventional sexual praxis are widely condemned even when their "transgression" takes the form of rape.

DRAUPADI'S POPULARITY

Today in South India, Draupadi's transgressive desire for Krishna is celebrated by showing her holding a closed lotus bud symbolizing virginity (as opposed to the open lotus of fertility) in one hand and in her other hand, clasping a parrot that represents Kama, the god of erotic desire. Draupadi is admired and even worshipped in southern India because of her verbal challenges to male characters in the *Mahābhārata*, for her unfaltering devotion to her husbands, which is shown when, after the dice game, King Dhritarashtra, Duryodhan's father, prevents Draupadi from putting a curse on the kingdom by promising to fulfill her wishes and she requests that her husbands' honor be restored. She is also well-regarded because, like me (and unlike Doniger O'Flaherty), many devotees see Draupadi as less divine and earthlier—an ambitious woman whose primal energy and sexuality is untamable. Draupadi is often identified as Virpanchali (*vir* meaning "warrior" in Hindi and "virility" in Latin and *panchali* because she was the princess of Panchal).[25] Her virility is presented in a new dimension by Mahasweta Devi in her short story "Draupadi" from the *Breast Stories*[26] series, where we see the much-worshipped, ambitious Draupadi who aspires to seek revenge of her husband's murderer and the rapists who tortured her fighting for her tribal community. This tale is set in West Bengal where Maoist guerrillas known as Naxalites are engaged in a violent insurrection against feudal landlords and government officials who exploit poor laborers and indigenous populations in the area. Draupadi, nicknamed Dopdi, is depicted as a feminist, indigenous, subaltern, outcast Naxalite who is challenging and protesting against the hegemony, demanding basic human requirements like food, shelter, medicine, and land denied to her tribe for long.[27] The government has identified Dopdi and her husband among the "most wanted" guerrillas. The army chief, Senanayak, a Duryodhan-like figure, successfully murders Dopdi's husband and then participates in a gang rape of Dopdi in their custody. Deprived of food and water, Dopdi's spirit cannot be diminished as she tears her clothes, revealing her naked, bruised, dark body and her "thighs and pubic hair matted with dry blood" (23). Here she is a figure of resistance in the face of the authorities whose *dharma* is to subordinate Dopdi and her tribe for claiming her rights, which appeared as aggressive to the oppressor. She "pushes Senanayak with her two mangled breasts, and for the first time Senanayak is afraid to stand before an unarmed target, terribly afraid" (23). This is earthly Draupadi who uses her bruised body as a weapon, but this time she does not even invoke any Krishna or appeal to humanity but fights her own battle.

CONCLUSION

Draupadi's polyamorous self is a model for the future women of India. In modern India, women are prioritizing human emotions over social institutions. Without entering into the indentured labor contract that is marriage, whether monogamous or polygamous, many women are now choosing polyamorous life, and they identify children born out of polyamory as "children of love" rather than "illegitimate children" like Karna, who was always a symbol of shame for Kunti.

I would like to end this chapter by referring to Girindrasekhar Bose, known as the father of psychoanalysis in India and a contemporary of Sigmund Freud. The founder of the Indian Psychoanalytic Society and author of the book *Concept of Repression* (1921), Bose develops a theory of opposite aspirations that explains how any given conscious wish is accompanied by an unconscious opposite. In his article discarding Freud's theory of castration and oedipal hatred, "The Genesis and Adjustment of the Oedipus Wish," Bose claims that Indian men do not produce oedipal hatred or castration anxiety; rather, they cherish an unconscious desire to be female and bear a child. Because he is not a westerner, Bose's revision of psychoanalysis to reflect cultural interpretive sensibilities is not well known in the West, though many Indian scholars are aware of his work. Few, however, have considered that the transformation of Freud's theory of castration fear to Bose's theory of desire to be castrated implicitly overturns Freud's correlative theory of "penis envy" among women and argues that men experience "vagina envy." A powerful woman like Draupadi perhaps provokes "the desire to be castrated" and reveals "vagina envy" in men like the Pandavas: in order to repress their vagina envy, they must be aggressive and *dharmic*.

NOTES

1 Commandant.

2 As a genre, the *Mahābhārata* is an epic, but it is also considered *itihasa* (history) and *smriti* (fables or biblical parables), and its passages are commonly quoted and referenced in texts and daily conversation. Written between fourth century BCE and the fourth century CE, the *Mahābhārata* is also called the fifth *Veda*.

3 In Hindu mythology, Draupadi is included in the Pañcakanyā hymn. Pañcakanyā is a group of five iconic heroines—namely, Ahalya, Draupadi, Sita, Tara, and Mandodari of Hindu epics who are venerated as ideal women and chaste wives. Draupadi is also called a "whore" by Karna, censured for her unquenchable desire in the *Mahābhārata*, and is thought to have caused the epic's great Kurukshetra war, a conflict over succession between the two sets of cousins, the Kauravas and Pandavas.

4 Stories concerning the previous births of Gautama Buddha in both human and animal form.

5 Also known as Bhil, they are the indigenous people in India's largest state, Rajasthan, which is located on the northwestern side of the country.

6 *Devi Bhagavata Puraana* is a Sanskrit text that belongs to the Purana genre of Hindu literature. It features Devi or Shakti, the incarnation of female power and the primordial creator of the universe.

7 Sita is the epic heroine from the ancient Indian epic *Ramayana*, attributed to Valmiki. She is the consort of the Hindu god Rama (avatar of Vishnu) and is an avatar of Lakshmi, goddess of wealth and wife of Vishnu. She epitomizes spousal and feminine virtues and is admired for her dedication, self-sacrifice, courage, and purity. She was kidnapped by the monster Ravana, and after being rescued by her husband, Sita undergoes a chastity test by walking in fire. Radha, also called Radhika, Radharani, and Radhikarani, is Hindu god Krishna's lover and his favorite *gopini* (female cowherd/female admirer). However, unlike Sita, Radha was not Krishna's wife, and popular myths say she was actually Krishna's distantly related aunt and married to another man.

8 The Panchal country, or Panchala, was an ancient kingdom in northern India located in present-day Uttarakhand and western Uttar Pradesh.

9 Durga is one of the many manifestations of the maternal principle in Hindu mythology. The story of Durga in Hindu mythology can be traced back to the *Shiva Purana*, which is one

of eighteen Sanskrit texts in the Purana genre. The *Shiva Purana* tells the stories of two goddesses, Shiva and Parvat. When the evil Mahishasura, the son of the demon Rambha, unleashes a reign of terror on earth, the gods he has defeated ask the Hindu trinity—Brahma, Vishnu, and Shiva—to intervene. Soon a mass of light emerges from Lord Vishnu's mouth, and it takes the form of a woman, Durga. After the gods give Durga their weapons, she rides into battle and, killing Mahishasura, rescues the world.

10 After Zeus married his first wife, Metis, he discovered that she was pregnant. According to a prophecy, the son of Metis would pose a threat to Zeus, so Zeus swallowed the child in order to protect his kingdom. Nine months after this incident, Zeus developed a severe headache and sought help from the blacksmith Hephaestus. When Zeus's head was split open, a fully grown Athena sprang out wearing armor, carrying a shield, and uttering war cries.

11 Krishna is a major Hindu deity and said to be the incarnation of Vishnu, one of the three creators in Hinduism. Krishna plays a crucial role in the *Mahābhārata*. He was born in human form in order to save humanity. Krishna's speech during the epic battle of the Kurukshetra War constitutes a critical passage in the Hindu scriptures.

12 Kunti's illegitimate son, Karna, was born before her marriage to Pandu, the father of the five Pandava brothers. Karna's father was Surya, the sun god, but Kunti did not disclose this to her five other sons until Karna died in the Kurushetra War. Her eldest son, Yudhisthira, curses Kunti and all women, saying that henceforth they will never be able to keep any secrets.

13 The Kuru kingdom was located in northern India in the present-day states of Delhi, Haryana, Uttarakhand, and western Uttar Pradesh. Its wars are represented in epic terms in the *Mahābhārata*.

14 For example, it is said that just like the *dharma* of fire is to burn, women's *dharma*—their nature—is to be a wife. When *dharma* is universal, it is *sanatan dharma*, and when it is relative or individual, it is *svadharma* (*sva* means "self"). There are many other types of *dharmas*, and they vary according to social location. The *dharma* for a woman can be different for a man, for example, or the *dharma* for a king can be different for a priest.

15 Noakhali is a district in present-day southeastern Bangladesh. In 1946, a year before India's independence from British rule, Muslims perpetrated a series of massacres, rapes, abductions, and forced conversions targeting Hindus. Additionally, Hindu properties were looted and destroyed by arson.

16 Kamadeva is the god of human love and desire (*kama* means "desire" and *deva* means "God"). One of his incarnations is Pradyumna, who is Krishna's son. Tales about Kamadeva from both Hindu and Buddhist traditions present desire as a powerful force continually redefining the boundaries of chaos and order and gently moving beyond the ephemeral lure of passionate longings.

17 It is said that when evil appeared on earth, the god Vishnu intervened by taking a human shape and, appearing as Krishna, slew demons and conferred salvation on select individuals by exempting them from further incarnations. Krishna is considered the guide in the *Mahābhārata*'s account of the human drama.

18 The *sakha-sakhi* concept of relationship became more prominent in the Vaishnavism tradition. Vaishnavism is one of the major traditions within Hinduism in which Vishnu, incarnated as Krishna, is preeminent. Vaishnavas believe that the ultimate reality is personal. Thus they believe that God is the supreme, all-attractive person—Krishna.

19 Sisupala was the evil king of Chedi, which is located in central India. Krishna kidnapped and married Sisupala's intended wife, Rukmini, who was being forced to marry Sisupala.

20 Aurobindo Ghosh is an Indian philosopher and a nationalist of the nineteenth century. Educated in Cambridge University, he returned to India to join the country's freedom struggle. During his imprisonment by the British government, Aurobindo practiced meditation, and entering into higher realms of consciousness, he began writing his philosophical text, *The Life Divine*, a comprehensive explanation of his yoga.

21 See note 17.

22 According to the *Rig Veda*, many gods desired Surya, but her father wanted her to marry the god Soma. Ultimately it was determined that she would marry whichever suitor won a race to the sun god. Twin gods—the Asvins—finished first, and from then on, Surya is depicted riding her two husbands' chariots.

23 Bali and Surgriv are brothers who rule the kingdom of Kishkindha at different times. Tragic mishap and misunderstanding pit them against each other, which prompts Bali to steal Surgriv's wife, Ruma, and keep her for himself.

24 Abū al-Rayhān Muhammad ibn Ahmad al-Bīrūnī, known as Al-Biruni in English, is a Persian Muslim regarded as one of the greatest scholars of the medieval Islamic era. He was well versed in physics, mathematics, astronomy, and natural sciences and distinguished himself as a historian, chronologist, and linguist.

25 The Draupadi Festival occurs in Melacceri, a village in South India, and the local interpretation of her character is based on the Tamil version of the *Mahābhārata* in which Draupadi is a heroine. Festivities include *Terukuttu* (village or street dramas), hero-cult rituals, construction of large effigies representing sacrificial events from the *Mahābhārata*, and fire-walking.

26 Translated by Gayatri Chakravorty Spivak.

27 "Naxals" or Naxalites are members of a communist guerrilla group (Maoist) in Bengal. The term *Naxal* derives from the name of the village Naxalbari in West Bengal, where the movement had its origin. Naxalites are considered far-left radical communists who adopt violent strategies against feudal landlords and governmental officers who exploit poor, landless laborers and indigenous populations in the region. The guerrillas claim they are fighting exploitation and oppression in order to create a society devoid of class structures and hierarchies. Dopdi and her husband are presented as Naxalites activists. In 2006, the growing influence of Naxalites prompted Indian Prime Minister Manmohan Singh to declare them to be the most serious internal threat to India's national security.

WORKS CITED

Divakaruni, Banerjee Chitra. *The Palace of Illusions*. Doubleday, 2008.

Doniger O'Flaherty, Wendy. *The Hindus: An Alternative History*. Oxford UP, 2010.

Forbes, Geraldine. *Women in Modern India*. Cambridge UP, 2006.

Gandhi, Mahatma. *Collected Works of Mahatma Gandhi Vols. 1–100* (e-book or CD ROM version), Government of India, Publications Division, 1999.

Ghosh, Sri Aurobindo. *Essays on the Gita*. Sri Aurobindo Ashram, 2000.

———. *The Life Divine*. Sri Aurobindo Ashram Trust, 2005.

Hiltebeitel, Alf. *The Cult of Draupadi*. U of Chicago P, 1988.

Hudson, T. Emily. *Disorienting Dharma: Ethics and the Aesthetics of Suffering in the Mahābhārata*. Oxford UP, 2013.

Jha, Manish. *Matrubhoomi: A Nation without Women*. 2003.

Joshi, Varsha. *Polygamy and Purdah*. Rawat, 1995.

Kannabiran, Kalpana. "Voices of Dissent: Gender and Changing Social Values in Hinduism," *Contemporary Hinduism: Ritual, Culture and Practice*, edited by Robin Inehart, ABC Clio, 2004, pp. 273–307.

Kishwar, Madhu. *Economic and Political Weekly*, vol. 20, no. 40, 1985, pp. 1691–702.

Kumar, Radha. *The History of Doing: An Illustrated Account of Movements for Women's Rights*. Zubaan, 1993, pp. 53–73.

Meckel, D. J. "Hinduism and Psychoanalysis." *Changing the Scientific Study of Religion: Beyond Freud?; Theoretical, Empirical and Clinical Studies from Psychoanalytic Perspectives*, edited by Jacob A. van Belzen, Springer Science and Business Media, 2009, pp. 215–16.

Patel, Sujata. "Construction and Reconstruction of Woman in Gandhi." *Economic and Political Weekly*, vol. 23, no. 8, 1988, pp. 377–87.

Ranjan, Radha. "Deconstructing Gandhi: Suicidal Prescriptions for Hindus." *Indiafacts Truth Be Told*. http://indiafacts.co.in/deconstructing-gandhi-suicidal-prescriptions-hindus/.

Ray, Pratibha. *Yajnaseni: The Story of Draupadi*. Rupa, 1995.

Rich, Adrienne. "When We Dead Awaken: Writing as Re-vision." *College English*, vol. 34, no. 1, 1972, pp. 18–30.

Singh, Sarva Daman. *Polyandry in Ancient India*. Vikas, 1978.

Sutherland, Sally J. "Sita and Draupadi: Aggressive Behaviour and Female Role-Models in the Sanskrit Epics." *Journal of the American Oriental Society*, vol. 109, no. 1, 1989, pp. 63–79.

Vyasa. *The Mahābhārata*. Translated by Kisari Mohan Ganguly, Manonmani, 1893.

———. *The Mahābhārata*. Translated by Bibek Debroy, vol. 2, Penguin, 2010.

6 DAMAGED GOODS! MANAGED GODS!

Indian Cinema's Virtuous Hierarchies

AMRIT GANGAR

In this chapter, Amrit Gangar surveys the trope of fallenness in the history of Indian cinematography. From silent movies of the 1920s through the present, popular Indian cinema is replete with misogynist images of women as "damaged goods," "impure" vamps, the violated, and nonvirgins. Gangar's analysis of the films and their reception interrogates the notion of the "fallen woman" through archetypes, mythologies, fabrications, linguistics, the male gaze, and new constructions of old stereotypes of fallen women in Indian popular cinema.

PROLOGUE: RAVANA. THE BODY. SACRED. PROFANE.

Six newlywed couples and a priestess meet after a mass wedding in a temple in India during a lunar eclipse. Still in their auspicious outfits, they theorize the significance of life milestones—"beginnings, endings, and everything in between" ("Production Notes"). One of the brides in this 102-minute, single-shot film, *Rati Chakravuh* (*Spirals of Love*; 2013), directed by Ashish Avikunthak, matter-of-factly discloses that Valmiki and Tulsidas,[1] revered Hindu sages believed to have authored two of the ancient heroic epics that shape Indian cultural consciousness, the *Ramayana* and *Ramcharitmanas*, respectively, are her lovers.[2] When they reach sexual satisfaction, they regale her with stories, and she has learned that the epics, which relate the god Rama's ascent to kingship in the form of allegories that teach ethical and philosophical principles, are untrue. The young bride explains that a key episode, the antihero Ravana's kidnapping and rape of Rama's wife, Sita, who in the Indian collective imagination embodies female sexual purity, sanitizes a tale of Rama's impotence and the sexual pleasure that Sita attains with Ravan, a multi-limbed, ten-headed demon. The bride, without inhibition, explains that Sita reveled in Ravana's lovemaking: he caressed her with his twenty hands and hundred fingers and kissed her in ten places at the same time. Though at first she resisted, Sita is exhilarated when Ravana's ten tongues lick her body simultaneously. "Any woman would have liked this," the bride says, quoting Sita's justification of infidelity: "My lord Ram, you are an impotent man. You are an impotent God. Ravana is not. He is a demon, I am in love with. He is in love with me, because he fulfils me. He makes me whole. He is the one who is God to me. I am euphoric when he touches me, kisses me, feels me and makes love to me" ("Production Notes"). The six couples and the priestess commit suicide.[3]

INTRODUCTION

Rati Chakravuh is one of the latest and perhaps most startling iterations of the female persona in a hundred-year history of Indian narrative film that started with D. G. Phalke's silent work *Raja Harishchandra* (*King Harishchandra*; 1913), in which all female characters were played by male actors due to social prohibitions against women in film, despite women's long history of public performance in South Asia. Throughout the history of film in India, representations of women respond—one way or another—to their changing sociocultural status in India. Consequently, the filmic female persona parallels contemporary norms established by the law-making apparatus of the state as well as cultural values about gender and womanhood even though her specific characteristics differ from region to region, time to time, and mind to masculine, *macho* (aggressive pride about masculinity) mind. A way to conceptualize the projectory of these fluctuations is to plot them on the persistently patriarchal graph of Indian culture.

Geometry, in Sanskrit, is *Bhoomiti*, where *bhoo* means "earth" or "body" and *miti* is the act of measuring. *Bhoo* is etymologically linked to *bhoo-gol*, which means "geography" as well as "landed property." *Bhoo* also conjures the personification of Mother Earth, variously named Bhumi, Bhuma, or Bhu Devi, who figures fertility in the *Ramayana* and other Indian mythologies and is Sita's mother and her refuge (literally and metaphorically) when she finally leaves Ram according to traditional renditions of *Ramayana*.[4] When these coordinates intersect, the cinematic Indian woman, understood as a social construct, is perpetually contained by patriarchal notions that her "nature" is established by ancient precepts articulated in ancient Indian myths whose import is nothing short of scriptural. Thus women are property, goods who must/should be managed by male kin (with the state often serving as their proxy) because they are easily damaged or (de-)spoiled by their choices as well as actions that external agents wreak upon them—rape, violence, and coercion—and, according to patriarchal logic, responsible for their own violation. Variables such as caste and class status and specificities such as time period and locale can move this woman up or down the vertical axis (y axis) that in this scheme measures her morality—as pure or "fallen."

Consequently, representations of women in Indian film typically oscillate between bifurcated patriarchal stereotypes: they are either pure, maternal, nurturing, balanced, loyal, self-sacrificing, and sexually virtuous or transgressive, violent, sexually unruly, unfaithful women who put their interests above their families and, if they are mothers, abandon or harm their children. Ultimately, then, Indian cinema, from its birth through the present, is a *godown* (warehouse) of dichotomized women—goods who are managed by the "gods," whether those gods take the form of mythological male divinities, family patriarchs, state apparatus, or social norms.

VEERĀNGANĀ AND *VĀRĀNGANĀ*: VIRGIN AND THE VAMP

Cinema draws on a melodramatic framework to embed archetypal allegories or allusions, ellipses, and encryptions in the stories it tells. Such melodrama thrives on binaries of good and evil, which, in the context of patriarchal constructions of gender, are often articulated as representations of women as virgin or vamp—in Indian cinema as *veerānganā* (heroic woman) or *vārānganā* (harlot). This false binary has two striking features in Indian film: it correlates with the caste-class hierarchy, though irregularly and in different patterns, and it is almost always rooted in ancient Hindu narratives that originally were recorded in Sanskrit and are the lynchpins of Hindu-Indian cultural sensibilities.

Sita, the female protagonist in the *Ramayana*, is frequently upheld as the ideal model of feminine morality, but unlike the Western stereotype of the "good" woman based on the figure of the Virgin Mary, Sita contains and resolves opposites and contradictions within her persona rather than representing one pole of the *veerānganā*/*vārānganā* binary.[5] Her moral counterpart is Kunti, one of two major female characters in the *Mahābhārata*, who differs from Sita in that she is solidly condemned for her "fallenness" although her actions are no more vampish than Sita's. One reason for this difference is that Sita occupies a higher status than Kunti in India's sociomythological hierarchy.

Sita, the daughter of the powerful *Bhu* (Mother Earth), was adopted by a mortal king and queen. She is married to Prince Rama of Ayodhya, the *Ramayana*'s hero. Soon after the marriage, Rama's evil stepmother, Kaikeyi, machinates against the prince in order to secure the throne for her son, Bharata, forcing Rama into exile in the forests of Dandaka and Panchavati. Sita follows Rama but is kidnapped by the demonic ten-headed King Ravana, who harbors a grudge against Rama. Rama then embarks on a protracted war against Ravana and, after defeating him, returns to Ayhodhya, where he rules with Sita as his queen. However, Rama, influenced by others, begins to doubt Sita's chastity, but she proves her sexual purity by walking through fire unscathed. In a later episode, Rama's doubts about Sita return, and he banishes her to the forest where she gives birth to male twins. As adults, the twins are reunited with Rama, and Sita again proves her sexual purity by returning to Bhumi's womb—that is, to Mother Earth. Thus Sita endures the meanest form of humiliation at the hands of her own husband! Although she is a complex character in the *Ramayana* who resists being categorized as either *veerānganā* or *vārānganā*, patriarchal narratives historically have appropriated Sita, depicting her as the ideal daughter, wife, and mother. During India's independence movement, for example, Mahatma Gandhi employed Sita as a symbol of moral force. Today, popular cinema and other visual arts use her figure to promote nationalist propaganda as well as to perpetuate traditional roles for women and misogynist thinking about sexual mores.

In contrast, the *Mahābhārata*'s mythological Kunti, who marries a king but is not royal, has been transposed into Indian popular cinema as the *vārānganā*, the unwed mother who later attains respectability only through the legitimizing institutions of patriarchal marriage and motherhood. When the sage Durvasa visits Kunti's foster-father, in appreciation for the host's generous hospitality, he gifts Kunti a *mantra* that enables her to bear a divine child. She invokes it out of curiosity and inadvertently conceives a son with Surya, the sun god. Kunti names the child Karna, but because she fears the stigma of being an unwed mother, she abandons him. Commoners find Karna and raise him as their own. Kunti later marries King Pandu of Hastinapur but is ashamed to tell him about Karna. After Pandu inadvertently murders the sage Kindama, the dying man curses Pandu to death if he has sexual intercourse with Kunti, which leaves Pandu heirless. Kunti then uses the *mantra* that Durvasa gave her to bear three sons by different gods. These sons are known as the Pandavas, and later they battle their cousins, the Kauravas, for the throne in the Kurukshetra War. During the war's final battle, one of the Pandavas kills Karna without realizing that Karna is his brother. Heartbroken, Kunti reveals the truth, including the fact that each Pandava's father is a different god. The eldest Pandava, Yudhishthira, who later becomes king, is enraged and retaliates by cursing women with the inability to keep secrets. Kunti later dies in a forest fire.

Although in motive and deed, both Sita and Kunti are equally "pure" sexually, in the nineteenth century, Sita became an icon of the Indian nationalist movement if not Indianness itself, but Kunti does not achieve the same prominence. To explain their different treatment in the national imagination, we must turn to the most salient difference between Sita and Kunti, which is class status. The *Mahābhārata* employs a complex caste-class hierarchy that consists of four major categories: Brahmins, priests, are at the top, followed in descending order by Shatriyas, warriors; then Vaishyas, the business class; and finally Shudras, the so-called Untouchables. Each of these categories has multiple subdivisions. The *Mahābhārata* is primarily about the Kshatriyas, the ruling class that consists of kings and warriors and is a subgroup of the Shatriyas. Kshatriyas, in turn, are also hierarchically organized, with powerful kings whose empires are vast and rich at the highest level and less wealthy kings presiding over smaller territories, again in descending order. In the *Mahābhārata* (though not all the many Hindu texts that feature her), Kunti is the daughter of Shurasena, a minor king, essentially a minister whose primary responsibility likely would have been to serve as administer of a small village. Furthermore, Kunti was raised by a distant relative who had no position in government. While Kunti's marriage to Pandu, a powerful monarch to whom many secondary kings and ministers answered, elevated her class status, she could never equal Sita, who derives from a far more important family line. Indeed, Sita's father, Janaka, was, as the king of Mithila (modern-day Nepal), very powerful. He was also seen as a philosopher of Vedic culture and was said to have accrued divine power through continuous, prolonged meditation and worship. At every juncture in her long, arduous life, Sita's actions, reactions, and instincts are deemed exemplary in Indian popular cinema, no matter the form she takes.

In this case and as a pattern in Indian film, class status largely determines which "fallen woman" is reincorporated into the respectable social mainstream as well as whether Indian cinema represents her as *veerānganā* or *vārānganā*. This phenomenon reveals the play of Hindu mythology in the Indian cinematic tradition, how it provides the *Bhoomiti* (a multiplexed geometry composed of intersections of gender, class, and caste) that attracts the mass audience and shapes its views. The different regard shown to Sita and Kunti in Indian film, the former elevated and the latter fallen, stems from their representations in mythology, its complex weaving of legends and imaginations that has created characters who have negotiated centuries of sighs of the poor and the oppressed! Still today, as Kunti's filmic characterizations show, the disenfranchised are vulnerable to manipulations by the powerful and the dominant.

INFERTILITY AND POLYGYNY

A cultural schema linked to Kunti that commonly appears in Indian film is the wife who is not able to conceive or is perceived as such when her "failure" is actually the result of her husband's unrecognized or unknown infertility. This woman is treated as an outcast, a person worthy of hate, and in other words, a fallen woman. Often she is controlled or castigated by her husband's family, which usually is presided over by the patriarch, the husband's father.[6] *Gharwali Baharwali* (*Beloved Outside Home*; 1998), directed by David Dhavan, is an example. The film is a remake of the Tamil film *Thaikulame* (1995), which was produced in Telugu as *Intlo Illalu Vantintio Priyuralu* (1996) and in Kannada as *Nannu Nanna Hendithiru* (1999). The Hindi film starred Anil Kapoor, Raveena Tandon, and Rambha in lead roles while the Tamil version featured Pandiarajan. Daggubati Venkatesh starred in the Telugu, and Veeraswamy Ravichandran was featured in the Kannada-language remake. As the film opens, a young couple—Arun and his wife, Kaajal—undergo tests that show Arun is infertile, but the couple are misled into believing that their inability to conceive is Kaajal's fault. The story becomes convoluted when Arun travels to Nepal and is tricked into marrying Manisha, a young, single woman who, unbeknownst to Arun, is pregnant (this implausible plot twist is explained by Arun's lack of familiarity with the local language and customs). When Manisha gives birth to a son, Arun believes it is his. Later, Manisha and the boy accompany Arun to

India where she, posing as a housekeeper, is ensconced in Arun's and Kaajal's home. Kaajal discovers the truth, but she, Arun, and Manisha end up living in blissful polygyny. The patriarchal nature of this happily-ever-after ending is underscored by the joy that Arun's father, who, at the beginning of the film urged Arun to divorce Kaajal, expresses at finally attaining a grandson—or so he thinks, because, ironically, the child has no biological relationship to either Arun or his father.

Not only does *Gharwali Baharwali* offer a twentieth-century update of the ancient practice of scapegoating women for their husband's infertility, but it endorses a form of marriage in which one member, inevitably a woman, has little or no agency in determining her role in the relationship. Significantly, such representations of sexuality reveal a double standard in Indian cinema's moral code. While fallen women are castigated in movie storylines, works featuring patriarchal forms of polygyny get a pass from the Central Board of Film Certification (CBFC) without whose certification films may not be screened publicly ("About CBFC"). For example, two films, *Saajan Chale Sasural* (*My Lover Goes Back to His Family*; 1994) and *Juddai* (*Separation*; 1997) that celebrate bigamy presented no problems for the CBFC, which approved them readily. As Shoma A. Chatterji comments, "This reversal of *Indecent Proposal*[7] is an indecent assault on our intelligence and morality. Worse, these are the most regressive films produced by a film industry which uses its heroines as sex objects to titillate and then makes them mouth *Sati Savitri* sentiments [idealized, unrealistic praise] about husbands who are to be worshipped."[8]

RAPE

Rape entered Indian cinema early during the silent film era, as exemplified by B. P. Mishra's 1925 *Devi Ahilyabai* produced by Royal Art. It retells the fall of Ahalya, one of the five *Panchkanya*—iconic virgins featured in the *Ramayana* and the *Mahābhārata* along with Draupadi, Tara, Sita, and Mandodari.[9] The *Panchkanya* are venerated as ideal women and chaste wives. Ahalya, who is played by an actress called Dwarki, heads the *Panchkanya* because of her nobility, her extraordinary beauty, and the fact that she is chronologically the first *kanya* (literally "first daughter" but used here to mean "first girl"). The name Ahalya has a double meaning: one who is flawless; it also means unploughed—that is, virginal. Her origin myth states that Brahma, the god who created the universe, having fashioned Ahalya as a flawless beauty, handed her over to Gautama, one of Hindu's seven greatest sages, in order to keep her safe until she reached puberty.[10] When Gautama returns her with her undespoiled, the Creator is so pleased that the sage restrained himself from violating Ahalya that he gives her to Gautama permanently and the two marry. But the king of the gods, Indra (comparable to the Roman king of the gods, Jove/Jupiter), who assumed different shapes to seduce and impregnate women, was infatuated with Ahalya's beauty and, when the sage is away, disguises himself as Gautama. Depending on the version consulted, Indra either requests or orders

Ahalya to have sexual intercourse with him. In the *Ramayana*, she sees through the deception but still complies out of curiosity. In later iterations of the story, Ahalya is said to be raped or to fall prey to Indra's trickery. Whether Indra is a lover or rapist, in all the narratives, Gautama curses the couple. Although there are many different explanations of the nature of this curse, all stipulate that Ahalya is severely punished. Early texts describe how Ahalya must atone by undergoing severe penance while remaining invisible to the world and how she is purified by offering hospitality to Rama, the epic hero. In the most popular retelling that develops over time, Ahalya is transformed into stone and regains her human form after she is brushed by Rama's foot. Some versions also mention that she was turned into a dry stream and that she would be relieved of her guilt when the stream eventually starts flowing again and merges with the Gautami (Godavari) River.[11] Indra was cursed with castration or covered by a thousand vulvae that turn into a thousand eyes.[12]

Ultimately these minor variations regarding the nature of Ahalya's punishment have little bearing on how she is represented in Indian film or how we can/should interpret these representations. What is significant is that popular Indian film as a whole will not explore the psychological complexities of the myth, its stigmatization of female desire, and its perpetuation of the idea that women who transgress social norms to satisfy their sexual desire should be stricken with guilt and punished harshly.[13]

This psychological legacy of the Ahalya myth is the reason that it haunts the Indian social imaginary and accounts for the emergence of the myth's many versions as well as a multiplicity of current interpretations of it.[14] Another indication of Ahalya's importance in Indian cultures is the attention that feminist scholars have lent the myth as they reexamine and revise patriarchal narratives in order to offset the negative consequences of these tales' misogyny. For example, Pradip Bhattacharya writes in "Five Holy Virgins, Five Sacred Myths: A Quest for Meaning," that Ahalya was true to her independent nature, fulfilling her womanhood in a manner that she found appropriate, although she is never able to assert herself. Taking another tack, the critic Shoma A. Chatterji maintains that in the Ahalya myth there is both evidence of an earlier gynocentric stage in human history and of its suppression by androcentric patriarchalism. She goes on to explain that this shift from gyno- to androcentrism accounts for the sexual double standard, which continues today, that stipulates women are naturally monogamous while men are natural philanderers and the coexisting yet inconsistent belief that untethered women are promiscuous.[15]

A second context in which rape plunges women into moral fallenness in Indian film is when it is perpetrated at the whim of the gods. The Hindu scriptures—the *Vedas*, the *Ramayana*, the *Mahābhārata* in which the Upanishads are found, the *Bhagavad Gitā*, and other sometimes disputed texts—are full of mythical incidents in which women are depicted as sexual bait who distract both human ascetics, holy men, and divine entities from penance and sacred meditation. Temptresses or not, women are frequently victims of the gods' rapaciousness and are rendered fallen—become damaged goods—as a result. An example of one such female figure is Rambha, who appears in the *Ramayana*, the *Bhagavad Puranas*, the *Vedas*, and the *Mahābhārata*. Rambha is the queen of the Apsarasees, who are exceptionally beautiful, young, ethereal female divinities. She is often tasked by Indra, a higher-order god in the Hindu divine hierarchy who rules the heavenly paradise of Svargaloka, where the righteous await their next incarnation, to tempt devout men from their meditations in order to test their spiritual purity. In the *Ramayana*, Rambha is raped by her villainous father-in-law, Ravan. According to some versions of this story, Nalakuvara, Rambha's husband and Ravan's nephew, curses Ravan so that if he touches any woman without permission, his ten heads will explode.

There are at least ten Indian feature films about Rambha, as she offers a ready-made rape sequence straight from epic mythology. They include *Yathabhavishya* (*Rambha's Love*), a Tamil movie made in 1992 and directed by B. N. Rao; *Maya Rambha* (*Illusionary Rambha*), a Telugu movie dating to 1950 that was directed by T. P. Sundaram; and *Bhooloka Rambha* (*Forgetful Rambha*), another Teluga film that was directed by D. Yoganand in 1958. Episodes such as Rambha's rape provide fleshy meat to Indian film and titillate male viewers, who, forming a big chunk of the audience, bring a huge reservoir of mythical collective consciousness to the cinematic meaning-making process. Without doubt, this category of film perpetuates the patriarchal idea that raped women are to blame for men's violation of them.

MENAKA-VISWAMITRA MYTH

Another narrative often exploited to eroticize Indian cinema's warehouse of fallen women is the Menaka-Viswamitra myth. In this tale, Indra commands Menaka, a beautiful, heavenly nymph, to seduce Viswamitra, a revered sage who has undertaken a multiyear meditation to atone for his sins, as some versions of the tale suggest, or to enhance his piety (this mission parallels Rambha's assignment to lure pious mystics from their spiritual devotions). Menaka succeeds in interrupting Viswamitra's meditation, but the two fall in love. Only after many years does Viswamitra realize that Indra tricked him and the part that Menaka played in the deception. Enraged, Viswamitra opts to banish Menaka forever not only because he loves her but also because he realizes that her love for him is genuine despite her initial intention of diverting him from his devotions.

This myth was reconstituted in Indian cinema in the hugely popular 1941 film entitled *Chitralekha*, directed by Kidar Sharma and based on the 1934 Hindu novel of the same name by Bhagwatie Charan Verma. It starred Mehtab, Nandrekar, and A. S. Gyani. The plot centers on a sexual triangle involving King Chandragupta (340–298 BCE), regent of the large, powerful Iron Age Maurya Empire; his courtier, Maurya Aryaputra Samant Bijgupta; and Chitralekha, the king's beloved courtesan.[16] Bijgupta refuses to marry and fulfill his duty to produce an heir because he is so deeply in love with Chitralekha, which prompts his father to enlist a celibate yogi, Kumargiri, to intervene. When Bijgupta ignores Kumargiri's advice to avoid Chitraklekha, Kumargiri reprimands the courtesan. Rather surprisingly, she joins his *ashram* (retreat) and lives with the yogi's celibate male disciples. Kidar Sharma directed a remake of the movie in 1964 starring Ashok Kuma, Meena Kumari, and Pradeep Kuma, which was far less popular, but is notable for a scene in which Chitraklekha tells Kumargiri that abandoning the body is an insult to the Creator:

> What is sin and what is virtue
> They are customs with the seal of religion
> How will you find a higher ideal
> In beliefs that change with time?
> Sensual pleasure is a form of test too
> You cannot know this by giving it up
> It's an insult to the creator
> If you reject forms of creation.
> I say the world is our reality
> You say it's a false dream
> I will live my life before I go from here
> you may waste yours before you go.
> If you run away from the world
> How will you ever find the higher one?
> If you cannot accept this world's reality
> You will regret in the next one too.
>
> —"Song from Chitralekha: A Translation"

A similar sentiment is expressed in *Amrapali* (1966), which takes its name from the female protagonist whose character is based on the life of a courtesan who lived in Vaishali (present-day Bihar), the capital of the Licchavi Republic located in the Magadha Empire and ruled by King Ajatashatru. Ajatashatru falls in love with Amrapali and razes Vaishali in his desire to possess her. But Amrapali has a mysterious relationship with Gautama Buddha and becomes his disciple rather than acceding to Ajatashtru. Ultimately, she earns the designation of Arahant, a holy person who has attained a high degree of, but not perfect, enlightenment in the Buddhist tradition. Directed by Lekh Tandon and starring Vyajanthimala and Sunil Dutt, the film is remarkable for a sequence in which Amrapali declares that her place is where affectionate, caring, loving sexuality is a form of worship.

In these examples and many other films, the Menaka-Viswamitra myth perpetuates the stereotype of the fallen woman as a temptress, specifically a woman who lures even the holiest, wisest men away from their devotions. *Amrapali*, though it employs the stock figure of the temptress, deviates from it somewhat by offering an ending in which the temptress-turned-ascetic critiques (but does not wholly deconstruct) the opposition between the holy, cerebral male and the polluting, female body on which the stereotype is built. This ending is significant in two respects. It suggests that sexual pleasure and spirituality are not dichotomous. Additionally, it proposes that this pleasurable amalgamation of body and "spirit" is available to women as well as men, a radical notion. Finally, the film implies that these two possibilities are not facilitated by Hinduism in that Amrapali has turned to Buddhism in order to discover them.

FALLEN WOMAN WITH A HEART OF GOLD

Some of the earliest representations of the "fallen woman" in Indian cinema came out of Kolkata-based New Theatres, which, established in 1931, was one of the leading film production companies and studios in India. In 1935–36, adapting the 1917 Bengali novella *Devdas*, which was written by Saratchandra Chattopadhyay, New Theatres produced two films of the same name, one in Bengali (1935) and the other in Hindi (1936). Both were directed by P. C. Barua. Devdas, the male protagonist, an upper-caste-class Brahmin, and Paro (also called Parul), a young woman from a middle-class family, are childhood friends who fall in love when Devdas returns home from university.[17] Paro, believing that Devdas will marry her, reverses traditional gender roles and woos him. But Devdas's mother rejects a marriage proposal from Paro's family, who subsequently arrange for Paro to be married to a wealthy but elderly widower. Blaming Paro for this turn of events, Devdas departs for Kolkata where he begins drinking heavily and takes up with a sex worker named Chandramukhi. Chandramukhi falls so deeply in love with Devdas that she not only takes care of him but tries to persuade him not to condemn Paro, ostensibly her rival for Devdas's affection. However, Chandramukhi's defense of Paro only causes Devdas to turn his anger on Chandramukhi. Nonplussed, Chandramukhi dedicates herself to Devdas. Despite Chandramukhi's self-sacrificing (some would say codependent) love, the upper-caste-class Devdas cannot bring himself to violate social norms and marry her even though she makes him the center of her life: not only are Devdas and Chandramukhi separated by caste and class, but she is a sex worker, a member of the lowest social and moral category in India. Ultimately, Chandramukhi remains loyal to Devdas regardless of his abuse, thus embodying the figure of the fallen woman with a golden heart.

Indian popular cinema has a large reservoir of such stereotyped "golden-hearted" characters who are often drawn from ancient theatrical traditions, such as Sudraka's Sanskrit play *Mrcchakatika* (*The Little Clay Cart*). This ten-act play, one of the earliest texts in world literature that features the trope of the "moral courtesan," was written between the second and fifth centuries CE and remains one of the most widely celebrated and oft-performed Sanskrit plays in the West. In *Mrcchakatika*, Chārudatta, a married Brahmin with a young son whose fortune has dwindled due to his excessive charity, falls in love with a wealthy courtesan, Vasantasena. She reciprocates his love, but soon the play's villain, Samsthānaka, who is backed by an evil king, becomes violently obsessed with her. The plot is complicated by a series of ill-fated misjudgments and misidentifications that cause

Chārudatta to be convicted for a crime he did not commit. Vasantasena goes missing, and it appears that Chārudatta murders Vasantasena, but in reality she is sequestered under the care of a Buddhist monk. She reappears on the brink of Chārudatta's execution, not only saving him, but also his wife, who is set to die on his funeral pyre. Ultimately, Chārudatta forgives and rehabilitates Samsthānaka, and the evil king is toppled by a good prince.

This stock figure—the sex worker who falls in love with an impoverished yet upper-caste-class lover, patron, or client who catapults her into a tragic crisis—pervades Indian literature and drama and, as the film *Devdas* illustrates, migrated to Indian cinema at its inception. Indeed, it has acquired archetypal contours that reveal the complexities embedded in cultural ideas about sexual decency and moral character. If anything, filmic representations of "golden hearts" have extended the reach of this and related tropes due to cinema's mass circulation patterns. Consequently, *Devdas* exerted phenomenal influence on the pan-Indian psyche as well as the film industry, and it has been remade in many South Asian languages, with the most recent iteration directed by Chashi Nazrul Islam in 2013. In fact, Devdas's persona has been woven into South Asia's popular cultures, and viewers to this day remain attracted to the figure of the golden-hearted fallen woman who endears the nation's heart. "The story has since become one of the touchstones of popular Indian cinema," explains film scholar Corey K. Creekmur ("The Devdas Phenomenon"). As such, the film perpetuates the ancient equation of female fallenness with low caste-class status, rendering it appealing by depicting the woman as infinitely munificent despite her mistreatment by her dissolute, upper-caste-class lover.

DAMAGED GOODS

Another prominent trope for fallen women is "damaged goods," and it was introduced to Indian audiences by New Theatres's 1938 bilingual (Bengali/Hindi) film *Abhigyan/Abhagin*, probably the first Indian film to apply the phrase to sexually transgressive women. Prior to its debut in India, this moniker was associated with sexually transmitted disease in two silent films produced in the West, both entitled *Damaged Goods*, which were based on Eugene Brieux's 1901 *Les Avaries*, a play about a young couple who contract syphilis. The US version was a short film directed by Tom Ricketts that appeared in 1914 starring Richard Bennett. Triggering a sex hygiene-venereal disease film craze, it was followed by the British adaptation in 1919, which was directed by Alexander Butler. Later in 1937, a sound film directed by Phil Goldstone that was also entitled *Damaged Goods* focused on premarital sex without mentioning venereal disease.[18] *Abhigyan/Abhagin* adds its own socially and morally loaded prescriptions binding upper-caste-class women to chastity to the Western films' themes.

Abhigyan/Abhagin is based on a story by Bengali novelist Upendranath Ganguly (b. 1881–1960), a follower of the well-known and more popular novelist Saratchandra Chattopadhyay (b. 1876–1938). Directed by Prafulla Roy, the construct of *abhagin* (the unfortunate, wretched one, a "fallen" woman) that lends the film its title is entrenched in the most popular Indian film genre—mainstream Bollywood cinema featuring *masala* songs, dances, and magical realism. As with *Devdas*, mass distribution patterns played an important role in perpetuating the moral codes embedded in *Abhigyan/Abhagin*. However, in this case, the effect was to extend a morality previously specific to upper-caste-class women to the middle classes.

Bimal Roy, who had already shot *Devdas* in 1935, filmed both the Bengali- and Hindi-language versions of *Abhigyan/Abhagin*, and Rai Chand Boral composed the music. Phani Majumdar wrote the script while Ajoy Bhattacharya penned lyrics for the Bengali version and Munshi Arzoo for the Hindi counterpart. The story opens with a tenant attacking the villainous landlord Jawaharlal Choudhury (Manoranjan Bhattacharya plays the role in the Bengali version and Nemo Mirza Muhammad Begg in the Hindi), injuring Choudhury's adult son, Pyarelal (Sailen Choudhury/Vijay Kumar), and abducting his daughter-in-law Sandhya (Molina Devi plays the role in both films). Sandhya escapes unharmed, seeking harbor with her relative, the engineer Prakash (Bhanu Bannerjee/Bikram Kapoor), but her father-in-law refuses to take her back, believing her to be "damaged goods." Sandhya then finds shelter with Promode, one of her husband's friends, and the two have an affair. After trials, tribulations, and eye-moistening melodrama, Sandhya's husband, Pyarelal, eventually accepts her back although she is torn between affection for her savior, Promode (Jiban Ganguly/Prithviraj Kapoor) and her marital obligations.[19] Ultimately, Sandhya reaffirms her commitment to her husband and chooses him over Promode. Consequently, the film's closing endorses patriarchal values, particularly the notion that women's moral honor requires them to subordinate personal happiness and individual fulfillment to their wifely responsibilities—they must privilege the good of the family over their own.

BRIDES FOR SALE; BRIDES IN DONATION

No examination of films that belong to the "fallen woman," "damaged goods" discourse can be complete without looking at Indian cinema's treatment of *kanyavikraya* (bride selling) and a related practice, *kanyadaan* (gifting a bride to the husband's family).[20] *Kanyadaan* is authorized by its appearance in Hindi scriptures and continues to be an important ritual in marriage ceremonies today. It is considered a holy, pious act through which the bride's father, with great emotion (he often cries), transfers ownership of his daughter to the groom. Failing to do so is akin to committing a sin, and a woman who has not been properly gifted—presented to the groom by her father or another senior male family member—is "fallen." Feminists argue that *kanyadaan* is a disguised form of *kanyavikraya*. Certainly, both practices figure women as damageable goods—commodities that can be ruined, especially sexually, if not properly handled—and men as managing "gods" who own and regulate them. Today's films typically represent *kanyadaan* as something to be cherished.

Kanyavikraya is often practiced in the context of child marriage, making it doubly oppressive, and it was common when the first silent films were made (1912–34), thus ensuring its presence in that era's productions. For instance, in 1923, Dadasaheb Phalke's Nasik-based Hindustan Cinema Film Company produced a silent film, *Kanyavikraya*, also known as *Sharada*, directed by V. S. Nirantar. The following year, Dwarkadas Sampat's Kohinoor Film Company issued *Kanya Vikraya* (1924), directed by Homi Master. And exactly a decade after that, yet another, more expressive version of *Kanya* was released by the Punjab-based Pioneer Film Company under the titles *Vikraya*, *Lobhi Pita*, and *Lobhi Baap* (*Greedy Father*; 1934), directed by Mohammed Hussain. In 1968, *Kanyadaan* (*Daughter's Marriage*) was a box-office success. Directed by Mohan Segal and produced by Rajendra Bhatia for Kiron Productions, the film starred Asha Parekh, Shashi Kappor, Om Prakash, Achala Sachdeve, Dilip Raj, and Sayeeda Khan. The protagonists, Rekha and Amar, are married as children but are too young to remember the ceremony by the time they are young adults, and in fact, the families who arranged the marriage have lost touch with each other. A second man coincidentally named Amar Kuma falls in love with Rekha. Rekha's mother reveals that the young woman is already married and forbids the relationship with "second" Amar. He then persuades Rekha that he is the original child groom. The deceit is made more striking by the fact that the Amar, who is in love with Rekha, knows that the child-groom Amar has married a woman named Lata who is unaware of his previous marriage. Convinced that her beloved Amar is actually her childhood groom, an innocent Rekha moves into his family home but does not marry him. Soon she learns the truth and intends to commit suicide, but the original Amar and his wife, Lata, take her into their home. When Rekha realizes they are happy and in love, she forgives the duplicitous second Amar and returns to his family home. In yet another twist, Lata learns of the child marriage for the first time and is outraged. This prompts Rekha to try suicide again, but happily, her mother arrives on the scene and pronounces the child marriage invalid because neither bride nor groom had consented to it. All characters are reconciled when Rekha's mother endorses the idea that *kanyadaan* and marriage are legitimate and binding only when the bride and groom are consenting adults. Interestingly, a more recent film springing from the *kanyadaan* genre is *Baabul* (*Father*), which, released in 2006, invokes the traditional notion of *kanyadaan* to advocate for widow remarriage, which may be problematic depending on caste and class status though certainly more so in the past than today (Johnson and Shyamala).

Directed by Ravi Chopra and dubbed in Telugu as *Premabhishekam*, it stars Amitabh Bachchan, Rani Mukerji, Salman Khan, John Abraham, and Hema Malini. In *Baabul*, Avinash (Avi) and Malvika (Millie) fall in love and marry to the dismay of Millie's childhood friend, Rajat, who is deeply in love with her. Avi and Millie are happy and have a child, Ansh. However, while driving to Ansh's birthday party, Avi is in an accident and dies. Seeing Millie's grief, her father-in-law, Balraj, seeks out Rajat and asks him to marry Millie. While some family members, believing that widow remarriage is a sin, object strongly—namely, Avi's mother and uncle—Balraj persists and the marriage takes place. The couple are happy, and in the end, Avi's spirit visits them, blessing Balraj in thanksgiving for caring for Millie. While the sentiment that a deceased husband loves his wife to the degree that he wants her to be happy above all else is appealing, this endorsement of widow remarriage hangs on the convention of *kanyadaan*, which is, of course, deeply rooted in a patriarchal desire to control women—paradoxically, the male "gods" persist in managing women even when subverting the norms that contain them.

SATI

Sati, the traditional, Hindu practice of widow suicide by choice or force, often through immolation on her late husband's funeral pyre, is equally prominent in Indian film. Significantly, *Sati* is also the name of the goddess who was the deity Shiva's first wife. Shiva, entitled "The Auspicious" and who is transcendent, benevolent, limitless, immutable, and formless, is one of the three most important deities in Hinduism and Sati, Sathi, or Suttee (the feminine of *sat*, or "truth") is the goddess of marital fidelity who embodies feminine goodness and virtue. She voluntarily burned herself on Shiva's funeral pyre to preserve his honor.[21]

Sati is a measure of female "goodness" and "fallenness," and the Hindu patriarchy sanctioned it as a means of regulating women's behavior. From the 2013 *Rati Chakravyuh* (*Spirals of Love*) to *Raja Harishchandra* (*King Harishchandra*) of 1913, there are no fewer than 110 "*sati* films."[22] The *sati* phenomenon was more pronounced in films made in the region of feudal Kathiawar, which was ruled by the Rajput Dynasty from 875 to 1473 (present-day Gujarat), an important film center during the silent and early "talkie" movie eras. Many cultural norms in the area were influenced by the Rajputs' militarism, particularly the extreme measures they took to create a large mass of male warriors, including *sati*.[23] Consequently, *sati* films targeting rural audiences were among the first talkies. In total, over thirty Gujarati films prefixed the word "*sati*" to their titles, and most of them source from Kathiawad folklore.

One legacy of these *sati* films is a preponderance of violence against women in Indian cinema. For example, in a study of 1970s-era films entitled "Bharatiya Chitrapatoma Narinu Pratibimba," Elaben Bhatt, a Ghandhian feminist and founder of the Self-Employed Women's Association (SEWA), and others examine forty-six female characters' roles in twenty-six Gujarati films, and they could not find a single one featuring a woman in professional employment. In thirty-nine roles, women were not depicted as being intelligent even as housewives or mothers—on the contrary, they were helpless, completely dependent on men, and insecure. Additionally, the study found innumerable instances of atrocities toward women.[24] These narratives are a breeding ground for the idea that women's "fallenness" warrants violence against them.

One example is *Sati Savitri* (1932), directed by Chandulal Shah and starring M. Bhagwandas, Ghori, and Keki Adajania. This film is based on the *Mahābhārata*'s story of the pious wife Savitri who rescues her husband, Satyvan, after he is taken away by the King of Death, Yamraj. Yamraj was forced to change his decision by giving back Satyvan's life after he witnesses Savitri's love, demonstrated by her willingness to commit *sati*. Another movie with this theme is *Akhand Saubhagyavati* (*May You Never Become a Widow*; 1963), which is about a virtuous wife, Usha, who falls in love with Arun. But the villain, Pankaj, who has an eye on Usha, spreads rumors about her infidelity and causes Arun to disappear on their wedding night. The excessively dramatic scenes that follow feature other characters, including the sexy vamp, Maya, and sequences in which Usha's house is burned down before she is proven innocent and forgives her now-repentant husband.

The *sati* tradition continues in so-called modern, postindependent India, and it is still present in relatively recent films, such as Anand Patwardhan's *Father, Son and Holy War* (1995), a two-part documentary that examines the intersection of Hindu nationalism, violence against women, and constructions of masculinity in urban India. Part I, which is entitled *Trial by Fire* (referring to Sita's trial by fire in the *Ramayana*), includes the case of Roop Kanwar's immolation in Rajasthan in 1987. In this incident, Roop Kanwar, an eighteen-year-old Rajput woman was burnt alive, whether by force or willingly is unclear, on the funeral pyre of her husband, Maal Singh Shkekhawat. At the time of her death, she had been married for eight months to Shekhawat, who had died a day earlier when he was barely twenty-four. They had no children. Several thousand people attended the *sati* event. After her death, Roop Kanwar was hailed as *Sati Mata* (a *Sati* Mother), almost a goddess.

DIRECT DIALOGUE WITH THE GODS

While Indian cinema's appropriation of ancient patriarchal myths that thematize gender and prescribe traditional roles for women (and men) usually flatten any complexities or nuances embedded in the original narratives, one exception occurs when "Direct Dialogue with Gods" (DDwG) is a key element in the film and it showcases female fallenness.[25] DDwG is a device that is pervasive in Indian cinema, particularly in Bollywood crime films, and villains often use it cleverly to justify their evil actions.[26] Essentially, the male antihero wreaks chaos—he murders, rapes, rampages, plunders, and deceives—throughout the work. The police or other representatives of "good" are always too late to stop him, and by the time they intervene, the antihero has violated a female character, rendering her "fallen," at least according to conventional social, familial, and legal mores. Despite the police's inability to prevent the woman's "despoilment," they usually manage to catch the villain, and he is punished. Notably, "good" always wins in the end but not before audiences have been privy to feature-length displays of violence and pandemonium.

Divya Shakti (*Divine Power*; 1993), for instance, shows the psychotic and brutal Tau (Amrish Puri) confessing his misdeeds to a statue of Lord Krishna that Tau keeps in a shrine in his home. Tau admits that he has raped and killed a girl, Kanya, and the scene is remarkable for the deeply twisted logic that he uses to imbue himself with the wisdom of God and effectively absolve himself on his own behalf. In a dramatically constructed episode, Tau sobs loudly, telling God, "I have tortured her a lot, God,

I am the only one responsible for her death. I know, killing one girl is equal to killing one hundred mothers. God, my life must end now. Fini . . . sh!" (my translation).

Thus apparently guilt- and remorse-ridden, Tau paces restlessly within his home shrine, takes out a revolver, loads it, and aiming the revolver at his temple, pulls the trigger, but nothing happens because, unbeknownst to Tau, the bullet is fake. Laughing crookedly and staring at God Krishna's icon, Tau exclaims, "Now I understand why you don't want to kill me. I am not a sinner at all. Death and life are in your hands. You are the reason for whatever is happening, and you are the reason for whatever is going to happen, so how could I be the sinner? *Jai ho, dinbandhu dinanath, jai ho* [Let victory prevail, friend and lord, let victory prevail]" (my translation).[27]

Such God-to-villain dialogue (DDwG) in Indian popular film is crucial and significant, for it deconstructs the oversimplifying, patriarchal binaries that dominate so many representations of women—sacred/profane, good/evil, and *veerānganā/vārānganā*. It complicates Indian cinema's representations of morality and the moral, including prescriptions governing gender that categorize female characters as virtuous or fallen.

REVERSE GEOMETRY

In recent years, as traditional constructions of gender are increasingly challenged in public discourse in India and globally, additional exceptions to Indian cinema's typically flat, dichotomizing representations of women have emerged on the screen. For example, *B.A. Pass* (*Bachelor's Degree*; 2012), based on the book *The Railway Aunty* by Mohan Sikka, examines the gigolo culture in Delhi and looks at the underbelly of the men's sex trade. When teenaged Mukesh's parents die in an accident in this Ajay Bahl-directed film, he is sent to live in Delhi's Paharganj neighborhood where he can complete his bachelor's degree. Friendless and made to feel like a freeloader in a hostile household, he finds sanctuary in the quiet confines of a Christian cemetery where he spends his days reading about new chess moves. The cemetery's caretaker, Johnny, befriends him, and the duo become regular chess partners. One day, when he visits his aunt Sarika's house to pick up some apples, she seduces him. She subsequently pimps him out, and his life takes a downward spiral that can end only one way—in tragedy.[28] Toward the end, Mukesh barges into Sarika's home seeking money that she owes him. Her husband arrives to find the doors locked from inside. He suspects adultery and threatens to expose Sarika in public. In order to persuade her husband that she is not having an affair with Mukesh, Sarika asks the teen to slash her lightly—to wound her slightly as proof that she was attacked—but in a state of shock, Mukesh repeatedly stabs Sarika forcefully until she dies. Facing arrest, Mukesh commits suicide. This startling gender reversal—the female authority figure pimps a vulnerable young man—certainly complicates the fallen woman motif in Indian cinema, not only subverting traditional gender roles of male and female characters, but also giving them some texture and dimensionality. Nevertheless, the basic architecture that historically has shaped depictions of women and gender in Indian film is preserved in *B.A. Pass*, for Sarika, like so many celluloid women before her, fears exposure and feels a deep sense of shame for being adulterous, a "fallen" woman. And of course, in traditional style, she is punished with death.

MAHATMA GANDHI AND CINEMA ITSELF AS A "FALLEN WOMAN"

If cinema as oeuvre were feminine, she would stand as a "fallen woman" herself in the eye of the father of the nation, Mahatma Gandhi, who was never favorably disposed toward her. This is significant in the metatext of this chapter because when present-day India was established as a state, the newly independent nation's film policy was affected by Gandhi's worldview and morality despite his dislike for the medium and his concomitant "hands off" posture toward cinema.

Gandhi compared cinema with social evils such as gambling and horse racing. When the Indian Cinematograph Committee (the Rangachariar Committee)—which the British colonial government convened and in 1927–28 charged with investigating "the adequacy of censorship and the supposedly immoral effect of cinematograph films"—consulted major public figures as part of this project, Gandhi's response evidences his dislike for cinema. Stating that he had never seen a film and calling it a "sinful technology," he wrote, "The evil it has done and is doing is patent. The good it has done if at all, remains to be proved" (46).

Later in 1938 (the year of *Abhagin*'s release) on the occasion of the Indian film industry's anniversary, a Mumbai trade paper asked Gandhi for a congratulatory message. Tejaswini Ganti notes that Gandhi's secretary responded, "As a rule Gandhiji gives messages only on rare occasions–and those only for causes whose virtue is ever undoubtable. As for the cinema industry he has the least interest in it and one may not expect a word of appreciation from him" (44). The next year, in celebration of Gandhi's seventy-first birthday in October 1939, journalist-turned-filmmaker Khwaja Ahmed Abbas published an open letter in the journal *Film India* asking him to change his poor opinion of the film industry. According to Manju Jain, in *Narratives of Indian Cinema*, Gandhi did not respond (25).[29]

Gandhi clearly did not hide his disapproval of cinema, and it's not clear whether he ever saw a film though he is purported to have viewed *Sant Tukaram* (*Saint Tukaram*;[30] 1936) and *Ram Rajya* (*Ram's Kingdom*; 1943), directed by Vijay Bhat. Nevertheless, Gandhi influenced many a filmmaker and continues to do so today.[31] Hypothetically, had leaders like Gandhi taken a positive interest in Indian cinema, the character of the medium would have been different.[32] For example, if Gandhi considered film a medium of nation building, as did Nehru, the first Prime Minister of independent India, and wielded film's power to shape national policies, Indian cinema might have adopted Gandhi's moral vision. If so, representations of women and gender in Indian film would be very different today, as demonstrated by Gandhi's response to *tawaifs*' (sex workers) contribution to his noncooperation movement in the early

1920s—specifically their participation in a boycott of British-produced goods prompted by the Jalliansala Bagh massacre in 1919 when British Indian Army troops fired on religious pilgrims who unintentionally violated martial law prohibiting public protests. As Saba Dewan's documentary film, *The Other Song*, recounts, "When told [of the *tawaifs*' participation in the noncooperation movement], Mahatma Gandhi was furious with them. He would not accept them as workers, or take their donation, unless they gave up on the 'unworthy profession that made them worse than thieves'" (Gupta). Obviously, the sex workers were fallen women in the Mahatma's eye.[33]

What Indian cinema would be like today if Gandhi had not considered it a vice and had been more involved in the development of the medium in the new state is a matter of speculation. Would filmic representations of women be less sexist? Would film have devolved into didactic, propagandistic moralizing? Would film reinforce and perpetuate ancient mythological beliefs about gender, class, and caste or revise them to tell new stories? There are no answers to these questions, but the possibilities are tantalizing to consider.

CONCLUSION

Ultimately, the *Bhoomiti*—geometry—of Indian film is determined by a patriarchal morality that maps the axes and criteria of women's relative purity and fallenness. In this manner, both celluloid and actual Indian women are plotted on a complex grid of vertical and horizontal intersections derived from the graph paper of Indian mythology. The result is that womanhood is constructed as a damageable good, a product that can easily rot and spoil if their male owners, serving as stand-ins for the managing gods of mythology, do not control them. This in turn engenders the *veerānganā/vārānganā* binary and its many permutations that lend Indian films their dramatic tension. From its silent period in the 1920s until now, the massive warehouse of popular Indian cinema has been overstuffed with the "damaged goods" and "impurities" of the vamp, the violated, and the nonvirgin. This warehouse has all shades and grades (ratings)—A, B, and C—officially censored or uncensored. Ironically, early in its history, cinema itself was considered fallen as it was a transgression for women to act in film, and they were stigmatized for doing so. Even Mahatma Gandhi considered cinema impure and sinful. Nevertheless, popular Indian cinema continues to "play" women as *veerānganā* or *vārānganā*, virgin or whore.

NOTES

1 Sage Valmiki is said to have lived in the first millennia BCE and to have authored the epic *Ramayana*. Tulsidas (b. 1532–1623) is best known as the author of the epic *Ramcharitmanas*, a retelling of Valmiki's Sanskrit *Ramayana* into vernacular Awadhi, which is spoken chiefly in the Awadh, or Oudh, region of Uttar Pradesh (North India) and Nepal. Another important source that has shaped the figure of Sita is the *Adbhuta Ramayana* (Amazing Ramayana), one of the two Ramayanas associated with Valmiki. This text might be the source of the Shakta (a Hindu sect) view that Sita is the amazing One, the source of all wonders.

2 *Rati Chakravyuh* is a digital single-shot film based on an original English-language script by Ashish Avikunthak, translated into Bengali by Sougata Mukherjee. As background for the present chapter, read my analysis of Rati Chakravyuh in Aicon Gallery's catalogue, "Rati Chakravyuh: Dissolving Nothingness into Nothingness."

3 Rati is the goddess of love, passion, and sexual pleasure. The *Kalika Purana* narrates the tale of her birth. The term *chakravyu* in also called a *padmavyuh*, which is a military formation that looks like a labyrinth or lotus (*padma*) when viewed from above. This is a reference to the *Mahābhārata*'s tale of Abhimanyu, Krishna's nephew, who entered the *chakravyuh* during a battle in the Kurukshetra War between the Pandavas and Kauravas (see in this volume) but did not know how to exit, which led to his death.

4 Bhu Devi is also the consort of Varaha, an avatar of Vishnu, one of Hinduism's three main male gods.

5 While associated with a single author, the *Ramayana* is a composite work that evolved over time and earliest estimates date it to 500 BCE. The *Mahābhārata* was written after the *Ramayana* (c. 400 BCE).

6 During my recent visit to the National Film Archives of India in Pune, its former director, P. K. Nair, told me that in southern India, if a wife fails to produce a male child from her first pregnancy, she is looked down on. This is true of many other parts of India, though of late, the situation has changed to a great extent.

7 *Subject: Cinema, Object: Woman: Study of the Portrayal of Women in Indian Cinema*, Shoma A. Chatterji, Parumita, Calcutta, 1998. *An Indecent Proposal* (1993) was an American feature film that was an adaptation of Jack Engelhard's novel of the same name. It was directed by Adrian Lyne.

8 The legend of Savitri and Satyavan is found in the *Mahābhārata*, as told by the sage Markandeya. Savitri is the ideal wife and has, in Indian narrative, become a symbol for a loyal and devoted wife. There are at least twenty feature films (including silent) based on the Savitri myth made in different languages. Some of these films also show married Hindu women performing a ritual called the *Vata Savtri vrata*, in which the *vata*, or "banyan tree" (*ficus bengalensis linn*), is worshipped by tying a thread around it, fasting, and praying. This *vrata* (vow) is performed on the night when the moon is full in the Hindu month of Jyeshtha (around June) in honor of Savitri, who like the Greek queen Alcestis brought her husband back from the dead. By observing this *vrata*, women hope to prolong their husbands' lives.

9 Film scholar Virchand Dharamsey's *Indian Silent Cinema (1912–1934): A Filmography* in *Light of Asia*, ed. Suresh Chabria, Niyogi, 2014. There are at least six feature films (including two silent) named *Devdasi*.

10 According to Hindi mythology, Tilottama is an Apsara (celestial nymph). In the *Mahābhārata*, she is described as being created by the divine architect, Vishwakarma, at Brahma's request. She was responsible for bringing about the mutual destruction of the Asuras (demons) Sundra and Upasundra. Even Siva and Indra were enamored of Tilottama. The *Padma Purana* had Tilottama as an ugly widow named Kubja in her previous birth.

11 The river derives its name from Gautama, who, with his disciples, bathed there to purify themselves of sin. According to the Kotirudra Samhita of the Shiva Purana, Gautama's enemies were also eager to be cleansed of their sins, but when they sought absolution in the Ganges, known as Mother Ganga, she was initially reluctant to purify them because of their cruelty to Gautama. However, Gautama convinced Mother Ganga to relent, and he dug a ditch from whence she emerged and purified the sages.

12 This is reminiscent of the Greek myth of Argus (Argos), the hundred-eyed giant, and Hera, the Queen of the Olympian gods and goddesses, who commanded Argus to watch over Io. Io was a woman with whom Zeus, the ruler of the Olympians, had a passionate sexual affair. However, in order to protect his mistress from the wrath of his wife, Hera, he transformed Io into a heifer. Hera commands Argus to guard the heifer. Displeased, Zeus sends the god Hermes to

dispatch the monster, and Hermes manages to subdue Argus. This myth has also acquired different versions. Some sources suggest that Hermes lulled Argus to sleep, while others state that Hermes killed the monster.

13 A recent exception is a fourteen-minute short directed by Sujoy Ghosh, *Ahalya*, which stars Soumitra Chatterjee, Tota Roy Chowdhury, and Radhika Apte. This film, dubbed a feminist revision of the original Ahalya myth by the Hindustantimes, depicts Gautama as a trickster who manipulates a hapless Indra into having sex with an unsuspecting Ahalya. In the end, Indra is turned to stone, and Gautama is revealed as a serial "killer," so to speak, of his wife's gullible lovers.

14 A manifestation of the fascination that Ahalya's story holds is Rabindranath Tagore's poem, which addresses her directly: "What were your dreams / Ahalya, when you passed / Long years as stone, / rooted in earth, prayer / And ritual gone, / sacred fire extinct / In the dark, abandoned / forest-shram? Earth / Merged with your body; did / you know her vast / Love, did hazy awareness / haunt your stone?" (trans. William Radice).

15 *Subject: Cinema, Object: Woman: A Study of the Portrayal of Women in Indian Cinema*, Shoma A. Chatterji, Parumita, Calcutta, 1998.

16 During this period, a courtesan was primarily a dancer, singer, and poet—an artist who could aspire to become queen and who might have sexual relations with the king. Nevertheless, the dance performances in *Chitralekha* and other elements of the film suggest that the courtesan entertained the king sexually.

17 The first adaptation of the novella was as a silent film directed by Naresh Mitra and starring Phani Sarma and Tarakbala Niharbala, released in 1928 by Eastern Films Syndicate of Calcutta. However, this chapter deals with the Bengali and Hindi "talkies" that date to 1935 and 1936, respectively, because they were far more popular and influential than the earlier silent version.

18 Thomas Schatz, in his book *Hollywood: Critical Concepts in India and Culture Studies*, Routledge, 2004, refers to some of these films.

19 *Encyclopedia of Indian Cinema*, new revised ed., ed. Ashish Rajadhyaksha and Paul Willemen, Oxford UP, 1999. See the song-synopsis booklet of the film's Hindi version, courtesy of Osian's Archive & Library Collection. Music composer and singer Pankaj Mullick also played a role in this film.

20 The expression *kanyadaan* is still used in contemporary Hindi wedding vocabulary in many parts of the country.

21 Derived from mythology, *A Sanskrit-English Dictionary* gives various alternative meanings of the word *sati*, viz. Viswamitra's wife, goddess Durga or Uma; sometimes described as Truth personified or as a daughter of Daksha and wife of Bhava (Siva), and sometimes represented as putting an end to herself by Yoga or, at a later period, burning herself on the funeral pyre of her husband; one of the wives of Angiras.

22 *Encyclopedia of Indian Cinema*; *Gujarati Film Geetkosh 1932–1994*, ed. Harish Raghuvanshi, Surat, 1995. There could be innumerable films alluding to the *sati* aspect.

23 Another Rajput practice was Doodh Peeti, drowning female infants in their milk. *The Rajputs of Saruashtra* by Virhadra Singhji offers a detailed explanation of *sati* among the Kathiwad Rajputs.

24 Elaben Bhatt, "Bharatiya Chitrapatoma Narinu Pratibimba," in *Strini Manomurtinu Roop*, Foundation for Public Estate, Ahmedabad, 1979; *Gujarati Cinema: Stories of Sant, Sati, Shethani and Sparks so Few*, Amrit Gangar, in *Routledge Handbook of Indian Cinemas*, ed. K. Moti Gokulsing and Wimal.

25 My term.

26 DDwG is as commonly employed—particularly in Bollywood films—as shooting, killing, dance, and song are used to signal "the forces of good" and to effect a cathartic cleansing of evil and immorality that restores social order.

27 The crooked, cruel Tau utters the word *finish* in highly stylized English while the rest of his speech is in Hindi (my translation). *Divya Shakti* (1993), directed by Sameer Malkan, starred Ajay Devghan, Raveena Tandon, Amrish Puri, and Satyendra Kapoor, among others.

28 "Seeking Redemption in the Sordid World of 'BA Pass,'" G. Sampath, *Live Mint*, 16 Aug. 2013.
29 Abbas's open letter stated,

> Today I bring for your scrutiny—and approval—a new toy my generation has learned to play with, the CINEMA!–You include cinema among evils like gambling, *sutta*, horse racing etc. . . . Now if these statements had come from any other person, it was not necessary to be worried about them . . . But your case is different. In view of the great position you hold in this country, and I may say in the world, even the slightest expression of your opinion carries much weight with millions of people. And one of the world's most useful inventions would be allowed to be discarded or what is worse, left alone to be abused by unscrupulous people. You are a great soul, Bapu. In your heart there is no room for prejudice. Give this little toy of ours, the cinema, which is not so useless as it looks, a little of your attention and bless it with a smile of toleration. (25)

Gandhi did not respond, which caused another outburst. *Narratives of Indian Cinema* by Manju Jain, p. 25.
30 Tukaram is a prominent saint and spiritual poet of the Bhakti movement in India.
31 Jay Prakash Chowksey, in his book *Gandhi Aur Cinema*, says he was inspired to write about the "Father of the Nation" after reading an anecdote in Charlie Chaplin's autobiography that said Gandhi opposed industrialization because he believed it facilitated Indians' economic colonization and oppression by the West.
32 *The Movies They Missed*, Amrit Gangar, *Independent* (*Times of India*), 4 June 1985.
33 Delhi-based filmmaker Saba Dewan's documentary *The Other Song* is about the life of Rasoolan Bai, a *tawaif*. It features her more famous song "Lagat karejwa ma chot, phool gendwa na maar," a 1935 gramophone recording.

WORKS CITED

Abhigyan/Abhagin. Directed by Prafulla Roy, performances by Molina Devi, Jiban Ganguly, and Sailen Choudhury, New Theatres, 1938.

Ahalya. Directed by Sujoy Ghosh, performances by Soumitra Chatterjee, Tota Roy Chowdhury, and Radhika Apte, Royal Stag Barrel Select Large Short Films, 2015.

"Ahalya: Watch Sujoy Ghosh's Feminist Take on an Epic Tale." *Hindustan Times*. 23 July 2015, http://www.hindustantimes.com/regional-movies/ahalya-watch-sujoy-ghosh-s-feminist-take-on-an-epic-tale/story-icp4uPvCsSMoaAF7pvFDlO.html.

Akhand Saubhagyavati. Directed by Manhar Raskapur, Rajat Films, 1963.

Amrapali. Directed by Lekh Tandon, performances by Vyajanthimala and Sunil Dutt, Eagle Films and Shemaroo Video Pvt. Ltd., 1966.

B.A. Pass. Directed by Ajay Bahl, FilmyBox Movies and Tonga Talkies, 2012.

Baabul (*Father's affection for his daughter*). Directed by Ravi Chopra, performances by Amitabh Bachchan, Rani Mukerji, Salman Khan, John Abraham, and Hema Malini, B. R. Films, 2006.

Bhatt, Elaben. "Bharatiya Chitrapatoma Narinu Pratibimba." *Strini Manomurtinu Roop*. The Foundation for Public Estate, Ahmedabad, 1979.

Bhattacharya, Pradip. "Five Holy Virgins, Five Sacred Myths: A Quest for Meaning." *Manushi*, no. 141 (Nov.–Dec.), 2004, pp. 25–33.

Bhooloka Rambha (*Forgetful Rambha*). Directed by D. Yoganand, Ashoka Pictures, 1958.

Central Board of Film Certification India. Central Board of Film Certification, cbfcindia.gov.in. Accessed 1 May 2016.

Chabria, Suresh, editor. *Light of Asia: Indian Silent Cinema 1912–1934*. Niyogi, 2014.

Chatterji, Shoma A. *Subject: Cinema, Object: Woman: Study of the Portrayal of Women in Indian Cinema*. Parumita Publications, 1998.

Chitralekha. Directed by Kidar Sharma, performances by Mehtab, Nandrekar, and A. S. Gyani, Film Corporation of India, 1941.

Creekmur, Corey K. "The Devdas Phenomenon." *Indian Cinema*. U of Iowa, http://www.uiowa.edu/indiancinema/devdas.

Damaged Goods. Directed by Tom Ricketts, performances by Richard Bennett, Adrienne Morrison, and Maud Milton, American Film Manufacturing Company, 1914.

Damaged Goods. Directed by Alexander Butler, G. B. Samuelson Productions, 1919.

Damaged Goods. Directed by Phil Goldstone, Criterion Pictures Corp., 1937.

Devdas. Directed by P. C. Barua, New Theatres Limited, 1935.

Devi Ahilyabai. Directed by Bhagwati Mishra, Royal Art, 1925.

Divya Shakti (*Divine power*). Directed by Sameer Malkan, performances by Ajay Devghan, Raveena Tandon, Amrish Puri, and Satyendra Kapoor, Sonu Films International, 1993.

Dutt, Manmatha Nath. *Markandeya Purana*. Elysium Press, 1896.

Gangar, Amrit. "Dissolving Nothingness into Nothingness." *Rati Chakravyuh: A Film by Ashish Avikunthak*. Aicon Gallery, 2013, prod-images.exhibit-e.com/www_aicongallery_com/Rati_Chakravyuh_Catalog_Web.pdf.

———. "Gujarati Cinema: Stories of Sant, Sati, Shethani and Sparks so Few." *Routledge Handbook of Indian Cinemas*. Edited by K. Moti Gokulsing and Wimal Dissanayake, Routledge, 2013, pp. 88–101.

———. "The Movies They Missed." *Independent* (*The Times of India*), 4 June 1985.

———. "Myth, Metaphor, Mirth, Memory, Mayhem: A Bollywoodian Replay on the Swiss Landscape." *The Indian Cinema and Switzerland*, edited by Alexandra Schneider, British Council, 2001. Hochschule fur Gestaltung und Kunst Zurich, 2002.

———. *Rupantar*. Arunoday Prakashan, Ahmedabad, 2014.

Ganti, Tejaswini. *Producing Bollywood: Inside the Contemporary Hindi Film Industry*. Duke UP, 2012.

Gharwali Baharwali (*Wife at home, lover in the kitchen*). Directed by David Dhavan, performances by Anil Kapoor, Raveena Tandon, and Rambha, Tutu Films, 1998.

Ghosh, Manomohan. *Natyasastra*. Translated by Bharata-Muni, The Royal Asiatic Society of Bengal, 1951.

Gosvami, Tulasidasa. *Sri Ramacaritamanasa* (*The Manasa Lake brimming over with the exploits of Sri Rama*). Gita Press, 1972.

Gupta, Rajesh. "Rasoolan Bai: The Other Song." Indian Raga. 31 Oct. 2009, indianraga.blogspot.com/2009/10/rasoolan-bai-other-song.html.

Intlo Illalu Vantintlo Priyuralu. Directed by Satyanarayana E. V. V., performances by Daggubati Venkatesh, Sri Durga Arts, 1996.

Jain, Manju, editor. *Narratives of Indian Cinema*. Primus, 2009.

Johnson, Emmanuel Janagan, and Shyamala. "Widow Remarriage: A New Dimension of Social Change in India." *International Journal of Humanities and Social Sciences*, vol. 2, no. 3, 2012, pp. 195–205.

Juddai (*Separation*). Directed by Raj Kanwar, S. K. Film Enterprises and Eros Entertainment, 1997.

Kamdar, Seema. "In 'Safe' Mumbai, Women Remain on Edge." *DNA*. 23 Mar. 2007, http://www.dnaindia.com/mumbai/report-in-safe-mumbai-women-remain-on-edge-1086755.

Kanyadaan (*Daughter's marriage*). Directed by Mohan Segal, performances by Asha Parekh, Shashi Kappor, Om Prakash, Achala Sachdeve, Dilip Raj, and Sayeeda Khan, Kiron Productions, 1968.

Kanya Vikraya. Directed by Homi Master, Kohinoor Film Company, 1924.

Kanyavikraya. Directed by V. S. Nirantar, Hindustan Cinema Film Company, 1923.

Maya Rambha (*Illusionary Rambha*). Directed by T. P. Sundaram, Modern Theatres Limited, 1950.

The Other Song. Directed by Saba Dewan, Aakar, 2009.

Pitra, Putra Aur Dharamyuddha (*Father, son and holy war*). Directed and distributed by Anand Patwardhan, 1995.

Rajadhyaksha, Ashish, and Paul Willemen. *Encyclopedia of Indian Cinema*. New Revised Edition, Oxford UP, 1999.

Rajagopalachari, C. *Ramayana*. Bharatiya Vidya Bhavan, 1996.

Raja Harishchandra (*King Karishchandra*). Directed by D. G. Phalke, Phalke Films, 1913.

Ram Rajya (*Ram's kingdom*). Directed by Vijay Bhat, performances by Prem Adib, Chandrakant, and Badri Prasad, Prakash Pictures, 1943.

Rati Chakrayuh (*Spirals of love*). Directed by Ashish Avikunthak, performances by Mishka Halim, Joyraj Bhattacharya, and Sharmistha Nag, welt | film, 2013.

Saajan Chale Sasural (*My lover goes back to his family*). Directed by David Dhawan, Sony Entertainment Television, 1994.

Sampath, G. "Seeking Redemption in the Sordid World of 'BA Pass.'" *Live Mint*. 16 Aug. 2013, http://www.livemint.com/Opinion/FP5vkw7w2hQVglUoToJ5IO/Seeking-redemption-in-the-sordid-world-of-BA-Pass.html.

Sant Tukaram. Directed by Vishnupant Govind Damle and Sheikh Fattelal, performances by Vishnupant Pagnis, Gauri, and B. Nandrekar, Prabhat Film Company, 1936.

Sati Savitri. Directed by Chandulal Shah, performances by M. Bhagwandas, Ghori, and Keki Adajania, Ranjit Movies, 1932.

Schartz, Thomas. *Hollywood: Critical Concepts in India and Culture Studies*. Routledge, 2004.

Singhji, Virbhadra. *The Rajputs of Saurashtra*. Popular Prakashan, 1994.

Vikraya, Lobhi Pita, and *Lobhi Baap* (*Greedy father*). Directed by Mohammed Hussain, Pioneer Film Company, 1934.

Williams, Sir Monier-Monier. *A Sanskrit-English Dictionary*. Oxford UP, 1960.

Yathabhavishya (*Rambha's love*). Directed by B. N. Rao, Kalpana Kala Mandhir, 1992.

7 ⑥ ROOP TARAASHI

Sex, Culture, Violence, Impersonation, and the Politics of the Inner Sanctum

NAINA DEY

I fear to speak about the way, that look I fear to behold
How *rakshashis*[1] turn into humans
Chomp-chomp she ate the son of her womb
Where did you find O farmer the egg of iron and the egg of gold?

—*Roop Taraashi, Thakurmar Jhuli* (my translation)

Naina Dey's chapter examines evil women in a nineteenth-century collection of Bengali folktales called *Thakurmar Jhuli* (*Grandmother's Bag*), published during a nativist revival among Bengal's intellectual elites that correlated with the ongoing nationalist movement to end British rule in India. In it, Dey argues that these tales domesticate girls and promote "feminine" submissiveness while also protesting the Anglicization of Bengali children. The dangers of female unruliness, she asserts, are borne out by the opposition between a stock character, the virtuous mother-queen, and a grotesque, demonic, monstrous stepmother whose attempts to seize power for herself or her sons inevitably end in self-destruction. Dey points out that rivalries between the demonic stepmothers and nurturing, submissive queens document anxieties about women's lack of agency under patriarchal institutions such as primogeniture and polygamy. Dey further suggests that evil stepmothers' cannibalistic rage against their stepsons and sometimes even sons reflects masculine fears of female sexuality even as *Grandmother's Bag* resists Indian children's Westernization. Dey's chapter on vicious fictitious female characters in Bengali folktales exposes the falseness of patriarchal idealization of motherhood and that dangerous purposes lurk behind children's folktales' veil of naïveté.

INTRODUCTION

Thakurmar Jhuli (*Grandmother's Bag*)[2] is a compendium of *roopkatha* (folk tales)[3] that, passed down across the generations, circulated orally in Bengal for hundreds of years before Dakshinaranjan Mitra Majumder collected and published them in 1907. When *Thakurmar Jhuli* first appeared, it was lauded by none other than Rabindranath Tagore[4] himself, who had already published two volumes of Bengali folk rhymes, one in 1894 and another in 1895.[5] In fact, Tagore wrote the preface for *Thakurmar Jhuli*, praising it in verse for embodying the essence of nearly forgotten tales: "All the princes and princesses of a thousand ages ago / Have come again, swimming over the ocean of charms / *Hau mau kau* [commotion][6] the kingdom of demons resounds / Who knew in which land, who knew how far" (Majumder 19). Tagore appreciated that the collection reflected the rural simplicity of Bengal, a quality that today's critics continue to admire: Dakshinaranjan captured "the inflections of her [grandmother's] voice, the nuances of her speech, and the archaic simplicity of her world" (Bhattacharya). In this respect, the stories contrast with the European fairy tales that the British introduced to India during colonial rule, and for this reason, Tagore considered the *Thakurmar Jhuli* an artifact that resisted Anglicization of Bengali children under British rule. Indeed, the book may convey a covert protest against the effects of foreign education in its depictions of the monstrous women in book 2, entitled *Roop Taraashi*, who inevitably perish after their malicious, sometimes murderous attempts to secure advantages for themselves or their children fail spectacularly. Indeed, such resistance is consistent with Dakshinaranjan's belief that patterning Indian education on the Western model was a colonial imposition, whether advocated by the British or Indians. He was particularly opposed to educating women. According to Dakshinaranjan, education polluted women by inducing in them a desire to move beyond the domestic and into public spaces, which violated many cultural practices including *purdah*. Thus at the same time the tales resist colonialism, they also lay down conservative codes of conduct that push back against changing women's status and role in nineteenth-century India. This put Dakshinaranjan at odds with Tagore, who belonged to a group of public intellectuals and artists who promoted women's education (which renders Tagore's enthusiasm for *Thakurmar Jhuli* somewhat ironic). Consequently, the book is part of a larger, complicated discourse about India, colonial rule, and gender in which Dakshinaranjan and Tagore represent two major factions, and unfortunately, women were caught between them.

The British, of course, imposed an alien culture on indigenous ways of life in India, and in urban centers like Kolkata, British influence was so profound that the entire sphere of Hindu domestic life and its most intimate relationships had become contested ground in the nineteenth century. Dakshinaranjan belonged to the adamantly anti-Western, nationalist Swadeshi movement that congealed in the mid-1850s and primarily relied on exerting economic pressure on Britain and fostering *swadeshi* (self-sufficiency) in India to secure the country's independence.

Tagore, on the other hand, belonged to the Brahmo Samaj, meaning "Divine Society," an organization founded by Raja Rammohan Roy (b. 1772–1833) in Bengal in the nineteenth century. Its main purposes were to replace orthodox Hinduism's "superstitious" polytheistic worship with a monotheism informed by reason and science and, second, to end the caste hierarchy. As a result, Brahmo Samaj members espoused Western education for both women and men and worked to end practices such as *sati*, and to a degree, these positions aligned the organization with the British. This, of course, was a significant difference between the Swadeshi and Brahmo Samaj movements, and mass sentiment was on the Swadeshis' side because the Brahmo Samaj, with well-to-do members such as Raja Rammohan Roy (its founder, who some consider a feminist), Debendra Nath Tagore (Rabindranath's father), and Keshab Chandra Sen, who were thought to be sycophants of the British.

STORIED ENCULTURATION

Folk tales, as do many discourses, explain the world and humans' relationship to it and to each other. The specific character of this explanation depends on local contingencies, such as communal values, a people's historical experiences, and the conditions and institutions that shape daily life. Hence folk and fairy tales are products of and represent a particular conjunction of cultural forces and social elements, and they socialize audiences into the values and beliefs represented in them.

Roopkatha depicts and socializes readers into a patriarchal world, implies Sreekumar Bandopadhyay, when, relying on Freudian theory, he argues that they "penetrate the inmost recesses of our soul and stirs those secret, unnamed desires concealed therein" (my translation; 4). While Bandopadhyay exhibits an obvious lack of concern with feminist interpretations of the stories when he imagines the meaning-making process as an act of male sexual desire and fulfillment, he makes a valuable observation when he implies that the stories situate readers in a masculine subject position and render female characters objects of the male gaze. As he says, "The princess who reclines on the bed of coral in the secluded land of the *rakshashas* across the thirteen rivers and seven seas, is the beloved who we all pine for in the secrecy of our inner sanctum; the obstacles and dangers that the prince of the *roopkatha* overcomes to attain his love, are the sighs of resentment of the romantic lover hidden within us at the present materialistic marital alliances" (my translation; Bandopadhyay 4). Here, Bandopadhyay raises the possibility that *roopkatha* is particularly masculinist, a trait that is particularly conspicuous in *Thakurmar Jhuli*'s tales in part because they, like almost all folklore worldwide, were originally composed in a patriarchal society. At the same time, because the tales in *Thakurmar Jhuli* were textualized and published in nineteenth-century Bengal, they also register the values and anxieties of that era and place. Likewise, the stories' socializing function was repurposed as they migrated from their initial milieu and were adapted to meet the needs and desires of their new audience (defined broadly) in different contexts.

In *Fairy Tales and the Art of Subversion: The Classical Genre for Children and the Process of Civilization*, Jack Zipes sheds light on the effects of transferring Western folk stories from their natural environment into a different setting. For instance, he explains that when oral tales are extracted from their original contexts and recirculated in a later historical epoch, they may be redesigned to fulfill the needs and desires of the new era's authorities. He also suggests that such stories' social function accrues additional purposes, such as distracting audiences from restrictions that authorities have imposed on them, thus becoming more conservative than their oral predecessors (6). Examining how these processes are inflected by gender, feminist critic Marina Warner explains that when female characters are severed from the original web of tensions in which they were developed—the local contingencies that shape the stories—these figures are reduced to flat archetypes, that is, culturally denuded stereotypes.

Such stereotyping is conspicuous in *Thakurmar Jhuli*, which, of course, transferred oral *roopkatha* from their natural environment—a storyteller addressing a limited, intragenerational audience consisting of family members or others connected by family-like bonds—and circulated them in the form of a text that signaled political resistance rooted in nationalism to a mass audience. Hence the good queen who the king wrongfully banishes turns into a *ghunte-kuruni dasi* (a poor woman who makes her living by drying cow dung for fuel). The lonely princess languishes in the classic feminine pose of *rekhe shonar khate gaa, aar rupar khate paa* (her body reclined on a golden bed, her feet resting on a silver bed) waiting for her prince. The *rakshashi* (a monstrous woman like a witch) is always the outsider of unknown origin. Two women vie against each other to secure an advantage for their offspring, unabashedly victimizing their rivals and their rivals' children, often by means of necromancy, but good triumphs over evil in the end.

The origin of the word "fairy" in the context of Western "tales" is instructive. Thomas Keightley in his *Fairy Mythology* (1828), and later in the appendix of his *Tales and Popular Fictions*, explains that "fairy" derives from the Latin *fatum*, "to enchant." In old French romance, *fee* was a "woman skilled in magic." Women who maintained their beauty, youth, and riches through enchantment were called "Fays." This was true also of the Italian *fata*. In the English literary tradition, "fay" came to signify a "wicked witch" because of the association with magic and spells that, even if benevolent (love potions, for example, or charms to induce pregnancy), challenged Christian precepts and, by implication, institutional religion's power. Consequently, the malevolent sorceress featured in Thomas Malory's *Le Morte d'Arthur*, a medieval romance about the legendary King Arthur and his knights that derives from earlier chronicles telling the mythological history of England, is named Morgan La Fay, Arthur's sister and a practitioner of necromancy.

Significantly, these stereotypes are conspicuously patriarchal, particularly in the case of stories *Roop Taraashi* (book 4) that feature *rakshashi*, who is often disguised as a mother or stepmother figure and, in "Sonar Kathi Rupar Kathi" ("The Golden Rod and Silver Rod"), as a beautiful young woman who marries the king.

The *rakshashi* inflicts her greatest malevolence on her stepchildren who typically are her rivals in a patriarchal society that uses primogeniture to transfer family wealth and power from one generation to the next. The *rakshashi* trope is also present, albeit in the character of the wicked stepmother, in English fairy tales that, like those collected in *Thakurmar Jhuli*, were transmitted from generation to generation over a period of several hundred years. In the English tales, a father marries a new wife after his first wife dies, and the second wife, insanely jealous of a stepdaughter, sets about getting rid of the child often by means of magic. Hence the English fairy tales and Bengali *roopkatha* share some important features despite Tagore's celebration of *Thakurmar Jhuli*'s indigeneity. For example, in the English tale, "The Laidly Worm of Spindleston Heugh" a widower king marries a new wife who is jealous of his daughter, Princess Margaret, considered the most beautiful female in the kingdom. The stepmother queen, who is actually a witch, casts a spell turning Margaret into a *laidly worm* (a dragon). When Margaret's brother, Childe Wynd, who is away from the kingdom, learns of the crisis, he returns to rescue his sister. After some obstacles, Childe Wynd kisses Margaret three times, and she returns to her former self. He also touches the stepmother with the leaf of an enchanted rowan tree, turning her into a hideous toad. The story ends when Childe Wynd assumes the kingship.

In "The Well of the World's End," an envious stepmother sends her daughter on an impossible task—filling a sieve with water from the well of the world's end—and forbids her to return home until she is successful. When the girl arrives at the well, she despairs that she will never be able to accomplish her mission. But a frog tells her how to seal the sieve with mud and moss if she will do what he commands for one night. The girl returns home, and the frog soon turns up. Somewhat unwillingly, the girl keeps her promise, even his request for her to chop off his head. As it turns out, a prince jumps out of the decapitated frog, for he had been under a spell that could only be broken if a girl did his bidding an entire night and then chopped off his head. In the end, the prince marries the girl, and they live happily in his kingdom. The stepmother is left behind.

These representative English fairy tales employ the trope of the wicked stepmother in a manner similar to its performance in four *roopkatha* in *Roop Taraashi*, "Sheet Basanta" ("Winter Summer"), "Neelkamal ar Lalkamal" (the protagonists' names), "Dalim Kumar" (the protagonist's name), and "Sonar Kathi Rupar Kathi" ("The Golden Rod and Silver Rod"). In both sets of stories, English and Bengali, the stepmother uses sorcery to establish a unique position—the greatest beauty, the favored lover, the queen regent, or otherwise most powerful woman in her environment. This bespeaks the tales' depiction and facilitation of psychological processes of maturation, particularly children's separation and individuation from the mother. It also draws attention to the ways that the patriarchal family and numerous other social institutions deprive girls and women of agency, which, in turn, pits women against each other as they struggle to attain security and survive their marginalized status whether in Western or Bengali contexts.

Cynthia Burack offers an explanation of psychological maturation that is useful in understanding the stepmother figure's murderous rage. Burack builds this argument on Jessica Benjamin's contention, in "The Bonds of Love: Rational Violence and Erotic Domination," that the "differentiation of self from (m)other and the recognition of independent selfhood received from the (m)other together structure both the nature of selfhood and of relations between selves" (1994, 82). Burack goes on to suggest that when differentiation and individuation processes constitute a power struggle marked by rage, as they are in the mother-child dyads featured in the evil stepmother topos, it is indicative of some damage or deficiency: "The characters in the drama of domination and submission use one another to repeat and to cope with their psychic disfigurement and the rage that underlies it" (1994, 84).

While Burack is primarily interested in singularized forms of "disfigurement" rather than the social, Warner's work focuses on how fairy tales convey the dangers of womanhood itself, particularly within the disfiguring contexts of patriarchalism in the West. As she writes in *From the Beast to the Blonde: On Fairy Tales and Their Tellers*, when European fairy tales were first composed (often long before their transcription), absent mothers were a frequent feature of family life largely because death in childbirth was a common cause of female mortality. Surviving orphans were often raised by their mother's successor, and Warner suggests that the inclusion of the harmful stepmother may have started as a warning, for history is full of heirs and heiresses murdered by a new spouse, ambitious for their own offspring. Moreover, the enmity of stepmothers toward children from husbands' previous marriages that marks so many tales from around the world is, Warner stresses, the product of patrilineal systems that arrange women's marriage and obstruct their autonomy.

Zipes's work, following earlier research by Heide Göttner-Abendroth on the history of Western fairy tales, arrives at a similar conclusion. Zipes argues that in Europe as pre-Christian cultures were eclipsed by medieval feudalism and then early modern capitalism, the stories' original, community-wide audience was narrowed to "children of the upper classes" and the tales were successively patriarchalized so that the goddesses featured in early tales were replaced by malevolent female figures (qtd. in Sellers 12). Reflecting the conditions of feudal society, the goddess was recast as evil witch, bad fairy, or malevolent stepmother, and the stories' maturation and integration function was subordinated to the exploits of a male protagonist intent on domination and wealth (7).

Despite the commonalities between the *roopkatha*'s and English fairy tales' uses of the wicked stepmother trope, there are some important differences between the *rakshashi* in *Roop Taraashi*'s stories and the fairy tales' stepmother. For one thing, the *rakshashi*'s rival is a cowife due to polygamous marriage. Second, the *rakshashi* as well as her rival have sons rather than daughters, which reflects the influence of primogeniture. Finally, the *rakshashi* is often cannibalistic, capable in one instance of consuming even her own sons.

When *Thakurmar Jhuli* was published, complications that polygamy created in the family were well recognized, as demonstrated by late eighteenth-century articles and pamphlets extolling education for women: "Almost all of those with too many wives are . . . compelled to listen to bickering and quarrels until one's ears are ready to burst which means that there is no possibility of finding fulfillment in being the head of too many households" (my translation; Basu 74). Beyond causing "bickering" and decreasing the possibilities for husbands' "fulfillment," polygamy is a high-stakes institution for women and their sons. It increases the sheer number of competitors for resources, whether material or psychological and emotional. It also inserts boy children into the contest, for the privileged eldest son generally accumulates more resources than other offspring due to primogeniture (even when it is not strictly followed), and importantly, his mother can use this son's favored status to increase her own worth to the husband-father. Consequently, polygamy can exacerbate intrafamily conflicts whether they stem primarily from concerns about material wellbeing or a family member's status in the patriarchal hierarchy or relate to psychological processes of separation and individuation.

The precarity that polygamy engenders for women and children is evident in *Roop Taraashi*'s "Sheet Basanta," a story about Duo Rani, a queen neglected by a royal husband who is infatuated with his other wife, Shuo Rani, a manipulative woman. Shuo Rani is extremely competitive, and the high level of rage that she directs at her rivals, Duo Rani[7] and her two sons, Sheet (Winter) and Basanta (Spring), is commensurate with the degree of threat that they pose: "With her three twig-like sons, Shuo Rani burnt with suppressed rage. Her mind filled with spite, her stomach filled with gall—she served her sons varieties of dishes soaked in *ghee* [clarified butter]; Sheet and Basanta were given stiff rice without oil or salt, and vegetables over which she would throw a lump of ash and walk away" (my translation; Mazumder 75). Shuo Rani is uncontrollably jealous because she has little control of her situation in the polygamous family—she has neither material nor psychological security—and her ability to respond has been reduced to ruining her rivals' meals.

But Shuo Rani's revenge pales in comparison to the measures that other women in *Roop Taraashi* take against rivals. Significantly, in these stories, the *rakshashi* initially targets boy rivals of her son(s), and her jealousy is so extreme that she sometimes cannibalizes enemies. Indeed, she hankers for human flesh. For instance, the *rakshashi*'s craving is so intense in the most widely read story in *Roop Taraashi*, "Neelkamal ar Lalkamal," that she even turns against her own son. "Neelkamal ar Lalkamal" opens with an atmosphere of evil foreboding conveyed in an announcement that one of the king's two wives is a *rakshashi*, although none of the characters realize this. Day and night, the *rakshashi* longs to eat the son of her rival—the human queen—but is chagrined to find her own son, Neelkamal, always protectively hovering near the other boy, who is named Lalkamal. She secretly curses Neelkamal as her crimson tongue slabbers in anticipation of tasting Lalkamal's tender meat. Eventually, the good queen falls ill and takes to her bed. One night, unable to control her greed any longer, the *rakshashi*, in a fit of rage, literally petrifies the king and gobbles up both the boys as her husband looks on horrified and helpless. The story takes an almost predictable twist when a farmer accidentally unearths two unusual looking eggs—two balls of food composed of iron and gold that the *rakshashi* vomited after her meal—from which emerge the two princes. Lalkamal and Neelkamal, now finding it dangerous to return home, travel to a neighboring kingdom, where *khokkoshes* (another type of cannibalistic *rakshashi*) are terrorizing the population. The ruler of this realm had proclaimed that he would give away his two beautiful daughters to a suitor who would free his people from the *khokkoshes*, so Lalkamal and Neelkamal vow to destroy the demons. They put up in a village cottage and wait for the *khokkoshes* to arrive. When the demons attack Neelkamal, who, as a witch's son, is endowed with supernatural facilities, at first succeeds in driving them away with his quick thinking and presence of mind, but when it is time for Lalkamal to stand guard against the *khokkoshes*, he fails in a moment of drowsiness that betrays his identity as human. The *khokkoshes* spring on the two brothers, but Neelkamal ruthlessly slaughters them. The grateful king marries his two daughters to the princes. But the demon queen has not been idle. Hearing the *khokkoshes'* fate, she decides to put an end to the two princes forever. Upon her orders, two *rakshashas* disguised as royal guards deliver a message to the princes that their father has taken ill and will only recover if administered oil from a *rakshasa*'s head. The brothers set out for the *rakshashas'* homeland and on the way encounter the Byangama and Byangami, male and female birds that are a common feature in Indian folktales.[8] The birds are blind and pine for sight, so the princes draw blood from their own fingers and the droplets are magically transformed into eyes for the birds. The birds then carry the princes for seven days and nights until they reach the *rakshashas'* lair. When the *rakshashas* rush to devour them, the princes use trickery to save themselves. They are safe for the time being, but what they beheld horrified them: "What a kingdom!—what a land. This strange realm squirmed with *rakshashas* of every kind. They romped the earth and killed all creatures and had filled up the land with their carcasses. Lal and Neel rode on the shoulders of *rakshashas* and saw everything—piles and piles of the dead, mounds and mounds of decaying flesh. Festering, putrid, the kingdom was slimy, stinking—the stench drove away ghosts and ghouls, frightened angels and giants!" (my translation; Majumder 133). The princes eventually find two enchanted wasps that contain the lives of all the *rakshashas* including the demon queen. The story ends as the wasps—thus the *rakshashas*—are killed, but not before the true identity of Neelkamal's mother is revealed to all, and the king regains his health.

In the next story, "Dalim Kumar," a *rakshashi* who has seven sons gobbles up the real queen and then impersonates her. Only the real queen's young son realizes what has happened when he notices a drop of saliva rolling down the disguised *rakshashi*'s tongue when she serves him food. Here, the demon queen, jealous of her stepson, seeks a secure future for her seven sons. As in "Neelkamal ar Lalkamal," the *rakshashi* is not the only cannibal in the story. In the course of their adventures, the *rakshashi*'s sons encounter seven sisters who carve up and eat the princes. Meanwhile, the demon queen's machinations blind her stepson. The story ends when he regains his vision and rescues his seven stepbrothers from the sisters' clutches.

In "Sonar Kathi Rupar Kathi" ("The Golden Rod and Silver Rod"), a prince and three friends set out to make their way in the world. Hungry, they find a deer's head and decide to cook it for dinner. When one of them cuts it, a *rakshashi* leaps out and eats the prince's friends, but he hides in a mango tree. The *rakshashi* turns herself into a beautiful maiden, and the king (the prince's father), who is passing by, sees her, falls in love, and marries her. She remains determined to kill the prince and develops a scheme to cut down and burn the mango tree, where he still resides—she claims to be ill and persuades the king that only inhaling smoke from a burning mango tree will cure her. However, the mango tree saves the prince by turning him into a fruit, which falls into a tank when the tree is cut down and then eaten by a large fish. Later, he turns into a snail, which a princess who bathes in the tank finds and cracks open the shell, thus releasing the prince, after which she gives him refuge in her palace. The *rakshashi*, using her magical powers, learns what has transpired. She commands the king, who is now completely under her control, to capture and return the prince. The king's guards retrieve him, and the queen orders the young man to travel to the land of the *rakshashi* to obtain a list of items that the queen says will restore her health. The prince arrives at a palace ruled by a king and queen where they and all their subjects have been gobbled up by *rakshashi*. Only the princess had been spared but was kept under a spell. The story ends with the death of the *rakshashi*, the return of the prince and princess to the court of the foolish king, and the unmasking and killing of the *rakshashi* queen. In her death-throes, she vomits out the prince's friends and their horses.

The *rakshashis* in *Roop Taraashi* thus bear a resemblance to Lilith, a demoness who murders newborns in some iterations of her character in Jewish mythology and folklore, and Medea, who in Euripedes's eponymous Greek tragedy punishes Jason, her beloved, for his infidelity by murdering their sons, Tisander and Alcimenes (Gilbert and Gubar 39–42).

Like Medea, who is as an intelligent woman and an ethnic Other in Jason's Greece, these *rakshashis* suffer from the insecurity and guilt that springs from a desire to attain recognition and exercise power over a foreign dominion in which they have little agency. To wit, the *rakshashis* practice dark arts and entice foolish kings with their deceptively innocent beauty that masks sinister intentions. They murder anyone who stands between them and power, with stepsons in line for the throne a prime target. This pattern of weakness performed as maternal monstrosity directed particularly at children, as noted previously, is present in English fairy tales and folklore from around the world. However, few such discourses equal *Roop Taraashi* in the great emphasis it places on stepsons' and sons' murders by anthropophagistic queens and (step)mothers, although some mothers in classical Greek mythology murder their stepsons or sons with zeal. For instance, in Euripides's *The Bacchants*, Agave and other female devotees of Dionysus (Zeus's son and the god of wine, death, madness, and drama) attack and dismember her son, Pentheus, when they discover him spying on them (he opposed the cult of Dionysus). Another Greek mother who murders her son is Procne, the wife of King Tereus of Thrace. After Tereus rapes Procne's sister, she murders his son and serves the boy to his father for dinner. After the meal, Procne presents Tereus the child's head.

These representations of maternal ferocity in Greek myths, argues Philip Elliot Slater in his book *In the Glory of Hera: Greek Mythology and the Greek Family*, are propelled by Greek wives' subordination to their husbands: "Such vengeance is especially appropriate. . . . Since the direct expression of hostility to the husband would be inhibited by the wife's dependence on him . . . [and] her social inferiority" (28–29). Nancy J. Chodorow likewise argues that Greek mother-son relationships in the classical period, when marriages were fraught with sex antagonism and wives were isolated in their marital homes with children, were psychologically complex: "Mothers reproduced in their own sons the same masculine fears and behaviors that their husbands and the men in their society had. They produced in these sons a precarious and vulnerable masculinity and sense of differentiation by alternating sexual praise and seductive behavior with hostile deflation, ridicule, and intrusive definitions of their sons' intrapsychic situation" (105). Chodorow goes on to link literary representations of women as demons, vampires, and sorceresses directly to men's need to assert superiority during the process of their psychical and physical development. A boy fears his mother yet finds her seductive and attractive. However, he cannot escape his ambivalence toward the mother by simply dismissing or ignoring her. As a result, boys and men develop psychological and cultural/ideological mechanisms to cope with their fears without giving up women altogether. One is to create folk legends (and other discourses) that ward off their simultaneous dread of and attraction to the mother by externalizing and objectifying women: "It is not . . . that I dread her; it is that she herself is malignant, capable of any crime, a beast of prey, a vampire, a witch, insatiable in her desires . . . the very personification of what is sinister." Thus they banish their anxieties at the expense of acquiring realistic views of women. On one hand, they glorify and adore: "There is no need for me to dread a being so wonderful, so beautiful, nay, so saintly." But they also disparage: "It would be too ridiculous to dread a creature who, if you take her all round, is such a poor thing" (183). This analysis offers a useful frame for examining *Roop Taraashi* and, so doing, suggests that the extraordinary lengths that stepmothers in Dakshinaranjan's stories take in their conflicts with stepsons and sons enacts *masculinist* as well as maternal anxieties relating to the separation that occurs when boys differentiate from the mother by rejecting identification with her.

Burack alludes to the conjunction masculine and maternal apprehensions embedded in this developmental step: "Both in theory and in practice our culture knows only one form of individuality: the male stance of over differentiation, of splitting off and denying the tendencies toward sameness, merging, and reciprocal responsiveness. . . . To be a woman is to be excluded from this rational individualism, to be either an object of it or a threat to it" (83). It is no wonder then that *Roop Taraashi*'s *rakshashis* are thoroughly evil, rampaging boy-consuming cannibals. As Burack further explains, the masculine experience of psychological maturation vis-à-vis the mother, boys must reject the mother in order to assume an adult sense of masculinity: "Male development is structured through differentiation from mother, in fact, by rejection of identification with her. Instead, in spite of the emotional bond between them, boys 'dread' mother. Further, they strive to establish themselves as male by emulating abstract masculine role requirements rather than identifying affectively with fathers and other males, who are usually emotionally, if not physically absent" (72–73). For this rejection of the mother to happen, she must be transfigured into a monster. How better to do this than depict her as a threat to boys' and thus men's very existence?

The stories in *Roop Taraashi*, Bangla *roopkatha*, are a textualized, nineteenth-century mass-distributed representation of a vernacular culture in India that originally was performed and transmitted by women. Despite the fact that they were collected and published in an effort to reclaim and revive indigenous Bengali folklore to resist British colonialism, they share the trope of the wicked stepmother with English fairy tales though with some differences—the *rakshashi*'s female rival is a cowife, the *rakshashi* is a cannibal, and her victims are stepsons and sons rather than stepdaughters. Feminist psychoanalytic criticism of these tales exposes the traditional patriarchal values that were embedded in *thakumar* (grandmothers') versions of these stories and later reframed by their transfer into Bengal's nineteenth-century, nationalist milieu. Notably, *Roop Taraashi*'s representations of women exhibit extreme anxieties about the maternal, specifically, boys' simultaneous fear of and attraction to the mother as well as their need to destroy the mother in order to differentiate from her and successfully progress through the developmental stages leading to adulthood. The *rakshashis*, who embody these masculine anxieties as well as women's fears of losing all value due to primogeniture and polygamy, are demonized and ultimately silenced in *Roop Taraashi*'s tales, as are the women who initially narrated them when *Thakurmar Jhuli* was published in book form—when women were caught between nationalist factions' disputes about gender roles in the state-to-be. Consequently, the stories in *Roop Taraashi* remind us of us Spivak's question again and again: "With what voice consciousness can the subaltern speak?" (80). And as Spivak points out, the subaltern is not speaking from the Stone Age: the irony is that although the title of the book is *Grandmother's Tale*, the subaltern grandmother never speaks.

This silent grandmother thus symbolizes the Indian/Bengali women who are story tellers, healers, artists, and ascetics that the patriarchy will not be let heard. As Lee Haring says, "The challenge today is not to the subaltern to find a voice but for those in dominant positions to develop ears" (177). Writers such as Mahasweta Devi, author of "The Fairy Tale of Mohanpur," has executed feminist interventions in Indian *roopkatha* and undermined the simplistic identity politics of the subaltern woman by arguing that solid critique of nationalism, how male gendered nationalism can solve a young man's crisis and the realization that as time passes for a woman the ideology of love remains a memory but acknowledges defeat in the hands of hunger is an exquisite aporia. Likewise, Salman Rushdie, Arundhati Roy, and Chitra Banerjee Divakaruni have focused on the subjects of magic, fantasy, and negotiation of stereotyped gender and moral roles, as well as localized politics and globalized marketing. It's time to listen to what they say.

NOTES

1 The word *rakshas* might have indicated one of a non-Aryan anthropophagous race of India, appropriated and obliterated by the "fair-skinned" Aryans. The word came to mean "cannibal" or someone/something monstrous. *Rakshashi* is therefore a female monster who can devour anyone who crosses her path.

2 *Thakurmar Jhuli* has four parts. Book 1 is *The Ocean of Milk*, book 2 is called *Roop Taraashi* (Scary Beauty), book 3 is *The Nest of the Animals*, and book 4 is called *The Dessert*. In terms of theme and subject matter, *Thakurmar Jhuli*'s stories can be divided into four distinct categories: tales of adventure, tales of demons, animal tales, and humorous tales.

3 *Roopkatha* is also spelled *rupkatha* in English. Both words derive from Sanskrit.

4 Rabindranath Tagore (b. 1861–1941) is a major figure in Bengali intellectual and artistic production of the late nineteenth and early twentieth centuries. He was a poet but worked in diverse media—dance, drawing, painting, song, and music. He also employed different genres of prose, including essay, travel narrative, and autobiography. His work was innovative, particularly his use of the colloquial rather than classical Sanskrit, which transformed Bengali literature. Tagore was the first non-European to win the Nobel Prize in Literature.

5 Another important collection was published in 1899 by Jogindranath Sarkar. Dinesh Chandra Sen, a protégé of Tagore, is considered to be one of the foremost folklorists of Bengal. Sir Ashutosh Mukherji, the vice-chancellor of Calcutta University, appointed him a research fellow with funding to collect and document oral stories from the *Ramayana* in the 1910s and 1920s. Tagore's nephew, Abanindranath Tagore, and Aghorenath Chattopadhyay published collections of stories customarily narrated in domestic rituals—bedtime, for example—in 1897 and 1919, respectively. Dakshinaranjan Mitra Mazumdar's collection of folk tales was included in the anthropology syllabus of Calcutta University and was translated into German in 1919.

6 *Hau mau* may mean "commotion," but since there is no concrete etymological meaning, one can interpret *hau* as "a mouth wide open," *mau* as "mouth," *kau* as "to eat." Therefore, *hau mau kau* uttered by the *rakshashes* (demons) might convey something after all.

7 *Shuo* means "one who is fortunate" or "one dearly loved by her husband." *Duo* is the "unfortunate or wretched woman shunned by her husband."

8 Byangama and Byangami are common places in Indian folktales.

WORKS CITED

Bandopadhyay, Sreekumar. "Roopkatha" (Bangla Sahitya Parikrama). U of Calcutta, 2003.

Basu, Swapan, editor. *Unish Shatake Stree Shiksha*. Bangiya Sahitya Parishad, 2006.

Bhattacharya, Chandrima. "The Fairytale Femme Force." *The Telegraph—Calcutta, India*, 11 Dec. 2006, http://www.telegraphindia.com/1061211/asp/calcutta/story_7117602.asp.

Burack, Cynthia. *The Problem of the Passions: Feminism, Psychoanalysis and Social Theory*. New York UP, 1994.

Chodorow, Nancy J. *The Reproduction of Mothering*. U of California P, 1978.

Devi, Mahasweta. *Old Women Statue and the Fairy Tale of Mohanpur*. Seagull Books, 1999.

Gandhi, Leela. *Postcolonial Theory: A Critical Introduction*. Oxford UP, 1998.

Gilbert, Sandra M., and S. Gubar. *The Madwoman in the Attic*. Yale UP, 1979.

Haring, Lee. "Creolozation as Agency in Woman Centred Folktales." *Fairy Tales and Feminism: New Approaches*, edited by Donald Haase, Wayne State UP, 2004, pp. 169–78.

Mitra Majumder, Dakshinaranjan. *Thakurmar Jhuli*. Mitra O Ghosh, 1907.

Sellers, Susan. *Myth and Fairy Tale in Contemporary Women's Fiction*. Palgrave, 2001.

Sengupta, Jayita. *Refractions of Desire: Feminist Perspectives in the Novels of Toni Morrison, Michèle Roberts and Anita Desai*. Atlantic Publishers, 2006.

Slater, Philip Elliot. *The Glory of Hera: Greek Mythology and the Greek Family*. Princeton UP, 1992.

Spivak, Gayatri Chakravorty. "Can the Subaltern Speak?" *Can the Subaltern Speak?: Reflections on the History of an Idea*, edited by Rosalind C. Morris, Columbia UP, 2010, pp. 21–80.

Thorner, Alice, and Maithreyi Krishnaraj, editors. *Ideals, Images and Real Lives*. Orient Longman, 2000.

Walsh, Judith E. "As the Husband, so the Wife: Old Patriarchy, New Patriarchy and Misogyny in One Late Nineteenth-Century Domestic Science Manual." *The Indian Family in Transition*, edited by Sanjukta Dasgupta and Malashri Lal, Sage, 2007.

Zipes, Jack. *Fairy Tales and the Art of Subversion: The Classical Genre for Children and the Process of Civilization*. Routledge, 2012.

PART III POLITICAL ECONOMY AND QUESTIONING TRADITION IN THE FAR EAST

8 ◎ MORE THAN JUST AN EXCHANGE OF FLUIDS

Southeast Asian Prostitutes and the Western Sexual Economy

LOUIS BETTY

Louis Betty in this chapter offers a conservative alternative to feminist critiques of sex work that revises the stigmatization of female prostitutes in the Far East by examining representations of international sex tourism in Thailand in novelist Michel Houellebecq's novels. As a scholar specializing in French utopian thinkers such as Restif de la Bretonne, the Marquis de Sade, and Charles Fourier, Betty proposes a formulation of sex tourism as a type of erotic charity that provides sexual satisfaction to Westerners who are unable to compete—find unremunerated partners—in the Western sexual economy. For this reason and in order to resist "political correctness," Betty uses the terms *prostitute* and *prostitution* throughout the chapter rather than "sex worker" and "sex work." The author does not imply that prostitution is an unproblematic practice; rather, his argument shows that the so-called fallenness of Asian sex workers is produced by a struggle for sexual satisfaction, which he argues is in itself "fallen." This struggle, suggests Betty, is the result of the so-called sexual revolution in Western cultures, a shift in values that led to the proliferation of pornography and a dramatic increase in infidelity. Betty thus concludes that the Asian prostitute serves a constructive role, at least insofar as she highlights the inadequacies and injustices of the posttraditional sexual morality.

INTRODUCTION

I have always found somewhat curious the endlessly repeated claim that prostitution is the world's oldest profession. Whatever Kipling might have had in mind when he first made it—and likely the sentiment is as old as the profession itself—I suspect, or at least hope, that the beloved creator of Mowgli, Shere Khan, and Rikki-Tikki-Tavi was giving his readers what the French refer to as the second degree—an ironic commentary.[1] Among the most formative experiences of childhood and adolescence is the constant pressure to decide what one will be when one grows up. Children want variously to be doctors, lawyers, teachers, athletes, firemen, and police officers; in some rare and ethically dubious cases, they will even express a desire to become politicians. In no conceivable instance, however, will a child declare that he or she is considering *prostitution* as a viable career path. Prostitution is, rather (and to echo the language of this volume), a line of work that one simply *falls into*. Exceptions exist, of course—one could speculate that some female prostitutes operating in rarefied environments derive a feeling of seductive power from their work. But I imagine little argument would be made were I to suggest that the decision to sell one's body for sex is rarely accompanied by the same planning and general commitment to a goal that goes along with the choice of other professions.

Be that as it may, my aim in this chapter is not to debate definitions with Kipling and his appropriators. Rather, I want to question (or "problematize," to succumb to the jargon) the stigmatization of prostitution as a "fallen," and thus presumably sinful, enterprise. I also aim to imagine a way that the practice might be understood to play a constructive, though perhaps not desirable, role in the global sexual economy.[2] In the Western and specifically French tradition, a number of writers spanning the Enlightenment to the twenty-first century have imagined and in some cases even prescribed sexual economies in which a minimum of erotic gratification was guaranteed to all and free reign was granted to even the most idiosyncratic fantasies. French utopian thinkers as disparate in sensibility and moral compunction as Restif de la Bretonne, Charles Fourier, and the Marquis de Sade, for instance, have called for sexual regimes in which (respectively) marriage is compulsory for all young men and women, orgy serves as an antidote to middle-class erotic monotony, and the government is required to establish public brothels where both men and women may summon a person of their choosing to fulfill a sexual fantasy. Today such proposals constitute little more than curious remnants of somewhat perverse utopian zeal (especially in the case of de Sade), but the objective to which they aspire—the equitable sating of sexual desire and the limitless indulgence of erotic fantasy—is a thoroughly contemporary concern that finds, I would like to argue, one of its best expressions in sex tourism.

Accordingly, in this chapter, I will first explore prescriptions for sexual equality in the works of Restif de la Bretonne and Fourier, then test their affinities with Michel Houellebecq's 1994 debut novel *Whatever*, which, echoing the works of these utopian forebears, offers a critique of sexual economies that fail to guarantee *equality of erotic opportunity* to every member of society. From there, I will move on to an examination of de Sade's treatment of prostitution and pederasty and their bearing on sexual fantasy, then, returning to Houellebecq, suggest a link between de Sade's thought and Houellebecq's treatment of sexual frustration in his 2001 novel *Platform*, which imagines an attempt on the part of three French citizens to create a sex resort in Thailand for erotically disenchanted Westerners. Crucially, I will argue that sex tourism's appeal to the West can be understood as a commentary on the "fallenness" of the Western sexual economy, where a regime of pervasive erotic liberalism compels every man and woman to "compete" for sexual gratification and where excessive individualism and consumerist-driven narcissism forbid the sentimental and physical abandon necessary, as Houellebecq suggests in *Platform*, for true erotic fulfillment. In this economy, the sex worker, I argue, plays a potentially redemptive role by providing erotic pleasure to Westerners who would not be able to find it, or at least not find it to their satisfaction, in their home countries. I will not, of course, be making any empirical claims about the nature of sexual labor, nor will I champion it; rather, my intention is simply to imagine ways that the practice of prostitution, especially in the context of sex tourism in Asia, might be destigmatized as a "fallen" profession and understood to serve a constructive function in Western culture's sexual economy.

Before moving on, I should point out that the term "fallen" strikes me as a somewhat problematic choice of words for this analysis, since its religious and particularly Christian connotation suggests that the moral questions surrounding prostitution should be adjudicated in theological terms. At least in scholarly and progressive discourses of the contemporary, secular West, questions of right and wrong have for some time ceased to be reckoned as matters of sin. Instead, for political moderates, progressives, and intellectual elites, sinfulness has largely ceded to competing discourses of political incorrectness and insensitivity, with the moral reprobate no longer identified as the adulterer, the thief, or the murderer, but as the racist, the sexist, and the homophobe. If the female prostitute is "fallen," this is not because she is sexually impure, sinfully promiscuous, or otherwise displeasing to the Almighty but because she is caught up in a regime of economic and sexual exploitation that impedes her erotic agency.[3] The fallenness of the prostitute is, in other words, passive rather than active, and her flight from moral dissoluteness will involve the *recuperation of her agency* rather than her obedience to the Christological injunction that she should "go and sin no more" (King James Version, John 8:11).

SEXUAL EQUALITY

That an interest in erotic equality and sexual utopia finds particularly acute expression in the French tradition should surprise no one. France is in many respects the principal incubator of anxieties about modernity and freedom, whether the latter is construed in economic, moral, or epistemological terms. Maximillian Robespierre, for example, the greatest of all revolutionaries, was famously aware of the dangers that too swift a flight from tradition might pose to the nascent Republic. The corrupt clergy of the Old Regime may have been guilty of supporting a repressive nobility that left its subjects to starve; even so, it was of vital importance that civilization not be deprived of its metaphysical consolations, a consideration that led Robespierre to declare in 1794 that the French believed in a Supreme Being and the immortality of the soul (329). This schizophrenia about liberation—the simultaneous rapture and anguish of freedom—is distributed throughout the post-Enlightenment French literary and philosophical canon. Certain authors (i.e., Sartre) tremble at the moral implications of total existential liberty, and others (we might think of poet Paul Éluard) celebrate freedom in unproblematic, categorical terms.[4] In the domain of the erotic, utopian theorists such as Charles Fourier and Restif de la Bretonne concerned themselves with guaranteeing (or, more precisely, with devising utopian scenarios that would attempt to guarantee) a minimum of erotic satiety to those in society to whom it would have been forbidden in a laissez-faire sexual economy—that is, to those unfortunate few (or not so few) who would be unable, for reasons of either nature or custom, to "compete" successfully among their peers for sexual satisfaction. Below, I will examine the chief contentions of both de la Bretonne and Fourier regarding sexual equality with an eye to drawing them into a contemporary discussion about the often dark underbelly of the modern West's discourse of sexual freedom.

Restif de la Bretonne

A contemporary of Rousseau, Nicolas-Edme Restif de la Bretonne was widely known in late-eighteenth-century France for sexually explicit novels that earned him the sobriquet "The Rousseau of the Gutters." Something of a debauchee and self-loather, Restif authored a series of utopian tomes spanning several decades that were, according to Frank and Fritzie Manuel, embellished with a "nightmare of Deuteronomic prescriptions" for social order (553).[5] In his 1782 work *L'Andrographe*, Restif calls for obligatory monogamous marriage for "all young people of both sexes," arguing that "matrimony [was] the state for which Nature, religion, and the social laws intended them" (qtd. in Manuel and Manuel 175). He also advocates for the selection of a marriage partner based on a strict system of moral merit and physical beauty, and couples were to be matched during marriage festivals occurring four times a year. Girls refusing the boy to whom they had been assigned either had to show cause for their refusal or would be punished by marriage to a member of the class "last in merit and good looks" (qtd. in Manuel and Manuel 176). Somewhat curiously, Restif orders that couples be separated and made to live with their respective parents until age thirty-five. The ruse that husband and wife would have to undertake to see each other would, Restif predicts, maintain a level of erotic interest that would reduce rates of adultery.

Restif was aware that not every boy and girl would be a desirable candidate; indeed, some members of the community, due to either ugliness, deformity, or ill character, would be thoroughly undesirable, if not repulsive to their peers. In the case of anyone with a "bodily defect" who was excluded from the "legitimate classes" (176), Restif sets out procedures for guaranteeing a marriage partner: "Every boy who has some bodily defect will be excluded from the legitimate classes, and different classes of cripples will be constituted, in accordance with their degree of infirmity. . . . Selection among the malformed will have as many divisions as among the robust. Priority will be given to those uniting the least deformity with the greatest merit; the rest will be ranked in accordance with the merit which offsets their deformities, until that subject is reached who has the least merit and the greatest deformity" (177). One necessarily encounters some difficulty in determining whether Restif is in earnest when making these rigid prescriptions for sexual equality. The language of deformity, as well as the peremptory tone in which it is conveyed, is both darkly funny and slightly horrific; unless he was an utter prude, Restif no doubt took some delight in such rhetorical obnoxiousness. Even so, Restif was clearly aware of the existence of an economy of competition in sexual relations. Without his system of matchmaking, some boys and girls would enjoy broad erotic "success" thanks to their physical and moral worth, while others, curtailed by a less prepossessing or altogether repellent nature, would be erotic losers left on the sidelines to observe the frolicking of their more fortunate peers. Restif's concerns were, in other words, thoroughly if not incipiently modern—the rearrangement of social relations already well under way at the end of the eighteenth century would create separate classes of erotic haves and have-nots, and no less than an unbending system of "Deuteronomic prescriptions" for sexual equality would be necessary to guarantee everyone a minimum of sexual satisfaction.

Charles Fourier

Charles Fourier has the reputation of being the nineteenth century's most idiosyncratic social reformer. As appalled by the injustices of capitalism as he was by the monotony and oppressiveness of bourgeois marriage, Fourier imagined an ideal community, which he named Harmony, where orgies, partner swapping, and various forms of erotic charity would constitute a new sexual regime far removed from the evils of monogamous domesticity. On the subject of marriage, Fourier spares no flourish in communicating his horror of the institution: "For one who attains happiness through a rich marriage, how many others find the torment of their lives! The unhappy are able to recognize that the enslavement of women is hardly to man's advantage. What dupes men are that they have compelled themselves to wear a dreadful chain; what punishment they endure for having reduced women to bondage" (204).

Furthermore, the expectation of monogamous marriage was so fraught with hypocrisy that one did not have to look far to uncover its contradictions. The "prudish world" of fidelity, writes Fourier, ironically referring to it as "high society," was no more than a "heap of libertines and intriguers" who "disguised themselves behind a verbiage of fidelity" (221). In reality, such a world was "bigamous, trigamous, and polygamous" (221) in every way, and reason declared that accommodation be made for humanity's insuperable desire to flee fidelity for the pleasures of erotic variety.

Despite the regime of orgy and libertinage that was to govern erotic interactions within the Phalanstery,[6] Fourier knew that not everyone in Harmony would enjoy equal access to sexual satisfaction. The old, the sick, the deformed, and all those otherwise disgraced by nature rather than inhibited by custom would be excluded from sexual encounters; thus, Fourier's system called for the establishment of an "erotic nobility"—sexual philanthropists—who would ensure that physically repulsive inhabitants were not excluded from attaining erotic pleasure. Fourier scholar Jonathan Beecher explains,

> Fourier's solicitude for the elderly, the poor, the perverts, for all those to whom civilization denied sexual gratification, led him to create a variety of corps and institutions specializing in sexual philanthropy. . . . The members of these groups naturally had passionate inclinations for the tasks they performed. But Fourier recognized that just as there were some forms of truly loathsome work, so too there were forms of sexual philanthropy that had little intrinsic appeal. If there had to be Little Hordes to do the dirty work in the Phalanx, there also had to be an amorous nobility in each Phalanx whose main responsibility would be the providing of sexual gratification to all those whom age or physical deformity would have condemned to loneliness in civilization. (309)

As Fourier writes, "In Harmony no one is poor and all may be admitted to love's favours until a very advanced age" (my translation; 236). Much like Restif's system of obligatory marriage, Fourier's prescriptions for erotic charity and, in particular his call for the establishment of an amorous nobility, bespoke his recognition of a competitive sexual economy flush with various classes of winners and losers who ranged from those most commended by natural endowment to those most condemned by it. Just as Fourier intended economic life within the Phalanstery to furnish a countermeasure to the inequalities inherent in the capitalist system, so, too, the erotic elite within the commune were to provide an antidote to the often gross disparities in sexual satisfaction that resulted from natural inequality.

Michel Houellebecq: *Whatever*

Houellebecq's critique of the Western sexual economy makes a rather blunt appearance in his 1994 debut novel *Whatever*, which tells the story of an anonymous computer programmer struggling with loneliness and depression after the failure of a relationship. During a trip to the French provinces to teach a computer software program to employees of the French Ministry of Agriculture, the narrator muses about the erotic futility of his work partner, Raphael Tisserand, a remarkably ugly twenty-eight-year-old virgin with "the exact appearance of a buffalo toad" (54). Sexuality, the nameless narrator tells us, represents a "second system of differentiation" (99). Just as men and women may be distinguished in terms of wealth and material prosperity, they may also be distinguished in terms of sexual satisfaction: "Just like unrestrained economic liberalism, and for similar reasons, sexual liberalism produces phenomena of *absolute pauperization*. Some men make love every day; others five or six times in their life, or never. Some make love with dozens of women; others with none. It's what's known as the 'law of the market'" (99).

Moderation of the prohibition on adultery and the marriage obligation in the West since the mid-twentieth century is thus an "extension of the domain of the struggle" for wealth in a world where it and sex are now subject to market forces.[7] Those who possess significant erotic capital—the young, the beautiful, the strong—will accumulate a considerable sexual fortune; those with marginal capital—the old, the ugly, the weak—will enjoy little or none. Both Tisserand and the narrator have had relative success in the economic sphere; they are gainfully employed and enjoy a "tidy purchasing power" (13). But in the sexual sphere, they are radical losers. Tisserand's improbable ugliness denies him the slightest interest from women while the narrator's cynicism, fueled by deep bitterness following a failed relationship, results in an affective paralysis that impedes any effort to remedy his sexual misery.

While Fourier's and Restif's directives for sexual equality may seem like peculiar relics of an all-but-forgotten age of utopian fancy, Houellebecq, on the other hand, might reasonably be accused of making much out of what is, after all, very little. Certainly sexual injustice—if such a thing even exists—is not on par with economic or social injustice, and one imagines that Tisserand, despite his repulsiveness, would be well served by directing his energies toward finding someone of similar caliber as himself (or equal in degree of deformity, as Restif would have put it) rather than chasing after adolescents in nightclubs (111–16). One could also make the further, broadly Platonic objection that such preoccupation with sexual satisfaction constitutes a somewhat craven capitulation to the tyranny of the body and that all this worry over the equitable provision of erotic fulfillment is really only so much moral weakness, if not perversity. Be that as it may, we should be careful not to dismiss these utopian critiques of sexual economy simply on the grounds that they give rise to unfeasible and at times rather ridiculous solutions to erotic malaise. The problem of sexual inequality, though largely ignored in popular discourse, often comes to the fore in horrific fashion, as in 2014 when a male university student, ostensibly dejected by a lack of attention from women, murdered six people in a mass shooting in Santa Barbara (Dewey). In the case of sex tourism, then, we may theorize that, far from being limited to an erotic condiment for men and women in search of novel carnal adventures, the practice is also the result of *sexual insolvency* at home—that is, of a kind of erotic poverty that the Western sexual economy, which guarantees its actors no minimum of sexual gratification, inexorably produces.

PROSTITUTION, FRUSTRATION, AND FANTASY

If prostitution offers a last recourse to those like Tisserand who have been disgraced by nature, it is also an institution uniquely suited to the fulfillment of erotic fantasy. The modern proliferation of pornographic websites, sex shops, swingers' clubs, and escort services all bespeak the potential for sexual tedium that may afflict the Western man or woman. Affairs, infidelities, and other polyamorous excursions indicate the degree to which the erotic can too easily become another form of monotony, while criminalized forms of desire such as pederasty confront us with the dark biological underbelly of sensual yearning. To this point, I have only addressed the problems of the Western sexual economy in terms of *quantity*; that is, I have been largely concerned, as in the case of Tisserand, with erotic haves and have-nots. In this section, however, I will examine sexual economy in terms of *quality*, paying particular attention to the Marquis de Sade's writings on erotic servitude and Houellebecq's novel, *Platform*, which imagines the creation of a sex resort in Thailand. As I hope to show, the critique of sexual economy from the point of view of quality creates room for entertaining a constructive role for prostitution in the context of sex tourism even as it places a check on the *hubris* of sexual openness and moral tolerance in general.

The Marquis de Sade

Perhaps no thinker in the modern tradition went to greater lengths to imagine the sating of every form of erotic desire than the Marquis de Sade. To a great degree, the Marquis appears to be mocking Rousseau, who adamantly believed in the inherent goodness of the state of nature. If man in his natural state was morally immaculate, de Sade suggests, then surely such natural predilections as rape, incest, and murder were beyond censure. He writes, "It is beyond question that we have the right to establish laws which will force woman to yield to the ardours of him who desires her; violence itself being one of the results of this right, we can legally employ it. Has not Nature proved to us that we have this right, by allotting us the strength necessary to force them to our desires?" (qtd. in Manuel and Manuel 228). Beyond this evident lampooning of Rousseau, however, the Marquis was particularly bent on making sure that every form of sexual desire should have its day, even if, according to conventional norms, it seemed wholly aberrant. Men were to have the right to summon a "woman or girl" of their choosing to a designated "temple of Venus," where in "complete meekness and submission" she would be obligated to "satisfy all the caprices he wishes to indulge with her" (qtd. in Manuel and Manuel 228–29).[8] In fact, within these "health establishments," "all sexes, all ages, all creatures possible" were to be "offered to the caprices of the libertines who wish pleasure" (qtd. in Manuel and Manuel 226); in other words, both pederasty and, it would seem, bestiality were to be acceptable practices in de Sade's brothels.

It would, of course, be something of a stretch to impute to the Sadean sexual project the sort of philanthropic concerns that we find, for example, in Fourier. De Sade was admittedly hostile to any form of exclusive love, referring to such sentimentality as a "madness of the soul" resulting in "egotistical and privileged enjoyment" for some but not for others (qtd. in Manuel and Manuel 228). Nevertheless, the Marquis's decree that men be able to punish "immediately and arbitrarily" whatever woman might refuse their demands, however perverse, is a far cry from the erotic nobility of the Phalanx, and certainly his apology for pederasty moves from the realm of the naïvely utopian to the squarely criminal. De Sade's interest lies rather in identifying an *economy of quality* (rather than equality) in sexual relations in which true fulfillment of fantasy and desire requires much more than the inevitably tedious arrangements of monogamous domesticity. Civilization denies, and in many cases even criminalizes, the satisfaction of certain sexual fantasies; thus we can expect the emergence of various erotic marketplaces, either officially sanctioned (as the Marquis wished) or legally forbidden, suited to meet demand. Such, at least in bare form, is the thesis we find in Houellebecq's *Platform*, which I examine in the following section.

Houellebecq: *Platform*

The sexual have-nots of Michel Houellebecq's third novel are neither frog-faced, twenty-eight-year-old virgins like Tisserand nor sentimental rejects such as *Whatever*'s sullen narrator. Rather, *Platform* assumes that sex is abundantly available to whoever wants it; the only problem is that the erotic products available in the contemporary West turn out not to be particularly satisfying. The novel places the blame for such "bad sex" on the culture of rampant individualism that grew up in the wake of the 1960s cultural revolution—a revolution that, as several French intellectuals have argued, set the stage for the victory of consumerist-driven narcissism in the 1980s and beyond.[9] The novel's narrator, aptly named Michel,[10] states apropos of contemporary sexuality,

> Offering your body as an object of pleasure, giving pleasure unselfishly: that's what Westerners don't know how to do anymore. They've completely lost the sense of giving. Try as they might they no longer feel sex as something *natural*. Not only are they ashamed of their own bodies, which aren't up to porn standards, but for the same reason they no longer feel truly attracted to the body of the other. It's impossible to make love without a certain abandon, without accepting, at least temporarily, the state of being in a state of dependency, of weakness. . . . We have become cold, acutely conscious of our individual existence and of our rights; more than anything, we want to avoid alienation and dependence. . . . These are hardly ideal conditions in which to make love. (174–75)

Sexuality in the West has, in other words, been spoiled by egotism; thus the sort of intimacy, both physical and emotional, necessary for sexual satisfaction has become not only progressively impossible but also largely undesirable. Constantly subjected to idealized images of physical beauty and sensual fulfillment, but paradoxically goaded on by the ethos of individualism toward ever-increasing degrees of independence and self-determination, the Westerner is inevitably alienated from his or her sexuality—it becomes both a source of bodily shame and psychic paranoia, at once threatening his or her physical confidence and emotional independence. Narcissism drives us to want more to be desired than to be pleasured, more to be looked at than loved, and what pleasure we do experience is always laced with the anxiety of dependency. What is the result of this sorry state of affairs? As Michel tells us, "You have several hundred million Westerners who have everything they want but no longer manage to obtain sexual satisfaction. They spend their lives looking for it without finding it, and they are completely miserable" (173).

And what is *Platform*'s solution to this entrenched erotic malaise? Sex tourism—but of course! Certainly, the novel suggests, the sexuality of the non-Western world has not been corrupted by the excesses of individualism. On this point, Michel remarks, "You have several billion people who have nothing, who are starving, who die young, who live in conditions unfit for human habitation, and who have nothing left to sell except their bodies and their unspoiled sexuality. It's simple, really simple to understand: it's an ideal trading opportunity" (173).

Thus far from being a fallen enterprise, prostitution accomplishes two salutary goals; first, it grows the coffers of the developing world; and second, it relieves the West's erotic disaffection by providing a sensual outlet free from physical shame. The prostitutes of Thailand, for instance, are presumably unconcerned about whether their bodies conform to the Western ideal of beauty or are up to "porn standards," and neither are they burdened by the fear of sentimental dependency that stands in the way of erotic fulfillment. Following this unassailable logic, *Platform*'s three protagonists, Michel, Valérie, and Jean-Yves, open a sex resort in Thailand where "the people get to fuck" (171). Unfortunately, the club's opening ceremonies are interrupted by a murderous terrorist assault by Malay Muslims who look unfavorably on the operation of a tourist brothel on the other side of their border. Significantly, the media christen surviving tourists who return to France "Not So Innocent Victims" (244). The novel, having introduced a clever if not curious suggestion of moral ambiguity into the question of prostitution, leaves us to wonder whether this is truly the case.

Sex tourism is thus capable of not only solving the quantitative erotic dilemma of those so lacking in attractiveness that they are left out of the sexual marketplace; it also promises to resolve the qualitative problem of making sex not simply available but also *good*. The issue is, granted, somewhat delicate. Few people will want to admit to *not getting any*, and just as many will likely deny that their sex lives are unsatisfying. Such things are, in other words, taboo. But does not this taboo explain in the most patent way the stifling anathema that has always surrounded the question of prostitution? That if the practice is "fallen," this is because, rather scandalously, it proves that things in the domain of sexuality are *not as good* as we would like to imagine? Perhaps the most potent myth of Western modernity is that with ever increasing degrees of liberation—from economic subjugation, from family life, from religious truth—comes a corresponding increase in human happiness. To doubt this is to doubt progress, to become antimodern, even premodern. But can we truly say with unabashed confidence that liberation is so unequivocally positive? Is there no room for suspicion, for teasing out the ambiguities of freedom? Unwillingness to engage in such soul searching may go a long way toward explaining the stigma surrounding sex tourism that we find, for example, in Houellebecq's *Platform*: that, in our rapacity for ever more liberation, sexual and otherwise, a great many people have been *left in the lurch*, with sex tourism naturally stepping in as an alternative market for erotic fulfillment. If the prostitute is fallen, this can only be the result of disingenuous sublimation, for the truly fallen party is Western sexuality, which excels in producing more desires than it is capable of satisfying. Vilification of the prostitute is thus hypocrisy. To admit her constructive role in the Western sexual economy shines an uncomfortable light on the shortcomings of our ever more liberated—and presumably happier—society.

CONCLUSION: WHOM ARE YOU CALLING FALLEN?

As I indicated in my introduction, the use of the term "fallen" to describe the work of prostitution (as well as "transgressive" female behavior in general, be it erotic or otherwise) is already fraught with problematic assumptions about the bases of moral judgment. Fallenness, after all, carries with it a clear theological connotation. In its most basic sense, it is a synonym for sin, inherited from an ancient system of religious ethics that must do constant battle with secular legal norms. Despite dogged opposition in many quarters of Western society, sexual freedom of all sorts is now legally sanctioned, homosexual marriage has become the law of the land in the United States, and birth control, abortion, and other forms of contraception enjoy juridical protection. These developments may be provisional, but in an ethical and legal dispensation where the sole notion of "sin" is no longer a sufficient means of adjudicating the moral, a purely *secular* legal argument for criminalizing prostitution will be increasingly difficult to elaborate. The prohibition against prostitution may indeed be one of the final legal anachronisms held over in the West from its presecular past. Assuming the continued ascendency of secular values in the adjudication of moral behavior, little justification will soon remain for proclaiming "fallen" or criminal the work of prostitutes who choose actively to engage in this "profession."

This is, of course, only half the story. Many prostitutes—and this is especially true of sex tourism—are forced into their "trade" through either enslavement or economic conditions that threaten their survival. In these cases, the designation of "fallenness" is much more apposite, though it is more appropriately applied to *consumers* of sex tourism than to the prostitutes who serve them. In secular and academic terms, prostitutes who have been compelled to take up such work are no longer sinners but victims: the moral onus thus shifts to consumers and facilitators—pimps, slavers, and tourists, essentially—who perpetuate the system of exploitation. Here we have a clear demonstration of the growing shift in moral judgment, at least in progressive circles, from traditionally religious to secular juridical norms: the sinner has now become the victim; she has fallen not into sin but into oppression. The escape from fallenness, then, depends not on repentance but on the *recuperation of agency*; that is, on the prostitute's playing an active, willful, and self-determined role within the erotic market. Prostitution may never be liberated from the more basic degradation inherent in giving one's body to a person one does not desire, but it can at least be freed from the fetters of sin and crime and reimagined to play a constructive role—if only discursively—in a globalized sexual economy.

NOTES

1 Kipling calls prostitution the "most ancient profession in the world" in his 1888 work "On the City Wall."

2 My argument here is akin to that made in *Sex Tourism: Marginal People and Liminalities* by Ryan and Hall, who write that one purpose of their volume is to "remove some of the marginality from the lives of [sex workers], and yet in cases where women are degraded and exploited, to argue that the marginalities are not those inherent in the status of 'sex worker' but arise from an abuse of economic and cultural power" (xv).

3 See Derks (2004) for a discussion of this shift in terminology in the context of the Cambodian sex trade. The issue of a general cultural transition in the West from a religious to a secular moral regime

calls, naturally, for further analysis (indeed it would be better to speak of competing moral regimes, one traditional, and one postreligious). However, the evolution of terminology describing the trading of money for sexual pleasure from prostitution to "sex work" indicates a secularization of moral notions at least in the minds of scholars who address themselves to the issue of sexual labor.

4 Paul Éluard is best known for his poem in praise of freedom, "Liberté," in which he repeats the sentence *J'écris ton nom* (I write your name).

5 The book of Deuteronomy is the fifth book in the Hebrew Scriptures. In it, Moses delivers three sermons to the Israelites before they enter the "Promised Land," part of present-day Israel, after their exodus from Egypt. Current scholarship suggests that the sermons collate traditions that emerged over time rather than the work of a single author. Much of Deuteronomy codifies religious and juridical practices and criminal and civil law and is often perceived as overly strict and authoritarian.

6 Fourier coined the term *phalanstery*, which now has two meanings: it refers to a community based on Fourier's principles and a self-contained residence—a building—whose architecture is designed to promote the type of communal living Fourier proposed and a community based on Fourier's principles.

7 The French title of Houellebecq's novel is *Extension du domaine de la lutte* (Extension of the domain of the struggle).

8 Venus is the goddess of love, beauty, sex, fertility, prosperity, victory, and desire in Roman mythology.

9 See, for instance, Lipovetsky, *L'Ère du vide* (1983); and *Public Enemies: Dueling Writers Take On Each Other and the World* (2011) by Houellebecq and Bernard-Henri Lévy.

10 Houellebecq has on numerous occasions echoed much of his novels' polemical material in his public comments; thus it is no coincidence that several of his protagonists have taken his first name.

WORKS CITED

Beecher, Jonathan. *Charles Fourier: A Visionary and His World.* U of California P, 1990.

Derks, Annuska. "The Broken Women of Cambodia." *Sexual Cultures in East Asia: The Social Construction of Sexuality and Sexual Risk in a Time of AIDS*, edited by Evelyne Micollier, Routledge Curzon, 2004.

Dewey, Caitlin. "Inside the 'Manosphere' that Inspired Santa Barbara Shooter Elliot Rodger." *Washington Post*, 27 May 2014, http://www.washingtonpost.com/news/the-intersect/wp/2014/05/27/inside-the-manosphere-that-inspired-santa-barbara-shooter-elliot-rodger/.

Fourier, Charles. *Harmonian Man: Selected Writings of Charles Fourier*. Edited by Mark Poster, Anchor, 1971.

———. *La Théorie des quatre mouvements.* J.-J. Pauvert, 1967.

Holy Bible. King James Version. World Bible, 2001.

Houellebecq, Michel. *Platform.* 2001. Vintage International, 2002.

———. *Whatever.* 1994. Serpent's Tail, 2011.

Lévy, Bernard-Henri, and Michel Houellebecq. *Public Enemies: Dueling Writers Take On Each Other and the World.* Random House, 2011.

Lipovetsky, Gilles. *L'Ère du vide.* Flammarion, 1983.

Manuel, Frank E., and Fritzie P. Manuel. *French Utopias: An Anthology of Ideal Societies.* Free Press, 1966.

———. *Utopian Thought in the Western World.* Belknap, 1979.

Robespierre, Maximilien. "Sur les rapports des idées religieuses et morales avec les principes républicains et sur les fêtes nationales. Rapport présenté au nom du Comité de Salut Public (18 floréal an II/7 mai 1794)." *Robespierre: Écrits*, edited by Claude Mazauric, Messidor/Éditions Sociales, 1989, pp. 308–36.

Ryan, Chris, and C. Michael Hall. *Sex Tourism: Marginal People and Liminalities.* Routledge, 2001.

9 REPRESENTING BAD WOMEN IN *WU ZETIAN SI DA QI'AN*

Political Criticism in Late Qing Crime Fiction

LAVINIA BENEDETTI

Lavinia Benedetti considers gong'an xiaoshuo (公案小说; *gong'an* for "court case" and *xiaoshuo* for "fiction"), a popular Chinese genre that consists of detective stories about criminal court cases. She analyzes the novel Wu Zetian si da qi'an (1890) which celebrates the exploits of Di Renjie, a detective who investigates murder and corruption during the Tang Dynasty (618–907 CE). Benedetti traces the texts' misogynous representations of female characters and their crimes and how these representations influence society.

A BRIEF INTRODUCTION TO THE TRADITION OF CHINESE CRIME NARRATIVE

The court case is a narrative genre that in China boasts a very long tradition. Stories of criminal cases brought to trial, of murder, theft, deception, or disputes, and tales of honest and upright judges performing a variety of legal duties or of corrupt judges who abuse their power emerged as early as the sixth century. A diverse genre that includes oral stories, ballads, dramatic performances, short stories, novellas, and chaptered novels, court-case narratives were composed in the vernacular. This kind of traditional Chinese detective narrative is called *gong'an xiaoshuo* (公案小说; *gong'an* for "court case" and *xiaoshuo* for "fiction"). The magistrate is usually the protagonist (Liu 1), and representing the emperor on an in loco basis, he investigates cases and issues judgments. The stories accurately depict the administration of justice, which was one of the most important duties of a county official in China.

Scholars offer different views on the development of *gong'an xiaoshuo* as a genre. A predecessor may be found in the ancient tradition of Chinese myths and legends, as well as in Chinese classical prose, which contained some short court-case stories that can be considered prototypes of *gong'an xiaoshuo*. Novellas composed in Classic Chinese of the Six Dynasties Period (220–589 CE) and the Tang Dynasty (618–907 CE) included stories of criminal cases, although most scholars believe that these works are not representative of the genre's evolution (Huang 3), and the Song Dynasty (960–1279) gets more credit for contributing to the development of *gong'an xiaoshuo*. During this era, an extraordinary expansion of crafts, industry, and trade favored the development of big cities and the emergence of a new urban elite. In these more cosmopolitan areas, *chantefables*, or *shuohua* (说话; raconteurs), sang and recited court-case narratives in what might be called "entertainment quarters." These performances satisfied a broader and growing audience, and the tales' themes varied to suit its tastes (Miao 39–40).

The Song Dynasty also saw the textualization of oral court-case narratives with the emergence of *huaben* 话本, stories written in the vernacular. This shift infused court-case narratives of this period with colloquialisms, and the stories describe the most quotidian aspects of urban life. The inclusion of seventeen court-case stories in Luo Ye's (罗烨) *Commentary Notes of an Old Drunk* (*Zuiweng tanlu*; 醉翁谈录), the most comprehensive collection of plays and *huaben* of that period, indicates that they were popular (Miao 27–39). *Gong'an* narrative further developed during the Yuan Dynasty (1271–1368). In this period, the dramatic genre known as *zaju* (杂剧; a miscellanea of forms that involve recitation, dance, and song) flourished, and some *huaben* stories featuring crimes were adapted to the stage (the so-called *gong'an ju*; 公案剧).[1] This is when the figure of the "pure official," Bao gong (Lord Bao or Judge Bao),[2] emerged. Bao gong was based on the historical Song Dynasty official, named Bao Zheng (包拯; b. 999–1062), and thanks to literary representations of him in this period, he became one of the stock characters of the next generation of crime literature: the "pure official" (*qingguan*; 清官) who solves any kind of criminal case.

In the Ming period (1368–1644), the court-case novella developed again, particularly during the reign of the Wanli Emperor (1572–1619),[3] when economic expansion and advances in papermaking technology led to an increase in printers in cities. Higher living standards, especially in the South, also contributed to a rise in demand for literature in the vernacular, prompting publishers to collect and reprint hundreds of texts. Several anthologies entirely dedicated to short court-case stories (*duanpian gong'an xiaoshuo ji*; 短篇公案小说集) were published during this period.[4] Because these texts were based on preexisting narratives, it was common to find the same stories in different anthologies, sometimes differing only with regard to elements such as setting and characters' names. One of the first collections was *Baijia gong'an* (百家公案; 1594), which included one hundred crime stories featuring Bao gong as the protagonist.[5]

The success of vernacular literature, including court-case stories, during the Ming Dynasty can also be ascribed to the *literati*. They collected an immense number of *huaben* from preceding epochs into anthologies and began to write imitations (*nihuaben*; 拟话本—namely, pseudo-*huaben*) to attract a larger readership. These *literati* include Feng Menglong 冯梦龙 (b. 1574–1646), whose trilogy of collected short stories, known as the *Three Words* (*Sanyan*; 三言),[6] contained old and original stories, and Ling Mengchu (凌濛初; b. 1580–1644), who compiled two compendia, known collectively as the *Two Slaps* (*Erpai*; 二拍).[7] Both authors included short *gong'an* stories in their collections although they did not classify them as such. According to scholars, among the one hundred twenty stories in "Three Words," eighteen were original *gong'an* stories, while the *Two Slaps* contains twenty-five (Huaiming 76).

With the transition to the Qing Dynasty (1644–1911), the first Manchu sovereigns consolidated power by imposing heavy-handed ideological control over literature and instituting a repressive cultural policy, especially with regard to vernacular narrative. As a consequence, vernacular narrative lost its characteristic lively expression, and *literati* began to use the vernacular as an instrument reinforcing the importance of traditional values.[8] The *gong'an* stories written during this period often condemn behaviors contrary to traditional ethical principles, lavishing on the reader all kinds of advice and admonitions (Benedetti 17–37).

In the mid and late Qing period, the development of the oral literature market, especially in Beijing and northern areas, fostered a renaissance in court-case literature. New genres of *gong'an xiaoshuo* arose from oral performances and surfaced sometime later in the publishing landscape, including adventure-detection novels (*gong'an xiayi xiaoshuo*; 公案侠义小说),[9] a kind of fusion of the court-case stories written during the Ming, such as those included in the aforementioned *Baijia gong'an*, and the adventure novel (*xiayi xiaoshuo*; 侠义小说),[10] another type of novel popular in that period. The introduction of Western innovations in publishing technology that helped knock down prices and improved the printing press's efficiency also boosted the desire for fiction; hence, *Gong'an xiayi xiaoshu*o circulated widely during the last decades of nineteenth century.[11]

The new adventure-detection novels were very long chaptered novels in which the protagonist, the "pure official," investigates and solves a number of intricate criminal cases. Unlike the stories written during the Ming period, the pure official does not investigate criminal cases alone but is helped by several *xiake* (侠客; knights-errant),[12] stock characters borrowed from adventure novels. In adventure and detection novels, however, the character of the *xiake* plays a different role. In adventure novels, the knight-errant is a type of "honorable" outlaw who helps people fight officials' and aristocrats' abuse of power. In the new novels, they are instead granted pardon by the pure official and serve the government by fighting crimes. The adventure-detection novels were also very different from earlier court-case stories, especially those written during the last years of the Qing Dynasty (the late nineteenth and early twentieth centuries) because they imbibe the shared aesthetic, thinking, and "spirit" of a period in which China faced enormous problems.[13] After nearly a century of wars, revolts, and invasions by foreign armies, the country was debilitated politically and economically and corruption permeated the central government. As Lu Xun (b. 1881–1936), one of the most important writers and literary critics of modern China, once observed, at the turn of the twentieth century, the Chinese were disappointed with their governance, thus "the trend in fiction was to expose social abuses and lash out at contemporary politics, sometimes at social conventions as well" (Lu 352). Crime narrative was no exception. While adventure-detection novels of the previous periods celebrated important officials and the outlaws who served them, this submissive, passive attitude was ill-suited to the needs of a population that desired change. Consequently, late Qing adventure-detection novels, such as *Wu Zetian si da qi'an*, while still centered on an idealized government official and celebrating the existing regime, became one of the most effective venues for criticizing the imperial government and other rulers of the time.

WU ZETIAN SI DA QI'AN: A LATE QING DYNASTY NOVEL OF ADVENTURE AND CRIME DETECTION

In 1890, the Shanghai *Shuju* (上海书局; Shanghai Press) published a book entitled *Xiuxiang Wu Zetian si da qi'an* (绣像武则天四大奇案; *Fine-Lined Portrait of Four Strange Cases Solved during the Period of Wu Zetian's Reign*), later retitled *Wu Zetian si da qi'an* (武则天四大奇案; *Four Great and Strange Cases from the Era of Empress Wu Zetian*) and *Di gong'an* (狄公案; *Cases Solved by Di gong*).[14] This was a lengthy adventure-detection novel consisting of four volumes. The setting of *Wu Zetian si da qi'an* is also drawn from history, for the novel takes place during the reign of Empress Wu Zetian and features historical figures such as Yan Liben (阎立本; b. 600–673), a painter; the esteemed official, Yuan Xingchong (元行冲; b. 653–729); Empress Wu Zetian (武则天; b. 624–705);[15] the eccentric abbot, Xue Huaiyi (薛怀义; b. ?–694); and the empress's beloved brothers, Zhang Changzong (张昌宗; b. ?–705) and Zhang Yizhi (张易之; b. ?–705).

Sixty-four chapters of *Wu Zetian si da qi'an* center on the very popular character, Di gong (狄公), who like Bao gong in earlier short court-case stories was a stock "pure official" character. Interestingly, Di gong was the fictional counterpart of a Tang Dynasty (618–907) official named Di Renjie (狄仁杰; b. 618–907), one of the most celebrated officers of the imperial government. Note that these names are used interchangeably throughout the remainder of the chapter, and both Di gong and Di Renjie refer to the same character. The first of five children in a family of bureaucrats (his father and the grandfather were government officials), he began studying Confucian classics and medicine when he was just a boy. In his twenties, he followed his father's footsteps into the civil service. During his time in office, Di Renjie was regarded a "living legend." He was credited with solving more than seventeen thousand legal cases in just one year (675–76) while serving as the Secretary General at the *Dalisi* (大理寺; the Imperial Court). According to the records, Di Renjie displayed extreme caution when investigating a case, avoiding hasty decisions when evidence raised even the slightest doubt about the suspect's guilt. He even overturned unjust verdicts, which actually raised peoples' confidence in the legal system.[16]

The fictional Di gong of *Wu Zetian si da qi'an* is based on representations of him in three works: the semifictional biography compiled by Tang calligraphist Li Yong (李邕 b. 678–747)[17] entitled *Di lianggong zhuan* (狄梁公传; *Biography of Di Renjie*), stories included in the *Taiping guangji* (太平广记; *Extensive Records of the Taiping Era*),[18] and thirty-eight acts in plays by Ming *literatus* Jin Huaiyu (金怀玉; dates unknown) entitled *Di lianggong fanzhou wangyun zhongxiao ji* (狄梁公返周望云忠孝记), or simply *Zhongxiao ji* (忠孝记; *Records of Loyalty and Filial Piety*). In the latter, as suggested by the title, Di Renjie is depicted as a cultivated man whose conduct is guided by moral principles.

Formally, *Wu Zetian si da qi'an* is conventional at a time when new fiction was experimenting with narrative techniques inspired by Western and Japanese novels. During the last two decades of the Qing Period, at least one hundred seventy publishers printed Chinese translations of Western detective fiction for an audience estimated to be between two and four million readers.[19] Some Chinese authors even tried to combine Western detective stories with the traditional Chinese *gong'an* novel. Resisting these trends, *Wu Zetian si da qi'an* used the older *zhanghui*-style *xiaoshuo* (chaptered novel) structure, dividing the novel into several chapters, each one having a heading of about two lines that briefly describe the contents. Moreover, throughout the novel, the narrator uses stock phrases of introduction, connection, and conclusion, and the main story (or stories) are placed after an opening poem in the vernacular and a long introductory sermon, which is the same organizational pattern used by traditional, vernacular short court-case stories and other traditional oral genres that were later textualized.

In terms of narrative, *Wu Zetian si da qi'an* follows a sequence that can be subdivided into six parts, one for each criminal case. It employs various techniques typical of vernacular narration, the most common being a repetitive format: the magistrate finds evidence of a crime and opens an investigation during which he learns of another crime that forces him to interrupt the previous investigation and begin an inquiry related to the new case. In this way, the solution of every case is delayed, and the reader remains engaged.[20] As the Dutch sinologist Robert Hans van Gulik (b. 1910–67) noted, *Wu Zetian si da qi'an* has two different parts, each one nearly thirty chapters, that are clearly distinguished from each other by style and content (225). He opines that part 1, which consists of the first thirty chapters, originally was a complete novel in itself, while part 2 was a later addition. The novel's content supports his theory, since the first murder cases are recounted in the classical manner, and after chapter 30, another story begins in which Di gong fights corruption and is implicated in a coup. Thus each part embraces a different type of crime and criminal. Thus in part 1, Di Renjie investigates three murder cases that involve ordinary members of local communities (*putong xingshi an*; 普通刑事案; "ordinary cases") with the help of his assistants, Ma Rong (马荣), Qiao Tai (乔泰), Tao Gan (陶干), and Hong Liang (洪亮).[21] The next thirty-four chapters—part 2—concern three criminal cases as well, but the type of crime and the personality of the criminals are very different from part 1. The cases in part 2 are all related to abuse of power and corruption by politicians and bureaucrats (*zhengzhi xing an*; 政治性案; "political cases"). Another difference between the sections is that historic events take place off-stage in part 1, but in part 2, historical events play a direct role in the narrative, and as noted previously, the majority of the characters are fictional versions of historical figures.

Significantly, parts 1 and 2 are connected by a scene that occurs in chapter 31: Di Renjie, having solved the three murder cases in part 1, gets a promotion and is invited to the capital. On the way to his new office, he overhears some men complaining about the behavior of a local magistrate who does not protect the citizenry and encourages abuse of power: "Di gong had just arrived in the prefecture. He was carrying out his personal investigations, when suddenly, over in a local village, he saw many people surrounding an old man in his fifties and passionately arguing. Almost unconsciously he and Ma Rong approached the crowd, hearing a man say: 'You do not know how terrible he is; last month Wang Xiaosan's son, because of what happened to his wife, was nearly beaten to death!'" (my translation; 180).

Di gong looks for clues to determine whether such crimes have taken place, and once he finds out that the criminals are all related to members of the ruling class close to Empress Wu, he bravely accuses them as if they were ordinary people. Doing so, he proves not only that he is honest and incorruptible but that he is guided by a Confucian sense of justice and governance. On one hand, Di gong's stance enacts the Confucian concept that justice is a matter of individual and eschews, in this instance, propagation of the interests of a corrupt state. Second, as a member of government without a great deal of power, Di gong exemplifies the Confucian principle that moral conviction earns trust—the peoples' trust—and is a more effective method of rule than legalism and harsh punishment: his honorability and morality bring to justice even the most powerful members of the royal court. In short, in this passage, Di Renjie demonstrates that he is a virtuous, pure official.

Having established his moral credentials, Di gong investigates many other cases of abuse throughout part 2 as he attempts to reduce the damaging effects of political corruption. The first thing that catches the reader's eye in part 2, however, is not the protagonist's moral integrity but the leeway that decision-makers give administrative malpractice and corruption. Here the novel highlights an important point, which is that government reform is very much needed. Specifically, the book suggests that ending corruption and restoring the country requires a new outlook, which must be based on the revival of traditional Confucian values. If the country's rulers do not embrace these values—moral integrity, a sense of justice, social responsibility, compassion, and benevolence—China will be thrown into an unprecedented crisis. The two parts of the novel, even if they may have been extracted from different narrative material and assembled into one publication, as van Gulik suggests, should therefore be read as two essential components of a single novel that expresses a particular view of government and morality.

THE NEGATIVE INFLUENCE OF WOMEN ON PUBLIC LIFE: DECONSTRUCTING THE AUTHOR'S MISOGYNY

Significantly, both parts of the book include a villainous (albeit different) female character who plays a major role in each section's story. In part 1, she is the adulteress and murderer Mrs. Zhou, and in part 2, she is the depraved Empress Wu Zetian.

Mrs. Zhou appears in chapter 4. In this chapter, the narrator introduces the case of "The Strange Corpse" about the murder of a young man, Bi Shun (毕顺), who dies suddenly on the night of the Dragon Boat Festival while accompanied by his wife, Mrs. Zhou.[22] Di Renjie learns of the incident almost by chance when, disguised as a doctor in order to collect evidence for another case, he meets Bi's elderly mother. Made desperate by her precarious financial condition, the old woman shares the story of her son's death with Di Renjie, who she thinks is a doctor. This immediately stimulates his curiosity. Determined to examine the matter more deeply, Di Renjie tells the old woman that he will deliver medication to her house whereupon she warns him not to anger her daughter-in-law, Mrs. Zhou: "At my house there is only my daughter-in-law and me. During the day we are together, but in the evening each of us returns to our room. If you come to our home sir, you may prepare the medicine in the central room, but once it is ready, I ask that you leave swiftly to avoid that she gets angry at me again" (my translation; 20).

These bizarre circumstances increase Di Renjie's suspicions, and on entering the home, he tries to meet her daughter-in-law. In just one glance, he decides that Mrs. Zhou is responsible for her husband's death:

> Judge Di peeked out from the room and caught a glimpse of the daughter-in-law. She was a woman under thirty years of age, wearing no make-up and dressed in a simple manner, but even so one succeeded in perceiving the voluptuousness of her eyes and the radiance of her person. She was so beautiful that one could lose their soul. Her eyebrows slightly curved, her face white as snow, with a timid blush on her cheeks. . . . After seeing her expression, Judge Di understood: "This woman must not be a good person. Certainly there is something hidden beneath this façade." (my translation; 21; van Gulik 35–36). Essentially, Mrs. Zhou is too charming, beautiful, and seductive to be a good wife and a grieving widow: her attractiveness is evidence that she murdered her husband.[23]

Notwithstanding this "proof" that Mrs. Zhou is the murderer, the story's dialogue offers readers other clues that she is a malevolent character. Di Renjie speaks to her in a harsh, condemning manner from the beginning, using phrases such as "you, lascivious woman" and "you, ignoble and depraved woman."[24] Mrs. Zhou is quick-tempered and responds in an insolent, tone, addressing the magistrate as "you, dog of a magistrate." She also verbally assails her mother-in-law, who, as the head of the family in the absence of male members, should be addressed deferentially. Mrs. Zhou's disrespectful discourse marks her as "fallen" in Confucian society, where relationships are organized hierarchically and respect is considered the most important component needed to maintain human bonds, be they with one's ancestors, rulers, officials, elders, parents, or friends. The performance of respect is gendered in this hierarchy, with women enacting a form of filial piety that is rooted in obedience to male family members. According to this doctrine, a woman's relationship to the family should be shaped by "three ways of obedience" (*sancong*; 三从): she must mind her father reverently before marriage (*weijia cong fu*; 未嫁从父), serve her husband diligently after marriage (*jijia cong fu*; 既嫁从夫), and lastly, listen to her sons during widowhood (*fu si cong zi*; 夫死从). Significantly, Mrs. Zhou's lack of deference to her mother-in-law, who, though not male, is the senior member of a female-only family, violates the key cultural imperative of filial piety. This, along with Mrs. Zhou's disrespect for Di Renjie, shows readers that she is neither a good woman nor a good citizen.

While the dialogue may be sufficient to convince the audience that Mrs. Zhou is guilty, Di Renjie, of course, must make a plausible case for his suspicions; hence, he opens an enthralling investigation that sniffs out the existence of a young lover, Xu Detai (徐德泰), who is portrayed as a naïve victim seduced by the manipulative Mrs. Zhou. Xu Detai cannot help but fall into her trap, because, according to the story's logic, any man may be incapable of resisting a beautiful woman's wiles. Once she snares her prey, Mrs. Zhou, as in most traditional Chinese ghost stories, reveals herself to be a malevolent monster, and she proposes murdering her husband. Thus she draws Xu Detai into the scheme, which leads to his death at the end of the story.

Once Di Renjie identifies the criminals, he brings both lovers to court and questions them. While Xu Detai acknowledges his guilt immediately, Mrs. Zhou is determined not to admit her crime. As a result, the biggest obstacle Di gong faces in solving the case is extracting information from Mrs. Zhou, who is so clever that she has killed her husband without leaving any trace of the corpse.

Di Renjie, in episodes that would undermine his "pure official" ethic among today's readers, tortures Mrs. Zhou to get the evidence he needs. She is stripped, bound, pierced, revived, and tortured again as in the following scene:

> When he finished his speech, Judge Di ordered that she be put again into the press: she was immobilized on the ground while both her legs were placed through the holes. As soon as the cord was tight and the stick inserted, a howl of pain was heard, before her eyes turned back in her head and she lost consciousness. . . . Judge Di, having witnessed the behaviour of Xu Detai, understood that he had not acted under his own free will, and so ordered that the bonds of Mrs Zhou be loosened and that fresh water be sprinkled on her face. After some effort, the woman succeeded in regaining consciousness, stretched out in the pool of fresh blood that flowed from her legs and covered her feet. (my translation; 159–60)

At the end of her trial, Mrs. Zhou is sentenced to a lingering death, and her head is mounted on the city gate. This drastic measure serves as a deterrent to criminal behavior, but Mrs. Zhou's disemboweled body also symbolizes her lack of filial piety, for Confucian teachings require the integrity of the body to be preserved.

The book's other villainous woman, Empress Wu Zetian (b. 624–705), initially appears at the beginning of the novel, and she dominates part 2, which is solely dedicated to a scathing critique of her administration of the country. *Wu Zetian si da qi'an,* like most contemporary accounts as well as traditional Confucian histories, represents Wu's reign as corrupt, despotic, violent, and chaos-inducing although historians today are split in their assessments of her reign, some arguing that the empire's expansion and a decline into internal rebellion suggest that Empress Wu was more effective than *Wu Zetian si da qi'an* purports. Be that as it may, Wu, who governed as empress dowager after the death of her husband, Emperor Gaozong, rose to power by murdering or otherwise eliminating rivals, including sons that Gaozong had with other women. When her son Li Zhe came of age to rule but exhibited some independence from her, Wu deposed him; put her youngest son, Li Dan, on the throne; and ruled as regent thereafter.

A vast number of stories ranging from folktales to historical chronicles such as the aforementioned *Ruyijun Zhuan* stereotype the empress as an oversexed, vicious tyrant because of her well-known sexual liaisons and her reliance on brutal violence to maintain power. It is also possible that these representations were influenced by Ming and Qing erotic fiction. However, the story in *Wu Zetian si da qi'an* differs in that it centers primarily on Di Renjie and does not lend much attention to the empress's infamous sexual exploits, focusing instead on her misrule and its negative consequences. In fact, Di gong's main objective in the second half of the novel is to restore the Tang Dynasty and return the throne to Crown Prince Li Dan.

The book thus opens with a complaint that Wu Zetian created disorder as soon as she seized power: "This book is about the reign of Emperor Zhongzong, when Empress Wu rose to the throne and there was confusion in every place" (my translation; 2). This is no idle gripe about the state of civil society, however. Rather, it registers a serious concern that Empress Wu's rule violates the Confucian principle that, as we have seen, everything in the cosmos, including human relations, must be in a perfect balance that is achieved by right order. Wu's violations, as outlined in part 1, include disturbing the Confucian framework of positional and proportional relationships, which upends the cosmological order, by crowning herself emperor and occupying a position—head of government—hitherto occupied solely by men, an unprecedented event in Chinese history. A second charge is that the empress sets a poor example, a serious abrogation of the Confucian exhortation to lead others to goodness through example, an action that preserves order: "If you set an example by being correct, who would dare to remain incorrect?" (Analects, 12:17; *Lun yu* 110). By her bad example, *Wu Zetian si da qi'an* Wu leads her courtiers astray and brings chaos to the kingdom: "From the time that Empress Wu usurped the throne, ignorant and incapable men have risen to power, they destroyed good and honest men, killed sisters and brothers, assassinated gentlemen and mothers. Here are exposed many bizarre cases, all that have been solved by Judge Di" (my translation; 3). Part 1's emphasis on Wu's responsibility for creating disharmony and chaos points to her fallenness, and part 2 follows up by building the case against her.

From the beginning, part 2 adds to the evidence that Empress Wu's abrogation of Confucian principles has disrupted the country. In fact, the narrator introduces a new case-story by criticizing Wu Zetian's political course and reiterating his dissatisfaction with the state of the country: "[Wu Zetian's] wicked deeds increased: she killed Empress Wang and the concubine Xiao, then took the place of empress in the palace. From that moment on began her dissolute and tyrannical reign, which brought confusion and obscenity to the palace. After the death of Gaozong, she even exiled the son of Heaven Zhongzong,[25] who was reduced to the title of Prince of Luling" (my translation; 172). This theme is further developed in passages in which characters who model goodness criticize Wu. For example, Yan Liben, an official whose virtue is established in part 1 when he recognizes Di Renjie's elevated moral sensibility and serves as the younger man's mentor, castigates the empress: "Now that Empress Wu has ascended the throne, there is confusion and obscenity at court, but you cannot say it!" (my translation; 178). Later in the novel (chapter 32), one of Di Renjie's confidantes, Yuan Xingchong, voices similar concerns about the breakdown of morality at court: "Who would ever have imagined that just in a few years the emperor would die and the empress would ascend the throne? State affairs are no longer the same, corruption grows each day and the greater part of the experiences and expectations of the preceding emperor have vanished" (my translation; 178). Both men's unimpeachable moral standing underscores the import of their complaints and lends credibility to the novel's indictment of the empress.

Another strategy that *Wu Zetian si da qi'an* uses to attack Empress Wu is to describe the ruling class's corruption and abuse of power. This indirect evidence of her misrule is presented in three episodes in part 2 that thematize abuse of authority. The figures featured in these passages have obtained prestigious positions thanks to their relationships—either familial or "friendship"—with the empress. They are the so-called *nanchong* (男宠; empress's pets) who enjoy absolute protection from her (308). They include the Wu's ambitious nephews, Wu Sansi (武三思; b. ?–707) and Wu Chengsi (武承嗣; b. 649–698); the monk Xue Huaiyi; and Wu's young lovers, Zhang Changzong and Zhang Yizhi.[26] In the novel, these men comprise a clique that sustains itself by maintaining a strong sense of solidarity, leveraging its members' status to enhance their power and committing ignoble acts against ordinary people. The *nanchong*'s victims have no way to defend themselves because they have no recourse to justice in the country's corrupt legal system. One example of the *nanchong*'s abuse of power appears in the case-story entitled "The Abduction of the Beautiful Miss Wu," which recounts how the daughter-in-law of an honest man, Hao Ganting (郝干庭), is kidnapped by the influential Ceng Youcai (曾有才), the son of Zhang Changzong's servant. Hao Ganting reports the kidnapping at the magistrate's office (*yamen*), but the local magistrate does not pursue the kidnapper, who is his good friend. In contrast, when Di gong arrives in the district, he takes charge of this case and quickly unmasks the kidnapper. Although the kidnapper has ties to one of Empress Wu's powerful courtiers, Di gong does not hesitate to imprison him and use physical force in the process. Di Renjie goes further, in fact, on one occasion insulting Wu

Sansi, who was Empress Wu's nephew and exercised a great deal of influence over how she governed. He says, in no uncertain terms, "Wu Sansi, you dog head" (my translation; 287) and also permits his assistants to show open disrespect to powerful characters. For instance, Ma Rong, who is one of Di gong's lieutenants, doesn't refrain from insulting corrupt superiors. When Ma Rong meets Xue Aocao (dates unknown), one of the empress's lovers,[27] he bumps into him deliberately and then addresses him with the rude words: "You, dog head, why don't you use your eyes—it's as if you were blind!" (308). Showing a subordinate upbraiding a member of Wu's inner circle signifies the extent of the corruption in her court.

CONCLUSION

Importantly, *Wu Zetian si da qi'an* renders both Mrs. Zhou and Empress Wu personifications of social and political disorder. In both cases, the author emphasized the importance of womanly virtue for maintaining social and cosmological order by illustrating the ill effects of their behavior on society. Mrs. Zhou lacks filial piety; hence, her transgressions, adultery and murder, are inexcusable acts against not only the family but also society, and she is punished severely. Part 2 takes a broader perspective, cataloguing Empress Wu's transgressions, which range from inducing social chaos through her bad example to fostering corruption. As a composite, these critiques suggest that violating the Confucian gender hierarchy in which women are subordinate to men has undesirable effects on the public sphere and, in fact, that women's participation in governance is destructive.

Nevertheless, the novel indirectly offers grudging admiration for Mrs. Zhou and Empress Wu in that they test Di Renjie's abilities as a detective. Their crimes and moral transgressions cause chaos, and he must use wisdom and moral integrity to restore order and harmony. As the narrator implies in the following passage, for example, Empress Wu is as capable as Di Renjie is capable and morally pure: "Empress Wu, though dissolute and tyrannical, knew well that only a man of extraordinary talent and celebrated for virtue could supervise the area around the capital, and for this reason she nominated Di Renjie as governor of Henan." Thus the book gives credence to women's mental capabilities, although disorder is the result of female cleverness.

As we have seen, one way to understand *Wu Zetian si da qi'an*'s negative representations of women is to recognize the sexism embedded in the Confucian idea that in a well-ordered society a woman's role in fostering harmony and balance in the public sphere is indirect, limited to obediently submitting to her father, husband, and son. At the same time, the novel implicitly recognizes women's cleverness, and this represents a departure from Confucian conservatism.

NOTES

1 The *huaben* of the Song and Yuan periods survive today only in posterior collections—that is, the short stories collected in Hong Pian's *Sixty Stories* (1550) and Feng Menglong's *sanyan* (published at intervals in the 1620s). Even if we no longer have the original texts, the

relationship between the stories included in these collections and Song-period narrative is universally accepted by Chinese and international scholars.

Patrick Hanan, in his book on Chinese vernacular literature, tackles the question whether *huaben* were written to be recited and served as mnemonic support for storytellers or if they were texts conceived primarily to be read silently (1981, 28–30). Most scholars agree that *huaben*, although they could have been spoken before an audience, were most likely printed (Hanan 1981, 29–30; Hu Shiying 2011).

2 For a study on the figure of Bao gong in the theater of Yuan and Ming periods, see Hayden (1978) and He Feng (2010, 28–32).

3 The Wanli emperor was a recluse disinterested in governing. This encouraged corruption and the kingdom lapsed into chaos. Popular discontent prepared the ground for the rise of the Qing Dynasty, and the first Western entities to establish themselves in China arrived during this period, essentially initiating China's colonization.

4 According to Miao, the leading publishers of *gong'an xiaoshuo* were in the cities of Jianyang (Fujian) and Nanjing (62–63).

5 An extensive literature exists regarding Judge Bao. For the historical Bao Zheng, see Cheng Rufeng (2009) and Ding Zhaoqing (2000, 13–58). For a theoretical treatment of the vernacular stories based on Bao gong, see Wolfgang Bauer (1974, 433–49); Susan Blader (1977); Patrick Hanan (1980, 301–23); and Wilt L. Idema (2010).

6 Feng Menglong is one of the best-known writers and novelists in China and worldwide. He composed works in the vernacular and classical Chinese. *Sanyan* is one of his most famous collections of vernacular short stories, and it has been published in three volumes that include tales dating back to the Song and Yuan periods, a few Ming imitations, and some original stories that he authored. The three *Sanyan* anthologies include *Yushi mingyan* (喻世明言), also called *Gujin xiaoshuo* (古今小说), *Jingshi tongyan* (警世通言), and *Xingshi hengyan* (醒世恒言).

7 Ling Mengchu was a scholar from southeast China (Zhejiang), who after a failed bureaucratic career devoted himself to writing and publishing short stories. His anthologies include *Chuke pai'an jingqi* (初刻, 拍案惊奇; 1628) and *Erke pai'an jingqi* (二刻拍案惊奇; 1632).

8 Manchu rulers' heavy ideological control on the literary production culminated in the so-called literary inquisition (1772–88), during which thousands of works were destroyed for being dangerous to the security of social institutions and morality. Historians estimate that some 10,231 works were identified as subversive and 2,230 destroyed (Santangelo XXIII–XXIV). For a discussion of the relationship between intellectuals and power between the two dynasties, see Sabattini and Santangelo (2006, 95–101).

9 The first adventure-detection novel is believed to be *Shi gong'an* (施公案; *Judge Shi's Cases*). The oldest edition available today dates to 1824 (Miao 98–99).

10 The best example is *Shuihu zhuan* (水浒传; The Water Margin: Outlaws of the Marsh), an adventure novel completed during the Ming era and perhaps one of the best-known Chinese novels abroad. The protagonists are a group of rebels who struggle against abuses of power and corruption. At the end of the novel, the rebels surrender and then join the imperial army to defend the northern borders of the empire from barbarian invasions.

11 The most active publication centers were Beijing and Shanghai, and among publishing houses, the *Wuben tang* (务本堂) in Beijing and the *Shanghai shuju* (上海书局) stand out. More traditional methods were used in the capital, while publishing houses in Shanghai were already benefitting from lithographic printing, which is why Shanghai was the major publication center in the country (Miao 107; Fu 20–26).

12 The terms most frequently used to translate *xiake* are "knight," "knight-errant," "swordsman," or "hero." This nomenclature is meant to suggest the similarity between the chivalric figures of medieval Europe and the *xiake*, since both groups of warriors wield arms expertly in hand-to-hand combat and are honorable in their conduct. The main difference is that they are outlaws who fight injustice alongside the weakest members of society (Liu 193–208).

13 See Lu Hsun (1976, 336–52); and Cao Yibing (2005).

14 See Du Wenyu (2000, 283–317).
15 For a semifictional biography of Empress Wu largely based on historical documents about the Tang Dynasty, see *Lady Wu: A True Story* (1957), written in English by Lin Yutang (林语堂; b. 1895–1976).
16 The literature on Di Renjie, popularly referred to as Di gong (狄公; Lord Di or Judge Di), is not as voluminous as that on Bao gong. His biography is found in *juan* 89 of the *Jiu Tangshu* (*Book of Tang*), the official history of the Tang Dynasty. For a contemporary biography, see Du Wenyu (2000).
17 Li Yong was an important scholar and officer of the Tang Dynasty. His calligraphy was known for its exceptional semicursive script.
18 *Taiping guangji* is a comprehensive collection of stories and unofficial historical biographies (from the Han to the early Northern Song eras). It was compiled by Li Fang (李昉; b. 925–96) and others during the third year of the Taiping Xingguo Period (978).
19 The famous stories of Sherlock Holmes were the first Western detective stories that appeared in the Chinese market. The earliest was "The Final Problem," which was published in Liang Qichao's *Shiwubao* in 1894. In 1902, many others appeared in *The Adventures of Sherlock Holmes* in a section entitled "Translation from English Newspaper," but the first complete collection appeared only in 1916. In the 1920s, Cheng Xiaoqing (程小青; b. 1893–1976) wrote a series of novels strongly influenced by Conan Doyle's Sherlock Holmes series. Not coincidentally, Cheng Xioquing's private detective, Huo Sang, had the same initials as the famous English detective. For further information, see also Liu Weimin (2011, 5–7); Der-wei Wang (1997, 1–3); and Wei Shaochang (1966, 127–30).
20 On the narrative models of *gong'an* vernacular stories and novels, see Ding Can, and Hu Heping (2007, 91–93).
21 This section was translated into English by Robert Hans van Gulik, who titled the three cases "The Double Murder at Dawn," "The Strange Corpse," and "The Poisoned Bride." For a discussion of van Gulik's translation, see Benedetti (2014, 11–42), who gives a title to each of the three cases in part 2: "The Abduction of the Beautiful Miss Wu," "The Crazy Monk," and "Di gong Fights for the Restoration of the Tang Dynasty."
22 Zhou is the maiden name of Bin Shun's wife.
23 A wife's murder of her husband was considered one of the most serious homicides. See T'ung-tsu Ch'u (1969, 119–24).
24 Please note that Mrs. Zhou is often verbally abused. Throughout the novel, Di gong speaks to her in a harsh and offensive manner, using phrases such as "you, prostitute" (*ru zhe yinfu*; 汝这淫妇) and "you, cheap prostitute" (*ru zhe jian yinfu*; 汝这贱淫妇). Even the narrator describes her with offensive adjectives such as "vicious prostitute" (*eyin*; 恶淫) or "depraved and brutish" (*yinpo*; 淫泼). In van Gulik's translation, on the contrary, most of the time, Judge Di simply addresses her by her name, "Mrs Zhou."
25 Emperor Zhongzong (b. 656–710) was the son of Emperor Gaozong and Empress Wu. He succeeded his father in 684, but Wu Zetian deposed him in less than two months in favor of his younger brother, Emperor Ruizong (b. 662–716). As in the novel, he was demoted to a princely rank, sent into exile in the provinces, and put under house arrest.
26 As recorded in the *Old Tang Book*, Empress Wu's brought her young male favorites to the palace to fulfill her every need. Her first "favorite" was Xue Huaiyi, a businessman originally named Feng Xiaobao (冯小宝), whose name she changed to Xue and who she made a monk, appointing him head of the Temple of the White Horse in 685. As many narrative works recount, Wu Zetian had a sexual relationship with Xue Huaiyi but was dissatisfied with his sexual performance and his rude manners, prompting her to seek other lovers. That is how the young brothers Zhang Changzong and Zhang Yizhi were introduced to Empress Wu. They soon became her favorites and were granted official positions (*Jiu Tangshu* 47, 50, 183). See also X. L. Woo (2008, 151–59).

27 This character also appears in the aforementioned *The Biography of Lord Complete Satisfaction* (*Ruyijun zhuan*). In this novel, the character Xue Aocao, the lord of complete satisfaction, is a man with an unusually large penis who loyally serves the empress's sexual needs. Paradoxically, he is also a virtuous Confucianist official who is very frustrated because he is only valued for his sexual performance. See Stone (2003).

WORKS CITED

Alford, William P. "Of Arsenic and Old Laws: Looking Anew at Criminal Justice in Late Imperial China." *California Law Review*, vol. 72, no. 6, 1984, pp. 1180–256.

Altenburger, Roland. "Early Qing Yangzhou in Shi Chengjin's Vernacular Vignettes." *Lifestyle and Entertainment in Yangzhou*, edited by Lucie Olivová and Vibeke Børdahl, NIAS Press, 2009, pp. 149–76.

Anonymous. *Di gong'an. Zhengzhou.* Zhongzhou guji, 2008.

A Ying (阿英). *Wanqing xiaoshuo shi* (晚清小说史; *History of Late Qing Fiction*). Renmin chubanshe, 1980.

Backus Rankin, Mary. "'Public Opinion' and Political Power: Qingyi in Late Nineteenth Century China." *Journal of Asian Studies*, vol. 41, no. 3, 1982, pp. 453–84.

Bauer, Wolfgang. "The Tradition of the 'Criminal Cases of Master Pao' Pao-kung-an (Lung-t'u kung-an)." *Oriens*, vol. 23/24, 1974, pp. 433–49.

Benedetti, Lavinia. "Justice and Morality in Early Qing Crime Fiction." *Ming Qing Studies*, no. 2, 2013, pp. 17–46.

———. "Killing Di gong: Rethinking van Gulik's Translation of Late Qing Dynasty Novel Wu Zetian Si Da Qi'an." *Ming Qing Studies*, 2014, pp. 11–42.

———. "The Supernatural and Chinese Crime Fiction." *Asian Journal of Literature, Culture and Society*, vol. 4, no. 2, 2010, pp. 117–34.

Blader, Susan. *Tales of Magistrate Bao and His Valiant Lieutenants*. Chinese UP, 1998.

Brook, Timothy, Jérôme Bourgon, and Gregory Blue. *Death by a Thousand Cuts*. Harvard UP, 2008.

Cao, Yibing (曹亦冰). *Xiayi Gong'an Xiaoshuo Jianshi* (侠义公案小说简史; *A Brief History of Novels of Adventure and Detection*). Renmin chubanshe, 2005.

Chang, Wejen. "Classical Chinese Jurisprudence and the Development of the Chinese Legal System." *Tsinghua China Law Review*, vol. 2, 2009, pp. 207–72.

Cheng, Rufeng (程如峰). *Bao gong zhuan* (包公传; *Biography of Lord Bao*). Huangshan shushe chuban faxing, 2009.

Chiang, Sing-chen Lydia. *Collecting the Self: Body and Identity in Strange Tale Collections of Late Imperial China*. Brill, 2005.

Ch'ü, Tung-tsu. *Local Government in China under the Ch'ing*. Council on East Asian Studies—Harvard U, 1988.

Collotti Pischel, E. *Storia della rivoluzione cinese*. Editori Riuniti, 1982.

Dien, Dora Shu-fang. *Empress Wu Zetian in Fiction and in History: Female Defiance in Confucian China*. Nova Science, 2003.

Ding, Can (丁灿), and Hu Heping (胡和平). "Woguo gong'an xiaoshuo xushu moshi tanxi" (我国公案小说叙述模式探析; "On the Narrative Modes of Chinese Detective Stories"). *Journal of Hunan Public Security College*, vol. 6, 2007, pp. 91–93.

Ding, Zhaoqing (丁肇琴). *Suwenxue de Baogong* (俗文学中的包公; *Bao Gong in Vernacular Literature*). Wenjin chubanshe, 2000.

Du, Wenyu (杜文玉). *Di Renjie pingzhuan* (狄仁杰评传; *Commented Biography of Di Renjie*). Sanqin, 2000.

Elman, Benjamin. *From Philosophy to Philology: Social and Intellectual Aspects of Change in Late Imperial China*. 2nd rev. ed., U of California at Los Angeles P, 2001.

Elman, Benjamin, and Alexander Woodside, editors. *Education and Society in Late Imperial China, 1600–1900*. U of California P, 1994.

Fu, Xianglong (傅湘龙). "Wanming, wanqing shangye yunzuo yu xiaoshuo kanyin xingtai zhi bianqian" (晚明, 晚清商业运作与小说刊印形态之变迁; "On the Changes in the Publishing Business and Commercial Operations of Novels in the Late Ming and Late Qing"). *Zhongguo wenxue yanjiu*, vol. 4, 2009, pp. 20–26.

Fung, Yu-lan. *Storia della filosofia cinese*. Mondadori, 1990.

Hanan, Patrick. *Chinese Fiction of the Nineteenth and Early Twentieth Centuries: Essays by Patrick Hanan*, vol. 2. Columbia UP, 2013.

———. *The Chinese Vernacular Story*. Harvard UP, 1981.

———. "Judge Bao's Hundred Cases Reconstructed." *Harvard Journal of Asiatic Studies*, 1980, pp. 301–23.

Hegel, Robert E. *True Crimes in Eighteenth-Century China: Twenty Case Histories*. U of Washington P, 2009.

Hegel, Robert E., and Katherine Carlitz, editors. *Writing and Law in Late Imperial China: Crime, Conflict, and Judgment*. U of Washington P, 2007.

Hu, Shi (胡适). *Hu Shi gudian wenxue yanjiu lunji* (胡适古典文学研究论集; *Collection of Hu Shi's Essays on Classical Literature*). Shanghai Guji Chubanshe, 1988.

Hu, Shiying (胡士莹). *Huaben xiaoshuo gailun—quan liangce* (话本小说概论—全两册; Introduction to *Huaben*—Two Volumes). Commercial Press, 2011.

Huang, Yanbo (黄岩柏). *Gong'an xiaoshuo shihua* (公案小说史话; *History of Detective Fiction*). Liaoning jiaoyu, 2000.

Hucker, Charles O. *China's Imperial Past: An Introduction to Chinese History and Culture*. Stanford UP, 1975.

———. *A Dictionary of Official Titles in Imperial China*. Stanford UP, 1985.

Idema, Wilt Lukas. *Judge Bao and the Rule of Law: Eight Ballad-Stories from the Period 1250–1450*. World Scientific, 2009.

Ko, Dorothy, JaHyun Kim Haboush, and Joan R. Piggot. *Women and Confucian Cultures in Premodern China, Korea, and Japan*. U of California P, 2003.

Li, Shixin (李世新). "Xiayi xiaoshuo he gong'an xiaoshuo heliu de shehui wenhua tanyuan" (侠义小说和公案小说合流的社会文化探源; "Social and Cultural Roots Causes of Confluence of Chivalry Stories and Detective Stories"). *Journal of South-Central for Nationalities*, 15, no. 1, 2006, pp. 160–62.

Li, Xiang, and Lisa Rosenlee. *Confucianism and Women: A Philosophical Interpretation*. SUNY P, 2012.

Lin, Yutang. *Madame Wu*. Garzanti, 1966.

Liu, Shengli, editor. *Lun yu*. Zhonghua shuju, 2007.

Liu, Weimin (刘伟民). *Zhentan xiaoshuo pingxi* (侦探小说评析; *Discussion on Detective Novel*). Dongnan daxue, 2011.

Liu, Xu. *Jiu Tangshu*. Zhonghua shuju, 1924.

Lu, Hsun. *A Brief History of Chinese Fiction*. Foreign Language, 1976.

Lü, Xiaopeng (吕小蓬). *Gudai xiaoshuo gong'an yinsu de wenhua tanxi* (古代小说 中公案因素的文化探析; *Cultural Analysis of* Gong'an *Elements in Ancient Narrative*). Dissertation, Capital Normal U, 2002.

Ma, Yau-Woon. "Kung-an Fiction: A Historical and Critical Introduction." *T'oung Pao, Second Series*, vol. 65, no. 4/5, 1979, pp. 200–259.

———. *The Pao-Kung Tradition in Chinese Popular Literature*. Yale UP, 1971.

Meng, Liye (孟犁野). *Zhongguo gong'an xiaoshuo yishu fazhanshi* (中国公案小说艺术发展史; *History of the Development of Chinese Detective Fiction Art*). Qunzhong chubanshe, 1999.

Miao, Huaiming (苗怀明). *Zhongguo gudai gong'an xiaoshuo shilun* (中国古代公案小说史论; *History of Ancient Chinese Detective Novels*). Nanjing U, 2005.

Sabattini, Mario, and Santangelo, Paolo. *Storia della Cina*. Laterza, 2005.

Santangelo, Paolo. *Il pennello di lacca: la narrativa cinese dalla dinastia Ming ai giorni nostri*. Laterza, 1997.

———. *Zibuyu, "What the Master Would Not Discuss," According to Yuan Mei (1716–1798): A Collection of Supernatural Stories*. Brill, 2013. 2 vols.

Stone, Charles R. *The Fountainhead of Chinese Erotica: The Lord of Perfect Satisfaction (Ruyijun zhuan)*. U of Hawai'i P, 2003.

Su, Xing (苏兴). "Wu Zetian si da qi'an sanlun" (武则天四大奇案散论; "Essay on *Wu Zetian si da qi'an*"). *Journal of Dalian University*, vol. 27, no. 1, 2006, pp. 39–41.

Sun, Kaidi (孙楷第). "Bao gong'an yu Bao gong'an gushi" (包公案与包公案故事; "Judge Bao and Judge Bao Stories"). *Cangzhou houji* (沧州后集), vol. 2, Zhonghua shuju, 1985.

Tang, Xiaobing. *Global Space and the Nationalist Discourse of Modernity: The Historical Thinking of Liang Qichao*. Stanford UP, 1996.

van Gulik, Robert Hans, editor. *Celebrated Cases of Judge Dee: An Authentic Eighteenth-Century Chinese Detective Novel*. Courier Dover, 1976.

Wei, Quan (魏泉). "Gong'an yu zhentan: cong Di gong'an shuoqi" (公案与侦探: 从狄公案说起; "*Gong'an* and Detective Fiction: The Case of di Gong'an"). *Journal of Yunnan University* (Social Science Edition), vol. 5, no. 4, 2006, pp. 65–70.

Weisl, Annabella. *Cheng Xiaoqing (1893–1976) and His Detective Stories in Modern Shanghai*. GRIN Verlag, 2009.

Williams, Paul. *Mahayana Buddhism: The Doctrinal Foundations*. Routledge, 2008.

Woo, X. L. *Empress Wu the Great: Tang Dynasty China*. Algora, 2008.

Zito, Angela. *Of Body and Brush: Grand Sacrifice as Text/Performance in Eighteenth-Century China*. U of Chicago P, 1997.

10 ⊚ THE PROBLEMATIC MATERNAL IN MOTO HAGIO'S GRAPHIC FICTION

An Analysis of "Iguana Girl"

TOMOKO KURIBAYASHI

This chapter on Japanese graphic fiction thematizes the unmotherly in the works of Japanese manga author Moto Hagio. Kuribayashi historicizes the graphic narrative in Japanese gender norms of the 1970s, the period in which it is set, suggesting that it exposes the harms these gender roles wrought on family dynamics. Specifically, she argues that the deeply troubled mother-daughter relationship featured in "Iguana Girl" exemplifies women's and girls' internalization of fallenness when they cannot meet the impossible-to-achieve ideal of Japanese motherhood. The story is loosely based on Hagio's childhood but goes well beyond it, looking at social structures and institutions. As an aside, the story's title offers insight into the problematics of translation, for it is published as "Iguana Girl" in the United States, but a more faithful rendition is "Iguana Mother." Clearly the disparity between the two titles is significant, each one signifying different protagonists and sets of concerns. This chapter refers to the text as "Iguana Girl"; however, the author strongly prefers "Iguana Mother."

Moto Hagio is a major Japanese manga author whose career has spanned over forty years; some even call her "the Great Mother of *shojo manga*" (*Bungei Bessatsu* back cover).[1] This chapter focuses on her well-known short narrative called "Iguana no musume" ("Iguana Girl"), first published in 1991. Hagio has stated that this is the most autobiographical of her works ("Hagio Moto vs. Nagashima Yu" 142). It features a problematic maternal figure who appears to be based on her own mother, as are similar characters in Hagio's corpus of graphic fiction, whose origins lie in the difficult relationship she had with her mother both as a child and as an adult. The mothers in her works other than "Iguana Girl," however, appear in narratives that are far from autobiographical, usually set in a foreign location, and often the problematic relationship is between mothers and sons rather than mothers and daughters. In this sense, "Iguana Girl" has a special place in Hagio's oeuvre.

Hagio was born and raised on the main southern island of Japan called Kyushu several hundred miles west of Tokyo, which is rather far from manga's central place of production in Tokyo.[2] She was an avid reader of fiction and attended a fashion design school but had already decided that she wanted to become a manga author while in high school. Though her parents were not at all supportive of her manga aspirations, Hagio sent manuscripts to Tokyo publishers, who encouraged her to submit more, and she eventually relocated to Tokyo. She became a member of the core group of *shojo manga* authors who are often referred to as the "Twenty-Fourth-Year Flower Group" (the twenty-fourth year in Japan's calendar was 1949, and these female authors were all born in or around that year.) The group included other notable authors such as Keiko Takemiya, Ryoko Yamagishi, and Yumiko Oshima.[3] Prior to these women's debut in the late 1960s and early 1970s, manga authors whose target audience was teenage girls were men (and, perhaps needless to say, most authors of manga meant for teenage boys were also men), and when they were first published, the Twenty-Fourth Year Flower Group were not much older than their readers. Their *shojo manga* can be said to have successfully revised the image of the girl (*shojo*) that had been created by men and reflected men's views of young girls. As Takemiya stated, "We began to present ideas about *shojo* from our own point of view" (qtd. in Ogi 148–85).

Initially, editors considered most of Hagio's manga narratives too gloomy and inappropriate for the intended audience, but some of her earliest works whose themes were more lighthearted were published in major magazines. Her career took off with a serialized narrative about a family of vampires called *Po no ichizoku* (*The Poe Clan*). This series, whose title explicitly connects it to Edgar Allan Poe (furthermore, the two main characters, teenage male vampires, are named Edgar and Allan), was wildly popular when it was published in book form. After *The Poe Clan*, Hagio went on to publish a wide variety of manga narratives, many of which are quite long and complex. They include science fiction and speculative narratives, works in the category of "Boys' Love," romantic comedies, and socially oriented narratives that deal with child abuse, war, or the everyday lives of ordinary people. Her most recent works include *Barubara ikai* (*Otherworld Barbara*) and *Zankoku na kamiga shihai suru* (*After Us the Savage God*), both of which may be considered psycho thrillers even though the latter is much more realistic than the former (and all the more disturbing in its depiction of brutal sexual abuse). At the time of this writing, Hagio was hard at work on a new science fiction narrative called *Awei* (*Away*), in which adults and children are suddenly and inexplicably divided into two separate universes, and a historical narrative (her first of this genre), called *Ouhi Marugo* (*Queen Margo*), which is based on the life of France's Queen Margaret (b. 1553–1615). Hagio is one of the rare manga authors who continues to be prolific in her sixties and whose work is still evolving with one innovative narrative after another.

As has already been stated, Hagio often depicts problematic maternal figures in both her fantastical and realistic *manga* narratives. In the aforementioned *After Us the Savage God* (whose title is a quotation from William Butler Yeats by way of the title of a book by A. Alvarez),[4] which was serialized from 1993 to 2001, a beautiful, youthful mother sacrifices her only son, a teenager who adores her, to the sadistic sexual demands of her new husband so that this wealthy and seemingly loving man does not reject her. In *Marginal*, a futuristic narrative written in the 1980s, Hagio presents Holy Mother, who is the only woman on earth after a deadly epidemic that only men survived. The aging and no longer fertile Holy Mother is worshipped with what some feel is an excessive passion, which leads to her assassination. In the end, Holy Mother is revealed to be a sham concocted to manipulate the men into exploiting the earth's mineral resources. On the rare occasions when Hagio's maternal character is nurturing, she is often of foreign origin, as in *Umi no Aria* (*The Ocean's Aria*; 1991), a story about two teen brothers, Colin and Abel. An alien life-form invades Abel's body, causing erratic mood shifts and leading to the discovery of dark secrets.

Hagio's abusive or otherwise "unmaternal" mothers figure the author's relationship with her mother who, it seems, was desperate to please her husband—a father whose rigid, idealized views of family life were unrealistic and unattainable. Having suffered childhood deprivation, Hagio's father demanded perfection and insisted that his daughter never deviate from her parents' expectations (Thorn 178–79). Hagio admits that she was afraid of her mother, which might explain why mothers often die in her narratives (Thorn 177), and Hagio's portrayals of problematic mothers may shock readers. Nevertheless, the mother-child relationships she depicts are anything but exceptional or aberrant. In addition to reflecting the author's individual experience of domestic trauma, Hagio's maternal figures highlight the influence of often unquestioned and unchallenged cultural forces, including gender expectations placed on women that create and preserve destructive family environments in Japan and other societies.

It was a surprise when I realized, as I began to examine the short narrative closely, that "Iguana Girl" was written in the 1990s, well after Hagio's position as a major manga artist was firmly established rather than at a previous point in her career.[5] My surprise that Hagio did not produce an autobiographical work earlier was somewhat based on a perhaps naïve assumption that in the initial years of their careers many authors produce works that are at least somewhat autobiographical, especially in light of the dominant Japanese genre of *shishosetsu* (I-novel), which is an autobiographical novel. Hagio has addressed this issue, affirming, as previously stated, that it is the most autobiographical of her works, and her comments imply that she could not have drawn a narrative so reminiscent of her own traumatic mother-child experience when she was younger and less self-assured:

> For a long time I had wanted to depict a conflict between mother and daughter, but since I had not solved my own problem all ideas that I could come up with sounded like complaints about one's own family problems. The issue was very painful to think about, so often I would begin working on it and then give it up. In the end I decided to resort to animals. I said to myself that the parent-child relationship was in trouble because the child was not human. . . . It helped me become resigned to my own failed relationship to my parents, at least temporarily. (my translation; "Hagio Moto and Nagashima Yu" 142)

Indeed, when Hagio discusses the short narrative, she always acknowledges its autobiographical nature.[6]

In terms of plot, "Iguana Girl" centers on the life of the elder of two daughters of an ordinary, middle-class family living in late twentieth-century Japan, apparently in the Tokyo area. What is not very ordinary about this family is that there is a major conflict between the mother and the eldest daughter, or more precisely, given that mother-daughter conflicts are commonplace, the nature of this clash is out of the norm: the mother believes that the eldest daughter, Rika, is an iguana. In fact, the mother cannot stop screaming when she gives birth and first sees the baby because in her eyes the girl is an iguana (166). All other people, including the father, consider Rika pretty (if somewhat dark-skinned, which is not considered attractive in Japan) and smart, but the mother persists in believing that the child is an ugly iguana; therefore, try as she might, she is unable to love Rika. When the second child, also a daughter, is born a few years later, the mother has no trouble loving her, which underscores the problematic nature of the mother's treatment of Rika: it is not that the mother is incapable of loving her children but that she cannot love Rika, and Rika only. Rika internalizes her mother's belief that she is an iguana to the degree that she sees herself as an iguana when she looks in the mirror. Thus Rika is convinced that she is ugly and unattractive no matter how much romantic attention boys give her during her teenage years (187). Feeling her mother's disapproval and often unfairly disciplined by her mother, Rika nevertheless manages to develop into a functional adult: she marries after graduating from college and moves away from her family. When Rika gives birth to her own daughter, she is relieved that the baby looks human but also fears that one day she might begin to dislike the child. Later, Rika gets news of her mother's sudden death, returns to Tokyo, and to her surprise, discovers that her mother is actually an iguana, although none of the other characters realize this (204). While waiting for the funeral, Rika drowses off and dreams that her mother was once an iguana princess who fell in love with a human male and had herself transformed into a human woman in order to win his love. This revelation helps Rika understand why her mother hated her—the mother was worried that Rika's iguana-like appearance would reveal the mother's real identity, causing her to lose her human "prince's" love. Rika develops compassion for her mother and begins to feel capable of loving her own daughter.[7]

When I read "Iguana Girl" for the first time several years ago, I was fascinated by its graphics (the piece begins and ends with scenes from the Galapagos Islands where the iguana princess originated) and the sociocultural implications of the difficult mother-daughter relationship. As related in the plot summary, the mother in "Iguana Girl" finds it impossible to love her oldest daughter because in her eyes the child is an iguana. There are three ways to explain why the mother is unable to love the daughter. One is to treat the story as a fairy tale or myth in which supernatural forces act upon humans in fantastical ways. The second is to employ psychoanalytics to examine the story, while a third possibility is to proceed by merging both strategies. The case for treating "Iguana Girl" as a fairy tale rests on the narrative's last few pages (it is also hinted at in the first few pages even though the reader may not understand the full meaning at that juncture), which suggest that the story is a myth about womanhood: the mother was originally an iguana who, like Hans Christian Andersen's Little Mermaid, had herself magically transformed into a human female in order to win a human male's love (167).

On the other hand, feminist psychology suggests that the mother's fears are a manifestation of the self-hatred that women develop as they attempt to fulfill impossible social expectations to be beautiful and otherwise perfect mothers, daughters, and wives. In a 2008 discussion with Moto Hagio, Tamaki Saito, a renowned (male) Japanese psychoanalyst, highlights the centrality of the body to women's sense of themselves, asserting that sharing strong awareness of that centrality of physicality makes mother-daughter relationships different from other parent-child relationships (father-daughter, mother-son, and father-son) (Saito and Hagio 51). In Saito's view, women, unlike men, are seldom free from being conscious of their own bodies. Additionally, femininity is often defined via bodily traits such as how one dresses and how one moves one's body, which means that raising a girl to become feminine equates to raising her to become feminine in her bodily appearance. At the same time, femininity entails being (physically) passive, giving up "masculine" (or active) desires. Thus a woman is required both to learn to repress her desires and to achieve a body that is desired by men. That split physicality is shared by mother and daughter, which makes their relationship particularly complex and conflicted (Saito and Hagio 52). Whether they like it or not, mother and daughter are inseparably bound through their sense of themselves as grounded in their female bodies. Hence the inability of Rika's mother to love her first daughter stems from her hatred of—or at least insecurity about—her own nature and/or appearance as a woman. Rika in turn sees herself as an iguana when she looks in the mirror because she embodies her mother's fear of being ugly and lacking in other qualities that society deems desirable in women.

In this manner, Hagio's narrative poses questions about what is expected of mothers in Japanese society not only when "Iguana Girl" was published but also during the post–World War II era in which it is set. In her book *The Other Women's Rib. Gender and Body in Japanese Women's Fiction*, Julia C. Bullock discusses expectations placed on Japanese women in the 1960s and 1970s.[8] According to Bullock, even though US-initiated postwar reforms included providing equal educational opportunities for women, this period of high economic growth for Japan, 1955–73, saw a "resurgence of pre-war 'good wife and wise mother' ideology" (2). Bullock elaborates that "a strictly gendered division of labour . . . required women to take full responsibility for the domestic sphere so that their husbands could devote themselves to rebuilding the nation's economy through paid labour" (2). She continues, asserting that "the term 'femininity,' as understood in Japan during the 1960s, thus primarily denoted qualities associated with women's nurturing and supportive functions vis-à-vis men," and "it was also understood that . . . women were expected to respond to male activity and self-assertion with passive and self-effacing behavior" (2). Significantly, writes Sumiko Iwao, the parents' relationship to each other becomes asexual once children are born, at least in the presence of the children, and they call each other "father" and "mother" rather than by their first names because they are expected to be parents before they are wife and husband (135). Iwao also asserts that too much pressure is placed on mothers to build a warm and nurturing family with close ties (152).

Not surprisingly, a number of women writers in the 1960s actively questioned such expectations. For example, Yumiko Kurahashi evinced a "long-standing animosity towards all things maternal" in her fictional works (qtd. in Kleeman 51). Writing in the early 1990s, Iwao argues, "The Japanese woman's consciousness of her role in the family centers on motherhood" (125), which in Japan is considered far more important than being a wife. Psychologically, therefore, the problematic mother-daughter relationship in "Iguana Girl" is rooted in both characters' fears of falling short of patriarchal expectations and reflects the stress women experience vis-à-vis motherhood as a social institution.

To recap, viewing "Iguana Girl" as a myth underscores its fantastic elements, such as its fairy-tale treatment of the human-animal divide, while a psychological approach points to sociocultural reasons for the female figures' fears. Notably, those two explanations are interrelated by the story's use of a human-animal hierarchy to cast animals as inferior to humans, who, in contrast, are more civilized and less "natural." Fairy tales often use this human-animal hierarchy to reveal what society considers ideal feminine behavior—as well as what it deems unacceptable behavior in women—with the objective of socializing the audience into the dominant society's values about gender (or at least teach girls and women how to avoid disgrace or disaster). Along these lines, fairy tales show the sacrifices women may have to make to be considered feminine and thus objects of romantic love capable of snagging marriage proposals from desirable men. When a human-animal hierarchy is present in such a tale, it often involves a nonhuman woman who, if not an animal, is limited by her animal characteristics. For instance, to be considered an ideal woman, Andersen's Little Mermaid, who has a finned tail rather than legs, must give up her voice and endure the great pain of walking like a human female (which I have always seen as a metaphor for the torture of high heels). In "Iguana Girl," the mother, originally a princess in the iguana kingdom, gives up her royal position so that she can be transformed from an animal to an ordinary human female who, married to an ordinary man, is ordinarily—but not glamorously—happy. Obviously, she sees being an average human as superior to being a member of a royal family of animals.[9] The iguana princess-turned-human-housewife, however, is constantly fearful that her "beastly" nature might be revealed to the world, especially to her human husband, as she believes that the discovery will cost her his love as well as her ordinary human happiness.

This association of femininity with animals, particularly in the context of women's sexuality, occurs not only in fairy tales, mythology, and folklore in diverse cultures but also in specifically Japanese contexts. For instance, the trope of women's beastliness appears in the postwar Japanese genre called *nikutai bungaku* (literature of the flesh), in which "the [male] protagonists are able to project onto woman all of the negative qualities that are associated with the corporeal" (Bullock 36). Accordingly, womanhood and women's sexuality is represented as animal-like—that is, uncontrollable. Notably, one thing that these disparate genres have in common—and indeed share with many other genres that feature human-animal hierarchies—is that women's association with animals reflects their subordinate social status. That is to say that women are animalized because as "less than male," they are less than human. While men occupy the superior realm of culture, women are relegated to the lower domain of nature. Consequently, a woman may find it of utmost importance to suppress and hide her "beastly" nature in order to be acceptable and desirable—that is, properly feminine—but ultimately it is impossible for her to fully eradicate her animalism because the culture in which she lives believes that she is controlled by her flawed bodily nature, whereas men are in control as a result of their superiority to all nature.

Thus treating "Iguana Girl" as a twentieth-century fairy tale and employing psychoanalytics to examine the human-animal hierarchy on which the mother-daughter conflict hinges offers important insights into why the mother abuses Rika. Keeping in mind Japanese norms that "good" mothers' sexual activity should be minimal, it is possible that the mother's attitude toward Rika stems from fears that she will be discovered as having active sexual desires, as being too sexually assertive. This is supported by Bullock's claim, noted previously, that in postwar Japan "the only morally acceptable outlet for women's sexuality was motherhood" (20). Another fear that might have plagued the mother is that she would be exposed for having other "unwomanly" desires, perhaps in the public or social realm. As Bullock writes, during the period in which the story is set, the dominant "models of femininity . . . stressed marriage and motherhood as woman's 'natural' roles" (20), and if a mother had any ambitions beyond the domestic sphere, she might be considered a "bad" mother and aberrant woman.

Casting aside these arguments for a moment, even if the mother's fear stems solely from the prospect of being revealed, literally, as an iguana, her anxiety renders her psychologically and figuratively beastly: she neglects and abuses her oldest daughter because Rika seems to embody everything that is unfeminine and undesirable in herself. In this respect, at least where Rika is concerned, the mother (paradoxically) engages in a common maternal practice in Japan, which is for a mother or other older woman to try to control or even dominate a daughter or younger woman to the most minute detail (Nobuta and Ueno 75). There are many reasons that Japanese mothers adopt this problematic approach, though conventional wisdom decrees that it is undertaken in the hopes of helping young women acquire a demeanor and behavior that will protect them from social failure and personal unhappiness (Saito and Hagio 52). Anecdotal evidence suggests that the older female may perceive something of herself in the younger woman, for example, characteristics or tendencies that the older woman has been taught to dislike, and she may feel compelled to extinguish or suppress them, which is a pattern that Tomoko Yamada identifies in Hagio's works (207).[10] Another possibility, again based on anecdotal evidence, is that the older woman's harshness may be an attempt to curry the father's favor—and the favor of patriarchal society in general—by making the daughter conform to the feminine ideal, which was the case with Hagio's real-life mother.

Regardless of her motives, the iguana mother's abuse of Rika has all the outward appearances of attempts to socialize the girl into the Japanese ideal of womanhood, at least until the reveal at the end of the story.[11] For instance, the mother prefers the younger daughter, called Mami, over Rika because Mami is fair-skinned (she looks good in pink), whereas Rika is darker in a society where darkness connotes ugliness and light skin is a valued physical trait.[12] The mother also prefers Mami because her behavior is more feminine. Mami likes to bake cookies, but Rika is a tomboy. (She is a promising softball player in elementary school, and her athletic prowess is respected by neighborhood boys.) Moreover, Rika possesses the "masculine" characteristic of intelligence and makes good grades in school. In contrast, Mami is "girlishly" less gifted and has to attend an inferior university. Thus it is significant that, as readers learn after the mother dies, Rika strongly resembles the mother. This information emerges when Rika, looking at her mother's corpse, screams, "She looks just like me!" Rika's paternal aunt confirms the likeness, replying, "I've always said you look like Yuriko, but she used to get so angry when I said that" (205). Obviously, all along the mother had seen herself in Rika and feared that her own beastliness would be exposed by the only "abnormal" characteristics that others could perceive in Rika, namely, her "ugly" dark skin, her athleticism, and her intelligence. And, of course, if the mother's secret had been exposed by Rika's deviance from the womanly ideal, the mother would become undesirable and subject to male disapproval and might have lost both her husband's love and her "happy" family life.

The difficult relationship with her mother scars Rika, all the more so because the mother is very fond and proud of Mami. Rika is so traumatized by her mother's abuse that when she gives birth to a daughter, she fears she will be unable to love the baby even though the newborn does not look like an iguana. Yet at the end of the story, Rika realizes that her mother was as traumatized by her inability to love Rika as Rika is terrified that she will not love her own daughter. The discovery that the mother was an iguana and feared being detected and that the mother's hostility to Rika stemmed from the older woman's overwhelming fear of society's disapproval and the possible loss of her husband's affection enables Rika to overcome the trauma of maternal rejection. It also empowers Rika to prevent the disastrous, dysfunctional mother-daughter relationship from being replicated in her relationship with her infant daughter and to ensure that self-hatred and fear are not handed down to the baby girl.

While Rika sees the problem as individualized rather than broadly social, Hagio's narrative suggests that the maternal neglect and abuse Rika endured result from patriarchal oppression that women suffer in contemporary Japanese society and that unattainable expectations of women can lead to a traumatic family climate for children, especially daughters. While the fairy-tale framework conspicuously visible at the beginning and end of this short text downplays the main narrative's challenge to the patriarchal precept that motherhood is the ideal form of femininity and categorizes Rika's experience as an isolated, idiosyncratic case, "Iguana Girl" leaves the reader with disturbing but ultimately liberating questions regarding mother-daughter dynamics.[13] After all, astute readers are aware that fairy tales are far from apolitical and that the lessons of social and gender conformity that they teach are often more debilitating than beneficial, especially for young women.

Importantly, Rika's damaging relationship with her mother is not a unique product of Japanese culture and society. Mothers or maternal figures are often entrusted (or burdened) with young women's cultural training, which too often turns out to be limited to passing on an oppressive ideology with suffocating restrictions. Instead of helping the younger generation reach its potential, mothers' efforts often focus on keeping girls in line and ensuring that they conform to traditional standards. Granted, some of the gender expectations imposed on Rika's mother (and both of her daughters) in Hagio's short narrative are culturally specific, and Hagio's story must be considered in Japan's sociocultural contexts. However, women throughout the world experience pressure to perform traditional qualities that are desired in women, such as willingness to pretend to be inferior to men in gendered endeavors—usually those that entail academic, political, or economic leadership or involve "masculine" abilities like athleticism, mechanical facility, or mathematical and scientific reasoning—or an obsessive and even paralyzing concern with one's appearance. If the force of these expectations can be said to be somewhat diminished in today's world, they were ubiquitous in recent history and have not yet disappeared completely.

Whether one subscribes to the mythological or psychological explanation of the mother's inability to love her daughter in "Iguana Girl" or opts to merge the two approaches, the mother's rejection of the daughter is representative of problematic mother-daughter (or, more generally, mother-child) relationships that abound in Hagio's manga narratives. Thus "Iguana Girl" offers a suitable entry point into an extensive study of Hagio's explorations of powerful social and psychological factors—the most pertinent being gender expectations—that give rise to the disturbing family dynamics that mark her works. The story also serves as a vantage point from which to study the ways in which femininity, specifically motherhood, is culturally defined and leveraged to regulate women's behavior not only in Japan but in many other societies. While it is true that the short narrative is based loosely on the author's childhood experiences, it is far from representative of an idiosyncratic case. Nor does it represent a singularly Japanese phenomenon; instead, it exposes the damaging effects of mothers' internalization of oppressive gender expectations and their subsequent imposition of such norms on daughters—in the name of tradition and social propriety, or out of a desire to protect a loved one from failure. While *shojo manga* can be rightly criticized for helping to perpetuate mainstream if not patriarchal ideals of feminine appearance and behavior, it also, sometimes, highlights the problems caused by such standards. It can also challenge or at least question patriarchal measures of womanhood, as do many of Hagio's narratives.

NOTES

1 *Shojo manga* is the term for graphic narratives whose target audience is teenage girls. Graphic narratives produced for the teenage male audience are *shonen manga*.
2 Most major publishers in Japan, including those specializing in manga magazines and books, are located in or near Tokyo.
3 Keiko Takemiya was one of the first manga writers whose works feature romantic or sexual relationships between young adult males. Dubbed "Boys' Love," this genre's target audience is female rather than gay men. Her best known work in the "Boys' Love" genre is *Kaze to ki no uta* (*The Song of the Wind and the Trees*; 1976–84). She is also well known for science fiction narratives such as *Watashi wo tuki made tsuretette* (*Fly Me to the Moon*; 1981–87) and *Tera e* (*To Terra*; 1977–80). Ryoko Yamagishi's manga often includes occult themes and reflects her early training in classical ballet. *Hiizuru tokoro no tenshi* (*The Son of Heaven in the Land of the Rising Sun*; 1980–84) follows the life of a man, based on a historical figure, who has supernatural powers, and *Maihime: Terepushikora* (*Dancing Girl: Terpsichore*) exposes the harsh lives endured by young girls and boys who aspire to become ballet dancers. Yumiko Oshima often explores psychological issues and fantastic themes in her usually short narratives. One of her representative works, *Banana bureddo no puddingu* (*Banana Bread Pudding*; 1977–78), depicts a sensitive young woman spiraling into seeming madness.
4 Matt Thorn explains that Hagio named her narrative after Alvarez's book without knowing that the title was a quotation from Yeats. See Thorn's preface to the interview with Hagio that is included in *Moto Hagio's Drunken Dream and Other Stories* (x).
5 I did not initially notice the narrative's composition date because I found it only after it was anthologized in a collection of Hagio's shorter texts in 1991.
6 Information about Hagio's childhood is also available from other sources—in fact, her two sisters and parents agreed to be interviewed for a special journal issue on Hagio, *Bungei Bessatsu: Hagio Moto Tokushu*.
7 In 1996, a few years after its original publication, TV Asahi made "Iguana Girl" into a dramatic television series of eight to ten hours total, or eleven episodes, with a much-expanded script. It was later released as a set of DVDs. Two high-profile actors in their forties played the parents, and the teenagers who played the main character and her friends went on to have successful acting careers.
8 As in many other societies, gender expectations placed on women as well as the roles available to them changed rapidly in the second half of the twentieth century, and it is challenging to select the "right time period" against which to discuss Hagio's "Iguana Girl." The short narrative was written and published in the early 1990s, but Hagio's own experience with her mother, during her childhood and teenage years, occurred in the 1950s and 1960s. It seems, therefore, reasonable to focus on the stereotypes of femininity from the 1950s into the 1960s. On the other hand, based on her research in Japan from 1991 to 1993, Christine R. Yano contends that popular songs in Japan, specifically those belonging to the *enka* (modern ballad) genre, emphasize that

"motherhood is a source of strength for a woman . . . and part of a woman's duty and destiny" even in the 1990s (241).

9 This human-animal hierarchy is common in western literature but is not a feature of Japanese narratives. In "Iguana Girl," in contrast, the ex-princess portrays being a human female as more desirable than being an iguana princess.

10 Though probably not applicable to "Iguana Girl," the mother or older woman may try to keep younger women in line because they are consciously or unconsciously envious of the opportunities offered to the daughter or the younger woman that were never available to the elder. Particularly during the 1960s and 1970s in Japan, despite conservative views about gender, that was exactly the case: young women had many more educational and professional options than those previous generations of women enjoyed, affecting interactions between the two. Mari Hayakawa discusses at least two examples from mid to late twentieth-century Japan where a mother tried to impress on her daughter the importance of personal beauty and feminine behavior in order to secure a husband while the daughter felt she could support herself by obtaining a profession (119–22).

11 While the father does not encourage the mother to discriminate against Rika and declares that both of his daughters are pretty and lovable, he does intervene actively to correct his wife's favoritism (in the television series, which provided more details over the course of eleven weekly episodes, the father tries to console Rika after the mother hurts her feelings, but he is not effective in lessening the mother's antipathy toward Rika).

12 Setsu Shigematsu discusses the idealization of whiteness as a female beauty standard in the 1970s in Japan (568).

13 A number of contemporary Japanese theorists assert that Japanese women, especially mothers, are very powerful and have always been so, as discussed by Ayako Kano. For example, Kojin Karatani argues that Japan is a nation rooted in matrilinearity, having "originated" from a goddess, instead of a male god. Kano justly criticizes and disproves the view.

WORKS CITED

Bacchilega, Cristina, and Cornelia N. Moore, editors. *Constructions and Confrontations: Changing Representations of Women and Feminisms, East and West.* College of Languages, Linguistics and Literature—University of Hawaii, 1996.

Bullock, Julia C. *The Other Women's Rib: Gender and Body in Japanese Women's Fiction.* U of Hawaii P, 2010.

Bungei Bessatsu: Hagio Moto Tokushu, 30 May 2010.

Hagio, Moto. "Iguana Girl." *Moto Hagio's Drunken Dream and Other Stories.* Translated by Matt Thorn, Fantagraphics, 2010, pp. 163–212.

———. "Iguana no musume." *Iguana no musume.* 1991. Shogakukan, 2002, pp. 3–54.

"Hagio Moto vs. Nagashima Yu." *Bungei Bessatsu: Hagio Moto Tokushu*, 30 May 2010, pp. 138–54.

Hayakawa, Mari. "Jinsei no natsu no hi no aisukurimu" ("Ice Cream on a Summer Day of Life"). *Yuriika (Eureka)*, vol. 40, no. 14, 2008, 117–26. (Special Issue on the Mother-Daughter Plot: *The Curse by the Name of Mothers and Daughters*).

Iguana no musume (Iguana Girl). TV Asahi, Directed by Kazuhisa Imai and Shinjo Takehiko, screenplay by Kazue Okada, 15 Apr. 1996–24 June 1996.

Iwao, Sumiko. *The Japanese Woman: Traditional Image and Changing Reality.* Harvard UP, 1993.

Kano, Ayako. "Toward a Critique of Transhistorical Femininity." *Gendering Modern Japanese History*, edited by Barbara Molony and Kathleen Uno, Harvard UP, 2005, pp. 520–54.

Kimura, Saeko. "Haha to musume no kyuutei monogatari: Naze haha wa musume wo ijimeruka" (The courtly narrative of mothers and daughters: why mothers abuse their daughters). *The*

Curse by the Name of Mothers and Daughters, special issue of *Yuriika* (*Eureka*), vol. 40, no. 14, 2008, pp. 166–70.

Kleeman, Faye Yuan. "Sexual Politics and Sexual Poetics in Kurahashi Yumiko's *Cruel Fairy Tales for Adults*." *Constructions and Confrontations: Changing Representations of Women and Feminisms, East and West*, edited by Cristina Bacchilega and Cornelia N. Moore, College of Languages, Linguistics and Literature—University of Hawaii, 1996, pp. 150–58.

Kotani, Mari. "Space, Body, and Aliens in Japanese Women's Science Fiction." *Science Fiction Studies*, translated by Miri Nakamura, vol. 29, 2002, pp. 397–417. *MLA International Bibliography*. Accessed 17 Mar. 2013.

Nobuta, Sayoko, and Chizuko Ueno. "Suraimu haha to hakamori musume: Michi nimi michi yuku onnatachi" (Slime mother and grave-hugging daughter: women who take the path that is not a path). *Yuriika* (*Eureka*), vol. 40, no. 14 (2008): 71–88. (Special Issue on the Mother-Daughter Plot: *The Curse by the Name of Mothers and Daughters*).

Ogi, Fusami. "Shojo Manga (Japanese Comics for Girls) in the 1970s' Japan as a Message to Women's Bodies: Interviewing Keiko Takemiya—a Leading Artist of the Year 24 Flower Group." *International Journal of Comic Art*, vol. 10, no. 2, Fall 2008, pp. 148–85. *MLA International Bibliography*. Accessed 17 Mar. 2013.

Saito, Tamaki, and Moto Hagio. "Shojo manga to 'hahagoroshi' no mondai" (Shojo Manga and the problem of matricide). *Yuriika* (*Eureka*), vol. 40, no. 14, 2008, pp. 50–62. (Special Issue on the Mother-Daughter Plot: *The Curse by the Name of Mothers and Daughters*).

Shigematsu, Setsu. "Feminism and Media in the Late Twentieth Century: Reading the Limits of a Politics of Transgression." *Gendering Modern Japanese History*, edited by Barbara Molony and Kathleen Uno, Harvard UP, 2005, pp. 555–89.

Thorn, Matt. "Hagio Moto to watashi to sinkuronishiti to" (Hagio Moto, I, and synchronicity). *Bungei Bessatsu: Hagio Moto Tokushu*, 30 May 2010, pp. 175–79.

———. "The Moto Hagio Interview." *Moto Hagio's Drunken Dream and Other Stories*, translated by Matt Thorn, Fantagraphics, 2010, pp. ix–xxx.

Yamada, Tomoko, editor. "Haha to musume no monogatari: Bukku gaido manga hen" (The mother-narrative plot: book guide, *manga* version). *The Curse by the Name of Mothers and Daughters*, special issue of *Yuriika* (*Eureka*), vol. 40, no. 14, 2008, pp. 200–213.

Yano, Christine R. "Constructing Women as Agents of Non-Change: Motherhood and Nationhood in Japanese Popular Song." *Constructions and Confrontations: Changing Representations of Women and Feminisms, East and West*, edited by Cristina Bacchilega and Cornelia N. Moore, College of Languages, Linguistics and Literature—University of Hawaii, 1996, pp. 240–49.

PART IV UNCHASTE GODDESSES AND TRANSGRESSIVE WOMEN IN A TURBULENT NATION

11 A DARK GODDESS FOR A FALLEN WORLD

Mapping Apocalypse in Some of Bankim Chandra Chatterjee's Novels

MEENAKSHI MALHOTRA

India is one of the few places in the world where goddess worship is fervently practiced today, and part 4 examines the performance of female deification in the contexts of India's nineteenth-century liberation movement. Focusing on the Hindu feminine principle of Shakti, Meenakshi Malhotra, in her chapter "A Dark Goddess for a Fallen World," explores the major novels of pioneering novelist Bankim Chandra Chatterjee along a trajectory that traces linkages between Bankim Chandra's depiction of female characters and his attempts to reimagine and revivify an Indian culture battered by years of British rule. Malhotra argues that Bankim Chandra's use of woman as a trope signifying the variegated and contentious history of the putative state of India is specifically located within the cultural phenomenon of Kali-worship, the goddess of power who, prior to the nationalist movement, was primarily worshipped in the "fallen" world of criminals, misfits, and other marginalized populations. Malhotra concludes that Bankim Chandra's novels participate in recuperating Kali from racist, sensationalizing Western representations of her as a dark orgiastic and reconstitutes her in a form that empowers the nationalist movement.

This chapter explores linkages between Bankim Chandra Chatterjee's depiction of female characters and his attempts to foster the development of an Indian national consciousness capable of stimulating and sustaining a nationalist movement leading to India's independence.[1] In *Anandamath* (*Abbey of Bliss*; 1882) and *Debi*

Chaudhurani (*The Wife Who Came Home*; 1884), Bankim Chandra succeeds in forging a revolutionary trope of woman-as-nation based on nationalist reinterpretations of the goddess Kali, whereas previous novels, such as *Krishnakanter Will* (*Krishnakanta's Will*) and *Bishabriksha* (*The Poison Tree*), feature early versions of this figure that are tragic and incomplete because they—Rohini and Hira, respectively—are women situated precariously between regressive traditions and discomforting new models of womanhood imported from the West. As Sudipta Kaviraj points out, these early novels manifest an "unhappy contradictory consciousness," for women who exemplify the traditional ideal of Indian womanhood are shown as virtuous though oppressed, while the "fallen woman" who exhibits a "socially unsanctified form of passion . . . threatens the mapping and the whole architecture of the social world" (6). This impasse is finally resolved in *Anandamath* and *Debi Chaudhurani*, in a reformulation of the mythos of the wildly transgressive Kali that fashions a burgeoning concept of the nation as the motherland.

To make this argument, I rely on Fredric Jameson's theory that most postcolonial texts narrate and present an allegory of nation, an argument that is extended by critics like Sangeeta Ray and Makarand Paranjape who analyze the imbrication of the concept of "woman" with the putative Indian nation or nation-in-the-making. Jameson, in his monograph on Wyndham Lewis, *Fables of Aggression* (2008), and an article entitled "Third-World Literature in the Era of Multinational Capitalism," proposes that "the story of the private individual destiny is always an allegory of the embattled situation of the public third-world culture and society" (69).[2] Ray focuses on unravelling the intimate connections among nation-building, narration, the novel, and gender in her book *En-gendering India*, examining how the figure of the "Hindu woman" emerges as a site of contestation and debate: "After 1857, the figure of the Hindu woman begins to function as a crucial semiotic site in and around which the discourses of imperialism, nationalism, an Indian post colonialism and feminism are complexly inscribed" (3). Likewise, Paranjape, in his essay on *Rajmohan's Wife* (1864), Bankim Chandra's first and only novel in English, reads the character of Matangini (Rajmohan's wife), as a signifier that mirrors the narrative of the nation, metonymically representing a space or site where contradicting ideologies are played out. Building on their work, in this chapter, I will situate my argument about woman as trope and cultural symbol signifying the variegated, contentious history of the new nation in the cultural phenomenon of Kali worship, which gained a new popularity in fin-de-siècle Bengal. In doing so, I challenge the androcentric bias in most modern Indian national imaginings.

In his two explicitly political and historical novels, *Anandamath* and *Debi Chaudhurani*, Bankim Chandra represents the nation-in-the-making as the motherland by drawing on the specific mythos of the goddess Kali,[3] one of three mother goddesses associated with the nation. The first is Jagaddhatri,[4] a representation of what the motherland was in the past, the second is Kali,[5] what the mother has become in the present, and the third is an image of the mother in the future, Durga.[6] *Anandamath*, which was serialized in *Bangadarshan*,[7] a literary journal, and subsequently published as a full-length novel in 1882, is set during the

Bengal famine of 1771.[8] It depicts the state of Bengal as impoverished and reduced to misery by agrarian and other policies of the British East India Company, the corporation that governed India during this period. The novel also draws on the Sannyasi Rebellion of the 1770s[9] when Hindu and Muslim ascetics and monks, taking a vow to emancipate their country, rebelled against the East India Company. *Debi Chaudhurani* enacts a fantasy of female empowerment with the female protagonist, a rejected Bengali wife, Prafulla, training to take leadership of a band of bandits after being transformed into Debi Chaudhurani,[10] the queen of the *dacoits* (a band of armed robbers). However, the novel closes with her reunion with her long-lost husband, Brajendra, which is somewhat disappointing since Prafulla's choice to return to her life as a housewife valorizes traditional patriarchal ideologies.

Both *Anandamath* and *Debi Chaudhurani* merge political allegory and historical romance, but Bankim Chandra builds his narrative on slender historical evidence. The past they imagine is glorious and effulgent and hearkens to Bengal's past glories, whereas the future or the emergent bespeaks rejuvenation and revival of Bengal's lost glories and fortunes. The present dominates the novels in powerful tropes that represent Bengal's degraded and impoverished condition: in *Anandamath*, the figure of goddess Kali, specifically imagined as the mother, and in *Debi Chaudhurani*, Prafulla, who metamorphoses from an unfortunate victim into the powerful bandit leader, Debi Chaudhurani, simultaneously embody both powerlessness and emancipation. Consequently, cultural anxieties coalesce around these figures, paralleling the constellation of contentious national debates around a divinized construction of Mother India—disputes about authenticity and imitation, tradition and modernity, and religion and science—to which Sumathi Ramaswamy avers in her book *The Goddess and the Nation: Mapping Mother India*.[11]

BACKGROUND

Numerous scholars suggest that Bankim Chandra experienced the pull of conflicting ideologies that his novels manifest. His project was to write a history of Bengal, and he was convinced that only a Bengali could execute this task in an authentic manner, but as Kaviraj writes of Bankim Chandra's psyche in *The Unhappy Consciousness*, the author was torn between a rich but outworn religious tradition and secular modernity. As an ardent nationalist, Bankim Chandra maintained a similarly contradictory, paradoxical position vis-à-vis the colonial government, which provided him employment as a district magistrate for most of his career. Although conflicts with British rulers marked his years in the civil service, in 1894 he earned the designation of Companion, Most Eminent Order of the Indian Empire, an honorary organization founded by Queen Victoria. Parallel tensions resonate through Bankim Chandra's novels, and they mirror disputes occurring throughout India during the period.

These conflicts were sparked, of course, by British colonization and rule of India, which necessitated the cultural contacts between Britain and India that heralded modernity. Affecting disparate areas of life and existence, these interactions catalyzed the development of the Indian novel, and Bankim Chandra was one of the first practitioners of this new form. As such, he is credited with being one of the chief architects of the Bengal Renaissance, the nineteenth-century sociocultural and religious reform movement that transformed Bengali society and culture. Thus Bankim Chandra's novels chart a period when the fabric of India's traditional values and institutions was threatened by tumultuous, wide-ranging changes to everything from agrarian policies to caste structures. Passage of the Permanent Settlement Act of 1793[12] and outlawing sati,[13] for instance, betokened shifting values in a process led by Indian reformers such as Raja Ram Mohan Roy,[14] who exerted pressure on the British government to hasten the process. Others, including Ishwar Chandra Vidyasagar,[15] strived to legalize widow remarriage (1856), which was strictly prohibited, with widows (depending on their class status) forced to fast and live in isolation from their families and communities, their heads shaved, deprived of even small comforts, and reviled as harbingers of misfortune.[16] Contending that traditional norms shaping Hindu marriage were unjust to women, these men favored companionate marriage. This indirectly helped the cause of women's education (at least among the upper and middle classes) when a preference for educated wives emerged, and small but significant steps increased girls' access to formal schooling. Throughout the nineteenth century, in fact, a great deal of legislation ameliorated women's lot, triggering debate on the age of consent, for example, and polarizing public opinion. Significantly, the Bengali elite split into reformists and conservatives, and Bankim Chandra sided with the latter. Hence in his essay "Prachina o Nobina" ("The Traditional versus the New-Fangled Woman"), Bankim Chandra argues for maintaining tradition and custom and against the encroaching forces of modernity.

The new institutions of companionate and monogamous marriages provide Bankim Chandra rich opportunities to depict a particularly fraught moment of social transition. Many of his protagonists are young men from the landed gentry,[17] the *zamindari* or land-owning class, who are caught between two contradictory systems of morality. On one hand, Bankim Chandra's young men want to satisfy adulterous desires, yet the new conjugality demands monogamy, which was not universally practiced in the nineteenth century.[18] A recurring trope that appears in texts like *Bishabriksha* and *Krishnakanter Will* is a love triangle involving an unfaithful husband, a loving, morally pure wife, and a beautiful, seductive widow. The figure of the widow is problematic in both these novels and raises questions, as in some of Rabindranath Tagore's novels—*Chokher Bali* (*A Mote in the Eye*)[19], for instance—about widows' fates under oppressive social arrangements, such as prohibition of widow remarriage and *purdah* (women's confinement to domestic spaces).[20] In these works, the young, beautiful widow, who represents a threat to the established social structure and occupies the third point in the triangulated relationship, is constructed as Other. However, this character is developed along contradictory axes—beautiful and desirable on the one hand, but also embodying a desire that is dangerous and ultimately destructive. Bankim Chandra's novels likewise portray the widow dichotomously, both sympathetically—her condemnation to endless isolation and mourning evokes compassion—and censoriously because she seduces the husband character and lures him from his virtuous wife. This endows her with an ambiguity that is never resolved. In contrast, the wife emerges not only as the victim of a failed monogamous compact but also as a symbol of indigeneity and a custodian of the threatened values of purity and chastity. In sum, she is a protector of the nation. In this manner, Bankim Chandra's novels veer between condemnation of the widow's illicit desires and pity for her as well as the rejected wife. This oscillation reflects anxieties about social change and offers a mixed assessment of its consequences despite Bankim Chandra's conservatism.

KALI: BANKIM CHANDRA'S UNCONVENTIONAL STANDARD-BEARER FOR THE NATION

Where does this leave the question of the nation, Bankim Chandra's stated resolve to write a true history of Bengal, and his contradictory position vis-à-vis the colonial government? Obviously, a deep ambivalence marks his deployment of the trope of nation-as-women, particularly because it is foregrounded in the helplessness and powerlessness of the nation-in-the-making. Neither the heroines of classical Indian literature nor the modern woman, who is often seen as imitating her Western counterpart, provided an adequate blueprint or stage on which the discourse of nationhood could be performed. However, the goddess Kali, who was worshipped primarily by *dacoits* and bandits before the nineteenth century because she was considered destructive and sometimes associated with the occult, proves a potent signifier of feminized cultural nationalism and indigeneity, and her mythology offers Bankim Chandra a rich field of symbols and signifiers.

In the Hindu pantheon gods and goddesses, one finds Kali, a Sanskrit word that means "black one" and "force of time" because of her dark skin and her associations with Kali Yuga, a future epoch marked with chaos and struggle.[21] Kali was created by powerful male gods to defend the cosmos against demons who threatened to disrupt and destabilize it. According to sacred Hindu texts, the gods met this threat by consolidating their powers to produce Shakti (female creative energy). Shakti subsequently splits into two entities, the fair goddess Gauri[22] and the fierce Kali. Kali attacks and kills the demons and then launches a wild, celebratory dance that ends when she inadvertently trods on the god Shiva,[23] who has prostrated himself on the ground to stop her cavorting. When she realizes that she has landed on his chest, Kali's tongue protrudes from her mouth, and she crosses it in a sign of shame that she has harmed Shiva, who is her consort in some but not all versions of the story. "The goddess Kali," as David Kinsley points out, "is almost always described as having a terrible and frightening appearance." She is usually naked and has long, disheveled hair. Her belt is fashioned from ten severed arms, she is garlanded with freshly decapitated heads, and her bracelets are serpents. She has long, sharp fangs and fingernails, claw-like hands, and blood smeared across her lips. Her usual haunts are battlefields, where she is portrayed as a furious warrior, and cremation grounds, where she is pictured in the company of lowly animals like the jackal (Kinsley 116). In some myths, Kali incites Shiva to perform destructive acts that threaten the cosmos' stability. A stark contrast with the many lithe, beautiful, and elegant women, both divine and human, in classical literature, Kali is beyond the pale of canonical, institutionalized Hinduism and its icons.

REPRESENTATIONS OF KALI IN ANCIENT AND MEDIEVAL TEXTS

In most of Kali's literary incarnations prior to Bankim Chandra's novels, she is associated with the periphery of Hindu society. Her devotees are mainly low-caste or tribal people, and her temples are traditionally located far away from towns and villages, near cremation grounds and the dwellings of *Chandalas* (a low caste whose members perform death rites). The *Agni-* and *Garuda-Puranas* record that her worshippers petition Kali for success in war. In 5.9.12–20 of the *Bhagavata-Purana*,[24] as Kinsley documents, Kali is represented as a patron saint of outlaws, who invoke her in fertility rites that involve human sacrifice. Significantly, this vivifies her image and Kali turns on them:

> Kali is the patron deity of a band of thieves whose leader seeks to attain Kali's blessings in order to have a son. A thief kidnaps a saintly Brahmin youth with the intention of offering him as a blood sacrifice to Kali. The effulgence of the virtuous youth, however, burns Kali herself when he is brought near herimage. Emerging from her image, infuriated, she kills the leader and his entire band. She is described as having a dreadful face and large teeth and as laughing loudly. She and her host of demons then decapitate the corpses of the thieves, drink their blood until drunk, and throw their heads about in sport. (128)

Banabhatta's seventh-century drama *Kadambari*[25] contains a similar story featuring a goddess named Chandi, "an epithet used for both Durga and Kali." Here, a tribe of hunters worship Chandi, plying her with "blood offerings" (128).[26] This pattern of representation appears in numerous other texts, explains Kinsley. Vakpati's[27] *Gaudavaho: A Historical Poem* (late seventh and early eighth century) portrays Kali as an aspect of Vindhyavasini (an epithet for Durga).[28] She is worshipped by *sabaras* (hunters), is clothed in leaves, and receives human sacrifice (verses 285–347). In Bhavabhuti's *Malatimadhava*,[29] a drama of the early eighth century, a female devotee of Chamunda,[30] a goddess who is very often associated with Kali, captures the heroine, Malati, with the intention of sacrificing her to the goddess (128–30).

Like Kali, Chamunda is depicted as a terrible goddess, a *materna dentate*, a mother-goddess with a gaping mouth and bloody fangs. One hymn praising Chamunda describes her as "dancing wildly and making the earth shake" just as Kali did in the episode in which she defeated the demons who threatened to destroy the cosmos. Another text in which Kali appears is Somadeva's *Yasatalika*[31] (eleventh to twelfth century), which contains a long description of a goddess called Candamari that evokes Kali's iconography: "[Candamari] adorns herself with pieces of human corpses, uses oozings from corpses for cosmetics, bathes in rivers of wine and blood, sports in cremation grounds and uses human skulls as drinking vessels. Bizarre and fanatical devotees gather at her temple and undertake forms of ascetic self-torture" (130).

By far one of the most popular stories surrounding Kali features her dance competition with Shiva. Kali had been terrorizing the forest Thillai and its inhabitants.

Shiva intervenes, but Kali refuses to leave. They decide to settle the matter in a dance contest. They are evenly matched, and it appears that neither will win. But Shiva cheats by lifting his foot over his head, a move, ironically, that Kali cannot make lest it violate her feminine modesty. In a rare loss, Kali is at least temporality subdued.

Thus in the pantheon of Hindu goddesses, Kali represents an element, a force that is disruptive, wild, and uncontrollable. She threatens stability and order, and when she kills and subdues demons and other villainous figures, she becomes frenzied and drunk on her victims' blood, posing a threat to even "friendly" bystanders. She represents an aspect of reality that is not amenable to human control and, as such, is liminal and untamable. Kali is cast in the image of a mother goddess who resolutely resists domestication.

KALI WORSHIP

Kali worship can be traced to 500–600 BCE, but it is possible that she was venerated in earlier, matriarchal, pre-Vedic eras. Devotion to Kali, which was not widespread prior to the nineteenth century, increased in Bengal in the 1890s and the first decade of the twentieth century especially among militant nationalists, outlaws, forest-dwellers (tribal populations), and emerging fringe groups that discovered in Kali a powerful resource for protesting their poverty and downtrodden status and articulating their aspirations for political empowerment. As a mother goddess associated with fertility, birth, and creativity as well as violence, martial prowess, and anger, Kali offered the movement for independence a particularly apt narrative and iconography.

Another phenomenon that promoted Kali worship in Bengal in the nineteenth century was the emergence of a new sect that, merging classical Hinduism, Tantrism, and other forms of worship, rejected dualism. This sect, established by Ramakrishna Paramahamsa, a mystic and ascetic who was dedicated to Kali, offered devotees a space outside the domain of colonialism, which in turn helped trigger a Hindu revival. The middle class, argues Tanita Sarkar, had been emasculated by nineteenth-century colonial institutions so that it was predisposed to be attracted to Ramakrishna Paramahamsa's doctrine. She notes that with the expansion of education to the middle classes, increasing numbers of Bengali men had joined the lower echelons of colonial administrative service. This added one more layer to Indian men's long subordination to the British, putting them in the servile role of "service-providers" who came to be referred to as servants, *chakri* in Bengali and *naukri* in Hindi. While goddess worship might appear to be an internal contradiction in these contexts, Kali's fierceness—her performance of virile masculinity—is precisely what made her appealing, for devotees could reclaim a sense of manliness by associating themselves with Kali's masterfulness. She offered them an empowered sense of self that colonialism had eroded at a time when Indian men were increasingly characterized as cowardly and effeminate (Sinha 1995 and Chowdhury 1995). Consequently, the symbolic valences and resonances of Kali worship gained new meaning and significance while Ramakrishna's precepts offered the Bengali middle-class autonomy (or an illusion of it). In this way, Kali worship spread beyond the fringes and into mainstream Indian society.

KALI AS A SIGNIFIER OF CULTURAL NATIONALISM

Bankim Chandra both contributed to and was influenced by this expansion of Kali worship in Bengal. Departing from classical and medieval Indian literary conventions, *Anandamath*'s use of Kali to signify time and political change reveals a modern, secular, rationalist sensibility (despite Bankim Chandra's conservatism) that distinguishes the novel from previous works fraught with tensions between tradition and change. As Jasodhara Bagchi argues in "Positivism and Nationalism: Womanhood and Crisis in Nationalist Fiction Bankim Chandra's *Anandamath*," in Bankim Chandra's later novels, "order and progress are not discussed in terms of social analysis, nor in naturalistic psychological terms" (129). Instead, "Broad historical canvases are lit up by the lurid glow of a vengeful, often mythologized, order threatened from within and without" (129). Furthermore, argues Bagchi, womanhood is central to *Anandamath*'s challenges to order, attributing this innovation to Auguste Comte's influence. Comte's Positivist project, of course, was to "remove social phenomena from the sphere of theological and metaphysical conceptions" (Morley qtd. in Bagchi WS-50). Unlike Comte, however, Bankim Chandra did not believe that Indians would rally behind a secular independence movement. Rather, he concluded that a sense of nationalism could best be cultivated through religion, albeit a new, doctrinally unconventional religion. Hence he proposed that God inhabits all humans and is best worshipped by working for others—both locally and globally—with love of country being the highest good aside from love of the world, which Bankim Chandra considered an impractical pursuit. He also extended Comte's idea that women and feminine principle are particularly powerful forces for social change: equating the nation with the divine maternal, Bankim Chandra asserted that the homeland is all Indians' divine mother—Shakti—and argued that "she" should be the object of their devotion. This adaptation of Shakti's mythology to the Indian nationalist project lent the figure of the mother goddess a new militancy in *Anandamath*'s parable of national confrontation and rendered womanhood an emblem of resistance to the ravaged order engendered by India's oppression under British.

Significantly, *Anandamath* employs the figure of Kali, who is central to Bengali Shakti worship (she was born from Shakti and, like Shakti, is associated with motherhood) to embody "ravaged" India, marking the first time that Kali's iconography and imagery were employed for the purposes of political mobilization.[32] To recognize Kali's significance in India's nationalist movement and in *Anandamath*, it is necessary to understand Shakti, the maternal creative force.

Shakti, the divine mother goddess, embodies feminine creative power—a primordial cosmic energy. She is the creative force of the universe. She is motherly and sometimes ruthless; thus, she deconstructs the good/evil binary. This particular quality, that she transcends dualisms, was consistent with the rejection of dualism by the Hindu revivalists such as Ramakrishna. In Shaktism, which is a branch of Hinduism that privileges the maternal, Shakti's creative, feminine power undergirds all else, including the male principle. Similarly, in Tantrism, which is not a form of Hinduism but shares many of its icons and myths, Shakta is the creative force of the universe, and all women are symbols of the Divine Mother. Shakti is manifest in many Hindu goddesses, including Kali.

In *Anandamath*, Kali's darkness signifies India's degradation. An ascetic Hindu monk, Satyananda, tells Mahendra, the female protagonist, about the past state of the motherland, which, he says, was glorious. But in its present, impoverished form, India is like Kali, the dark mother. The ascetic narrates, "Look, what the mother has come to . . . Kali, the dark mother. She is naked because the country is impoverished, the country is now been turned into the cremation ground, so the mother is garlanded with skulls" (88). However, the monk asserts that this condition is temporary and will end once revolutionaries rescue the motherland from the clutches of foreign interlopers and restore India to its original pristine form and glory. In this passage, Kali's iconography is welded to a vocabulary of economic deprivation and colonial degradation, an important innovation in Indian literature as well as contemporary political discourses that metaphorically and metonymically use Kali to articulate a modern historical analysis. Aside from politicizing her figure, the novel infuses the trope of Kali with a twofold dynamic. As mentioned previously, she is associated with time, "*kala*," which is the etymological root of her name, and in *Anandamath*, Kali signifies two times, the current "fallen" time of colonial oppression and the incipient time of a revolution-in-the-making that will liberate India from the British Empire. Bengal's miserable state, says the monk, is not permanent, and a historical epoch will come when the nation's sons restore the motherland to its former glory. Here, Bankim Chandra encodes a warning to the colonial ruler that times—*kala*—will change and that Hindustan will emerge unfettered.

To wit, Bankim Chandra's later novels endow women with "demonic power" that conveys the intensity of India's crisis. Kali's iconography is particularly effective in this respect, for her unbridled ferocity manifests the vagaries of history and the damage of elapsing time (*kala*). She signifies the troubled present and gestures toward the better future promised by nationhood. Thus the motherland's resplendent past, her wretched present, and her radiant future are all tropes that "appeal for a rising nationalist consciousness" (129). In the final analysis, the complex female characters in Bankim Chandra's novels suggest that if woman—feminine principle—is the repository and custodian of the nation, then the only way to liberate and reconfigure the nation is to revise the figure of woman, to apotheosize her in the image of Kali, thereby birthing a "terrible beauty." The figure and mythology of Kali, as employed by Bankim Chandra and the larger nationalist movement in the nineteenth century thus exists at the interstices of religion, colonialism, and politics and, furthermore, locates these institutions at the site of gender. Without doubt, Bankim Chandra's novels depict, as he aspired, Bengal's history, or, as Kaviraj frames it, its mythic history (1995, 144).

CONCLUSION

To an extent, Indian feminism in the late twentieth and early twenty-first century, somewhat akin to nineteenth-century nationalism, faces competing pressures from religious ideologies, historical discourses, and contemporary narratives as it seeks a prototype for and space in the postcolonial feminine. The Hindu right's political mobilization of women in the 1990s reveals the complexities involved in this project.[33] Hindu conservatives, to further an agenda of imposing on India a definition of citizenship that equates Indian national identity and "belonging" with Hindu values and traditions, fostered women's public leadership, albeit through sex-segregated institutions, for the purpose of promoting traditional norms governing women, particularly conventions that contain them to the domestic sphere and limit their social roles to wife and mother (Berglund 397, 401). Feminist critiques of this tactic—whether used by feminists or Hindu conservatives—offer two insights. One is that the use of the figure of Kali and similar warrior-woman goddesses to represent Indian womanhood or female empowerment is problematic because it is exclusionary and limiting. As Flavia Agnes, a feminist lawyer and activist, argued in a landmark speech, the women's movement in India, for all its "secular pretensions, was normatively Hindu" in a nation of diverse religious affiliations (qtd. in Ray 7). Furthermore, the Hindu right's cooptation of the strategy of using sacred iconography to institute *anti*feminist social change shows that legitimization of violence can be among this approach's consequences. As Berglund explains, in the 1980s and 1990s, right-wing Hindu nationalist groups adopted "role models of Hindu women and goddesses acting as warriors, [which] replaced or supplemented the previous ideal of the women as primarily mothers, wives, and care-takers" (391). Conservative women such as Sadhvi Ritambhara subsequently took a leading role in fomenting violence against Muslims, as when the Vishwa Hindu Parisha and Bharatiya Janata Party destroyed the Babri Mosque in 1992.[34] This episode sparked riots throughout India and serial bombings in Mumbai in 1993, and conservative Muslim groups cite its demolition to justify their violence against Hindus. This result demonstrates that deploying warrior-women goddesses to create indigenous "feminisms" and politically mobilize middle-class Hindu women is problematic and hardly emancipatory.

The feminist critique, however, does not detract from the value of deploying Kali's story and symbolism to support the nineteenth-century nationalist movement, a crucial juncture in Indian history. As Kaviraj points out in his essay "The Imaginary Institution of India," until that time, Indian nationalism existed in "gerrymandering" narratives like the Mangal-kavyas[35] of geographically dispersed communities. Bankim Chandra and those who followed him in politicizing Kali transformed these scattered discourses into a national narrative that contributed to establishing independent India.

NOTES

1 Bankim Chandra Chatterjee or Chattopadhay (b. 1838–94) is generally viewed as the first novelist in Bengal. His first novel, *Rajmohan's Wife* (1864), was written in English, but his later novels, written in Bengali, made him a household name in Bengal.

2 Aijaz Ahmed has criticized Jameson's use of the term "Third World literature" in relation as reductionist in that it suggests that "Third World" literatures are nationalistic, which is problematic among Westerners who, from the perspective of "global American postmodernist culture," have a "tendency to remind us of outmoded stages of our development" (65). However, Jameson is keen to distinguish the national allegory of "Third World" literatures from the traditional Western conception of allegory as "an elaborate set of figures and personifications to be read against some one-to-one table of equivalences" (73).

3 See note 5.

4 *Jagaddhatri* literally means "the holder of the world," and associated with the morning sun, she is glorious and effulgent.

5 Kali is that aspect of the mother goddess that is terrifying, aggressive, and threatening. She is depicted as dwelling outside the pale of reason and law and is associated with power, energy, birth, death, and reincarnation. Her role is to destroy evil.

6 Durga is a popular form of the mother goddess. Ten-armed, she is associated with salvation.

7 Bankim Chandra founded *Bangadarshan* in 1872. Publication stopped in the 1880s, but Rabindranath Tagore revived it in 1901. The magazine was instrumental in fostering Bengali nationalism.

8 Between 1769 and 1773, approximately ten million people died, roughly one-third the population in the affected area, which included present-day West Bengal, Bengal, Bangladesh, and parts of Assam, Odisha, Bihar, and Jharkhand. The British East India Company, which governed the region, unnecessarily elevated the death toll by forcing farmers to replace food with cash crops like opium, monopolizing trade in food crops, and raising taxes to unpayable levels (sometimes by as much as fifty to sixty percent in a short period of time).

9 The term *sannyasi* means "ascetic." In the Sannyasi Rebellion, ascetics clashed with the British East India Company over taxes.

10 In the eighteenth century, Devi Chaudhurani was so well known for her efforts to elevate women's status in India that her name was used to insult others who shared this goal. Christine Garlough's "Transfiguring Criminality: Eclectic Representations of a Female Bandit in Indian Nationalist and Feminist Rhetoric" writes that in her lifetime Devi Chaudhurani was considered a criminal for violating "the law" and Victorian norms for female behavior. Later, Bankim Chandra appropriates her figure in his 1884 *Debi Chaudhurani*. Feminist writer, professor, and Communist Party politician Malini Bhattacharya features her in the 1987 street play, *Giving Away the Girls*. In this text, Devi Chaudhurani is a subversive character who deconstructs the nationalistic notion of Indian womanhood.

11 Mother India is an anthropomorphic personification of the nation. The usage of the term motherland evokes feelings of patriotic love toward the nation state, more so because it bespeaks a primal bond between a mother and a child: the nation state is the caregiver and mother, and citizens are her children. Depicting the state as a mother ravaged by external or internal antinationalist forces and needing protection is a particularly effective rallying strategy. Rabindranath Tagore's nephew, Abanindranath Tagore, a leading exponent of national (*swadeshi*) values in Indian art painted a portrait of Mother India, also known as Bharatmata, which depicted her as a goddess. Her four hands hold not weapons but promises of food, education, shelter, and salvation. Significantly, this new Mother India's eyes are downcast, suggesting that she is the married Hindu woman, chaste and committed.

12 The Permanent Settlement, an act initiated by Lord Cornwallis in 1703, was an agreement between the East India Company and Bengali landlords to fix the land tax without taking fluctuations in production into account.

13 *Sati* refers to a funeral ritual in some Indian communities in which a recently widowed woman commits suicide on the funeral pyre of her dead husband. It was outlawed in India in 1829.
14 Raja Ram Mohan Roy (b. 1775–1833) was a linguist and social reformer of vast repute. He founded the Brahmo Samaj.
15 Ishwar Chandra Vidyasagar was an educator and social reformer. Vidyasagar's efforts paved the way to widow remarriage in 1856.
16 See Radha Chakravarty's chapter in this volume.
17 The landed gentry was a wealthy, powerful, nonaristocratic class who derived income primarily from renting agricultural lands and housing.
18 See Naina Dey's chapter in this volume. Since the Vedic period, *Kulin* (of aristocratic and noble descent) institutionalized polygamy among high-ranking Bengali Brahmins. *Zamindari* also practiced polygamy.
19 See Radha Chakravarty's chapter in this volume. *Chokher Bali* is translated as both *A Mote in the Eye* and the more widely used title *Grain of Sand*, which is the variant that Chakravarty uses. One reason for the discrepancy in translation is that *bali* means both "female friend" and "sand." Tagore plays on this double meaning to suggest that the two women in the novel who are in love with the same man have an uneasy relationship that is as discomforting as the feeling of a mote or sand particle in one's eye.
20 *Purdah*, depending on the era, region, and religion, varies from strict sex segregation among relatives to confining women in the home. It can include sartorial regulations mandating that women cover parts or all of their bodies.
21 Sanskrit scriptures divide time into four phases. The first three are *Satya Yuga*, *Treta Yuga*, and *Dvapara Yuga*. *Kali Yuga* is the last of the four stages in this cycle. Here, the *Kali* of *Kali Yuga* means "strife," "discord," "quarrel," or "contention," not the goddess Kali.
22 Gauri is a name sometimes used to refer to the goddesses Parvati and Durga. All three are mother goddesses.
23 Shiva is one of the three major Hindu deities. The other two are Brahma and Vishnu. Shiva is also known as Maheshwara. These three gods form a *Trimurti* (Trinity) constituting of the supreme God who personifies the acts of creating, maintaining, and destroying the cosmos. Typically Brahma is the creator, Vishnu the preserver, and Shiva the destroyer and transformer. Shiva can be formless, limitless, transcendent, and unchanging as well as an omniscient Yogi who lives an ascetic life on Tibet's Mount Kailash, a sacred place in Hinduism and Buddhism.
24 Composed in Sanskrit, the *Agni-Purana*, *Garuda-Parana*, and the *Bhagavata-Purana* are three of eighteen texts that constitute a genre of their own. The earliest versions of these texts may have appeared in the first millennium CE, but they probably evolved over a much longer period. They treat a wide range of topics including, but not limited to, medicine, philosophy, law, education, and instructions for constructing civic projects. The *Garuda-Parana* centers on the god Vishnu, one of the three most important Hindu gods (see note 23). The *Bhagavata-Purana* promotes worship of Krishna, one of Vishnu's incarnations.
25 *Kadambari* is a lyrical prose romance in Sanskrit that narrates the love story of Kadambari, a princess, and Chandrapida, a prince who is the moon god.
26 The Sabaras are also known as the Sora tribe. Endogamous, they maintain a shamanic culture. The Sabaras live in western India, primarily along coastal areas but also inland.
27 In Sanskrit, Vakpati means "Lord of Speech." Vakpati was an eighth-century courtier in the court of King Yashovarman, the medieval ruler of Kannauj. His *Gaudavaho* tells how the king of Gauda (present-day Bengal) was slain.
28 Vindhyavasini is another name for the goddess Durga and literally means "she who resides in Vindhya," a mountain range in central India.

29 Bhavabhuti (c. 700 CE) was a poet and dramatist. His plays, written in Sanskrit, are noted for their suspense and vivid characterization. A romance, *Malatimadhava* combines the names of the woman and man who are the play's protagonists—*malati* and *madhava*.

30 Chamunda is a fearsome aspect of Devi or Kali, the Hindu Divine Mother and one of the seven Matrikas (mother goddesses). She is also one of the chief Yoginis, a group of Tantric goddesses, who are attendants of the warrior goddess Durga. Her name is a combination of Chanda and Munda, two monsters that she killed. Chamanda is often portrayed as haunting cremation grounds or fig trees.

31 Somadeva was a Kashmiri Brahman of the Śaiva sect who transcribed to Sanskrit much of India's ancient folklore in a series of tales written in verse.

32 Bankim Chandra Chattopadhay was one of the first writers, chronologically, to use religious icons as a marker of Hindu nationalism and Hindu cultural identity, but he was certainly not the last.

33 See *Women and The Hindu Right* (1995) by Urvashi Butalia and Tanika Sarkar for an analysis of the use and deployment of religious imagery in the politics of the Hindu right in the 1990s.

34 Centuries in the past, the Babri Mosque had been built on a Hindu place of worship, and Hindu rightists wished to reclaim the site.

35 The Mangal-kavyas are funerary verses sung in honor of gods and goddesses. Because Mangal poetry is noncanonical, these texts are unfixed and vary per performers' preferences and evolve over time.

WORKS CITED

Bagchi, Jasodhara. "Positivism and Nationalism: Womanhood and Crisis in Nationalist Fiction—Bankim Chandra's *Anandamath*." *Women's Studies in India: A Reader*, edited by Mary E. John, Penguin, 2008, pp. 124–31.

Berglund, Henrik. "Including Women: Strategies of Mobilization within the Hindu Nationalist Movement." *India Review*, vol. 8, no. 4, 2009, pp. 385–403, http://www.academia.edu/7168692/Including_Women_Strategies_of_Mobilization_Within_the_Hindu_Nationalist_Movement.

Bhattacarya, Malini. *Giving Away the Girls and Other Plays*. Seagull Books, 2001.

Butalia, Urvashi, and Tanika Sarkar, editors. *Women and the Hindu Right: A Collection of Essays*. Kali for Women, 1995.

Chattopadhyay, Bankim Chandra. *Anandamath, or The Sacred Brotherhood*. Translated by Julius Lipner, Oxford UP, 2005.

———. *The Bankimchandra Omnibus Vol. 1*. Translated by Radha Chakravarti and Marian Maddern, Penguin Classics, 2005.

Chowdhury, Indira. *The Frail Hero and Virile History: Gender and the Politics of Culture in Colonial Bengal*. Oxford UP, 1994.

Garlough, Christine L. "Transfiguring Criminality: Eclectic Representations of a Female Bandit in Indian Nationalist and Feminist Rhetoric." *Quarterly Journal of Speech*, vol. 93, no. 3, 2007, pp. 253–78.

Jameson, Frederic. *Fables of Aggression: Wyndham Lewis, the Modernist as Fascist*. Verso, 2008.

———. "Third-World Literature in the Era of Multinational Capitalism." *Social Text*, no. 15, 1986, pp. 65–88.

Kaviraj, Sudipta. *The Unhappy Consciousness*. Oxford UP, 1995.

Kinsley, David. *Hindu Goddesses: Visions of the Divine Feminine in the Hindu Religious Tradition*. Motilal Banarsi Das, 1986.

Mehrotra, Rajiv. *Thakur Sri Ramakrishna: A Biography*. Hay House, 2009.

Paranjape, Makrand. *Making India: Colonialism, National Culture and the Afterlife of Indian English Authority*. Springer Science and Business Media, 2012.

Ramaswamy, Sumathi. *The Goddess and the Nation: Mapping Mother India*. Chicago UP, 2009.

Ray, Raka, editor. *Handbook of Gender*. Oxford UP, 2012.
Ray, Sangeeta. *En-Gendering India: Women and Nation in Colonial and Postcolonial Narratives*. Duke UP, 2000.
Ricoeur, Paul. *Time and Narrative*. Translated by Kathleen McLaughlin et al., U of Chicago P, 1984. 3 vols.
Sarkar, Sumit. "Renaissance and Kaliyuga: Time, Myth and History in Colonial Bengal." *Writing Social History*. Oxford UP, 1998, pp. 186–215.
Sinha, Mrinalini. *Colonial Masculinity*. Oxford UP, 1995.

12 DESIRE AND DHARMA

A Study of the Representation of Fallen Women in the Novels of Bankim Chandra

CHANDRANI BISWAS

In this chapter, Chandrani Biswas continues the exploration of Bankim Chandra Chatterjee's novels, looking at *Kapalkundala* (1866), *Bishabriksha* (*The Poison Tree*; 1873) and *Krishnakanter Will* (*Krishnakanta's Will*; 1878). In her chapter, Biswas looks at Bankim Chandra's use of the fallen women motif vis-à-vis Bengal's rigid, patriarchal nineteenth-century milieu. By focusing on the concept of fallenness within the social and cultural complexities of the region where Bankim Chandra lived and analyzing the rationale for cultural practices that confine women to positions of subservience, Biswas examines female characters who dare to experiment with their own lives, violating the social codes, norms, and expectations of their society. Thus she considers concepts such as *satittwa* (women's chastity) to show that, paradoxically, Bankim Chandra's transgressive female characters are more empowered than stereotypical heroines who conform to traditional constructs of womanhood.

INTRODUCTION

This chapter examines—puts in critical perspective—"fallen" women in three novels by Bankim Chandra: *Kapalkundala* (1866),[1] *Bishabriksha* (1873), and *Krishnakanter Will* (1878). Bankim Chandra depicts a complex variety of female protagonists in these novels, works that highlight tensions between individual sensibility and social codes that delineated "correctness" in India's rigid, nineteenth-century patriarchal culture, and this chapter probes the performance of female fallenness against this background. Hence it analyzes the rationale for cultural practices that confined women to positions of subservience and interrogates the books' representations of a new type of female protagonist who dares to resist conventional social codes, norms, and social expectations.

BACKGROUND

The etymology of the Sanskrit word *upanyas* (novel) can be traced to the participle *upanyasta*, which means "placed" or "kept near." The *oupanyasik* (novelist), of course, is one who represents human experience and complex social situations fictionally. Yet the possibilities available to novelists for shaping their fiction and their flexibility to choose among these options are heavily dependent on the social fabric, values, and norms of the age. In the nineteenth century, Indian novelists had to mediate between two sets of mostly dichotomous social contexts—an alien literature and local social contingencies. In literature as in reality, women were conceived as the purveyors of domestic virtues, objects of procreation, nurturers, and keepers of the hearth. The ideal woman was a romantic image of frailty, delicacy, helplessness, and acquiescence. "Good" women ritually, mechanically performed their duties while their minds remained unenlightened and barren. A woman had no rights over her own property or products of her labor (until 1965). She was often stereotyped in literature either as the "angel" or as the "whore," the *sati*[2] or the *asati nari*. Interestingly, even language was assessed and categorized in terms of gender, with female virtue associated with elites' discourses and the vernacular depicted in terms of female sexual "fallenness": "Thus Mritunjoy Vidyalankar,[3] himself a teacher of Bengali, disparaged the vernacular as 'a naked and prostituted female' compared to Sanskrit—'a beautiful and virtuous woman'" (qtd. in Sangari and Vaid 12). John Stuart Mill's appraisal of Hindu society and women is noteworthy in this regard. According to Mill, Hindu women were in ". . . a state of dependence more strict and humiliating than that which is ordained for the weaker sex. . . . Nothing can exceed the habitual contempt which Hindus entertain for their woman. . . . They are held in extreme degradation, excluded from the sacred books, deprived of education and (of a share) in the paternal property. . . . That remarkable barbarity, the wife held unworthy to eat with her husband, is prevalent in Hindustan" (qtd. in Sangari and Vaid 35).

Though largely offering a prejudiced, Eurocentric view of Hindu society, Mill's argument was not completely deficient of truth. In fact, nineteenth-century social discourse was much influenced by Brahminical texts such as Manu's[4] code, which says, "Obedience to her husband is the beginning, and the middle and the end of female duty" (qtd. in Sangari and Vaid 43). And, as other chapters in this volume demonstrate,[5] Indian mythology, scripture, fairy tales, classical romantic tales, and other genres that idealized women's obedience to men had long shaped audiences' notions of conjugal love. For example, in the story of the Savitri and Satyavan—wife and husband, respectively—Savitri's promise to follow Satyavan even in death signifies the depth and purity of her love for him and, indeed, her moral character: when the god of death, Yama, attempts to collect Satyavan, Savitri says, "Where he goes, my path shall be, I will follow where thou leadest, listen once again to me" (quoted in Sangari and Vaid 44).[6]

But not all nineteenth-century scholars and public intellectuals agreed that Indian women were totally and absolutely "degraded." In sharp contrast to Mill's views on Hindu women, Romesh Chunder Dutt[7] in *History of Civilization in Ancient India highlights the honored status women occupied in the Vedic Period* (*1500–500* BCE)[8]: Do not such passages as these indicate that women were honored in ancient India, more perhaps than among any other ancient nation in the face of the globe? Considered the intellectual companions of their husbands, as their affectionate helpers in the journey of life, and as inseparable partners in their religious duties, Hindu wives received the honor and respect due to their position (qtd. in Sangari and Vaid 51). As this account documents, women were honored in ancient India. They were considered their husbands' intellectual companions, affectionate helpers in the journey of life, and inseparable partners in their religious duties.

Significantly, the intellectual climate in nineteenth-century Bengal was fraught with questions about women's status and gendered institutions to the degree that the period is associated with a crisis in values triggered by a tradition-bound society's exposure to a liberal, humanistic, European worldview. Thus Bankim Chandra began his literary career not only in the midst of monumental cultural conflict but also prior to the emergence of a fully mature novelistic fiction in India, and his efforts were directed at creating a new language, a new literature, and not incidentally, a new nation; although armed uprisings against the British had occurred since at least the 1750s, not coincidentally, the modern independence movement came into its own in the early nineteenth century as traditional cultural values were being questioned vigorously. One of Bankim Chandra's strategies for crafting the new literature was to transfer indigenous themes into the genre of the novel. In his nationalistic era, this maneuver contributed to the formation of an aggressive, militant masculinism endowed with the spirituality of a renouncer or *sanyasi*, a religious ascetic who has renounced the world by performing his own funeral and abandoning all claims to social or family standing.

KAPALKUNDALA

Kapalkundala (1866) centers on the character of Kapalkundala, a child of nature untainted by the complexities of civilized existence. Although the narrative primarily focuses on the heroine's rites of passage into an unknown social space—an urbanized human community—the book's representations of the "other" woman in the novel, Motibibi, a woman who transgresses norms governing women's behavior, shed light on tensions surrounding contemporary challenges to traditional notions of femininity.

Set during the reign of Mughal emperors Akbar and his son Selim, who was known as Emperor Jahangir (b. 1569–1627), *Kapalkundala*'s subplot centers on a young girl, Padmavati, the first wife of a character named Nabakumar. Padmavati's father forces her to convert to Islam, which prompts the Hindu Nabakumar to divorce her. Padmavati, who is given the name Motibibi when she becomes Muslim, seeks a new home in the Mughal court in Agra, the empire's capital city located near present-day Delhi on the Yamun River[9] where, assuming a new identity, she establishes herself as a woman of accomplishment and pursues a life of luxury under the name Lutfannisa. Driven by sexual passion for Agra's Prince Selim, she dreams of marrying him but faces competition from his first wife, Mehrunnisa. Notwithstanding her desire for the prince, Padmavati-Motibibi-Lutfannisa is seized by a desperate yearning to win back Nabakumar. She even attempts to destroy his relationship with his second wife, Kapalkundala, by, in order to convince Nabakumar that Kapalkundala is having an illicit affair, disguising herself as a Brahmin man seeking a meeting with Kapalkundala (an encounter of this nature between a woman and man violated social norms and gives the impression of sexual impropriety). Initially Nabakumar believes that Kapalkundala is unfaithful, and he decides to abandon her. When Lutfannisa's machinations are revealed, Nabakumar realizes his mistake, but Kapalkundala is distraught because she witnessed the depravity of the human mind and because her husband doubted her. She decides to end her life, leaps into the Yamun River, and Nabakumar, trying to save her, also drowns.

That Motibibi is the "fallen" woman in *Kapalkundala* is signaled early in the book by her conversion, albeit forced, to Islam. Significantly, the conversion fractures her identity, which is why her character changes dramatically over the course of the novel, each of her incarnations bearing a different name—Padmavati, Motibibi, and Lutfannisa. Padmavati is the soft spoken, innocent child wife of Nabakumar who wields little agency in her patriarchal Hindu society. Ironically, when she converts and acquires the name Motibibi, her access to the public sphere widens because in nineteenth-century India, "Hindu and Indian were synonymous terms . . . [so that] the Muslim was often conceived as the cultural Other" This belief helped create a new Hindu national consciousness, a consciousness that was a critical component for successfully resisting British colonialism (Gupta 250). Furthermore, among Hindus, Islam was associated with lecherous behavior, overindulgence, religious fanaticism, and other negative attributes. Charu Gupta observes, "Stories of rape and abduction highlighted the vulnerability . . . of Hindu women, who often appeared as passive victims at the hands of inscrutable Muslims" (250). While Padmavati-Motibibi-Lutfannisa is never raped or kidnapped in *Kapalkundala*, in the context of nineteenth-century Hindu Islamophobia, her conversion to Islam renders her "guilty by association" and implicates her in Muslims' purported sexual deviancy. She is, as a result, dislodged from her original social location and placed in a debased position in conservative Hindu society. But if she is shut out of her original Hindu stratum, as a "fallen" woman and Muslim, she enters a wider social space.

After her conversion and divorce, Padmavati-Motibibi-Lutfannisa (hereinafter referred to as Motibibi for convenience), as noted previously, takes up residence in the Mughal court where she acquires skills associated with feminine accomplishments, such as knowledge of foreign languages and training in fine arts, and is eventually transformed into an ambitious social climber known as Motibibi. Despite her newly acquired proficiency in "womanly" arts, Motibibi is morally deficient. She is indiscrete in matters of the mind and emotion and tainted by her countless amorous relationships. Considering marriage an entrapment, she gains notoriety for her fallenness, which completely estranges her father. Furthermore, Motibibi cunningly cultivates a friendship with Mehrunnisa, the wife of Agra's ruler, Prince Selim, solely in order to replace Mehrunnisa as empress, though she never manages to do so.

Significantly, Bankim Chandra portrays Motibibi as a debased *sexual* Other in relation to both Mehrunnisa and Kapalkundala, who are depicted as morally virtuous. Mehrunnisa, who ultimately is divorced from Selim and marries Sher Afghan,[10] genuinely loves the prince, whereas Motibibi is merely a lust-driven strategist who considers marriage to him a means of accruing power and wealth. And, compared to the conniving, seductive, avaricious Motibibi, Kapalkundala is a naïve "nature-woman" incapable of subterfuge and machination. As Sisir Kumar Das observes, "If Kapalkundala symbolizes Nature in its artlessness, Motibibi represents art and sophistication . . . while Kapalkundala represents timelessness" (Das 48). But ironically, the very qualities that demonstrate that Motibibi is morally deficient, her artfulness and sophistication, also empower her in the Mughal court. Not only does she acquire competence in negotiating the public sphere due to her education, she also exercises greater agency than she did as Nabakumar's Hindu wife. Her moral fall increases her autonomy and enables her to make relatively uninhibited choices about her own life.

When the plot takes another turn, the novel's critique of Motibibi intensifies by revealing that Motibibi's newly acquired empowerment is not emotionally gratifying, which becomes apparent as the result of her chance meeting with Nabakumar. After this encounter, Motibibi yearns to be Nabakumar's wife again even though he does not recognize her and her conversion to Islam precludes remarriage. As Motibibi explains, seeing Nabakumar again teaches her that her wealth and prominence in Agra do not provide true happiness:

> Of late I have come to know the reasons. I have spent three years in this royal palace vainly searching for happiness. What I could not find here in three years that I found that night on my journey from Orissa to Agra. Now I understand what happiness is. . . . All these years I have lived like a Hindu idol, its exterior decked with precious stores, its interior lifeless. I have looked for pleasure in wrong places. I have skimmed the surface. Now I have found the real thing. Now I must find out whether I have a human heart or I am just a cold, lifeless idol. (Das 49)

Here, Motibibi's desire to leave the royal court and reunite with her former husband is an expression of repentance. In this morally didactic passage, readers learn that although Motibibi has economic independence and sexual freedom, because they were obtained through transgression, these conditions are not emotionally or psychologically rewarding.

But this realization does not lead to a simple moral rehabilitation, for Motibibi does not recuperate her Padmavati personality. Rather, she continues to employ the postconversion, postdivorce logic and behaviors she has learned at Agra. For instance, she thirsts for Nabakumar's love not as his beloved but in order to reestablish her position as his wife. Indeed, she exhibits a sense of ownership of Nabakumar. In her mind, he rightfully belongs to her and Kapalkundala is an imposter who robbed her of her wifely status. Hence Motibibi launches a plan to discredit Kapalkundala by convincing Nabakumar that his naïve young wife is unfaithful. Disguising herself as a young Brahmin man, Motibibi tricks Kapalkundala into a "rendezvous," which, of course, flagrantly violates contemporary prescriptions governing women's interactions with men. The plan fails, and Motibibi gives up her claim on Nabakumar, but the damage has been done. Kapalkundala throws herself into the Yamun River, and Nabakumar tries to rescue her, but they both drown.

Unlike Kapalkundala who remains "unresponsive to the calls of love, unaffected by the pressures exerted by human institutions and unruffled by the fear of death," Motibibi's character undergoes numerous changes through a maze of circumstances in *Kapalkundala* (Das 50). Yet she never succeeds in regaining her former status as Padmavati. Once dislodged from her original social location, Motibibi remains in the margins of the Hindu mainstream because though she is an empowered woman, she belongs to another clan and culture. Consequently, she is not accorded the beauty of a romanticized death and fails to evoke sympathy from readers. Like the defeated party in a battle, Motibibi must submit to the very rival she wanted to defeat. Ultimately, *Kapalkundala* asserts that after achieving an artificial freedom through her fallenness, Motibibi can never be reassimilated into the social space from which she was displaced.

BISHABRIKSHA

Bankim Chandra's *Bishabriksha* (*The Poison Tree*) is another novel that explores, among other themes, women's fallenness in a rigidly gender-codified society. The novel centers around a love triangle involving Nagendra, a wealthy young landlord happily wedded to Suryamukhi, and a beautiful thirteen-year-old widow and orphan named Kundanandini who lives with the couple. A third female character is Hira Malini, who is also a widow. Approximately twenty years old, she is a sadistic, scheming maid who uses her beauty and sexuality for her own ends. Hira is in love with a wealthy male debauch named Debendra who lusts after Kundanandini. As the narrative unfolds, Nagendra becomes besotted with beautiful Kundanandini although he is well loved by his devoted wife Suryamukhi. When Nagendra takes Kundanandini as a second wife, Suryamukhi leaves Nagendra, and Hira sets about creating numerous problems for Kundanandini. Eventually the marriage sours, and Nagendra deserts Kundanandini when he realizes Suryamukhi's true worth. Meanwhile, Debendra charms Hira in the hope of seducing Kundanandini but leaves Hira in the lurch when his plan fails. Hira entices Kundanandini to poison herself, and before she dies, Nagendra rushes to her bed and asks for forgiveness. But Kundandini rebukes him and dies. Hira then becomes a hapless vagabond for the rest of her life.

Bankim Chandra offers two unconventional character types in the figures of Kundanandini and Hira. Kundanandini, although she is the "other" woman, is portrayed as a model of pristine purity utterly victimized by others' ill intentions through no fault of her own. But the murderous Hira is a far more interesting study in that she is irredeemably flawed by sexual jealousy. Nonetheless, she is depicted as an intelligent maid who has risen to the position of the household's chief attendant by virtue of her expertise and strategy. Furthermore, she exercises an extraordinary degree of agency and autonomy throughout *Bishabriksha*.

For example, although Hira was a child widow, she did not adhere to norms regarding widows' behavior.[11] According to Manu's code, writes Tanita Sarkar, the "wife was regarded as *ardhangini*—the half-body of her husband. This meant that a husband lived on in his wife even after his death; thereby, the marriage tie remained in place, and any subsequent relationship between the widow and . . . [another] man could only be adulterous. Manu prescribed for her a regime of harsh and continuous self-flagellation and self-deprivation, a renunciation of all pleasures of life—sexual, dietary, sartorial and ritual" (133–34). However, Hira attires herself to enhance her natural beauty. Her lotus-shaped eyes made her face appear like a full moon surrounded by her snake-like curls of hair. Hira also seeks rather than renounces pleasure, and worse than that, she derives satisfaction from teasing people, initiating quarrels among servants, and tormenting others. For example, Hira envies Suryamukhi's initial happiness in her marriage to Nagendra and sees no wrong in causing her ill in order to extract some money from her master's household by causing a row between Suryamukhi and Nagendra.

In this respect, she clearly violates the British-Indian ideal of femininity in the Victorian period, which, as Susie Tharu points out, stipulated that women should be asexual, childlike angels: "The Victorians laid great stress on sexual restraint and moral uprightness in women, for without systematic control, women's sexual powers and appetites were considered dangerous to 'civic society' as a whole. . . . For the Victorians, women . . . were really children . . . 'half-angel, half-child'" (qtd. in Sangari and Vaid 260). According to these values, Hira is certainly a transgressive woman. She is self-centered and "loves" without being willing to sacrifice anything for her "beloved," a behavior that Bankim Chandra considered sinful. She adorns herself with clothing and jewelry prohibited a widow—she jingles her bangles, wears bracelets on her arms and rings on her ankles, and sports a silver chain around her waist.

Nevertheless, Hira is intelligent, independent, and, interestingly, prosperous in relation to others with her class status, as evident in the description of the small hut that she calls home: "Hira's dwelling was surrounded by a wall. Inside were a couple of clean mud huts. The walls of the rooms were decorated with figures of flowers, birds, and gods. In the court-yard grew red-leaved vegetables, and near them jasmine and roses" (132). Furthermore, she is freer to exercise her choices than her mistresses, Suryamukhi and Kundanandini, who are dependent on men. And with her cunning, Hira sees through a plan Debendra proposes, paying Hira for helping him kidnap Kundanandini, realizing that he is taking advantage of her lower-class status to satisfy his lust for the younger woman. As Hira says when she rejects his offer, Debendra can make the proposal only because she is a maid servant.

Further evidence of Hira's intelligence and independence is provided in a striking piece of interior monologue that provides more evidence that she has an acute understanding of the role that her class status plays in shaping her life: "If I give Kunda[nandini] to Debendra . . . I shall get a large sum of money at once. But I can't do that. Why does Debendra think Kunda so beautiful? If I had good food, dressed well, took my ease like a fine lady in a picture, I could be the same. . . . Why should I trouble myself?" (140–41). Here, Hira compares the privileged life of the upper-class women in the novel with the hapless condition of its working-class women. She reflects that if she could lead the cloistered and protected life of wealthy women like Kundanandini, she, too, would be attractive to men—Debendra in particular, whom she acknowledges that she loves. However, she goes on to admit that she doesn't have the heart to hand Kundanandini over to Debendra regardless of the fee offered or her attraction to him. Notably, Hira does not consider her motives evil because she sees herself as a victim of class exploitation. That she is financially impoverished, materially disempowered, and lonely are Hira's chief accusations against the privileged upper classes epitomized by Nagendra, Suryamukhi, and Kundanandini.

While this appeal to pathos might have prompted sympathy for Hira, the *papistha* (the fallen, sinning woman), among readers, Bishbrikshaandini cuts short the audience's inclination to reflect that Hira, like Nagendra, who begged Kundanandini for forgiveness on her deathbed, should have a chance at self-amelioration and proceeds to vilify her as devious and manipulative in passages that feature Debendra's attempts to seduce Hira as he angles for Kundanandini. This episode is particularly complex. On one hand, it suggests that Hira is susceptible to Debendra's advances because she is a member of the suffering working class, which contravenes his assumptions that she is "available" because she is morally loose. Furthermore, her fiery rhetoric, which reveals her awareness of her vulnerability as a lower-class woman and bespeaks an attempt at self-definition, suggests that she has little choice but to submit to the wealthier, more powerful Debendra. At the same time, the text makes it clear that Hira realizes that Debendra is a degenerate who, as a self-indulgent, upper-class man, hunts for opportunities to satisfy his whims regardless of the ruinous costs to women. Despite this knowledge, Hira cannot avoid being allured by Debendra's physical and sexual charms, and she succumbs to him: Hira for a few minutes "forgot self, forgot Debendra's position and her own. She thought, 'He is the husband, I am the wife the Creator, making us for each other, designed long ago to bring us together, that we might both enjoy happiness'" (165). Despite her romantic fantasy that she and Debendra are destined to be together, as a widow, Hira does not have the luxury of indulging in what is actually a perverted relationship; nevertheless, she does just that.

Significantly, Bankim Chandra characterizes Hira's acquiescence to Debendra's seduction as tasting a forbidden fruit, likening it to an act of moral turpitude whose consequences will haunt her in due time (192–93, 238). The forbidden fruit refers to not only the myth of original sin in the Hebrew Scriptures—God forbids Adam and Eve to eat from the Tree of Knowledge, but they disobey and are cast out of paradise—but also the "poison tree" after which the novel is named. The metaphorical fruit of *Bishabriksha*'s poisonous tree, like that of the Tree of Knowledge, is the suffering that results from a moral lapse:

> This tree is very vigorous; once nourished it cannot be destroyed. Its appearance is very pleasant to the eye; from a distance its variegated haves and opening buds charm the sight. But its fruit is poisonous; who eats it dies. In different soils the poison bears different fruits. In some natures it bears sickness, in some sorrow, and other fruits. To keep the passions in subjection[,] will is needed, and also power. The power must be natural, the will must be educated. Nature also is influenced by education; therefore, education is the root of self-control. I [the narrator] speak not of such education as the schoolmaster can give. The most effectual teacher of the heart is suffering. (190–91)

For Hira, the promise of the poison tree is fulfilled when, for her many sins, including her responsibility in Kundanandini's death, she goes mad and spends the rest of her life as a beggar. In contrast, during the course of the novel, both Nagendra and Kundanandini, who are members of the upper class, have a chance at redemption. Nagendra begs Kundanandini for forgiveness when she is dying, and although she refuses, this moment still constitutes an opportunity for Nagendra to make amends. Kundanandini's first opportunity to redeem herself—to extricate herself from widowhood—is through a proposed marriage to a bachelor named Taracharan, a widow's son who teaches at the school that Nagendra had opened in the village. Taracharan is well respected for his learning and high moral standing. However, Kundanandini refuses. Her second opportunity to escape widowhood is when she marries Nagendra, but of course, this is a flawed option because she becomes his second wife, and this union ends in tragedy. Unlike Kundanandini and Nagendra, Hira never has a chance at redemption. As Humayun Kabir points out, "Bankim Chandra allows his rigid social ideas to dominate his artistic sympathies. Widow remarriage was condemned by contemporary Hindu society and therefore to Bankim Chandra it is an evil, even if the widow who remarries had lost her husband as a mere child" (qtd. in Das 86). This differential treatment—Kundanandini and Nagendra, who are given the possibility of recuperating from their transgressions, are made far more sympathetic than Hira—suggests that Bankim Chandra was strongly influenced by his era's more conservative mores, but this does not detract from his moral courage in showing Hira's transgressions in the book.

KRISHNAKANTER WILL

Although ancient Sanskrit literature abounds with stories of premarital or postmarital love affairs, these topics were, for the most part, considered too salacious to include in nineteenth-century Bengali fiction. However, erudite readers at the time were exposed to and developed a taste for narratives of romantic love from the English literary tradition. One device that Bengali writers used to skirt the taboo on illicit love yet satisfy the audience's desire for scenes of romantic love was to set these stories in the remote past, which ameliorated the tales' objectionably. The historical novel was ideally suited to this purpose, and emerging as a popular genre, it played a major role in transferring conventions of English romances to Bengali literature. Bankim Chandra, of course, pioneered the Bengali novel, and his historical romances (*Mrinalini*, *Chandrashekhar*, *Anandamath*, and *Debi Chaudhurani*) problematize the question of human love and temptation vis-à-vis an imposing, overpowering social authority, and although *Krishakanter Will* is not a historical romance, this theme is particularly evident in it.

The plot of *Krishakanter Will* revolves around three principle characters, Gobindalal, the rich landlord; Bhramar, his devoted, childlike wife; and a seductive, unhappy widow named Rohini. Rohini first encounters Gobindalal after she steals his uncle Krishnakanta's will. He becomes infatuated with her and leaves his wife, Bhramar. In the course of the novel, Gobindalal murders Rohini after he discovers her flirting outrageously with a casual visitor. Gobindalal finally returns to a grief-stricken Bhramar just in time for her to die in peace, leaving him the inheritance that Uncle Krishnakanta had left her when he died. But Gobindalal forsakes all worldly fortunes after Bhramar's death and leads an ascetic life to atone for his sins.

The roles that Rohini and Bhramar play in Gobindalal's decisions are rooted in his perceptions of them. He considers Rohini the *chira rahasyamayee* (eternally mystical woman), an ever-elusive woman with a dreamlike quality reminiscent of heroines in ancient Sanskrit dramas like Kalidasa's *Abhijñānaśākuntalam* (*The Sign of Śākuntalā*), which is based on an episode in the *Mahābhārata* and whose heroine, Sakuntala, is a dreamy, sylvan character who has been raised in a forest hermitage by a sage. To Gobindalal, Rohini is inscrutable, untamable, wild, and uninhibited. Bhramar, on the other hand, is domesticated, bound by the ties of devotion, love, and responsibility. Hence she represents "bondage" in love, whereas Rohini represents "freedom." Of the three, only Bharmar consistently fulfills the expectation attached to her social role as wife. In contrast, Rohini and Gobindalal attempt to carve out "alternative space" for themselves in a rigid, role- and rule-oriented social order. Rohini refuses to adhere to her *dharma*[12] and attempts to escape the constraints of widowhood by having an affair with Gobindalal, who throws off the garb of patriarch and husband to pursue his own interests—namely, Rohini.

Bhramar and Rohini occupy two poles on a moral spectrum built on an admixture of Hindu-Indian and English cultural and literary traditions ranging from the Rigveda's[13] misogynist representations of women, the English-inspired Victorian myth that asexuality signifies women's virtue, the social institution of widowhood, and the Indian class hierarchy. The first, the idea that women are intrinsically fallen, appears throughout the Rigveda and has influenced depictions of women in Indian literature for centuries. According to Mukherjee, the Rigveda[14] condemns women's many flaws, including fickleness and uncontrollability. Time and again, they are shown seducing men and coveting men other than their husbands. They are the gateway to hell: "Men, even if they are ugly or mean, should be on their guard against women, for no one is safe from then. Women were accused of being lascivious, devoid of love for their husbands and of always tempting men" (Mukherjee 11). By this measure, of course, Rohini is irrevocably fallen. In contrast, the second tradition—the Victorian myth of asexuality—marks Bhramar as virtuous: "The still familiar logic of the myth runs something like this proposition, 'a pure woman excites no sexual response.' Its corollaries: a woman who arouses a man is not pure, and second, a woman's infallible protection against male aggression is her 'virtue.' Bhramar is . . . 'the real, uncorrupted Indian woman is like her white counterpart,' 'childlike and angelic.' Her purity is 'God's purity.' She spreads a 'divine radiance'" (Sangari and Vaid 260). Whereas Rohini is sexually and temperamentally unruly, Bhramar, the dark, less-than-beautiful but devoted housewife who conforms to the image of the *Grihalaksmi* (a beneficent domestic goddess),[15] is an idealized model of domestic womanhood associated with the goddess Lakshmi. In short, Bhramar, whose name means "bee," although she is mild-mannered and acquiescent, is an angel.

Women's performance of widowhood, as noted in the previous discussion of *Bishabriksha,* in nineteenth-century Bengali fiction also reveals their moral character, and by this gauge, Rohini is irrevocably flawed. The widow, as a woman without legal—meaning male—proprietors, was perceived as embodying "unharnessed sexual energy" that threatened the social order (Mukherjee 103). As Tanika Sarkar points out in her essay "Wicked Widows," "Widowhood norms . . . expressed . . . a constitutive contradiction within Hindu domesticity. These norms outlawed desire for and of the widow, yet simultaneously made her a focus of desire, necessarily extramarital, that otherwise might be directed at prostitutes. In brothels, there was no certainty of reciprocity, or of meaningful relationships. Since both widow and prostitute functioned under the same sign of non-prescribed and undomesticated desire, it is no wonder that the same Bengali colloquial term (*ranrh*) denotes both kinds of women" (141). Complex socioreligious conventions designed to reduce this threat took the form of avoidance so that the widow's social relations were restricted, and she was forced into peripheral position in the social network of a village community. However, the pleasure-loving Rohini routinely violates the rules of widowhood by dressing stylishly and indulging herself, essentially flaunting her fallenness.

Third, women's ability and willingness to comply with gendered prescriptions for classed behavior indicates their relative moral purity, as Sumanta Banerjee implies when she reminds us that nineteenth-century Bengali women were a heterogeneous population: women of nineteenth-century Bengal, like women in other regions, were not an economically or socially homogenous group. Their lifestyles and occupations varied depending on whether they were "women of rich families," "women of middle station," or "poor women" (Sangari and Vaid 128). Bhramar, although she was born into a poor class, gains prestige when she marries the landowning Gobindalal while also losing some freedom because she must comply with middle- and upper-class restrictions on, for example, women's movements. Rohini, however, is lower class, and as such, her possibilities are severely limited.

Hence Bhramar and Rohini epitomize dichotomous concepts of Indian femininity and serve as centers of opposition in the novel: Bhramar is serene and loving and offers men a wholesome form of happiness, whereas Rohini is sensuousness and passionate and offers pleasure. Rohini is associated with sensory perception and colorful, dramatic aspects of nature—brilliantly blooming flowers, water (from the Baruni tank, the village's water source), humming bees of springtime, and the cuckoo's song. She is a great cook, loves gossip, and wields a flamboyant style: "Rohini was young. . . . She was a widow, but she never much cared to live as a high caste Hindu widow ought. She loved to pay attention to her passion and dress and she wore some of the ornaments that she was given when she was married. . . . Besides her personal attractions which were by no means inconsiderable 'she possessed certain accomplishments: for example, she excelled in culinary arts, could use the needle with skill, and was known to have a knack in certain other things requiring ingenuity'" (my translation; 111). She even chewed *paan*, which is made with mildly psychoactive stimulants, and guests traditionally present some of its ingredients as a hospitality or house gift to wives on special occasions.[16] Bhramar, on the other hand, though pious, is neither pretty nor attractive and is portrayed as domesticated and simple. She is likened to tranquil elements in nature. Her world, identity, and beliefs derive from her husband's. She enjoys a position of power because she is the wife of a rich landlord, yet she lacked the beauty, wealth, and accomplishments that in nineteenth-century Bengal defined a woman's identity in relation to her family and were thought to determine happiness. Because she lacked beauty and wealth, other women, including Rohini, were jealous of her good fortune in marrying a landlord. Their jealousy alienates Bharmar from the community, and Rohini irrationally blames Bharmar for her marginalized status as a widow in a patriarchal society.

Despite the simplicity of this opposition (Rohini is "vice" and Bharmar is "virtue"), *Krishnakanter Will* offers complex if not contradictory perspectives on Rohini's character, first soliciting sympathy and then castigating her as an ogress. Readers sympathize with her suffering, her feelings of deprivation, and her longing to escape the desolate tedium of widowhood. Her lament—"I am a widow. I have lost my *dharma* [harmony, balance, and right conduct], my happiness, my life, what shall I cherish?" (my translation)—is heartrending even though readers realize that according to conventional moral norms, it does not justify Rohini's transgressions, small or large. And, of course, all Rohini's actions constitute attempts to escape the oppressive confines of widowhood. She cooks, washes, and gossips but never worships her *grihadevata* (household god), the deity who protects the house.[17] She rarely stays in isolation and constantly moves about the neighborhood and in Gobindalal's garden where the couple meet and make love. She also aims to remarry a minor character named Haralal, even though widow remarriage is strictly forbidden, not for love or money, but in order to escape her widow's fate. In fact, her plan to marry Haralal prompts Rohini to steal Krishnakanta's will, and the theft sets the stage for her disastrous, illicit affair with

Gobindalal, the ultimate evidence of Rohini's fallenness. At the same time, all these signs of moral turpitude demonstrate that Rohini merits appreciation if not admiration for refusing to submit to her fate and lead a quiet life of *dharma*. Her courage to confess her desires, make choices, and ignore her *dharma* breaks barriers.

Krishnakanter Will proffers similarly complicated views of Bhramar. Unlike Rohini, Bhramar virtuously remains confined within her prescribed social roles—daughter, daughter-in-law, and wife. Additionally, class-based codes of behavior that restrict Bhramar's movements constrain her almost as much as widowhood confines Rohini, or would have if she adhered to the rules. Bhramar, as the wife of a privileged landlord, is constantly surrounded by maids, who not only assist her but also chaperone her, which, limiting her privacy and freedom, denies her an "individual space." Consequently, Bhramar's privilege confines her within the four walls of her house. She is always in the company of either maids or relatives and spends most of her time in the kitchen or her own room. She is both socially and spatially circumscribed by class status. Notwithstanding Bhramar's acquiescence to these constraints, her situation becomes more involved after she receives the inheritance—land and a house—from Krishnakanta. While it doesn't substantially increase her class status in the community, the inheritance catalyzes a significant power shift in her marriage. As a wife, she remains subject to her husband's authority, but she accrues power in the relationship and society when she becomes a property owner. But the contradictions between Bhramar's roles as wife and landowner generate conflict and increase her alienation. Ironically, she can make decisions about financial matters but not about her own life, because her social and economic roles constantly clash with each other. This has a disastrous effect on her marriage, for when Gobindalal no longer has complete control over Bhramar, he uses it as a pretext to abandon her for Rohini.

Another twist in the story complicates Bankim Chandra's representation of Bhramar. For most of the novel, she embodies *satittwa*,[18] a woman's unflinchingly chaste devotion to her husband; however, at one juncture, Bhramar pens an important critique of the institution of marriage just before Gobindalal leaves her for Rohini:

> That day when you returned from the garden after eleven o'clock at night, I inquired what made you stay away so late. You refused to tell me. When I insisted on knowing you said you would tell me, but not until a couple of years had passed. But I have got your secret. I wish I had never known it. Rohini called yesterday to show me the cloth and the ornaments you gave her. Such a wicked impudent woman she is. She did it to hurt and insult me, I know. But I bore with her and let her go unharmed. What will you say now? I had unbounded faith in you, you know I had. My heart is broken; I wish we should not meet when you come. Would you kindly drop a line to say when you are going to come home? I request this favor because I want to go to my father's house before your return home. (my translation; 511)

This letter from an otherwise perfect wife protests the traditional Hindu ideal of unconditional devotion of the wife to her husband and questions the institution of marriage. In this sense, it is reminiscent of Madhusudan Dutt's "Birangana Kavya" ("Valiant Ladies"; 1861–62), an epistolary poem[19] in which Dutt imagines the most noted female characters in Puranic literature—a huge collection of legends, myths, and scriptures composed in Sanskrit and other South Asian languages from the third through tenth centuries CE—would have written to their lovers or lords. Indeed, Bhramar's letter preempts Rabindranath Tagore's short story "Strir Patra" ("The Wife's Letter"), published in 1914, which is a wife's manifesto against patriarchal codes and an early critique of traditional marriage.[20] Thus the character of Bhramar, the ideal wife, is complicated by her single deviation from *sattitwa*, raising the possibility that she was not so perfect or that *sattitwa* itself is not ideal, the latter hypothesis supported by Bankim Chandra's objection to restricting women to the home—to private, domestic spaces—which he articulates in "Samya" ("Equality"): "Keeping women confined to their homes like animals in an animal house. We shall move freely in heaven and earth like the *chatak* bird [Jacobin cuckoo], they shall remain confined to one and a half *katha* [680.5 square feet] of land like someone kept in a cage" (qtd. in Haldar 195). Paradoxically, however, Bankim Chandra's novels could not grant equivalent degrees of mobility to both Rohini and Bharmar due to social and class constraints even though the man himself asks for more space, more air, and more mobility for women.

Ultimately, *Krishnakanter Will* does not address either possibility definitively—readers are never told if Bhramar's *satittwa* cracks momentarily—but the novel represents the nineteenth-century Hindu belief that preserving women's sexual chastity is coterminous with maintaining social order. Rohini and Bhramar represent two extremes, one woman's desire to satisfy herself only and a second woman's persistent commitment to her social role as wife. But this is no simple binary. To wit, in common social perception, Bhramar is the ideal woman who earns the designation of *satittwa* for her effacing nature and self-control, but she unconsciously perpetrates the very patriarchal conventions that cause her suffering. Likewise, Rohini is stigmatized as fallen, yet she is not a wholly unsympathetic character. This nuanced treatment of gender norms also surfaces in protests that Rohini and Bhramar register against patriarchalism as well as in any empowerment they may achieve in the course of the novel. For example, Bhramar accrues power from her inheritance and, ironically, from Gobindalal's abandonment, which to a degree frees her from the constraints of wifehood. But this is no happy solution, for Bhramar is uneasy in her new role and feels nostalgic for domestic life—her cage. In fact, had Gobindalal loved Bhramar without interruption, she would have been satisfied with her *sansar-dharma* (household *dharma*). Likewise, had Rohini not been a widow, she might not have protested the dominant social order given that Rohini's quest is not for a specific social identity. Rather, she voices frustration that her desires are thwarted by the oppression embedded in widowhood as an institution. Consequently, in both cases, the women's protests are contextual and "functional."

Of course, *Krishnakanter Will* also underscores the pronounced double standard applied to women and men in nineteenth-century Bengal. Though Gobindalal transgresses the code of ethics or *dharma*, he can resort to *sanyas* (renunciations) that provide him a means of escape. But the women who he caused so much suffering die, and this is a persistent pattern in Bankim Chandra's novels, which provides an ongoing space for Gobindalals, but Rohinis who voice dissent must be silenced. Curiously, Bankim Chandra's wry critique of the sexual double standard in "Samya" stands in opposition to his works' condemnation of Rohini and her fictional counterparts: "Men are not governed by the same hard and fast rules as women are. If a woman commits the slightest fault in matters of chastity, she cannot even show her face to others. . . . A man however can do such things in the open, can go back to his house in splendor and mirth driving a phaeton in the wee hours of the morning to provide his wife with occasion for touching the dust of his feet; his wife should be very happy at this" (qtd. in Haldar 201).

This contradiction between Bankim Chandra's prose and fiction points to the oft-observed tensions between tradition and social change in Bengal during the nineteenth century as well as his ideas about the purpose of literature. Bankim Chandra was often sympathetic to the idea of suffering but could not approve of social transgression. Furthermore, he believed that literature should catalyze *chittasuddhi* (purification of one's heart). While he did not suggest that the object of literature should be ethics, Bankim Chandra deemed ethics and literature to have the same end, which is to elevate the human heart. Clearly *Kapalkundala, Bishabriksha,* and *Krishnakanter Will,* whose tragedies result from unrestrained passion, advise readers that such "elevation" is achieved by eschewing excessive sexual desire. As Bankim Chandra observes in *Sitaram,* his final novel (1886),[21] "The satisfaction of desires for any purpose other than *dharma* is sin" (Raychaudhuri 112). Notably, Bankim Chandra was not the only contemporary novelist to take this position, for he and his fellow authors were eager to counteract colonialists' argument that Indian civilization was barbaric, passionate, and devoid of moral standards.

CONCLUSION

In all three novels discussed in this chapter, transgressive women are strong individuals who are acutely conscious of the deficiencies of the social world of which they are an integral part, and they work out idiosyncratic strategies for surviving it. In *Kapalkundala,* Motibibi is empowered by virtue of her conversion to Islam and exposure to the power and privileges of the Mughal Court. But in spite of her liberated status, mobility, and power to exercise choices, she yearns to reclaim her status as Nabakumar's wife. Hira in *Bishabriksha* is constrained by both widowhood and her low class status. Time and again, Hira regrets that her beauty and intelligence are all in vain owing to her class. Yet the novel shows a certain frankness and gusto in her candid confessions about her quest to win Debendra's love and attain a respectable social position. However, the transgressive outlaw who happens to be a woman has to be kept in the margins, thus she goes mad at the end of the novel. Rohini, the transgressive figure in *Krishnakanter Will,* also admirably denounces patriarchal society, and in her figure, readers encounter a courageous depiction of the desires of a widow who is oppressed and exploited in a rigidly codified social order. Nevertheless, Rohini cannot be shown as marrying or fulfilling her desires, and she has to die. As Sisir Kumar Das aptly points out in *The Artist in Chains*, "Such a world emerges out of the concerns of Bankim, as well as of the dilemma between the acceptance of an established order and the doubts about its stability and relevance . . . Bankim did not write moral tales ending in rewards for the virtuous and punishment for the wicked. He wrote stories about people who made choices out of their free will, which disturbed the apparently ordered universe, and suffered for their choice" (237).

Clearly Bankim Chandra was fascinated by the conception of empowered women in his own narratives in which "the ideal of *Veerangana* [whore or fallen woman] was jostling for space with the model of submissive, self-effacing woman in the political culture of the time" (Mukherjee 6). Thus the three novels discussed in this chapter attempt to represent two very different versions of ideal femininity, the empowered woman and the woman who embodies domestic if not patriarchal virtues. As a result, *Kapalkundala*, *Bishabriksha*, and *Krishnakanter Will* espouse contrary ideologies, "romanticism on the one hand and utilitarianism on the other" (Das 208). They recreate a world of human passions but impose order on it. Ultimately, they capture the innumerable cultural and ideological conflicts of nineteenth-century Bengal.

NOTES

1 Kapalkundala is the female protagonist's name.

2 The feminine of *sat* (true), also spelled *suttee*, refers to a funeral ritual in some Asian communities in which a recently widowed woman commits suicide by self-immolation, typically on a husband's funeral pyre. The practice is considered to have originated within the warrior aristocracy on the India subcontinent, gradually gaining popularity from the tenth century CE and spreading to other groups from the twelfth through eighteenth centuries. The practice was outlawed by the English Raj in 1892 in their territories in India and in India's Princely States (during the nineteenth century portions of India that had been allied with but not conquered by Britain were referred to as "Princely States") in ensuing decades. Queen Victoria issued a ban covering all of India in 1861.

3 Mrityunjay Vidyalankar (c. 1762–1819) was a Bengali writer and linguist who translated Sanskrit literature to Hindi and adapted Sanskrit stories in his Hindi-language fiction. He is considered the leading prose author of his time.

4 In Hinduism, Manu is the first or archetypal man, and he and his wife are believed to be humankind's progenitors. The Sanskrit text *Manava Dharma Shastra*, popularly known as the *Manu Smriti*, consists of Hindu laws, customs, and ethics and is said to have been composed by the Hindu mythological figure, Manu Svayanbhuva, the god Brahma's son. Translated by Sir William Jones in 1794 when Britain ruled India, the Manu code was used by the colonial government to formulate Indian law.

5 In this volume, see Devaleena Das, "Polyamorous Draupadi"; Amrit Gangar, "Damaged Goods!"; and Naina Dey, "*Roop Taraashi*."

6 Savitri, the daughter of the king of Madra, married Satyavan, the son of a blind king Dyumatsena, but as predicted in a prophecy, Satyavan died within a year of his marriage. When Yama, the God of Death, came to claim Satyavan's soul, Savitri persuaded Yama to spare Satyavan, and the god blessed them with eternal happiness.

7 Romesh Chunder Dutt was a nineteenth-century intellectual leader in the Bengal region of India. A civil servant whose politics were moderately nationalist, Dutt served as the president of his party, the Indian National Congress, in 1899. He translated the *Ramayana* and the *Mahābhārata*, two of the most important Hindu scriptures, into English and was dedicated to promoting Bengali-Indian literature. He was also an economic historian.

8 The start of the thousand-year Vedic period was first marked with tribal and then pastoral communities in northwestern India. Around 1200 BCE, these peoples expanded their territories to include the Ganges plain, developing a predominantly agricultural society. Greater urbanization, along with a monarchical state, emerged near the end of the period. The Vedic scriptures, the oldest Sanskrit texts and among the keystone documents of Hinduism, were composed during this era.

9 The Mughal Empire (1526–1862), spanned most of the Indian subcontinent and present-day Afghanistan. Agra, just south of present-day Delhi and site of the Taj Mahal, served as the capital city. Mughals were Muslim and, though not ethnically Persian, were strongly influenced by Persian (Iranian) culture.

10 Sher Afgan Khan, whose birth name was Ali Quli Khan Istajlu, was a Mughal courtier who had previously served one of the Safavid-Dynasty emperors in Persia. Prince Salim, Jahangir, gave him the title Sher Afgan Khan for meritorious service in Salim's war against the Rajput King of Mewar.

11 See Radha Chakravorty's chapter in this volume.

12 See Devaleena Das's chapter in this volume.

13 It is one of the four canonical sacred texts of Hinduism known as *Vedas*.

14 The *Rigveda* is the first of the four Vedic *Samhitas* which has a total of 1028 hymns divided into ten *mandalas* or sections. Each hymn has the name of a Rishi such as Vasishtha, Visvamitra, Bharadvaja, and others who received these texts in divine revelations. The *Rigveda* provides an account of Hinduism, society, and economy. It is usually dated between 1500 BCE and 1000 BCE (Dalal 310).

15 A common Hindu saying is that gods reside where women are respected, honored, and protected, and it is widely believed that goddess Lakshmi, who is associated with wealth, resides in every home in the form of the lady of the house, the *Griha-Lakshmi* (*griha* means "home").

16 *Paan* is made from the betel leaf which is spiced with a variety of condiments, usually imbibed after major meals according to Indian tradition.

17 *Grihadevata* refers to the concept of household gods. No house is supposed to be without its tutelary divinity. In Bengal, the domestic god is sometimes the Salagram stone worshipped as Vishnu, sometimes a plant, and other times a basket with a little rice in it.

18 *Satittwa* is the adverb of *sati*. Self-abnegation is the root of this quality, and its social function is to contain women within the patriarchy. If *mattrittwa* stands for motherhood, *satittwa* stands for ideal wifehood. The idealization of *satittiwa* among the urban, propertied class of Bengal during Bankim Chandra's lifetime is due to this population's growing misogyny.

19 Madhusudan Dutt was a nineteenth-century Bengali writer primarily known for his poetry and plays.

20 Mrinal, the protagonist in "Strir Patra" ("The Letter from the Wife") is a middle-class woman who, while traveling, writes a letter describing her dismal life at home. She concludes by declaring that she will not return.

21 His final novel, *Sitaram* (1886), tells the story of a Hindu lord who is torn between his wife and the woman he desires but is unable to attain. His arrogance leads him to make a series of arrogant, self-destructive mistakes. In the end, he confronts himself, takes responsibility, and motivates the few troops still loyal to him to defend his estate against an invading army.

WORKS CITED

Bagchi, Jashodhara, editor. *Indian Women, Myth and Reality*. Sangam Books Private, 1995.

Chatterjee, Bankim Chandra. *Bankim Rachanavali*, vols. 1 and 2. Dey's Publishing, 2006.

———. *The Poison Tree: A Tale of Hindu Life in Bengal by Bankim Chandra Chatterjee*. Translated by Miriam S. Knight, T. Fisher Unwin, 1884.

Dalal, Roshen. *The Religions of India: A Concise Guide to Nine Major Faiths*. Penguin, 2006.

Das, Sisir Kumar. *The Artist in Chains: The Life of Bankim Chandra Chatterjee*. Papyrus, 1984.

Gupta, Charu. *Sexuality, Obscenity, Community: Women, Muslims, and the Hindu Public in Colonial India*. Permanent Black, 2001.

Haldar, M. K. *Renaissance and Reaction in Nineteenth Century Bengal*. Minerva Associates Pvt., 1977.

Mukherjee, Meenakshi. *Realism and Reality: The Novel and Society in India*. Oxford UP, 1985.

———. "Story, History and Her Story." Nov. 1991, Centre for Historical Studies, Jawaharlal Nehru University. Lecture.

Mukherjee, Prabhati. *Hindu Women Normative Models*. Orient Longman, 1978.

Ray Choudhuri, Tapan. *Europe Reconsidered: Perceptions of the West in Nineteenth Century Bengal*. Oxford UP, 1988.

Sangari, Kumkum, and Sudesh Vaid, editors. *Recasting Women: Essays in Colonial History*. Kali for Women, 1989.

Sarkar, Tanika. *Rebels, Wives, Saints: Designing Selves and Nations in Colonial Times*. Permanent Black, 2009.

Srinivasan, Amrutur V. *Hinduism for Dummies*. Wiley, 2011.

13 THE FALLEN WOMAN IN BENGALI LITERATURE

Binodini Dasi and Tagore's *Chokher Bali*

RADHA CHAKRAVARTY

> There is no one in this world before whom I can lay bare my pain, for the world sees me as a sinner—a fallen woman. I have no kith and kin, no society, no friend—no one in this world whom I may call my own.
>
> —Dasi 49

This chapter focuses on writing by and about "fallen women" by juxtaposing the autobiographies of sex-worker-turned-stage-actress Binodini Dasi and Rabindranath Tagore's character Binodini in the novel *Chokher Bali (A Grain of Sand)*.[1] In nineteenth-century Bengal, the "woman question" became a central issue in a "culture war" that split Hindu reformists and the orthodoxy, despite their shared commitment to ending British rule. Alongside debates about child marriage, women's education, widow remarriage, and the *purdah* (gender segregation) system, questions of women's morality assumed a new importance in multiple discourses. The orthodox Swadeshi (self-sufficiency) movement brought many women out of *purdah*, but it also ascribed them a marginal place in the public sphere, while reformists advocated for women's education along a Western model. Chakravarty explains that in these contexts, the self-representations of famed actress Binodini constitute a complex negotiation of empowered voice and subjectivity on one hand and acceptance of the designation of "fallen woman" that society assigned her on the other. As a result, Binodini's text simultaneously submits to and subverts social norms regulating women, revealing the duplicity that a hypocritical patriarchy imposes on women. In contrast, *Chokher Bali*'s psychological approach to developing the character of the widow Binodini, whose interiority becomes a space for challenging social taboos, facilitates direct expression of *jouissance*, the pleasure of sexual transgression. These two models of womanhood, asserts Chakravarty, hearken to the past and the future while reflecting contemporary debates about nation and gender.

Legendary nineteenth-century stage actor Binodini Dasi's anguished outpouring in the preface to her autobiographical work, *Amar Katha* (*My Story*), expresses the pain and isolation of the "fallen woman" in Bengali society but also challenges that designation and the marginalization that accompanies it by laying claim to voice and subjectivity through the act of writing.[2] Another Binodini, the transgressive widow in Rabindranath Tagore's 1903 novel *Chokher Bali*, voices a similar desperation in her demand to be recognized as a person with individual needs and desires: "Am I an inanimate object?" she cries. "Am I not human? Am I not a woman?" (69). For both women, the social stigma attached to their "sinfulness" bars them from a "respectable" role in society, yet both interrogate the social mores that are responsible for their degradation.

The "fallen woman" in Bengali literature, particularly during the nineteenth century's protracted conflict over traditional and progressive and social values, occupies a troubled space where social taboos clash with a subversive impulse toward women's empowerment, creating the type of contradictions that drive a society in transition. As a result, the "woman question" became a central issue in the battle between the orthodoxy and reformists,[3] and in a society at war with itself, the fallen woman in literary texts emerged as a figure signifying liminality. Alongside debates about child marriage,[4] women's education, widow remarriage,[5] and the *purdah* system,[6] questions of women's morality assumed a new importance. In the rising tide of nationalism that coincided with these ideological clashes, women's position remained problematic, for while the nationalist Swadeshi movement of the early twentieth century brought many women out of *purdah*, it also ascribed them a marginal place in the public sphere.[7] As Partha Chatterjee points out, women in Bengal continued to be seen as the repositories of tradition, while the men sought a new modernity (233–53). In such a situation, the stigma attached to the "fallen" woman was directly proportionate to the value ascribed to female chastity. The *bhadramahila*, or respectable "lady" who epitomized the nationalist ideal of woman as "goddess" and "mother," was the polar opposite of the *patita*, or "fallen woman" (Chatterjee 248).[8]

It is easy to find parallels in England's Victorian literature and to argue that the *patita/bhadramahila* dichotomy is a construct borrowed from the West. In *The Femme Fatale in Victorian Literature* (2008), for example, Jennifer Hedgecock asserts, "The fallen woman trope is really meant to keep women subordinated to patriarchal power, and at the same time, to provide a convenient scapegoat for the existing moral turpitude in Victorian society" (49). The overlap between

Hedgecock's account of Victorian public morality and the social contexts of nineteenth-century Bengal appears obvious. Hedgecock, though, seems to identify the idea of the "fallen" woman primarily with the practice of prostitution, as distinct from the more ambitious figure of the *femme fatale* who leverages her beauty, sensuality, and charm for her own benefit. This points to an important difference between the Victorian and Indian conceptions, for in Bengali literature, the transgressive nature of the fallen woman involves more than questions of chastity and is framed within broader issues of class, caste, education, marriage, and the *purdah* system. In Bengali contexts, the fallen woman comes to be defined not only by her violation of the laws of sexual purity but also by her break with the social norms of marriage, domesticity, gender segregation, and confinement to the private quarters of the home. If the traditional woman, in her role as devoted wife (*pativrata*) and mother, comes to be celebrated as the epitome of Indian culture, the *patita* represents the very opposite: from her location beyond the pale of respectability, she poses a challenge to the stability of indigenous traditions at a time when these traditions were already under threat from the inroads of colonialist culture. Seen as dangerous to the existing order, the fallen woman is simultaneously blamed for her society's moral decline and subjected to strategies of containment that are intended to neutralize the threat she represents. Her marginalization is the means by which a patriarchal society negotiates its anxiety about women's empowerment, but the history of this process, its culturally specific nuances, and its entanglement with the politics of anticolonial resistance, cannot be understood as merely an indigenized version of Victorianism.

Likewise, the liminal space inhabited by the fallen woman, who has been denied a place in respectable society, offers multiple culturally specific possibilities for reconfirming, internalizing, or challenging and interrogating existing social structures. Binodini Dasi (b. 1863–1941), the iconic stage actor, and the fictional rebellious widow character Binodini in Rabindranath Tagore's novel *Chokher Bali* are examples of female figures who occupy this rich territory in the text, and in the case of Binodini Dasi, in actuality. Their narratives are complex and riven by internal contradictions, for they demonstrate both the fallen woman's subversive urge and her internalization of the "sinful" status ascribed her. These inner conflicts complicate the fallen woman's negotiations with a conservative, patriarchal society's attempts to contain the threat posed by her very presence. Thus representations of the fallen woman in Bengali literature are framed within broader issues of public morality and East/West relations and debates about women's position in a changing society.

Binodini, the protagonist in *Chokher Bali*, is a beautiful young woman with a burning sense of injustice about her plight as a widow. The story opens with the death of Binodini's father after which her mother, Harimati, frantically searches for a husband for Binodini but doesn't have sufficient funds to attract a rich son-in-law. Early in the novel, Harimati proposes that Binodini wed Mahendra, the son of a woman from Harimati's village, Rajlakshmi. Rajlakshmi accepts, but Mahendra is a whimsical egoist, and though he initially agrees with his mother's decision, he rejects the proposal at the last minute. Rajlakshmi loves Mahendra's close friend, Bihari, as a son, so she asks him to marry Binodini, but Bihari also refuses, saying that the "dessert" that Mahendra rejected is not meant for him either; he does not want Mahendra's leftovers. Hence Binodini marries an elderly man and is immediately widowed. As was the custom in British India in the nineteenth century, she returns to her home village. Meanwhile, Mahendra has married Ashalata, also referred to as Asha, a naïve, gentle, but illiterate girl who worships her husband. Mahendra begins tutoring Asha, but this is just a pretext to have frequent sex with her. When Mahendra performs poorly in medical school, the family blames Asha for distracting him. Feeling neglected, Rajlakshmi returns to her native village, where she encounters Binodini, invites the widow to live with her and, on returning home, uses Binodini to make Asha jealous. However, Asha befriends Binodini, who soon seeks sexual pleasure vicariously through Asha's tales of conjugal love. But Binodini uses Asha to seduce Mahendra, who initially resists his attraction to her, which insults Binodini, for she is keenly aware of her worth, beauty, and intelligence in comparison to the limited Asha. Soon Mahendra's friend, Bihari, sensing that Asha is in danger, ventures in, but he is equally smitten when Binodini beguiles him. Binodini revels in the attention of two men who initially refused to marry her, deriving a sense of power from their attraction to her, but Mahendra and Bihari quarrel over her. In the end, Binodini rejects both Mahendra and Bihari. She sees Mahendra for who he is, and though Bihari loves her, she rejects his marriage proposal because she realizes that the stigma of her widowhood will harm him as well as herself. She departs for Varanasi, an important spiritual center in northwest India where widows without other recourse lived during the nineteenth century. Asha, realizing that Mahendra never loved her, temporarily leaves him, but they are later reconciled.

The widow is a particularly prominent figure among the many fallen women in nineteenth-century Bengali fiction. Typically, these characters' development is foregrounded in the deplorable realities of widowhood in nineteenth-century Bengal. Widows were forbidden to remarry prior to the Hindu Widows' Remarriage Act of 1856, which endorsed widow remarriage, but even after this legislation was passed, social pressure maintained the remarriage ban. Furthermore, widows were expected to spend the rest of their lives as cloistered ascetics—celibate and contained within private spaces where they prayed, fasted, and abstained from even the smallest pleasures. *Sati*, widows' self-immolation (often forced) on their husbands' funeral pyres, was commonly practiced. Condemned to a life of austerity and self-denial, the widow, according to Dipesh Chakrabarty, represents the ultimate level of subalternity in a male-dominated society and, as such, provides a particularly cogent ground for the interrogation of a patriarchal ethos (66).[9]

Despite all these measures, whose purpose is to neutralize the threat that the widow poses the social order, Binodini is both the subject and object of desire in *Chokher Bali*, for, at the center of a complex intersection of desire and jealousy, she is the object of Mahendra's desire and a desiring subject who fantasizes about Bihari; hence, her eroticized body is a double signifier of subject and object. As such, Binodini enacts a scathing critique of the hypocrisy of a patriarchal culture that condemns widows to lives of abject self-denial without any possibility of voice, subjectivity, or agency.[10] Tagore, of course, is not the first Bengali novelist to address widows' sexuality in his fiction. His illustrious predecessor Bankim Chandra Chatterjee, in two novels—*Bishabriksha* (*The Poison Tree*; 1873) and *Krishnakanter Will* (*Krishnakanta's Will*; 1878)—portrayed the destructive effects young widows' sexual transgressions on their own lives as well as the lives of those around them. However, the typical widow in Bankim Chandra's works differs from *Chokher Bali*'s Binodini. Though not insensitive to the widows' plight, Bankim Chandra[11] "could not conceive of a young widow in the midst of a peaceful household except as a *femme fatale* wreaking havoc in the family" (Chatterjee 148). Thus the fate of widows in Bankim Chandra's novels is a symptom of the misogyny induced by coinciding fears of womanhood and social change that is manifest in *Sati*, prohibitions against widow remarriage, and other practices regulating widows' behavior (Nandy 1–35).

Binodini, however, differs from the traditional widow character, not only because she resists her victim status in order to claim the right to articulate her desires but also because the text offers a nuanced representation of her interiority. As Tagore asserts in his preface to the second edition of *Chokher Bali*, "The literature of the new age seeks not to narrate a sequence of events, but to reveal the secrets of the heart. Such is the narrative mode of *Chokher Bali*" (vii). Hence in Tagore's self-consciously "modern," psychological novel, Binodini maintains a sense of interiority that differentiates her from earlier heroines of Bengali fiction: she is portrayed as the object of male desire, but more important, she is also represented as a desiring subject, driven by her hunger for love and sexual fulfillment. This double view powerfully acknowledges woman's subjectivity but also represents it through the filter of the male gaze. Consequently, the fallen Binodini is simultaneously the object of male fantasy and the subject of her own erotic imagination, creating the supercharged atmosphere that marks *Chokher Bali*. For instance, in one highly emotional scene that exemplifies the novel's double view, Mahendra finds a flower-adorned Binodini dreaming of Bihari: "Through the open windows and doors, the moonlight streamed in, to fall upon the white bed. Weaving garlands of flowers plucked from the garden, Binodini had placed them in her hair, around her neck, and around her waist. Adorned with flowers, she lay on the moonlit bed like a vine laden with the weight of its blossoms" (341). Though objectified by Mahendra's gaze, here Binodini, as the desiring subject who yearns for Bihari, also *resists* objectification.

In her assertive articulation of her own needs and desires, Binodini defies the stereotype of the chaste *bhadramahila*. A convent-educated, intelligent, accomplished woman dissatisfied with her lot, she refuses to succumb to the passive self-denial conventionally prescribed the widow. She pursues her own desires, trying at first to seduce Mahendra, driving a wedge between him and Asha. Later, she switches her attention to Mahendra's close friend, the austere and severe Behari, who spurns her advances although he is strongly attracted to her. Significantly, the text adopts a bifurcated approach toward this bold expression of female desire, generating sympathy for Binodini's plight as a widow, but also positioning her as a "fallen" woman, especially in comparison to the innocent Asha. The latter view is expressed particularly emphatically in Behari's belief that Binodini is a threat to his moral uprightness, his conviction that she is an evil planet on his horizon who bodes ill. Consequently, Tagore's portrayal of this transgressive figure is ambivalent, implicitly critiquing the social oppression at the root of Binodini's suffering even while casting her wily nature in a negative light.

Chokher Bali employs various strategies to execute this twofold critique. While validating, for instance, Binodini's subjectivity and desire, it also highlights the destructive nature of her rebellious self-assertion. In her use, desire frequently functions as a weapon for revenge, and her struggle to resist the repressive strictures on widowhood has devastating effects on those around her. But the text also moves beyond conventional morality, offering a carefully crafted, complex depiction of Binodini. At certain points, for instance, her desire is legitimized by invoking the Vaishnavite tradition, which is steeped in the legend of the god Krishna's amorous relationship with Radha and their attendants, the Gopis.[12] In these passages, Binodini is compared to a Gopika,[13] a perpetually youthful figure who yearns for Krishna: she is "timeless and ageless, forever a Gopika. . . . With all her pangs of separation . . . she had traveled through so many songs, so many rhythms, to arrive at the shores of the present time" (340). This romanticized depiction of Binodini's desire places it beyond the realm of the mundane and, by emphasizing its timelessness, suggests that it transcends the narrowness of contemporary public morality.

A second strategy that produces the novel's dual critique of social conventions and Binodini's fallenness consists of highlighting her physical allure, describing it as simultaneously beautiful and dangerous. Traditionally, the widow's desexualized appearance signals the self-negation and abstinence that are her prescribed destiny. In contrast, in *Chokher Bali*, Binodini's body is the site of her resistance, for her beauty gives her power over men. Thus her rebellion is grounded in her adamant rejection of the self-repression expected of widows. She is also unconventional because she does not fit the stereotypes of either the traditional domesticated *prachina* (traditional woman) or the progressive, Anglicized, Western-educated *nabina*—the New Woman. In the nineteenth-century debate about social values that pit traditionalists against progressives, the hardworking *prachina* who wakes early, prepares a meal, and readies the household stood in contrast to the New Woman who conservatives depicted as lazy and narcissistic, a representation that Bankim Chandra popularized in "Prachina ebong Nabina" ("Old and New Woman"; Nanda 217). Neither *prachina* nor *nabina*, Binodini is hard to pigeonhole because she signals a new, more complex female character than had ever appeared in Bengali fiction.

Binodini's complexity is also apparent in her development over the course of the novel, for she grows out of her role as a destructive siren and, transformed by her love for Bihari, emerges as a self-sacrificing figure who puts his welfare above her own desires. As a result, at the end of the novel, when Bihari offers to marry her, Binodini refuses for his sake even though she is in love with him. She is aware that, despite the Hindu Widows' Remarriage Act of 1856, social attitudes have not changed much, and her marriage to Bihari would harm his image and reputation.[14] She realizes that she is "not simply a widow but deeply compromised, a fallen, stigmatized woman or *kalankini* [tainted woman] in colonial Bengal" (Dasgupta et al. 194). "I am a widow, a woman disgraced," Binodini tells Bihari, adding, "I cannot permit you to be humiliated in the eyes of society" (355). The fallen woman, who earlier refused to deny herself anything, sacrifices her own happiness for the sake of the man she loves. This is her redemption but also the end of her rebellion.

This nuanced portrayal of Binodini in *Chokher Bali* proved controversial in Tagore's own time, because of the book's amoral stance toward her fallenness. Later, critics attacked him for not being radical enough, as the ending left many readers dissatisfied with Binodini's change of heart: "Rabindranath's *Chokher Bali* had been frequently criticised, first for not being moral enough, and later for being too moral" (Dasgupta et al. 195). Tagore himself remained dissatisfied with the novel's ending, which he changed twice. In his social milieu, it was likely difficult to imagine a tidy resolution to the conflicts set up by Binodini's stormy intrusion into the lives of Mahendra, Bihari, and Asha. Given the narrative's realist style, Tagore was constrained from devising an ending that was compatible with the sociocultural reality of his times. The reconciliation of Asha and Mahendra, and Binodini's departure for a life of piety in Varanasi, strikes many contemporary readers as rather unconvincing. Despite her reformation in the final pages of the novel, it is Binodini the spirited fallen woman who lives on in the reader's imagination.

Binodini Dasi is another woman who in the Indian popular imagination is known for her fallenness, and in this sense, she is perhaps the fictional Binodini's material counterpart. Binodini Dasi was a fabled actor and sex worker whose clients and nonpaying lovers included prominent patrons of Bengali theater. Her life spanned roughly the latter half of the nineteenth century and the first half of the twentieth century. A low-caste woman born in a section of Kolkata inhabited by sex workers, she was raised by her mother and grandmother[15] and introduced to the stage when she was only ten. Because of her uncommon talent, she was cast as the heroine in her second play. Playing a wide variety of roles, Binodini was a pioneer in the evolution of modern Bengali theater, scaling the heights of her profession before her premature retirement. But betrayed, deceived, and eventually prohibited from the theater because she was a sex worker, she died in poverty and disease without anyone to look after her.

While Binodini's extraordinary talent brought her fame as an actor, the men in her life contributed to creating her reputation as a woman on the fringes of respectability who could not quite become a *bhadramahila*. Binodini writes about these relationships in *My Story* and *My Life as an Actress*, telling readers about her barely remembered child husband, her mentors, lovers, and fellow actors. Her narrative is dedicated to her *hridaydevata* (lord of her heart), the unnamed man who is her true love. She also speaks of her mentor, Girishchandra Ghosh, the renowned director, producer, and playwright, who cofounded the Great National Theatre and is considered the father of Bengali theater. Her relationship with Girishchandra was crucial to her emergence and evolution as an actor, and in fact, *My Story* takes the form of a series of letters addressed to him. In *My Story*, Binodini also recounts that she drew the approval of the sage Ramakrishna Paramahamsa, who, impressed with her portrayal of the male *bhakti* saint, Chaitanya,[16] is said to have redeemed her and, incidentally, the entire realm of Bengali public theater that she had come to represent. Additionally, Binodini describes her later years when she was as an unnamed client's cowife, living on his property but outside his house.

Despite her many successes, Binodini never escaped the stigma associated with sex work. Both her autobiographies, *My Story* and *My Life as an Actress*, offer a tantalizingly incomplete glimpse of her life in Bengali theater caught between the public glare and the private trauma of her existence on the margins of "respectability" and longing for the social acceptance that continuously eludes her. Nevertheless, the books differ in that *My Story* is a tale of pain and suffering, a *bedonagatha* (mournful verse), while *My Life as an Actress* is a celebration of the stage and Binodini's place on it.

For more than two thousand years before Binodini took the stage, the female performer was synonymous with sex worker. High caste-class male patrons sought out these women not only for sexual pleasure but also for their proficiency in music, dancing, and acting, skills that their virtuous, privileged wives did not and, according to conventional morality, should not possess (De Lamotte et al. 167). Prior to the advent of Proscenium Theatre in India, these shows were organized along the courtesan model, with performances staged in semiprivate spaces. When Proscenium Theatre developed during the colonial period and early prohibitions against women appearing onstage ended, female actors moved their performances to these public spaces, but they continued to be considered sex workers and, in fact, often were. Hence the word *nati*, which meant "actress" in the nineteenth century, accrued a second meaning, "sex worker." This and other similarly stigmatizing terms also indicated caste-class difference, underscoring the unbridgeable gap between "the upper-caste Hindu women as the embodiment of moral order" and "the moral decay brought about through the agency of sexually deviant women" (Chatterjee 162, 166). In the context of the nineteenth-century independence movement, the *nati*, as a public dancing woman, became "emblematic of the degraded morals of the metropolis" (Bhattacharya, "afterword" 188). Not surprisingly, Binodini never used this term to refer to herself, but the public tagged her "Nati Binodini," and this label gained wide currency, signifying both her talents as an actor and her fallen status. Paradoxically, however, being a *nati* gave Binodini a measure of freedom that "respectable" women in *purdah* did not enjoy. As De Lamotte explains, despite widespread condemnation of them, sex workers had privileges not accorded *bhadramahila*. They were "able to roam unveiled throughout the cities, [and] prostitutes and dancing girls remained free from the restrictions that respectable women endured over dress, behavior, sexual expression, and education" (167).

This *bhadramahila/nati* dichotomy shaped Binodini's life, and her autobiographies reveal a deep ambivalence about her status as a fallen woman. She longs for respectability but treasures the freedom that being a *nati* made possible. This ambivalence frames her self-representations and numerous topics tackled in the books. Consequently, Binodini emerges as a liminal figure with a split sense of subjectivity. Though she aspires to be acknowledged as a *bhadramahila*, she refers to herself in terms that signify traditional notions of women's sexual dishonor. She calls herself a *patita* (fallen woman), a *kalankini* (tainted woman), *samajpatita* (fallen in the eyes of society), and a *ghrinita barbonita* (despicable prostitute). For instance, about her writing, she says, "I am a prostitute, a social outcast; there is no one to listen to or to read what I feel within! That is why I have let you know my story in pen and paper. Like my own tainted and polluted heart, I have tainted these pure white pages with writing. But what else could I do! A polluted being can do nothing other than pollute!" (107). Clearly, she internalizes the stigma attached to her by a conservative society even though she wants to be free of its taint.

Despite subscribing to the stigma of fallenness, Binodini's autobiographies reveal that she feels no guilt. In fact, she is very clear that she is not to blame for her fallen status: sometimes she imputes her predicament to "fate," but in several passages, she faults "respectable" men as well as social conditions and norms for turning women into sinners. Indeed, Binodini writes that her autobiographies are motivated by her desire to tell the "truth" about forces—poverty, the caste-class hierarchy, and norms governing women's behavior—that create the sex trade and the personal suffering that being marginalized as a sex worker entails. For instance, regarding men's role in the sex trade economy, Binodini writes, "A prostitute's life is certainly tainted and despicable; but where does the pollution come from? . . . there are many who are taken in by the artfulness of men and trusting in them are doomed to carry an everlasting stigma and bear the pain of unending hell" (105). Binodini also points a finger at gender and class double standards: "Who are all these men? Are there not some among them who are respected and adored in society? . . . And it is these tempters of the helpless who become leaders of society and pass moral judgement on these insecure women in order to crush them at every step of their existence!" (105–6). Additionally, her critique of broader social institutions examines the intersections of class and gender. For instance, she relates the conditions that propelled her young brother into marriage with a toddler: "Our sufferings from poverty increased, and then our grandmother perpetrated a marriage between my infant brother of five years and a girl of two and a half and brought home a negligible quantity of ornaments. Then our livelihood was earned through the sale of ornaments" (qtd. in Spivak 147). Here, Binodini shows that poverty is a major cause of oppression. As Sumanta Banerjee points out, "Binodini is unsparing in her denunciation of those responsible for the plight of women like her, and shows an unerring understanding of the socioeconomic powers that operated in her society" (119–20). In one passage, for instance, Binodini describes the hopelessness that drives women to become sex workers and makes a point of humanizing them as mothers and beings afflicted by pain:

> Innumerable sighs hold together the heart of this luckless woman. An intolerable burden of pain has been covered by smiles, as despair fight hopelessness

> relentlessly day and night. How many are the unfulfilled longings, the wounds burning with pain that are alight in her heart; has anyone ever seen any of this? They become prostitutes forced by circumstances, lacking shelter, lacking space; but they too, first come into this world with the heart of a woman. The woman who is a loving mother. She too belongs to the same species! But we have been struck against stone from the very beginning and like the bit of iron which becomes magnetized having repeatedly struck against a magnet, likewise we have been struck against stone, have turned into stone ourselves. (104)

This appreciation of the role that poverty plays in subjugating women is one source of her hope that, conversely, wealth could extricate her from her position in society's margins. However, Binodini repeatedly found that money could not buy respectability. For instance, she became the mistress of a wealthy man in order to establish herself as the benefactor of a theater that she hoped would be named after her, but the Bengali theater establishment proved averse to the idea of naming a theater after a sex worker. As with so many of her attempts to gain social acceptance, Binodini found herself perpetually entrapped in the hinterland between respectability and fallenness.

Another factor that renders Binodini a liminal figure is the rupture between the roles she plays and her moral alterity, which, ironically, is a result of her presence on stage. Binodini, as Gayatri Spivak writes in "The Burden of English," believed that her success in the theater would override prejudice rooted in social norms stigmatizing sex workers: "For Binodini, the professional theater had promised an access to feminist individualism that resident prostitution denied" (150). However, this hope is perpetually frustrated, and "feminist individualism" as well as social acceptance prove elusive. For example, when she plays Chaitanya Mahaprabu, a sixteenth-century ascetic Hindu monk and social reformer in the Vaishnavite Bhakti sect that rejected the caste system and expanded lower-class' access to scriptures, Binodini crosses not only the gender divide but also the gulf between her "depravity" and the character's exalted moral position.[17] Her performance was so impressive that Ramakrishna Paramahamsa, a revered, influential ascetic who opposed religious and caste discrimination, is said to have blessed her and forgiven her sins. This incident was popularly characterized as Binodini's redemption and, by association, a legitimization of Bengali public theater that for so long had been excoriated for immorality.[18] However, this restoration of Binodini's morality, as it was perceived, did not lend her any more respectability than wealth did. Rather, nationalists in India's liberation movement and, to a lesser degree, Ramakrishna Paramahamsa coopted Binodini's performance, using her as prop for their causes, a phenomenon that occurred more than once during her career. Since the theater offered a counterpoint to Western cultural influence, Binodini's "purification" effectively shored up the cause of independence at a time when proponents were seeking a way out of a difficult dilemma: how to embrace aspects of Western culture without compromising their nationalist stance. Binodini's *bedonagatha*, her narrative of suffering perpetual personal and professional betrayal, lent resonance to the topos of betrayal by British colonizers that dominated liberatory, nationalist discourses. Yet nationalists did not acknowledge Binodini as one of their own, for as Chatterjee suggests, the putative state's emerging identity largely depended on differentiating between worthy insiders and unworthy outsiders. Consequently, betrayal was at the core of the nationalist agenda: "Because it could confer freedom only by imposing at the same time a whole set of new controls, it could define a cultural identity for the nation only by excluding many from its fold" (154). Similarly, after she was apotheosized as a celebrity, so to speak, icon of "Bhakti," Binodini effectively promoted the Vaishnavite Bakhti tradition to which she was faithful, yet she was denied full participation in its rites and services, for despite Ramakrishna Paramahamsa's praise, the stigma of being a sex worker kept Binodini from visiting holy sites and fulfilling her wish to join a religious order (Bhattacharya, "afterword" 202). Such contradictions, like so many others, contain Binodini in the nether space between acceptability and condemnation, but with the added twist that the very people and entities that rejected her because she was a sex worker also exploited her for their own ends. Binodini's texts do not indicate that she ever came to terms with this disjuncture between her success and her outsider status, for she continued to feel betrayed in her personal and professional life, and these feelings were compounded by her devastation at the death of her daughter: "I had found a reason for joy in this sorrowful life. But the karma of this wretched woman begrudged her even this pleasure! In order to punish me in the most extreme manner possible, the unsullied heavenly *parijat* flower [night-flowering jasmine] left me in eternal sorrow, returning to the heaven from whence she had come" (106). As these words imply, without her daughter, Binodini's sense of self is based solely on her status as a moral pariah with limited agency and simultaneously one of the most successful women of her time.

Although Binodini achieved fame as an actor and the episode of her redemption was renowned, until recently, historians have ignored Binodini's contributions to the theater and the nineteenth-century debate about women's social roles. Baidik Bhattacharya argues that this is due to her nonconformist stance: "She was sent into obscurity mainly because of her deviance from the norms" (57). In popular culture, however, several generations have iconized Binodini as a redeemed sinner rescued from sex work by her marriage, and today Binodini is increasingly recognized as a catalyst of social change: "Binodini . . . fought to participate in the career she loved and refused to accept her culture's reductive definition of her character?" (De Lamotte et al. 168). Her poetry and autobiographies celebrate women's creative power at a time when many women were illiterate, and these works persistently voice the need to change attitudes and institutions that oppress women, especially poor women and sex workers.

Nevertheless, Binodini remains an enigma to this day, her reputation created by a tissue of words, some spun by herself, and others conjured by those seeking to reclaim her for their own social and political agendas. Well-intentioned feminists, dramatists, and scholars have used her life and texts to further their causes, and film directors and stars have presented her in an erotic light rather than emphasizing her struggles and boldness. For example, the movie *Nati Binodini* focuses primarily on her love life, and another film, *Abohoman* (*Eternal*), shows how a director intends to make a movie based on Nati Binodini's autobiography *My Story* because he was Binodini's lover.

Thus Binodini's life story is obscured in the hands of others and also because her autobiographical narratives are incomplete. What she tells us overtly is important, but the gaps and silences in these accounts of her life and circumstances are even more eloquent. For instance, Binodini refused to include in the first edition of *My Story* the preface written by Girishchandra because it "faults Binodini's life story for being too personal, for containing too many details about herself, and for being a bitter social critique; it is simply not professional enough, and [he] wishes, it were, it were more concerned with the details of her performance" (Bhattacharya, "introduction" 19). This decision highlights Binodini's bitterness at Girishchandra's equivocation and his dishonesty in extricating her from poverty only to control and exploit her for his own benefit. That she chooses to include his preface in a subsequent edition published after his death is perhaps her concession to social expectations and an attempt to legitimize her narrative. But things left unsaid in Girishchandra's preface—Binodini's contributions to the development of India's national theater—destabilize the "truth claims" of her autobiographies, and Binodini's story remains fragmentary and incomplete.

The common ground between Binodini Dasi and Binodini of *Chokher Bali* is that both women articulate their bitterness about their circumstances but fail to alter the status quo as far as social attitudes are concerned. In the case of "Nati" Binodini, the narrative of her sin and redemption by Ramakrishna Paramahamsa tends to dominate the public imagination, while her autobiographical works testify to a ruptured subjectivity that is rooted in her fallen status and her rage and resentment at the price she pays for it—her utter failure to achieve social respectability. For in the final analysis, she was identified primarily as a sex worker but not as an actor or author, as illustrated by the criticism that her autobiographical narratives too heavily emphasize her professional achievements. In Tagore's novel, Binodini the seductress eventually undergoes a moral transformation through her chastening love for Bihari. At the end of the novel, she is shown in a penitent and reconciliatory mode and seeks the forgiveness of Asha, whose husband she seduced. Thus both texts ultimately fail to offer a satisfactory resolution to the conflicts that drive them. The Binodini in *Chokher Bali* disappears at the end of the novel, and Binodini Dasi never achieves the social acceptance she craves.

NOTES

1 *Chokher Bali* translates as "a constant irritant, like a grain of sand in the eye" (56). The term *chokher bali* in Bengali idiomatically refers to a relationship that is intimate, yet unbearable, and hard to dismiss or dislodge. In chapter 11 of this book, Meenakshi Malhotra translates *Chokher Bali* as *A Mote in the Eye*, but the more widely used title is *Grain of Sand*. One reason for the variance in translation is that *bali* means both "female friend" and "sand." Tagore plays on this

double meaning to suggest that the two women in the novel who are in love with the same man have an uneasy relationship that is as discomforting as the feeling of a mote or sand particle in one's eye.

2 Binodini Dasi (c. 1863–1941) was a famous actor on the Calcutta stage. She was also an accomplished poet and published the autobiographical works *My Story* and *My Life as an Actress.*

3 In the nineteenth century, the position of women in society became a raging social debate in Bengal, leading to a tussle between conservatives and liberal reformers who challenged various social evils such as child marriage, denial of education to women, ill-treatment of widows, and women's subjugation in the home. Later in the century, "the woman question" became connected with the rising tide of nationalism, as those struggling for freedom from British rule began to realize the contradictions between their claim to a new modernity and the backwardness of the women in their own homes.

4 According to custom, young girls of eight or nine were often married off to much older men and consigned to a life of extreme suffering upon the death of their husbands. In 1929, child marriage was outlawed in India. The minimum age of marriage was fixed at fifteen for girls and eighteen for boys.

5 Traditionally, the Hindu widow was condemned to a life of extreme hardship with no possibility of remarriage. Widowhood was regarded as inauspicious, and the widow was expected to live a life of prayer, fasting, celibacy, and self-denial. Reformers championed the cause of widow remarriage, and due to their efforts, the Widow Remarriage Act, which provided widows some legal protection, was passed in 1856.

6 *Purdah* refers to veiling and isolating women in the home—sometimes in one room—practiced in traditional Indian households. In Bengal, reformers and nationalists challenged these conventions during the late nineteenth and early twentieth centuries.

7 The Swadeshi movement began as a nationalist upsurge against the British attempt to partition Bengal in 1905. Emphasizing *atmashakti*, or "self-reliance," Swadeshi nationalists advocated boycotting British products in order to promote goods made in India. The boycott came to symbolize India's national dignity and the idea of freedom from foreign rule.

8 The term *bhadramahila*, or "respectable lady," became important for Indian nationalists with the opening of girls' schools in India by English missionaries in the mid-nineteenth century. At that time, reformers such as Rammohun Roy and Bhudev Mukhopadhyay were campaigning for women's education and the abolition of practices such as *sati*, widows' forced or voluntary self-immolation in their late husbands' funeral pyres. Partha Chatterjee argues that the definition of the term *bhadramahila* was gradually broadened by Indian nationalists to refer to a woman who was educated and refined but not given to "Western" habits like smoking, drinking, and mingling socially with men. The *bhadramahila* thus came to be seen as the preserver of Indian culture who defended its purity against foreign influences. She also came to embody a moral code that strictly emphasized woman's chastity and "honor." In contrast, *patita* (fallen women) were "invented by society to imprison them in an untouchable pigeon-hole," and it was assumed that they came from the "condemned fringes" of society (Banerjee 125). The *patita*'s marginalization and the figure of the *beshya* (female sex worker) were popular topoi in Bengali literature, providing writers and readers, as Ratnabali Chatterjee writes, much titillating material.

9 Ishwar Chandra Vidyasagar (b. 1820–91) was a social reformer, educator, scholar, and philosopher. He raised his voice against social evils such as polygamy and child marriage and promoted women's education. He pioneered the idea of widow remarriage, and it was largely due to the efforts of reformers like him that the Hindu Widows' Remarriage Act was passed in 1856.

10 I have explored some of these aspects of *Chokher Bali* in greater detail in *Novelist Tagore: Gender and Modernity in Selected Texts* (48–61).

11 The scholarly convention in India is to refer to some figures by their given rather than surnames. The editors have honored this practice to resist the West's dominance over scholarly practices and forms.

12 The Vaishnavas represent a branch of Hinduism devoted to the worship of Vishnu and his avatars or incarnations. Popular Vaishnava cults often center on two of these avatars, Rama and Krishna, along with their respective consorts, Sita and Radha. As Radha is married to another man, her relationship with Krishna is one of forbidden love. All the same, in Vaishnava lore, this erotic relationship is celebrated as an expression of *bhakti*, or pure devotion beyond the purview of worldly social mores. Tagore here plays on a central irony: widows are expected to follow the Vaishnava tradition, which celebrates the love of Krishna and his consort while embracing a code of ascetic denial of desire in their own lives.

13 The gopis or gopikas are the cowherd maidens of Vrindavana who are deeply dedicated to the Lord Krishna. Their unconditional devotion is represented in Vaishnavite lore through the erotic figuration of "Raas Leela," a dance in which Krishna engages playfully in ritual interactions with the gopis, especially with his consort, Radha.

14 The Hindu Widows' Remarriage Act was passed in 1856, making it legally possible for widows to marry again. The legislation was intended to safeguard the interests of widows, but it actually required these women to give up their claims on property inherited from their deceased husbands.

15 For a detailed account of Binodini Dasi's life and career, see Rimli Bhattacharya's afterword in *My Story and My Life as an Actress* (3–46).

16 Sri Krishna Chaitanya Mahaprabhu (b. 1486–1534), a Vaishnava, is a Hindu saint who promoted *bhakti* yoga, a spiritual practice cultivating love of God, in the sixteenth century. His devotees considered him an avatar of Lord Krishna and are known as Gaudiay Vaishnavas.

17 Rimli Bhattacharya tracks the evolution of Binodini's reputation through successive stages as "*dasi-nati-devi*" ("afterword" 189).

18 Ramakrishna Paramahamsa (b. 1836–86) was an ascetic spiritual leader in Bengal, a devotee of the goddess Kali. He opposed religious prejudice and caste discrimination, and his ideas had a major influence on the intellectuals of Bengal.

WORKS CITED

Albinia, Alice. "Womanhood Laid Bare: How Katherine Mayo and Manoda Devi Challenged Indian Public Morality." *SARAI Reader*, 2005, pp. 428–35.

Banerjee, Sumanta. *Dangerous Outcast: The Prostitute in Nineteenth Century Bengal.* Monthly Review, 1998. Seagull, 2000.

Bhattacharya, Baidik. "Domain, Domination and Domesticity: Nationalism, Gender and Women's Writing in Colonial India." *Signifying the Self*, edited by Malashri Lal, Sumanyu Sathpathy, and Shormishtha Panja, Macmillan, 2004, pp. 19–44.

Bhattacharya, Rimli. "Afterword." *My Story* and *My Life as an Actress*, by Binodini Dasi, Kali for Women, 1998, pp. 187–243.

———. "Introduction." *My Story* and *My Life as an Actress*, by Binodini Dasi, Kali for Women, 1998, pp. 3–46.

Chakrabarty, Dipesh. "Witness to Suffering: Domestic Cruelty and the Birth of the Modern Subject in Bengal." *Questions of Modernity*, edited by Timothy Mitchell, U of Minnesota P, 2000, pp. 49–86.

Chakravarty, Radha. *Novelist Tagore: Gender and Modernity in Selected Texts.* Routledge, 2013.

Chatterjee, Chanda. "Widows and Fallen Women: Gleanings from Nineteenth and Early Twentieth Century Bengali Literature." *Literature, Caste and Society: The Masks and Veils.* Edited by S. Jayaseela Stephen, Kalpaz, 2006, pp. 143–58.

Chatterjee, Partha. "The Nationalist Resolution of the Woman Question." *Recasting Women: Essays in Colonial History*, edited by Sudesh Vaid and Kumkum Sangari, Kali for Women, 1989, pp. 233–53.

———. *The Nation and Its Fragments*. Princeton UP, 1993.

Chatterjee, Ratnabali. "Prostitution in Nineteenth Century Bengal: Construction of Class and Gender." *Social Scientist*, vol. 21, no. 9–11, 1993, pp. 159–72.

Dasgupta, Sanjukta, Sudeshna Chakravarti, and Mary Mathew, editors. *Radical Rabindranath: Nation, Family and Gender in Tagore's Fiction and Films*. Orient Blackswan, 2013.

Dasi, Binodini. *My Story* and *My Life as an Actress*. Edited and translated by Rimli Bhattacharya, Kali for Women, 1998.

De Lamotte, Eugenia C., Natania Meeker, and Jean F. O'Barr, editors. *Women Imagine Change: A Global Anthology of Women's Resistance from 600 B.C. to Present*. Routledge, 1997.

Hedgecock, Jennifer. *The Femme Fatale in Victorian Literature: The Danger and the Sexual Threat*. Cambria, 2008.

Nandy, Ashis. *At the Edge of Psychology: Essays in Politics and Culture*. Oxford UP, 1980, pp. 1–31.

Panja, Shormishtha. "Rabindranath Tagore's *Chokher Bali*: The New Woman, Conjugality and the Heterogeneity at Home." *Signifying the Self: Women and Literature*, edited by Malashri Lal, Shormishtha Panja, and Sumanyu Satpath, Macmillan, 2004, pp. 211–25.

Spivak, Gayatri Chakravorty. "The Burden of English." *Orientalism and the Postcolonial Predicament: Perspectives on South Asia*, edited by Carol Appadurai Breckenridge and Peter van der Veer, U of Pennsylvania P, 1993, pp. 134–57.

Tagore, Rabindranath. *Chokher Bali*. Translated by Radha Chakravarty, Random House, 2012.

PART V THE MORAL FRONTIERS OF LESBIANISM IN THE EAST

14 ⑥ SHAKING THE THRONE OF GOD

Muslim Women Writers Who Dared

FEROZA JUSSAWALLA

When the earth quakes her violent shakings
And the earth bears forth her weighty burdens . . .

—Qur'an 99:1–8

This chapter debunks the idea that Islamic theology deems homosexuality a grave sin. By tracing early Islamic scholarship, historical documents, and literature, Jussawalla shows early acceptance of male same-sex relationships. Subsequently exploring works by four contemporary Muslim women writers—Ismat Chughtai, Roushan Jahan, Sara Suleri, and Sabiha Bano—Jussawalla traces lesbian desire, latent and conspicuous, in fiction by Muslim women writing and publishing in South Asia, which substantiates her claim that homosexuality is not antithetical to Islam. Third, Jussawalla proposes that *ijtihad,* an age-old practice of interpreting and reinterpreting the Qur'an, is being revived by Muslim scholars such as Scott Siraj al-Haqq Kugel and public intellectuals like Irshad Manji to reassess the scriptural validity of contemporary restrictions and attitudes that derive primarily from undue influence of local, non-Islamic cultural beliefs.

Muslims, whether of the Middle East, Persia, South Asia, Asia, and now the vast diaspora, believe that the Qur'an is the received word of God; that it was delivered through "the Messenger," the Prophet Muhammad; and that it cannot be questioned. Any questioning has been seen as blasphemy, and in recent years, punishments worse than any conceived in the religion's early years have been inflicted upon those who challenge the Qur'an's precepts, including prohibitions against homosexuality. Defying or challenging the Qur'an is commonly referred to as "shaking the throne of God," an expression based on verses in *Sura* 99 (*Book* 99), which is entitled "Surat al-Zilalal" ("The Earthquake"), that predict the earth will tremble and sinners will be separated from the virtuous on the "day of atonement," doomsday or judgment day (99:1–8). Thus in popular Islamic discourses, the phrase "shake the throne" is often used to categorize homosexuality as one of the worst sins of all, although, no such language exists in the Qur'an and is only found in an obscure hadith. According to James Bellamy, "Whenever a male mounts another male, the throne of God trembles; [and] the angels look on in loathing" (qtd. in Wafer 89). But attitudes about homosexuality, even among the Muslim faithful, are becoming more accepting and affirming today due to recent events—evolutions and revolutions intersecting with Western freedoms. Muqtada al-Sadr, one of Iraq's most influential and militant clerics, in April 2016 exhorted, "[You] must disassociate from them [homosexuals] and provide them advice [but] not attack them" (Bassem). Even in conservative Saudi Arabia, clerics such as Salman al-Ouda are now speaking out against persecuting homosexuals. Invoking the concept of free will in an interview in May 2016, he said, "Homosexuals are not deviating from Islam." He added that those who condemn them to death are the real deviants, and they commit the greater sin, since homosexuals do not need to be punished in "this world" (qtd. in Groisman). Additionally, a leading North American Muslim scholar, Hamza Yusuf, president and cofounder of Zaytuna College, the first Muslim liberal arts college in the United States, argues that same-sex desire alone is not sinful—he acknowledges that homosexuality is biological—although engaging in homosexual acts is immoral. Yusuf goes on to say that homosexuality is troublesome when it becomes a public matter because it is *al jahar* (corrupting of the public sphere) and leads others astray. At the same time, he argues that if homosexual acts are private, they do not merit punishment (Yusuf). In addition to these clerics, increasing numbers of openly homosexual Muslims and their allies are challenging homophobia. Nevertheless, conversations about homosexuality and Islam remain complicated.

This chapter contributes to this discussion by arguing that in Islam the word of God in the Qur'an does not define same-sex desire as a sin; rather, later interpretive traditions often based on dubious hadithic material[1] have fostered the false view that homosexuality is immoral. The chapter subsequently argues that homosexuality is indigenous to Islam. The basis for this argument is historical evidence, fiction by women that features lesbian desire, and recent nonfiction that reconsiders and revives the Islamic interpretive tradition of *ijtihad*. The chapter concludes by asserting that neither women writers whose fiction offers affirming representations of lesbianism or their lesbian characters are "fallen."

Homosexuality is often seen as a "gross" or major sin in Islam; however, the Qur'an has relatively little to say about homosexuality and mostly refers to it indirectly. The clearest-cut mention is "And as for the two of you [men] who are guilty thereof, / punish them both. / And if they repent and improve, then let them be. / Lo! Allah is Relenting, Merciful" (4:16). Another reference to homosexuality is in Surah 23:1–5, entitled "Al-Mu'minin" ("The Believers"), which lays out various actions a "good believer" should take and not take. This verse stipulates that men should engage in sexual behavior only with their wives (the Qur'an is addressed to a male audience): "They . . . who guard their private parts except from their wives, or their right hands possess, for indeed, they will not be blamed. But whosoever seeks beyond that then those are the transgressors." Additionally, the Qur'an's seven passages telling the story of the prophet Lot and the destruction of Sodom and Gomorrah, which are commonly cited as the Qur'an's strongest prohibition of homosexuality, relate that God sends the Prophet Lot to urge townspeople to desist from their sins, but they reject his message and the cities' men threaten to rape Lot's guests, travelers who, unbeknownst to the attackers, are actually angels. Conventionally, Lot is thought to exhort against homosexuality in one passage castigating the townsmen: "Will you commit lewdness such as no people in creation ever committed before you? For you come in lust to men in preference to women. No, you are indeed a people transgressing beyond bounds" (Qur'an 7:80–81). In another verse, Lot reprimands the townsmen for the adultery they would commit in the course of the threatened rape: "Of all the creatures in the world, will you approach males, and leave those whom Allah has created for you to be your mates? No, you are a people transgressing [all limits]!" (Qur'an 26:165–166, 27:54, and 29:28). When Lot is ignored, he flees, and God destroys Sodom and Gomorrah.

Since the Qur'an provides such sparse instruction on homosexuality per se, support for the position that it is a profound sin has been sought in the Qur'an's teachings on marriage. According to the Qur'an, marriage is humans' proper destiny and the cornerstone of Islamic society. Rather than a social institution, marriage is considered a divinely created, natural entity that gives shape and value to human relationships. Both sexual pleasure within marriage and reproduction are virtuous in that they are created by God. Homophobic interpretations of this doctrine construct homosexuality as the polar opposite of marriage, although there is no such language in the Qur'an. The logic these arguments employ is that homosexuality contravenes the natural order, undermines marriage and the family, leads people away from God, and subverts order, creating chaos as in Sodom and Gomorrah.

If the Qur'an has little to say about homosexuality, the *hadiths*, a collection of traditions that are based on Muhammad's sayings and customs as reported by others, are more expansive on the subject and, unlike the Qur'an, condemn homosexuality in no uncertain terms—to the point of criminalizing it. Some *hadiths* claim that Muhammad cursed homosexuals: "Narrated by Ibn 'Abbas: The Prophet cursed effeminate men; those men who are in the similitude (assume the manners of women) and those women who assume the manners of men, and he said, 'Turn them out of your houses.' The Prophet turned out such-and-such man, and 'Umar turned out such-and-such woman" (al-Bukhari 72:774). Other *hadiths* mandate capital punishment: "Narrated Abdullah ibn Abbas: If a man who is not married is seized committing sodomy, he will be stoned to death" (Abu Dawud 38:4448). Burning homosexuals alive is recommended, based on Ibn 'Abass's report that Ali, Muhammad's cousin and son-in-law, once decreed this sentence (*Mishkat al-Masabih* [*A Niche for Lamps*] 765). Another penalty is toppling a wall on homosexuals, something that Abu Bakr, Muhammad's close companion, was supposed to have done (ibn 'Abd Allāh Khatib Al-Tabrizi 765). These *hadiths* are the primary source of the belief that homosexuality is one of the most serious infractions in Islam.

However, much of this hadithic material on homosexuality, which is clearly not consistent with the text of the Qur'an, either is forged or has its source in folklore or cultural prejudice rather than scripture (Kugle). Furthermore, hadithic and current strictures against homosexuality *contradict* the Qur'an and bely a historical tradition of unspoken, gentle acceptance of same-sex desire. In fact, the Qur'an's depiction of paradise specifies that it is inhabited not only by *houri*, virginal young women who are companions of the pure, but also youth (Surah 56:17–18), and for most of premodern period, literature, the visual arts, and nonfictional records routinely documented or celebrated homosexuality throughout the Islamic Middle East and South Asia (Wafer 90).

According to Janet Afary, classical Persian literature dating from the twelfth century "overflows with same-sex themes" (87), including works by Sufi poets Sana'i (d. 1131), Khaquani (d. 1190), 'Attar (d. 1220), Rumi (d. 1273), Sa'adi (d. 1291), and Hafez (d. 1389). In Persia's Abbassid Dynasty (750 CE to 1258 CE), poetry frequently celebrated love of young boys, as exemplified by a verse written by the Persian-Arabic poet, Abu Nawas, who invokes the Qur'anic idea of a youth-laden paradise to develop this trope:

> I have a lad who is like the lads of paradise
> And his eyes are big and beautiful . . .
> His face is as the moon in its full perfection
> And you think that he is mysteriously struck by a magician
> Because he is so tender and pretty
> We spent the night together as if we were in paradise.
> Doing nothing except making love and pleasure. (132)

Likewise, early modern Islamic visual arts often feature scenes of same-sex coupling between men. For example, during the Safavid (1501–1736) and Qajar (1794–1925) dynasties in Persia, miniature paintings (a genre akin to the medieval Western tradition of illuminated manuscripts), depicted pederastic relationships in a highly romanticized style, as did South Asian Deccani and Moghul miniatures produced from the sixteenth through the nineteenth centuries. Among the most famous visual representations of same-sex desire is a painting by Muhammed Qasim, *The Portrait of Shah Abbas with Young Page* (1627), which shows the king embracing his beautiful, effeminate cupbearer.

Moreover, historians have identified numerous nonfiction reports documenting same-sex relationships. Afsaneh Najmabadi, in *Women with Mustaches and Men without Beards: Gender and Sexual Anxieties of Iranian Modernity*, notes that Persian elites routinely engaged in same-sex as well as heterosexual relationships up through the advent of the modern period when this practice abated in response to Western colonizers' disapproval. For instance, in the Safavid Dynasty, Shah Tahmasb II (b. 1704?–1740) was reported to have "preferred one Joseph-faced to thousands of Zulaykhas and Laylis and Shirins" (Rustam al-Humakma qtd. in Najmabadi 147). Azud al-Dawlah noted that Qajar ruler Fath'ali Khan (b. 1772–1834) had relationships with young men, and court poet Saba praised him for "liking both young men and young women" (Afary 20). Similarly, Abdul Karim Rafeq's meticulous examination of *shari'a* court records in the Ottoman Empire in the eighteenth century shows that same-sex relationships were not criminalized and that they were reported in positive terms in biographies of the elite, indicating that homosexuality was "widespread and socially accepted," at least among that class (188). Not to be overlooked, speculation over the centuries holds that Salman al-Farsi, the scribe that Muhammad entrusted to take down the Qur'an, was homosexual (Milani 158).

However, documentation of lesbianism[2] is far less ample largely because, as numerous scholars have argued, regardless of location or the nature of the dominant religion (if it is patriarchal), when women's status is low, their lives are not important enough to record. Furthermore, high levels of illiteracy among women in these societies ensure that only a few are able to record their experiences. Nevertheless, newly uncovered scraps of evidence are building a broad view of lesbianism in the Islamic world that argues same-sex relationships among women, whether situational or biological (if these distinctions are significant or even valid), were common in the premodern era and sometimes even institutionalized. For instance, As'ad Abu Khalil reports in "A Note on the Study of Homosexuality in the Arab/Islamic Civilization" that Andalusian poet Walladah bint al-Mustakfi (b. 1001–91), the daughter of Muhammad III of Córdoba, who was the last of the Umayad Cordoban Caliphs of Sothern Spain, wrote sexually explicit verses to her female lover, Muhya bint al-Tayyani, though most of this material has been lost (32–34). Afary relates that Jakob Polak, personal physician to Naser al-Din Shah Qajar (b. 1848–96) and the court gynecologist and obstetrician, documented the Persian institution of sister recognition, which formalized lesbian relationships: "Tribady—or *tabaq*—among women is widespread. . . . A certain friendship pact between women is performed within certain ceremonies in particular mosques on the last Wednesday before New Year's Day [*char shanbe suri*]. . . . Once the pact is entered into, the women maintain an inviolable commitment. This act is called *khahar khandegi* [sister recognition]" (Afary 103).

Muhammed al-Idrisi (b. 1100–1166), a Muslim cartographer and geographer originally from North Africa, reported in his travel narrative *Kitab Nuzhat al-Mushtaq Fi'khtiraq al-'Afaq* (*The Book of Pleasant Journeys into Faraway Lands*) that "mannish" women found it "difficult to submit to the wishes of men" and turned to "lesbian love." He adds, "Most of the women with these characteristics are to be found among the educated and elegant women, the scribes, Koran (sic) readers, and female scholars" (Murray 98). Khaquani (c. 1121–90),[3] a poet in the court of Persian ruler Abu'l Muzaffar Khaqan-i-Akbar Manuchiher who was a member of the Shivanshah Dynasty, penned this less than romantic ode about lesbian lovemaking in Baghdad:

> Look at Baghdad and you will see all classes of women performing sex [*tabaq zan*] with one another.
> You will see silver mortars for sifting saffron,
> But you won't see any pestles . . .
> When they place their plates [*tabaq*] on top of each other,
> You will hear wild screams all the way to the skies. (Afary 101)

Then there is the stunning seventeenth-century Mughal illustration, *Women with Dildo* (held by the Bibliotheque Nationale de France in Paris), that depicts two seated women facing each other. The figure on the right, slightly reclining, has spread her legs to expose her naked vagina and thighs. The figure on the left is aiming a bow loaded with a dildo (rather than an arrow) at her companion's vagina.

This combined evidence shows that the late twentieth- and early twenty-first century inclination to prosecute homosexuality exceedingly harshly is an extreme position that is justified only by *overreading* the Qur'an and excessively relying on *hadiths*. Another factor that accounts for the current draconian approach to homosexuality is *ijtihad*, the Islamic tradition of continuous study and reinterpretation of sacred texts by independent reasoning (much like *Midrash* in Judaism). As a practice, *ijtihad* lends Islam a certain plasticity that facilitates adaptation of ancient precepts to different times and conditions. On the other hand, this same permeability allows numerous forces to shape Islam. Samra Habib explains, "Every Muslim's relationship with Islam is shaped by class, geography and cultural context, resulting in different interpretation of the religion by its 1.6 billion followers. Yet, the complexities and the nuanced experiences are often overlooked" (Habib). One limit on the multiplicity of interpretations that *ijtihad* can engender is the notion that *ijtihad* closed (ended) or at least narrowed around 900 CE.[4] In practice, however, this closure of *ijtihad* around the time that the project of collecting *hadith* ended embedded them in Muslim cultures, and there have been few major shifts in how Islamic precepts have been interpreted from the classical period up through the beginning of the twentieth century when modernists began to argue that Islam needed to be renovated, so to speak, to suit the new era (Hallaq 3). Broadly speaking, these reformers took two different approaches to this project, advocating changes based on Western models of education and democracy or rejecting Western influences as corrupting. The latter position, which coincides with the emergence of Islamism, has dominated much of the Islamic world since Ayatollah Ruhollah Khomeini's rise to power in Iran immediately after that country's 1979 revolution. In fact, as much as Khomeinism appears to be "fundamentalist"—imposing a literalist reading of Islamic scriptures—the Ayatollah has been one of Islam's strongest proponents of *ijtihad* in that he used it to transform Iran into a theocracy[5] guided by Shi'a Islamic principles. Essentially, Khomeini relied on *ijtihad* to argue that *shari'a* (Islamic law revealed by God) does not apply just to individual actions but that it should also regulate society as a whole, a stunning prospect in the twentieth century, not just in the West, but in the Islamic world as well. This venture was possible, theologically speaking, because in *ijtihad,* Khomeini found (1) a strategy for articulating Islamic responses to conditions that did not exist in Muhammad's lifetime and (2) a means of rendering legal judgments on issues and actions not specifically spelled out in examples provided by the prophets: "Khomeini strove to bring about practical compatibility between *shari'a* and modern society.... Otherwise, Islam could not be claimed to be the ultimate religion" (Bahmanpour 123).

While Shi'ism and Sunnism historically have defined *ijtihad* somewhat differently, and despite the fierce competition between these sects in the past and as they battle (literally) to control the Middle East in the post-Hussain, post-Arab Spring era, Khomeini's use of it to establish Islamic governance in Iran has had a "revolutionary" impact on both Shi'a and Sunni communities (69). Indeed, Sunni groups seeking to institute Islamist theocracy in the Middle East—Al Qaeda, the Taliban, and the Islamic State in Iraq and al-Sham (ISIS)—though they consider themselves purists who practice Islam as it existed in Muhammad's time—have looked to the Khomeinist model to shape their movements. Troublingly, their "priority" targets include homosexuals who are most often subject to capital punishment, and if media reports are to be believed, Islamist hate speech has inspired homophobic vigilantism worldwide, as appears to be the case in the June 2016 mass shooting at a gay nightclub in Florida, Pulse.

Significantly, the counterpoint to such Islamism, though less widely embraced, also relies on *ijtihad* for legitimacy, with feminists, liberals, and progressives revising traditional teachings about women and proposing acceptance if not affirmation of homosexuals and homosexuality. Fiction writers in this latter tradition include Rokeya Hossain, whose 1905 novel, *Sultana's Dream,* includes an early reference to lesbian love; Sara Suleri, author of *Meatless Days* (1987); Ismat Chughtai, who wrote "Lihaf," a story featuring a young bride's situational homosexuality; and Sabiha Bano, a Pakistani writer whose *Chalawa* sets lesbian desire against the backdrop of Cold War tensions. Nonfiction writers whose works reconsider homosexuality in Islam are theologian Scott Siraj al-Haqq Kugle, who in *Homosexuality in Islam* challenges the scriptural validity of Islamic homophobia, *and* Irshad Manji, whose book *The Trouble with Islam Today: A Muslim's Call for Reform in Her Faith* invokes *ijtihad* to argue for greater acceptance of homosexuality.

Rokeya Hossain's *Sultana's Dream*, published in 1905, is one of the first feminist manifestos written in South Asia. Rokeya was a self-educated, upper-class Muslim Bengali who founded a girls' school in Kolkata in 1911 using funds that her husband, Syed Sakhawat Hossain, left for that purpose upon his death the year before. She wrote *Sultana's Dream* in English, her fifth language, and said she had two purposes, "to pass time" (1) and to wage *jihad* (holy war) against "the basic principles of her society" that oppressed women (3). In it, Rokeya dreams about a feminist utopia in which gender roles are reversed—men are put in *purdah* and women run the country. Later, she wrote *The Secluded Ones: Purdah Observed*, translated by Roushan Jahan. Its short journal-like vignettes were published serially in the *Monthly Mohammadi* beginning in 1929 and express the liberated Rokeya's horrors at *purdah*, the most shocking story relating that a burqa-clad woman who fell across a train track could not be rescued because men could not touch her. In addition to campaigning against *purdah* as early as 1908, Rokeya boldly advocated for woman's equal rights, including public employment: "By confining women to the household, men deliberately deprive women of equal opportunity to cultivate their minds and to engage in gainful employment, thus making them dependent and inferior in status" (47).

Significantly, *Sultana's Dream* offers faint hints of a progressive position on same-sex desire. The book opens with an explanation that the unnamed narrator—presumably Rokeya—falls asleep and dreams that a friend, Sister Sara, invites her to walk in the botanical gardens. But it turns out that the woman is not Sister Sara, and instead of heading to the gardens, the two stroll hand in hand through the city streets of Ladyland, a feminist utopia where virtue is omnipresent rather than enforced vis-à-vis patriarchal regulation of women and their bodies (7). There are no men in public (a reversal of *purdah*), but as the dialogue between the narrator and her friend shows, the narrator is attracting attention from passersby: "The women say you look very mannish," says the friend. The narrator asks, "Mannish?" The narrator's fingers tremble, and the friend responds: "'What is the matter, dear, dear?' she said affectionately . . . 'You need not be afraid here. . . . This is Ladyland free of sin and harm. Virtue herself reigns here'" (8). By the standards of today's lesbian literature, this passage would not attract attention, but in the context of lesbian cultures, history, and rhetoric, its very inconspicuousness resonates women's same-sex desire, for the subtle allusion that Sokeya crafts in *Sultana's Dream* parallels hints of sisterly love, intimate friendships, and enduring devotion to another woman that appear in women's "lesbian" writing in highly patriarchal societies.

In contrast to *Sultana's Dream*, more recent texts, such as Sara Suleri's *Meatless Days* (1987), thematize women's attraction to mannish women quite overtly.[6] Written in English and published by the University of Chicago Press, this autofictional novella told in nine vignettes is based on the experiences of Suleri's family during Pakistan's partition from India, after they immigrate to Connecticut, and as they move back and forth between the United States and Pakistan. Iffat, Suleri's sister, is attracted to a small but powerful woman from Tanzania called Mustakor. In fact, it seems that almost everyone is attracted to Mustakor: Perin Cooper, a small Zoroastrian woman who teaches drama; all the students at Kinnaird College in Lahore, an all-female school; and male characters who call her the Tanzanian Transvestite (63) even as they themselves are fascinated by her. The hidden, subverted desire that these many characters possess for Mustakor is linked to the book's theme of alterity, so aptly expressed when Suleri asserts, "Remember . . . I've lived many years as an otherness machine" (105).

Meatless Days, written in geographical and temporal dislocation, is embedded with social and political connotations. It records the memories of Sara Suleri and her protest against female subjugation and suppression through false, misconstrued, and wrong interpretation of Islamic laws in the Pakistani society. Suleri, with most of her formative years in Pakistan, has interwoven the turbulent phase of her country with the reminiscences of tragic events in her family and tried to theorize the problematic issues of gender, religion, and Pakistan as a postcolonial nation. The memoir further seeks to explore a patriarchal society where religion is used to circumscribe and exploit women. Each female character in *Meatless Days* reflects on the national scenario through her own lens, but none of them seem satisfied with the scheme of things in the social and political arena of Pakistan. The frustration of these characters is evident throughout the memoir, but the prospects of finding any means of catharsis are absent. They feel suppressed and suffocated. Sara's mother always seemed lost, absorbed and always succumbing to her husband by saying "what an excellent thing" in response to every query. Her grandmother found solace in food, which became a way for her to communicate with her son and family. Suleri's sister, Ifat, was always biting her lips, expressing her inability to harmonize with the male dominant society of Pakistan. All the female characters in the memoir are dominated by the male members of the household. Mr. Suleri, Sara's father, manhandled everybody at his home and particularly subjugated the women because of his domineering and authoritative personality.

The Otherness of women who do not belong begins to be accentuated. Thus we see, as stated previously, that overt and primarily covert same-sex desire is manifest in the literature of women from Muslim backgrounds as readily as it is in other religious traditions.

Ismat Chughtai's short story "Lihaf" ("The Quilt"), first published in 1942, takes a different tack, poignantly relating the consequences of arranged marriages and women's segregation behind the *purdah* while also addressing acceptance of homosexuality in South Asian Muslim communities. First published in the literary journal, *Adab-i-Latif*, "Lihaf" was written in Urdu and later served as the basis for Deepa Mehta's 1996 film, *Fire*. A young woman called Begum Jan—that is by her title, Begum (with Jan meaning "dear,")—is brought into an arranged marriage to a *nawab* (a title that Moghul rulers originally gave local governors that evolved into an honorary designation). Told in a light, satirical tone by a child narrator, Begum Jan's niece, it mocks contemporary social norms: "After marrying Begum Jan, and installing her in his house along with the furniture, the Nawab Sahib totally forgot her presence, leaving the frail young Begum to pine in loneliness . . . all her prayers and vows, her vigils and charms failed to move the Nawab" (130).

And so we see that having a young wife in his house does not have any impact on the *nawab*, who is clearly "gay." Begum Jan soon realizes the truth by spying on the *nawab* as he carries on with young men. She peeks through chinks in the blinds to see her husband and pines after him, but social strictures being what they were, she cannot do much more and divorce is not an option. Spurned by her handsome yet effeminate husband, jealous, and hurt, she initiates a relationship with her maid servant, Rabbu, although there is no indication that Begum Jan was born lesbian. In the midst of all this, Amiran, a nine- to eleven-year-old girl and the story's narrator, is entrusted to Begum's care for a few days. At night, she witnesses the gyrating quilt that covers the Begum and Rabbu as they make love. Amiran watches and listens: "When I awoke on the second night, I felt as though a dispute between Rabbu and Begum Jan were being silently settled on the bed. I could not make out anything, nor could I tell how it was decided. I only heard Rabbu's convulsive sobs, then noises like that of a cat licking a plate, lap, lap, lap, I was so frightened that I went back to sleep" (Tharu and Lalitha 133).

A hilariously irreverent scene occurs when the frightened little girl is asked to recite the most sacred of Qur'anic verse, the Aayat-al-Kursi, which is meant to ward off evil, to lull her to sleep in what would be considered a sinful atmosphere by Islamic standards! Significantly, the Aayat-al-Kursi is often referred to as "the throne" verse because near the end it states, "His [God's] throne extends over the heavens and the earth." (2:255). Clearly, the *hadith* stating that homosexuality shakes the throne of God refers to this verse from the Qur'an, and of course, the "shaking" alludes to the rhythm of Begum Jan's and Rabbu's lovemaking. To be sure, bringing such a supposedly impure act before the throne of God is the highest disrespect. But what "Lihaf" argues with this light-heartedness and humor is that homosexuality is integrated into the fabric of Muslim life in South Asia. In fact, some scholars argue that situational homosexuality among the region's women arises from institutionalized sex segregation in the form of *purdah* and polygamy. When women are kept veiled and in separate *purdah* quarters and men are allowed more than one wife, women satisfy their desires not as "fallen" women but as "unfallen" women. In other words, women keep themselves "pure" and safe from a charge of adulterous relationships with men by satisfying their desires in private, among themselves, and under their quilts or "lihafs" (Murray). In this sense, "Lihaf" is an artifact that attests homosexuality is so thoroughly embedded in the culture that it can be treated humorously in fiction.

Second, applying research that Matthew Hurley, Daniel Dennet, and Reginald Adams have conducted on cognition and humor to "Lihaf" suggests that the "shaking" scene, as fodder for comedy, also normalizes homosexuality. Their theory, articulated in detail in *Inside Jokes: Using Humor to Reverse-Engineer the Mind*, proposes that recognizing a false belief triggers laughter: "Humor involves a mental space that contains a false belief, a mistaken construction, and laughter indicates that someone is the maker of that mistake" (287). In other words, a joke is funny because it makes the audience aware of mistaken or faulty reasoning. Although Hurley, Dennet, and Adams do not go as far as to suggest that comedy has a socializing function, one of the founding principles of feminist literary theory is that texts indoctrinate readers into specific belief systems. In the case of "Lihaf," this process uses humor to argue that homosexuality is integral rather than antithetical to Islam.

Chalawa, a cold war, episodic, spy thriller written in Urdu by Sabiha Bano and set in Pakistan in the early 1980s, was initially serialized in a Pakistani magazine, probably before 1985, and published in book form in Karachi by Alif in 1985. At the time of this writing, it was available only online. The book, the link, and the information about *Chalawa*, was forwarded by Pakistani professor Massood Raja, of the "Pakistan Women's Rights Forum," an online Facebook group, where he noted that it was a very nationalistic narrative, narrated by a lesbian protagonist, where the author/narrator acts as a nationalistic agent/vigilante. In the 1980s, India was closely allied with the Soviet Union while Pakistan was in the US bloc. Consequently, the major focus of this series of frame tales is fighting corrupt Communist-inspired politicians and insurgents attempting to overthrow the country's US-backed government. Inspired by a sense of Americanized Pakistani nationalism, an unnamed lesbian narrator foils enemies of the state whose infractions include exploiting and sexually abusing young girls, usually by kidnapping and gifting them to politicians and other powerful men.

Notably, a *chalawa* is the Muslim equivalent of Keats's "La Belle Dame Sans Merci," or the German "Vilia," the witch of the woods who tricks her human prey. Mannish and long-legged, *Chalawa*'s narrator "fits the bill" except that she has a rather prurient interest in young girls, which she proclaims when she describes her same-sex instincts as natural. She openly dislikes men and routinely rejects their advances. She also lures young girls into same-sex encounters. Descriptions of these relationships initially suggest that she objectifies girls who pique her sexual interest, but as the tale evolves, she emerges as a savior figure who rescues them from patriarchal male lechery rather than exploiting the girls even if she is sexually attracted to them. The power differential between women and men lends this representation plausibility, as does the fact that in the Muslim world at the time the book was written, corrupt politicians and other powerful men frequently abused girls, as Nawal El Saadawi documents in *The Hidden Face of Eve*. Indeed, it was well known that politicians demanded sexual favors from subordinates, petitioners' young daughters, and other young women. So in this sense, the narrator, while seeming predatory, actually protects young girls.

The narrator is supposedly from an upper-class family, with a home on the beach. She drinks and smokes and is the very embodiment of the Americanized Pakistani under the regime of Ayyub Khan. She has a twinge of nostalgia for the way Pakistan was conceived in the late 1940s and expresses fondness for Muhammad Ali Jinnah, Pakistan's first president, the *Quaid-e-Azam* (father of the nation), who was married to a Parsi woman, Ruttie, renamed Maryam, and his sister, Fatima Jinnah, who was honored with the title *Madar-i-Millat* (mother of the nation). She has a car but chooses to take the bus so she can satisfy her desire to see young girls as they commute home from school: She likes to sit close to the girls, admiring their breasts, which she compares to firm, unripe oranges. She calls out to them, inviting the girls to sit with her, "*Idhar a jao* [come here], baby" (5). She is often successful and persuades them to accompany her to her beautiful home on the beach or another secluded location where she and the girl have sex. In the meantime, the young girls are also being hunted by politicians and members of the army who want to use them to bribe dignitaries and other powerful figures. One such girl is named Farah, and a politically connected military officer, Captain Ajaq, is planning to kidnap her and gift her to an Arab diplomat. This episode exemplifies the double-edged expression of lesbian desire, simultaneously overt and covert, that appears frequently in the book, for the narrator saves the girls from individual men's abuse while also saving the nation from corruption.

For 1150 pages, the frame tales go on, episode after episode, each involving a different girl, a Razia or a Zubeida. In each vignette, the story is the same. A little girl is kidnapped, and the narrator, while expressing her sexual desire for the girl, saves her from sexual exploitation. But there is a twist in one of these stories. The narrator takes two young girls, one named Sughra, who is the niece of a taxi driver, and another named Zubeida, to a hideaway in a rural village. At one point, she finds them hiding under a quilt having sex. This passage includes a detailed description of the girls' heavy breathing, blushing (*surkh*), and their intertwining bodies. Could Sabiha Bano have been familiar with Ismat Chughtai's short story? It's impossible to know, but at any rate, the strong female narrator, who, despite committing what she knows are considered transgressions against Islam, comes off as a savior—not a pervert—as she rescues young girls, whom she calls gold and diamonds, from predatory older men.

Very little, if anything, is known of Sabiha Bano, and this very well could be a pen name. Despite the author's reclusiveness, one prominent Pakistani woman author told me *confidentially* that she did not know of any women writers who "hadn't heard of Sabiha Bano!" This suggests that the book has attained a degree of popularity indicative of solid acceptance of Muslim lesbianism in Pakistani if not South Asian women's literature and implicitly acknowledges lesbianism as an integral feature of Islamic society in the region.

These fictional works by women affirm that representations of same-sex desire have very much been and still are part of the cultures of regions and countries considered Islamic. Yet today, with the rising dominance of extremist Islam, homosexuals and their allies find themselves in Edward Said's position when Ayatollah Khomeini, the Supreme Leader of the Islamic Republic of Iran at the time, issued a *fatwa* (judgment) on Salman Rushdie, whose *Satanic Verses*, a satire on Islam, includes an aside that the character of the Archangel Gibreel fantasizes about being in a homosexual relationship. Said, who fought hard to foster a positive understanding of Muslim culture in the West and worked to end Orientalist objectification of the Arab world, wanted to resist both the lack of "attention to detail, critical differentiation, discrimination and distinction" that the *fatwa* betokened *and* the Islamophobia that arose in response to it (311). He wrote extensively about this in a chapter "Challenging Orthodoxy and Authority" in his *Culture and Imperialism*. While his chapter is largely devoted to critiquing imperialism in Western arts and scholarship, Said emphasizes that institutions of power, regardless of their ideology and location, use the same processes and strategies—a "coercive orthodoxy" that, dichotomizing Self and Other, privileges Self, for instance—to control society, and he indicts extremist Islamic communities for this along with Western entities (311). He specifies that coercive orthodoxy, disallowing inquiry, investigation, and independent critical thinking, permits only "much coarser and more instrumental processes, whose goal is to mobilize consent, to eradicate dissent and to promote" unthinking adherence to group values and that "by such means the governability of large numbers of people is assured, numbers whose potentially disruptive ambitions for democracy and expression are held down or narcoticized" (310).

This response to the *fatwa* against Rushdie begs the question regarding how we are to "read" homosexuality at the intersection of "modernity" and "traditionalism" where the West and the East are perceived as pitted against each other (although from Said's perspective, they have far more in common than not) as the gay rights movement in the West is increasingly successful in challenging homophobia while extremist iterations of Islam are ever more radical in their condemnation if not persecution of homosexuality. How then should we analyze Islamic lesbian literature and the Qur'an (and other sacred texts)—in opposition to or in conjunction with each other? What contexts should we use to read literary texts? What does foregrounding analyses of these texts in Qur'anic and *hadithic* traditions mean? These are critical questions for both literary and cultural studies. Answers are many and varied. In his lesson on homosexuality, the cleric Yusuf repeatedly refers to "the West" and freedoms of choice that can run contrary to the collective good. He also uses a conventional interpretive tradition in Islam that synthesizes material from multiple sources, the Qur'an, the *hadith*, *shari'a*, and other legal discourses. And then there is *ijtihad*, which is a process of close reading of the divinely received text in order to access its meaning. But like its counterpart in current literary theory, Stanley Fish's reader response approach, the meanings *ijtihad* generates depend on the interpretive community. Who comprises that community in the case of Islam and homosexuality? Would it be, as Said envisions, an emergent postcolonial community driven not by "unthinking patriotism" but by "the improvement and non-coercive enhancement of life" that enables diverse communities to coexist? (310, 312). Or Islamic communities in the West? The answer lies in new uses of *ijtihad*.

Kugle, in *Homosexuality in Islam: Critical Reflection on Gay, Lesbian and Transgender Muslims*, articulates what these new uses entail: "Through *ijtihad* in scriptural interpretation and legal reasoning, Muslims can draw out the implicit meaning from the explicit words of revelation; it is our responsibility as ethical believers to do so" (195). This maneuver—relying solely on texts believed to be revealed by God—excludes the *hadith* from consideration because they are "man-made" sayings rather than divine revelation, and of course, it is wholly consistent with the core Islamic principle that the Qur'an is the preeminent source of knowledge about God.

Hence in *Homosexuality in Islam*, Kugle develops a Qur'anic-based understanding of homosexuality that is supported by his extensive research of *hadiths*, *shari'a*, and other extrascriptural material. An example of Kugle's careful scrutiny of the Qur'an occurs when he discusses lesbianism, concluding that the Qur'an in no way warrants lesbophobia. For one thing, he says, the story of Lot does not refer to lesbians. Second, the verse in the Qur'an most often cited to condemn lesbianism, explains Kugle, is vague and ambiguous: "As for those of your women who commit the immorality [*al-fahisha*] have four from among yourself bear witness against them. If they do witness, then confine them [the women] to their rooms until death causes them to perish or until God makes for them a way [of rescue]. And for any two from among you [men] who commit it then punish the two of them" (4:15–16). In fact, he argues that these two verses, the only ones in the Qur'an that have been invoked to censure lesbians "actually address financial honesty and fraud" in that the verses immediately before and after it consist of directions for distributing inheritance and providing material support for orphans. His logic, of course, is that "immorality" covers numerous activities and that the contextual reading actually points to a wholly different type of transgression than sexual intimacy between women.

Kugle also examines a wide range of scholarship produced by the earliest commentators on the Qur'an (a discourse distinctly different from the *hadiths*), looking at disputes and commonalities among these scholars, ultimately relying heavily on the work of Ibn Hazm, a medieval Andalusian Muslim jurist who addressed the concept of *al-fahisha* (immorality), and al-Tabari (b. 839–923 AD), a Persian commentator. Kugle relates that Ibn Hazm, "going back to earliest moments in the Qur'an," argues that the sin central to the story of Sodom and Gomorrah was the tribe's infidelity to God, which is manifest in its rejection of his prophet, Lot. Kugle also cites a major point in Ibn Hazm's general defense of same-sex love between men, which is that the townsmen threatened to *rape* Lot's guests, who were angels disguised as visitors to the area—rape being a far different sexual act than nonviolent male-to-male penetration. Ibn Hazm, relates Kugle, asserts that in addition to same-sex rape, the townspeople committed numerous other transgressions that most Islamic interpretations do not stigmatize to the same extent as homosexuality, which Ibn Hazm labels illogical and inconsistent. Kugle subsequently notes that another medieval scholar, al-Tabari (b. 839–923 AD), a Persian Qur'anic commentator, reinterprets the story of Lot's tribe as a condemnation of infidelity because the townsmen who try to rape the angels would, as married men, have been committing adultery while also violating hospitality norms and taking advantage of travelers' vulnerability. Kugle reinforces this claim in a close reading of the Qur'an that plays with the nouns and the article *al* (the; 27:55) in the passages dedicated to Lot. He concludes that the townspeople's sexual infidelity was driven by and signifies their spiritual infidelity, "their rejection of their Prophet" (Kugle 55).

A third tactic that Kugle uses is to consider the influence of extrascriptural homophobia in distorted interpretations of the Qur'an: "Antihomosexual bias can cause interpreters to read into scripture condemnations that are not necessarily there in the exact language and wider context of the Qur'an" (71). Ultimately, Kugle's work shows that claims that Islam deems homosexuality as sinful rest on scant evidence in the Qur'an and are primarily attributable to cultural rather than scriptural injunctions. Importantly, Kugle's method, starting directly with the Qur'an and drawing on the earliest scholarship on it, while rejecting the hadiths due to their lack of credibility, lends credibility to his conclusions.

Like Kugle, Irshad Manji, a public intellectual, recently has called for a new *ijtihad*. Manji is the author of *The Trouble with Islam Today: A Muslim's Call for Reform in Her Faith* and *Allah, Liberty and Love: The Courage to Reconcile Faith and Freedom*. Manji is a telejournalist reared and working in Canada. She shares Kugel's commitment to developing an Islamic method of interpretation that accommodates the needs of all humans (Said might be said to have this goal as well, though he believes that a global rather than solely Islamic hermeneutic is needed). A young Muslim lesbian, Manji has turned the concept of *ijtihad* on its head: "In Islam of a thousand years ago, the spirit of *ijtihad*—of discussion, debate and dissent—flourished. Not coincidentally, that's also when Islamic civilization led the way in ingenuity" (*The Trouble with Islam Today* 25). Not surprisingly, conservative Muslims have dismissed her work, and the book is banned in some countries. Additionally, some scholars, regardless of religious affiliation, claim her books are not sufficiently scholarly, although they are not intended to be theological treatises. Manji explains, "I'm calling only for the spirit of *ijtihad* to be broadened beyond academics and theologians. Get rid of the elitism that cements patterns of submissiveness among Muslims—submissiveness that stops us from speaking up about politicized and outdated dogma" (*Allah, Liberty and Love* 28). Thus Manji brings a multifocal approach to understanding and theorizing the female body in Islamic contexts, and her work creates an ideological space within Islam wherein progressive if not feminist notions of sexuality can flourish free of the oppressive restraints of interpretations clouded by homosexual bias rooted in extrascriptural sources.

Manji's general method of *ijtihad* is to start with the premise that God alone owns the full truth: "God and none other possesses ultimate Truth" (*The Trouble with Islam Today* 93). Very simply, Manji proposes that only God knows the meanings of his words. Second, she posits that God's words, because they are his, are not hateful. The process of codifying these basic precepts in a set of values that govern behavior, she says, must involve three steps. Every individual, writes Manji, ought to (1) keep in mind that culture is a human construct, imperfect, and therefore open to reform, (2) ask a particular question, and (3) ask it habitually. This key question is, "When I respect custom, what does that do to the weaker members of our group?" (*Allah, Liberty and Love* 100).

The consequences of interpreting the Qur'an this way are numerous. For one thing, it affirms God rather than diminishing him, the latter, according to Manji, being the consequence of rigid, punitive, dogmatic thinking ("coercive orthodoxy" in Said's words), as she explains when she writes, "I'll tell you what breaks *my* heart: that a fear-laced Muslim identity shrivels Allah. By defining ourselves so claustrophobically Muslims limit the possibilities of God's love" (34). In contrast, an accepting stance toward everyone in the community will uphold God and promote piety.

A second outcome Manji identifies is that Muslims can reconceptualize themselves and their relationship with God if they employ this new *ijtihad*. They will realize that they are not "sinners in the hands of an angry God,"[7] which contrasts with the Islamist doomsday orientation that views human nature as fundamentally flawed and relies on fear and coercion to compel, correct, or extinguish specific behaviors. Abandoning this cynical view of human nature, suggests

Manji, will strengthen Islam, promote its growth, and stand as a bulwark against Islamophobia.

But placing Islam in its historical context shows that such growth does not follow a straight and narrow path but follows a wide, meandering thoroughfare. Manji's form of *ijtihad* is her own *jihad* or holy war, as Rokeya Hossain described her resistance to her society's strictures. If the Qur'an could be interpreted with the recognition that at its inception Islam was a progressive religion that throughout history has been girded on all sides by strong women and their desires and that currently the religion is taking new root in diasporic soil, perhaps some of the resistance to and the violence provoked by interpretations distorted by extrascriptural influences can be mitigated and new understandings reached "among the believers."

NOTES

1 The *hadith* are collections of sayings attributed to Muhammad, and the authenticity of many are disputed because they were collected and recorded in the eighth and ninth centuries, many years after Muhammed's death in 632 CE.

2 This designation is used cautiously here because medieval and early modern Islamic cultures did not have a construct for "lesbian." The greater concern about women's sexuality focused on pre- and extramarital sex with men, and depending on region and era, much less import was given to erotic activity between women, in part because of patriarchal definitions of sex always involving penal penetration.

3 Khaquani was the pseudonym for Afzaladdin Badil (Ibrahim) ibn Ali Nadjar.

4 The idea that *ijtihad* ended around 900 CE has recently been challenged in the scholarship; however, the *perception* that interpretation had ceased is more significant to its revival than whether *ijtihad* completely ceased.

5 The term "theocracy" is used carefully here in recognition of scholarship debating whether the Islamic Republic is truly theocratic.

6 Bapsi Sidhwa's novel *Cracking India* where the poor aunt who is referred to as Slave Sister has some distinct tones of lesbian sexual desire.

7 Title phrase of Jonathan Edward's book *Sinners in the Hands of an Angry God and Other Puritan Sermons*. Courier Corporation, 2012.

WORKS CITED

Afary, Janet. *Sexual Politics in Modern Iran*. Cambridge UP, 2009.

al-Bukhari, Muhammad. "Book of Dress, Hadith 774." *Ṣaḥīḥ al-Bukhārī*, vol. 7. *Muflihun*. muflihun.com/bukhari/72/774.

al-Tabrizi, Muḥammad ibn 'Abd Allāh Khatib. "Prescribed Punishments" *Mishkat al-Masabih* (*A niche for lamps*), vol. 1. *Muhammadanism*. http://www.muhammadanism.org/Government/Government_apostasy_1.htm.

Bahmanpour, Mohammad Saeed. "On Religion, Politics, and Democracy." *Khomeini: The Life and Legacy; Essays from an Islamic Movement Perspective*. Islamic Book Trust, 2009, pp. 119–31.

Bano, Sabiha. *Chalawa*. Alif, 1985.

Bassem, Wassim. "Iraqi Cleric Urges Tolerance toward LGBT People." *AlMonitor: The Pulse of the Middle East*. 2 Sep. 2016, http://www.al-monitor.com/pulse/originals/2016/09/homosexuality-lgbt-iraq-iran-muqtada-sadr.html#ixzz4K4084xa7.

Bellamy, James A. "Sex and Society in Islamic Popular Literature." *Society and the Sexes in Medieval Islam*, edited by Afaf Lutfi Sayyid-Marsot, Undema, 1970, pp. 23–42.

Chugtai, Ismat. "Lihaf" (The quilt). *Women Writing in India: 600 B.C. to the Present, II: The Twentieth Century*, edited by Susie Tharu and K. Lalita, Feminist Press, 1993, pp. 129–37.

Crompton, Louis. *Homosexuality and Civilization*. Harvard UP, 2006.

Dawood, Abu. "Book 40, Hadith 4448." *Sunan Abu Dawood: Book of Prescribed Punishments*, vol. 5. *Muflihun*. muflihun.com/abudawood/40/4448.

El Saadawi, Nawal. *The Hidden Face of Eve: Women in the Arab World*. Zed Books, 2007.

Groisman, Maayan. "Saudi Cleric: 'Homosexuality Not a Deviation from Islam, Should Not be Punished.'" *Jerusalem Post*. 5 May 2016, http://www.jpost.com/Middle-East/Saudi-cleric-Homosexuality-not-a-deviation-from-Islam-should-not-be-punished-452957.

Habib, Samra. "Queer and Going to the Mosque." *The Guardian*. June 3, 2016, http://www.theguardian.com/lifeandstyle/2016/jun/03/unity-mosque-queer-muslim-islam-samra-habib.

Hallaq, Wael B. "Was the Gate of *Ijtihad* Closed?" *International Journal of Middle East Studies*, vol. 16, no. 1, Mar. 1984, pp. 3–41.

Hossain, Rokeya Sakhawat. *Sultana's Dream and Selections from the Secluded Ones*. Edited by Roushan Jahan, Feminist Press, 1988.

Hurley, Matthew M., Daniel C. Dennett, and Reginald B. Adams Jr. *Inside Jokes: Using Humor to Reverse-Engineer the Mind*. MIT P, 2013.

Khalil, As'ad Abu. "A Note on the Study of Homosexuality in the Arab/Islamic Civilization." *Arab Studies Journal*, vol. 1, no. 2, 1993, pp. 32–34.

The Koran. Translated by N. J. Dawood. Penguin Classics, 2014.

Kugle, Scott Siraj al-Haqq. *Homosexuality in Islam: Critical Reflection on Gay, Lesbian and Transgender Muslims*. Oneworld, 2010.

Manji, Irshad. *Allah, Liberty and Love: The Courage to Reconcile Faith and Freedom*. Simon and Schuster, 2012.

———. *The Trouble with Islam Today: A Muslim's Call for Reform in Her Faith*. Reprint edition, St. Martin's Griffin, 2005.

Milani, Milad. *Sufism in the Secret History of Persia*. Routledge, 2014.

Murray, Stephen O. "Woman-Woman Love in Islamic Societies." *Islamic Homosexualities: Culture, History, and Literature*, edited by Stephen O. Murray and Will Roscoe, New York UP, 1997, pp. 97–104.

Najmabadi, Afsaneh. *Women with Mustaches and Men without Beards: Gender and Sexual Anxieties of Iranian Modernity*. U of California P, 2005.

Qasim, Muhammad. *Shah Abbas I and His Page*. 1627, ink on paper, Louvre, Paris.

Refeq, Abdul-Karim. "Public Morality in Eighteenth-Century Damascus." *Revue du monde musulman et de la Mediterranee*, vol. 55, no. 1, 1990, pp. 180–96.

Rushdie, Salman. *The Satanic Verses*. Viking, 1988.

Said, Edward. "Challenging Orthodoxy and Authority." *Culture and Imperialism*. Vintage, 1994.

Semerdjian, Elyse. "Islam." *Homosexuality and Religion: An Encyclopedia*, edited by Jeffrey S. Siker, Greenwood, 2006, p. 132.

Sidhwa, Bapsi. *The Ice-Candy Man*. Penguin, 1989.

Suleri, Sara. *Meatless Days*. U of Chicago P, 1987.

Wafer, Jim. "Muhammad and Male Homosexuality." *Islamic Homosexualities: Culture, History, and Literature*, edited by Stephen O. Murray and Will Roscoe, New York UP, 1997, pp. 87–96.

"Women with Dildo." Seventeenth century, Bibliotheque Nationale, Paris. *Islamic Homosexualities: Culture, History, and Literature*, edited by Stephen O. Murray and Will Roscoe, New York UP, 1997, p. 101.

Yusuf, Hamza. "Homosexuality—Hamza Yusuf." YouTube, uploaded by Islam on Demand, 29 July 2011, http://www.youtube.com/watch?v=iXRnWTB2FRg.

15 HOMOEROTICISM AND REACCESSING THE IDEA OF "FALLEN WOMAN" IN KEVAL SOOD'S *MURGIKHANA*

KUHU SHARMA CHANANA

This last chapter, "Homoeroticism and Reaccessing the Idea of 'Fallen Woman' in Keval Sood's *Murgikhana*," asserts that the so-called straight fallen woman does not threaten heterosexual male dominion as radically as the lesbian does, an argument that implicitly invokes Judith Butler's theory that dichotomizing and then "Othering" homosexuality and transgenderism constitutes and gives definition to heterosexuality, for, as she writes, heterosexuality is that which nonnormative performances *are not*. Thus Chanana suggests that lesbianism mitigates heterosexual privilege by erasing men from women's sexual gratification, which challenges patriarchal social and familial structures at various levels. She further claims that sexuality is an expression of power and that by removing men from this domain through same-sex relationships, women rupture the structures of patriarchal subjugation. Analyzing Keval Sood's text *Murgikhana* (*Henhouse*), Chanana asserts that the figure of the nonnormative lesbian, not the sexually liberated heterosexual woman, transcends narrow boundaries that define "fallenness" and alleviate misogynist opprobrium of women. As a result, *Murgikhana*'s depiction of lesbianism is complex, simultaneously regressive and progressive, both giving impetus to and obstructing the production of a nonpatriarchal counterculture: while the book's portrayal of lesbianism resists hegemonic patriarchalism, its use of the lesbian figure to normalize heterosexual women's transgressions of traditional sexual mores undermines what could have been a profoundly radical text.

INTRODUCTION

Keval Sood's 2013 Hindi-language novel, *Murgikhana* (*Henhouse*), both showcases the radical potential of lesbianism to subvert the patriarchal hegemony and exhibits anxieties that reify homophobia. *Murgikhana* traces the relationship between two lesbians, Sheela and Savita, from its inception, when Savita rapes Sheela, to its tragic ending when Sheela murders Savita. Sheela is unmarried and childless, whereas Savita is a married mother, and as such, her sexual encounters with women constitute adultery. At the outset, the novel portrays Sheela sympathetically but quickly undermines this stance by depicting her as fraught with internalized homophobia. In contrast, the book treats Savita's double "fallenness"—her marital infidelity and her lesbianism—far less harshly. This difference is attributable to various factors. One is that Savita does not abdicate her role as mother as she gratifies her sexual desire for women. This disassociates Savita from lesbianism and aligns her with heterosexuality. While the book's depiction of Savita as "less lesbian" than Sheela is steeped in patriarchalism, the gentler treatment it allots her implies that the figure of the lesbian mitigates sexual opprobrium more effectively than the sexually liberated heterosexual woman. In Indian contexts, this phenomenon is due to the low status historically accorded "fallen" heterosexual women—those who transgress traditional sexual boundaries—whether in the *Kama Sutra*, an ancient Sanskrit tract on the philosophy of human sexuality, or today's legal codes, as evidenced by the fact, for instance, that neither acknowledge the existence of female adultery. Two additional factors that implant homophobic anxieties in *Murgikhana* and undercut its initially progressive approach to lesbianism are settings that are simultaneously queer and homophobic and the book's conspicuously stereotypical ending—one lesbian murdering another. This complex combination of sympathy and antipathy vis-à-vis character development, setting, and the conclusion embed *Murgikhana* with a set of countervalences—progressive and regressive—that lend it a disconcerting ambivalence about lesbianism.

That lesbianism is the ultimate marker of a fallen woman is not difficult to envisage. Lesbianism challenges heteronormativity, eliminates the male role in women's sexual gratification, and contests patriarchal family structures. Sexuality is a power assertion, and by excluding men from same-sex relationships, lesbians create significant ruptures in the structural subjugation of women in patriarchal society. This perforation of the heterosexual hegemony has intensified with the advancement of reproductive technologies ranging from test tube babies to assisted insemination. Not only do these resources make lesbian motherhood a reality, but they increase the numbers and forms of alternative family structures. In contrast, the so-called promiscuity and sexual liberation of heterosexual women can create ripples in the patriarchal structure but will never be the means of dismantling patriarchy's basic fabric. Hence the "fallen" heterosexual woman cannot threaten male domination in the same manner that the lesbian does.

LESBIAN AS INVISIBLE OTHER

One indicator of the greater threat that the lesbian poses the patriarchy, in Indian contexts, is that Section 377 of the Indian Penal Code (IPC), which dates back to 1860 and criminalizes sexual activities "against the order of nature,"[1] is completely silent about lesbianism despite identifying gay copulation as a criminal offence: the very acknowledgment of lesbian lovemaking is threatening to the core, thus lesbianism is erased from this and other discourses. In contrast, Section 497, which deals with adultery,[2] defines the male adulterer as the only criminal offender, while women in adulterous heterosexual relationships are treated solely as victims. At first glance, this legislation appears to favor women, but close scrutiny proves otherwise: "Whoever has sexual intercourse with a person who is and whom he knows or has reason to believe to be the wife of another man, without the consent or connivance of that man, such sexual intercourse not amounting to the offense of rape, is guilty of the offense of adultery, and shall be punished with imprisonment of either description for a term which may extend to five years, or with fine, or with both. In such case the wife shall not be punishable as an abettor" (IPC 497). Significantly, a woman cannot be charged under adultery not because the state desires to grant her sexual license but because she is considered a "movable object" without a will or sexual agency and thus assumed to have been misguided or tricked into the relationship. Strangely enough, even the National Commission for Women's (NCW)[3] plea against including women under adultery laws smacked of this bias (though unwittingly) by arguing that women are not offenders but always victims, a position that created a huge controversy in 2006 and 2007 ("NCW Rejects Proposal to Punish Women for Adultery").

The sexism manifest in IPC 497 has a long history in Indian literary production and can be traced in representations of women and gender in many ancient Sanskrit myths,[4] such as the *Ramayana* and the *Mahābhārata*. But for the purposes of this chapter, looking at the philosophy of sexuality articulated in the *Kama Sutra* is more to the point. In the West, the *Kama Sutra* is stereotyped as a "how-to" guidebook for sex acts; however, it is actually a philosophical tract on the erotics and ethics of sexuality. Consequently, it reveals sexual values, including beliefs about women and the "nature" of femininity, unfiltered by elements of literature, such as plot, narrative structure, character development, and setting.

The *Kama Sutra* was composed between 400 BCE and 200 CE and is strongly influenced by principles expressed in the *Vedas* and other pre-Hindu sacred texts of Vedic religion, a polytheistic belief system whose divinities are associated with natural phenomena. It is commonly attributed to Vatsyayana, a second-century Hindu philosopher who identifies himself as the author, although it is more likely that he edited rather than wrote the text. The *Kama Sutra*, he explains, is a resource for attaining mastery of the senses by cultivating virtue, wealth, and sensual pleasure: "This treatise was composed, according to the precepts of the Holy Writ . . . for the benefit of the world. . . . This work is not to be used merely as an instrument for satisfying our desires. A person acquainted with the true principles of this science, who preserves his *Dharma* [virtue or religious merit], his *Artha* [worldly wealth] and his *Kama* [pleasure or sensual gratification], and who has regard to the customs of the people, is sure to obtain the mastery over his senses" (Jones and Ryan 225).

With this aim, the *Kama Sutra* includes passages that clarify when it is permissible to violate traditional sexual norms, including adultery. In chapter 5, a subsection entitled "Talking about the Kind of Women Men Can Sleep With," which is part of a larger section entitled "Permissible Women and Adultery," the *Kama Sutra* permits adultery with women who have already been deprived of their virtue and when a sexual relationship with a married woman will produce material benefits:

> The fourth kind can optionally even be married to another man, but this depends on particular reasons. For example, she may already be known as a loose woman robbed of her virtue by many others. So, even though she is of a higher caste, sleeping with her is like with a courtesan or a previously married woman, and will not go against Dharama. . . . A variation may concern the woman's husband. "He is a great lord," one may consider, "and he is partial to someone who is my enemy. She has influence over him and, on becoming my intimate, she can turn him against that person out of love for me." Or, "her husband has the ability to harm me and now seems set to do so as he has turned hostile. She can improve the attitude towards me." Or, "winning his friendship through her, I will be able to help my comrades, repel my foes or accomplish some other difficult task." (21–22)

The language, tone, and imagery in this passage demonstrate that the *Kama Sutra*, which aims to produce sexual awakening in its readers and, as such, should address both sexes, is saturated with sexism, starting with the presumption that with rare exception the audience will consist solely of men. For one thing, it describes the means of achieving "sexual gratification" with men in mind and objectifies women in the process. Moreover, these instructions construct women as instruments of men's social and sexual interests, while representing the so-called fallen, adulterous woman as a commodity that fulfills the man's sensual and material desires.

Similarly, IPC 498,[5] entitled "Enticing or Taking away or Detaining with Criminal Intent a Married Woman," incessantly cloaks its chauvinism in a language of protectionism that suppresses feminine sexuality. This desire to protect women is rooted in the state's refusal to recognize women as able to make clear-cut, individual choices regarding their sexual needs. Of course, such an acknowledgement would be an admission that women are sexually aware desiring subjects, which, in turn, would threaten patriarchal order and opprobrium: "Whoever takes or entices away any woman who is and whom he knows or has reason to believe to be the wife of any other man, from that man, or from any person having the care of her on behalf of that man, with intent that she may have illicit intercourse with any person, or conceals or detains with that intent any such woman, shall be punished with imprisonment of either description for a term which may extend to two years, or with fine, or with both" (IPC 498).

On the surface, this paragraph takes a chivalric approach to the adulterous woman, depicting her as a victim of male aggression. In reality, however, such chivalry, as demonstrated by the law's use of the words "taking away" and "enticing," categorizes a woman not only as a man's property but as someone who cannot assert her own sexual choices and is easily manipulated into an adulterous relationship. Thus the law's "chivalry" is a sinister form of chauvinism founded on the prejudiced belief that women are sexually naïve and unable to resist or defend against men's illicit intentions. This repressive model of feminine sexuality has deep cultural roots. In the *Kama Sutra,* for instance, the chapter entitled, "The Arts Outlined," specifies that the married woman should read the treatise only with the consent of her husband. It further states that women should not be taught the "art of sexuality" because they are not intellectually capable of understanding it: "Some teachers say that instructing women in this knowledge is meaningless as they cannot comprehend science" (11). Essentially, this repressive model of feminine sexuality rests on the misogynist belief that women are so lacking in intelligence that they are unable to make choices about their bodies and sexual practices.

That two texts separated by approximately two millennia—an ancient philosophical tract on sexuality and the other a penal code defining sexual crimes in present-day India—so vehemently insist that women lack sexual agency (to the point that lawmakers offer them relief from prosecution) underscores how intimidating, destabilizing, it would be to recognize women as sexual beings. If heterosexual women's sexuality poses such danger to men's dominance, it is not difficult to imagine that lesbianism, which eliminates men's participation in women's sexual gratification, can be unnerving to the core. Lesbianism's potential to unravel the patriarchy is, in fact, so terrifying that historically it has been even less recognized or visible than heterosexual women's desire. In Western literature, for example, few works have thematized lesbianism until the twentieth century, a notable exception being Sappho's poems. Additionally, history has mostly been silent about lesbians until the advent of modernism in the West, though women's diaries and journals sometimes offer tantalizing hints of intimate "sisterhoods."[6] The same pattern marks criminal justice where antilesbian legislation is relatively rare, and few lesbians have been charged or convicted under such laws. As Lillian Faderman suggests in *Surpassing the Love of Men*, one reason for this aporia is that lesbianism is such an anathema to patriarchal culture. She cites the case of Woods and Jane Pirie v. Dame Helen to make her point. In Scotland in 1811, a troubled student, Helen Cumming, falsely accused Marianne Woods and Jane Pirie, owners of a girls' school in Edinburgh, of being lesbian lovers. Although the school failed and Woods's and Pierie's lives were ruined, they were acquitted at trial because, Faderman writes, the judge could not imagine women having sex without men:

> The lawyers for Woods and Pirie based their major arguments on that opinion. After establishing the good character of both these women, they demanded, "Is it no violent improbability that no less than *two* such persons should at last have been guilty of a crime so utterly abandoned, that it is totally unknown, and even doubtful that if it can exist?" That argument settled the case, in effect. Could two people engage in venereal activity though the male sex is absent? One judge asked, "Could murder be committed by hocus-pocus or paw-waving?" Without an instrument the act is impossible, the judge decided. (149)

This result, symptomatic of the nearly wholesale erasure of lesbians and lesbianism from history, strongly suggests that heterosexual women's sexual liberty is far less dangerous to the heteropatriarchal order than the so-called lavender menace.[7] Furthermore, lesbianism's radicalism may offer new paradigms for heterosexual women. For instance, lesbianism completely destabilizes norms that stipulate that monogamous marital sex is the only means by which heterosexual women can attain libidinal satiation. Hence it's not surprising that the Indian legal code would go so far as to exempt women from prosecution for adultery—rather than chivalry, this relief is actually motivated by a sinister agenda, a fear-driven wish to render women's sexuality invisible.

MURGIKHANA'S IRONIC AMBIVALENCE

Murgikhana is a controversial novel—it could not be published in India for fifteen years—because it showcases the potential disruptiveness of the lesbian to transcend narrow definitions of female fallenness and mitigate the sexual opprobrium and other hegemonic patriarchal structures. However, the text also manifests anxieties that blunt these possibilities or, more precisely, limits their radicalism. Sood's social location may account for these anxieties, or they may be attributable to a sense of audience—*Murgikhana*'s typical readers are Hindi speaking and generally consumers of mass fiction rather than English-speaking elites[8] and not immune to homophobia.[9] Thus, at one level, the writer posits the radical promise of feminine sexuality by drawing attention to the ways lesbians perform emotional and sexual intimacy, but at another level, the "new homonormativity"—accepting homosexuals only as long as they do not threaten the basic heterosexual patriarchal structure—and lesbophobia are so pervasive in the text that the disruptive potential of lesbianism is neutralized. In this light, the book implicitly suggests that the straight woman who is considered fallen because she indulges in forbidden relationships with men, such as extramarital affairs, is far more accepted, or *acceptable*, than the lesbian because the straight woman is at least heterosexual and a male partner contributes to her sexual pleasure. Hence *Murgikhana*'s depiction of lesbianism is convoluted even as it gives impetus to the production of a lesbian counterculture.

The story revolves around the protagonist, Sheela, whose internalized homophobia prevents her from coming to terms with her lesbianism. Her first sexual encounter occurs in a female-only hostel (a dormitory) where an absence of men has fostered a homosocial atmosphere. Savita, the hostel's manager, rapes Sheela, an act that initiates an ongoing sexual relationship between them. Prior to coming to the hostel, Sheela had plans to marry a man named Suneel, but they are abandoned due to the rape. Throughout the rest of the story, Sheela has rampant, incestuous, short-term homosexual relationships with numerous bisexuals and lesbians.[10] These relationships are bereft of any emotional or long-term commitment, two of the most cherished though often unfulfilled heterosexual ideals, and Sheela relentlessly explores her sexuality in these superficial encounters with other women. Thus at the outset, the novel seems to portray Sheela and her sexual choices sympathetically, but as the story unfolds, it consistently undercuts this tone. This endows the novel with a deep ambivalence about lesbians and lesbianism that culminates when Sheela murders her rapist and first lesbian lover, Savita, who was responsible for initiating many women into lesbian sex.

An early scene that highlights lesbianism's transformative capacity and offers a positive representation of Sheela focuses on her ability to be self-nurturing (my translation). Set in her home, this space is both a metaphor for her lesbian body and a place where she can "love herself," a phrase that, in the Hindi original, signifies both self-caring and masturbation: "Sheela strokes the pink walls of her room with her eyes and kisses her body all over. At times she feels a strong desire to kiss her own fair and pink body from top to bottom passionately" (my translation; 10). Her gaze caresses the walls as her hands or perhaps her tongue, if it could, stroke and arouse her body. Here, she embraces herself psychologically and physically, and her self-affirming mind-set is manifest in her fascination with her own body. In this passage, Sheela's self-loving transforms the domestic, traditionally a heterosexual site, into a radically queer domain. This appropriation of the domestic from the heterosexual realm underscores lesbianism's capacity to challenge the patriarchy. Clearly, this early passage casts Sheela in a positive light and, by demonstrating that lesbianism has the capacity to transvalue meaning—to claim heterosexual space and reconstitute it as a site of radical lesbianism—illustrates the lesbian woman's ability to upset the heterosexual status quo. Lesbianism is thus equated with self-loving within the book's opening pages and portrayed as posing a powerful challenge to heterosexism.

However, thereafter *Murgikhana* reveals a far more negative side of Sheela's character. For example, she is deeply jealous after she realizes that Savita is happily married with two children:

> Standing straight, she [Sheela] stares at the vacuum above the crowd and the long darkness over the sea. Within a few moments a strange tension appears in her eyes and then it evaporates. What should she [Sheela] tell Savita? [She considers the options], "That after pushing me into a deep water you have reached the shore?" Or, "Now you are in my grip, should I trap you?" Perhaps: "I am alone in my boat and your boat is filled. Yes, it is filled . . . and I know this for sure. But I will not be able to do this even if I wish. I will not be able to do this. . . . But you cannot be held responsible. There was a time when we both were in the same boat, but you escaped." (my translation; 48)

Furthermore, *Murgikhana* offsets depictions of Sheela's initial self-nurturing with passages that feature self-recrimination and self-loathing—that is, internalized homophobia. After her first sexual encounter with Savita, for example, Sheela rejects Suneel's advances by saying that she has corrupted herself and cannot be part of the fold again, meaning that she is a sexual outlaw, that she stands outside the boundaries of normative sexual morality. In essence, she is a sexual Other, and her deviation from the heteropatriarchal structure prompts her to exclaim: "No Suneel do not touch me, I am not worthy of it" (my translation; 57).

Unlike the masturbation scene, Sheela's language and descriptions of her as well as her sexual encounters take on a tone of disgust. For instance, Sheela's internalized homophobia is evident in constant fantasies that she will be killed brutally: "Sheela could foresee—a tiger is running and it has her living corpse in its mouth. There is an eagle that is hovering over that tiger. That eagle also has her living corpse . . . and she is crying vehemently to extract her dead body from the grip of the eagle; consequently, she is running and flying at the same time. Her own dead body is there on her shoulders" (my translation; 72). Such extreme responses to her desire and, specifically, her relationship with Savita offset the book's more positive representations of Sheela as self-embracing. This in turn reverses *Murgikhana*'s earlier affirming tone toward lesbianism. In so doing, the book diminishes the subversive potential of the lesbian woman to redefine and reevaluate the heterosexual definition of fallenness. Indeed, as the book takes an increasingly ambivalent stance toward lesbianism, it undermines the symbolic and actual power of the lesbian figure to disrupt heteropatriarchalism.

In contrast, Savita's status as a mother and wife is exculpating, for in Indian contexts where motherhood is a responsibility of citizenship as well as a highly idealized social role, she fulfills her duty toward the nation by being a "good" mother, by producing and raising the future body politic. Furthermore, Savita is able to navigate both lesbianism and heterosexuality and is rewarded for maintaining the heteropatriarchal framework even as she crosses its boundaries. For example, her homoerotic encounters are described in a language that affirms her passion: "The two pink bodies were floating in the river of flesh—traversing through one corner to another" (70). Moreover, *Murgikhana* implies that Savita's same-sex encounters are necessary for sustaining—refueling—her heterosexual identity. This is evident when, during one of their sexual encounters, Sheela states that she is attracted to Savita primarily because she is a mother. Sheela, however, does not mean that Savita is a revolutionary lesbian mother testing the limits of public tolerance by raising children with a same-sex partner. Rather, Sheela is referring to Savita's performance of heterosexual mothering, for Savita has children with a male partner and ostensibly maintains a conventional—heterosexual—family life.

In any event, the suggestion that Savita's lesbianism feeds or reinforces her heterosexual identity is a theme that recurs in the book. Specifically, Savita's lesbianism is sensually rejuvenating and, as such, fuels her performance of motherhood. Sheela reflects on this dynamic when she is in an introspective mood: "Sheela you are tired of this constant juggling and acrobats . . . yes you are tired . . . Savita wanted to say the same thing that night. Savita, the rugged one is still as fresh and spirited as she has always been . . . may be because she is following both the routes—the natural and the unnatural. . . . But no route is unnatural . . . we have seeds for both the routes" (my translation; 69). This passage implies that the homoerotic rendezvous of a married woman, Savita, with her lesbian lover strengthens the institution of heterosexual motherhood. Thus Savita's lesbianism does not render her fallen because she never abandons heterosexual mating or the patriarchal family. As such, she does not threaten the heteropatriarchal hegemony. In the figure of Savita, therefore, *Murgikhana* suggests that lesbianism is nothing more than a heterosexual woman's sexual resuscitation, for her same-sex relationships do not prevent her from fulfilling the duty to procreate, a responsibility that so often is cited as the basis of the belief that heterosexuality is natural and homosexuality is deviant. In other words, Savita's lesbianism does not prevent her from achieving full sexual citizenship because her relationship with Sheela, rather than diverting Savita from bearing and raising children, reinvigorates her will to produce future citizens, a woman's most important citizenship function in the patriarchal state. Consequently, Savita's lesbianism does not challenge the heteropatriarchal structure. Rather, it is merely a slight deviation outside marriage that is tolerated because, in comparison to the annihilating impact of the lesbianism on patriarchy, it is a much lesser evil. Ultimately, the book's more generous approach to Savita than Sheela suggests that because Savita performs the traditional social role assigned women, she is less threatening than the single, childless Sheela even though Savita is basically a rapist and an adulteress (if not legally, at least in terms of conventional morality).

This "softer" treatment of Savita calls to mind the heterosexist masculine gaze's construction of lesbian desire as a male-titillating performance. In this respect, *Murgikhana* is far less like "lesbian literature" and more like fiction that, Faderman contends, employs same-sex female relationships to satisfy heterosexual male fantasies: "Society did not object to the theme of passionate [female] friendship in literature because it appealed to male voyeurism" (109). Under such conditions, of course, descriptions of lesbian sex treat it as precursor to and part of heterosexual lovemaking. Faderman, quoting Pierre de Boudeille, Seignior de Brantome, explains that in these circumstances lesbian eroticism is "an apprentice to heterosexuality" (110). Hence any apparent acceptance of lesbianism is only another means of reinforcing heterosexuality and blunting the threat that the lesbian "outlaw" poses it.

Interestingly, a similar phenomenon exists in historic Indian visual and literary arts. Devdutt Pattanaik explains that same-sex relationships are depicted with moderate tolerance if not sympathy in age-old artifacts but primarily in order to redirect homosexuality into heterosexual desire (even if temporarily): "An overview of temple imagery, sacred narratives and religious scriptures does suggest that homosexual activities—in some form—did exist in ancient India. Though not part of the mainstream, its existence was acknowledged but not approved. There was some degree of tolerance when the act expressed itself in heterosexual terms—when men 'became women' in their desire for other men, as the *hijra* legacy suggests" ("Did Homosexuality Exist in Ancient India?").[11] *Murgikhana* combines these two approaches in its treatment of Savita. Her relationship with Sheela titillates male heterosexual desire even as it bespeaks lesbian eroticism. This, of course, erodes the book's initial celebration of lesbianism and exhibits palpable antipathy toward lesbianism.

Ultimately, *Murgikhana*'s voyeurism-inviting passages, combined with its contrasting characterization of the two major female figures—its condemnation of Sheela and relative tolerance of Savita—endow the text with crosscurrents, a combination of sympathy and antipathy that fosters a disturbing ambivalence about lesbianism and fails to acknowledge the extent of the threat that lesbianism poses patriarchal order.

A similar crosscurrent marks the book's settings as well. Throughout, the story of Sheela and Savita is told against a landscape that is simultaneously queer and homophobic. When the book opens, Sheela's rape takes place in the homosocial space of a hostel beyond the fringe of heterosexual society. That the hostel is depicted as being on the outside edge of society is one of the book's first expressions of lesbophobia. As the novel progresses, setting continues to intensify this lesbophobia. The location in which Sheela murders Savita—a henhouse—is the most extreme example. Symbolically, of course, the henhouse signifies female-only homosocial space, as is underscored when one of the characters asks how the hens can get along without roosters: "What is the life of these hens without roosters? Why have they been deprived of this primitive pleasure—how do they manage?" The question embarrasses her interlocutor, Mrs. Sharma, who, nonetheless explains that the hens have sex with each other. The narrator explains, "She [Mrs. Sharma] in a quite naughty fashion states that they do it among themselves." Then the lesson turns ominous as Mrs. Sharma adds that if "any rooster gets trapped inside it [the henhouse], these scoundrels [the hens] kill it" (my translation; 86). If the comparison of lesbians to hens seems innocuous at first, Mrs. Sharma reveals that, in fact, the hens are men killers, an assertion that invokes the negative stereotype that lesbians "hate" men, commonplace in the long catalogue of lesbophobic slurs. Furthermore, the hen analogy bestializes lesbians, a characterization that Savita reinforces as she repeatedly announces that she sometimes puts a rooster inside the henhouse just for the sadistic pleasure of witnessing the hens brutally mutilating him. These contrasting depictions of the henhouse—it is a space where hens "do it" without men (presumably happily and freely) and where male intruders are brutally killed—simultaneously valorizes and vilifies lesbianism. They depict lesbianism as the ultimate panacea for the patriarchy, while at the same time, undermining this characterization by representing the henhouse as a place where women destroy men. In the end, Sheela's murder of Savita, a stereotypical fate meted lesbians in heterosexist, homophobic fiction and other media as punishment for their transgressions completely overshadows the book's more progressive treatment of lesbianism in other passages. Sheela, torturing and murdering her mentor and paramour, Savita, reifies heteropatriarchal supremacy by performing lesbianism as depraved and dehumanizing.

CONCLUSION

In the final analysis, *Murgikhana* bears out the theory that in *lesbophobic* societies—and this caveat is critical—the figure of the lesbian challenges the heterosexual status quo *and* ameliorates the negative consequences of heterosexual women's fallenness because she is an extreme outlier in the field of unconventional, transgressive sexualities and, as such, serves as a lightning rod that normalizes heterosexuality. That is to say that lesbianism enables heterosexual women to exercise transgressive sexualities without suffering the full force of patriarchal opprobrium meted lesbians, for as long as heterosexual women comply with other patriarchal mandates, such as the duty to be a "good" mother, they are less threatening to the social order than lesbians. Thus lesbianism mitigates the worst consequences that fallen heterosexual women face and ruptures the stringent boundaries that regulate and police their sexuality. *Murgikhana*'s ambivalent depiction of lesbianism underscores this irony.

NOTES

1 Section 377 of the Indian Penal Code, an archaic, colonialist, nineteenth-century document, criminalizes sexual activities "against the order of nature." It states that "whoever voluntarily has carnal intercourse against the order of nature with any man, woman or animal, shall be punished with imprisonment for life or a term which may extend to ten years, and shall also be liable to fine." This clause covers homosexuality, but a further passages specifies that penetration is a necessary condition of such intercourse, which exempts lesbianism from the law's purview. AIDS Bhedbhav Virodhi Andolan, a movement that aims to end discrimination against AIDS patients, in 1991 launched an initiative to repeal Section 377. Their publication, "A Citizen's Report" catalogues the problems with 377. The Naz Foundation also worked with a legal team from the Lawyer's Collective to decriminalize homosexuality. In a momentous judgment in July 2009, the Delhi High Court overturned the 150-year-old section, legalizing consensual homosexual activities between adults. However, on December 11, 2013, the Supreme Court of India upheld Section 377. The decision recriminalizing homosexuality states, "We hold that Section 377 IPC does not suffer from the vice of unconstitutionality and the declaration made by the Division Bench of the High court is legally unsustainable" (Koushal 97).

2 Section 497 is found in chapter 20 of Indian Penal Code, which deals with the "offence related to marriage," and contains Section 497. The Supreme Court has affirmed that only a man can be prosecuted for adultery but not the wife, even as an abettor. Justices Aftab Alam and R. M. Lodha ruled, "Section 497 of the Indian Penal Code [which deals with adultery] is currently under criticism from certain quarters for showing a strong gender bias, for it makes the position of a married woman almost as a property of her husband. But in terms of the law as it stands, it is evident from a plain reading of the Section that only a man can be proceeded against and punished for . . . adultery. Indeed, the Section provides expressly that the wife cannot be punished even as an abettor" (Venkatesan).

3 The NCW is the national level organization of India to protect the interests of women. It was set up as statutory body in January 1992 under the National Commission for Women Act, 1990 (Act No. 20 of Govt. of India) to review the constitutional and legal safeguards for women and develop a mechanism for the redressal of grievances and to send recommendations to the government for constituting polices that affect the welfare of women.

4 See Chandrani Biswas's chapter in this volume.

5 Chapter 20-A of Indian Penal Code contains Section 498, which is "enticing or taking away or detaining with criminal intent a married woman." Sub-section A adds that whoever subjects the woman to cruelty will be fined and shall be punished with imprisonment for a term of up to three years. "Cruelty" is defined as (a) any willful conduct that is likely to drive the woman to commit suicide or to cause grave injury or danger to life, limb, or health (whether mental or physical) or (b) harassment of the woman for the purpose of coercing her or any person related to her to comply to an unlawful demand. This provision was enacted to combat dowry deaths and introduced to the Penal Code by the Criminal Law Amendment Act, 1983 (ACT 46 of 1983). By the same legislation, Section 113-A was added to the Indian Evidence Act to protect women from being harassed by their husbands or relatives (Mishra).

6 Some examples of lesbian subtexts in fiction include poems by Katherine Philips, the Anglo-Welsh poet known as "The Matchless Orinda," including "To My Excellent Lucasia, on Our Friendship," "Parting with Lucasia: A Song," and "Orinda to Lucasia." Other authors whose works hint at lesbianism are Aphra Behn, Sor Juana Ines de la Cruz, Queen Christina of Sweden, and Jane Addams.

7 Betty Friedan coined the term "lavender menace" 1969 when she served as president of the National Organization for Women, because she believed that associating feminism with lesbianism would undermine the women's movement in the United States.

8 Before the advent of European colonizers, Arabic, Urdu, and Sanskrit were the languages of the elites because they were taught only to upper class-caste Indians, but during colonization, India's ruling classes added English to their linguistic repertoire due to their interactions with the British. However, substantial debate about the desirability of English arose in the nineteenth century. Indian Orientalists favored Indian languages, and Anglicists or Occidentalists supported English, leading to a rift between intellectuals and British administrators. But the controversy ended when Thomas Babington Macaulay—who served in numerous government positions in England, including as Secretary of War, and held a seat on the Supreme Council of India between 1834 and 1838—published his "Minute on Indian Education" (1835) in which he called for the creation of an English-speaking Indian class of interpreters. This resulted in the adoption of English as India's official language. Sociolinguistics argue that this created an Anglophone subculture in India, rendering English a marker of elitist schooling, the key to powerful government positions, and an entrée into upper-class status. Nonelites did not favor English, and their dissatisfaction over linguistic policy was among the grievances that led to the unsuccessful Revolution of 1857. Today, upper-class parents pay heavy fees to send their children to English-language schools, while government schools provide instruction in Bengali, Hindi, or other regional languages. Students in these schools have poor English skills, and this is an impediment when they pursue higher education.

9 Dating to the colonial era, India's English-language readership was familiar with oblique and implicit references to homosexuality in fiction; however, after independence, homophobia emerged in public discourses, with debates about, for example, *Chocolate and Other Writings on Male Homoeroticism* by Pandey Bechan Sharma, a 1927 collection of eight stories that was the first Hindi fiction to focus on male same-sex relationships. Many prominent figures, including Gandhi, weighed in on the controversy, which lasted into the 1950s.

10 These relationships are considered incestuous because in Indian contexts the concept of family is expansive—the kinship network is heavily populated, so a sexual relationship with a distant relation would be incestuous.

11 Known by a myriad of names, including *khwaja sara, khusra, zenana, jhanka, khusa,* transgender, and transsexual, *hijras* are often men who have chosen to be castrated, have not fully developed sex organs at puberty, or were born hermaphrodites. They may also be biologically female and choose to live as males, or they may occupy an ambiguous sexual "identity" that has no parallel among western sexual categories. Neither men nor women, *hijras* have been considered members of a third sex in South Asia for the last three thousand years. At the same time, some *hijras* do not identify as a third sexual category outside the male/female binary. Instead they display mannerisms and signs of femininity that at times combine with traditionally masculine traits and behaviors. Furthermore, *hijras* do not always consider individual expressions of desire the sole defining feature of their lives. Instead, their histories move us toward an understanding of how sexuality is implicated in religion, community networks, and class. *Hijra* communities are present in both Hindu and Islamic enclaves in South Asia. Hindu scripture identifies gods who embody aspects of both male and female, like Lord Shiva who in his incarnation as Ardhanarishvara is half woman and who became the female Parvati, his wife and goddess of fertility, in the course of love play. In the *Mahābhārata*, Vishnu, another male god, is transfigured into Mohini, an enchantress who entraps her male lovers, dooming them to ill-fated endings. Hindu *hijras'* lineage is said to derive from the female goddess Mata Bahuchara, who, as legend has it, cut off her breast to save her virtue. Serina Nanda's book *Neither Man nor Woman: The Hijras of India* (1999) argues that the sanctity of this goddess is the source

of *hijras'* powers to curse or to confer blessings on male infants. In Pakistan, Muslim *hijras* are legitimated by Sura 42:49 of the Qur'an, which states, "To Allah belongs the dominion of the heavens and the earth; He creates what he wills. He gives to whom He wills female [children], and He gives to whom He wills males," and 42:50, "Or He makes them [both] males and females, and He renders whom He wills barren. Indeed, He is Knowing and Competent."

WORKS CITED

Faderman, Lillian. *Surpassing the Love of Men: Romantic Friendship and Love between Women from the Renaissance to the Present.* 1981. Harper Collins, 2001.

Koushal v. NAZ Foundation. "Civil Appeal 110792 et al. Supreme Court of India." *Judgements: The Judgements Information System*, 2013, judis.nic.in/supremecourt/imgs1.aspx?filename=41070. Accessed 31 Aug. 2016.

Macaulay, Thomas Babington. "Minute Recorded in the General Department by Thomas Babington Macaulay, Law Member of the Governor-General's Council Dated 2 Feb. 1835." *The Great Indian Education Debate: Documents Relating to the Orientalist-Anglicist Controversy, 1778–1843*. Curzon, 1999. Edited by Martin Moir and Lynn Zastoupil, Routledge, 2013, pp. 161–73.

Mishra, Richa. "Section 498 IPC." *Legal Service India*, http://www.legalserviceindia.com/article/l336-Section-498-IPC.html. Accessed 31 Aug. 2016.

Nanda, Serina. *Neither Man nor Woman: The Hijras of India.* 1990. 2nd ed., Cengage, 1999.

"NCW Rejects Proposal to Punish Women for Adultery." *The Hindu*, 26 Dec. 2006, http://www.thehindu.com/todays-paper/tp-national/ncw-rejects-proposal-to-punish-women-for-adultery/article3038719.ece. Accessed 31 Aug. 2016.

Pattanaik, Devdutt. "Did Homosexuality Exist in Ancient India." 2000. *Devdutt*, devdutt.com/blog/did-homosexuality-exist-in-ancient-india.html. Accessed 31 Aug. 2016.

Sharma, Pandey Bechan. *Chocolate and Other Writings on Male Homoeroticism*. Translated by Ruth Vanita, Duke UP, 2009.

Smith, Patricia Juliana. "'And I Wondered if She Might Kiss Me': Lesbian Panic as Narrative Strategy in British Women's Fiction." *Modern Fiction Studies*, vol. 41, no. 3–4, 1995, pp. 567–607.

Sood, Keval. *Murgikhana*. Shilalekh, 2013.

Vatsyayana. *Kama Sutra: A Guide to the Art of Pleasure*. Translated by A. N. D. Haksar, Penguin, 2011.

Venkatesan, J. "Women Can't Be Prosecuted for Adultery: Supreme Court." *The Hindu*. 5 Dec. 2011, http://www.thehindu.com/todays-paper/tp-national/women-cant-be-prosecuted-for-adultery-supreme-court/article2687809.ece. Accessed 31 Aug. 2016.

AFTERWORD

DEVALEENA DAS AND COLETTE MORROW

Eurocentrism is like white privilege—those who are entrenched in it don't feel it and can't recognize it without sustained, conscious effort. Nevertheless, Eurocentrism is omnipresent in the West, as Ella Shohat and Robert Stam write in *Rethinking Eurocentrism: Multiculturalism and the Media*, and we argue that it dominates intellectual production worldwide. By this, we mean that with rare exception, Eurocentrism determines modes of knowledge production and their outcomes—that is, the interpretations that knowledge-making processes engender and, equally importantly, the material consequences that these interpretations yield through practical application, whether they relate to political or economic policy, civil engineering, agricultural practices, or the less tangible, such as subject constitution. In other words, Eurocentrism, now propagated by the continent's "New World" surrogates, for example, in the form of "US exceptionalism," as well as Europe per se, establishes *how and what we know*, and this affects the material realities of our lives, regardless of geographic or social location.

To understand the pervasiveness and effects of Eurocentrism in intellectual production, we must first consider what it entails. Shohat and Sham offer a useful overview of Eurocentrism that explains it is not merely a frame through which the West views the world, though it is that. Eurocentrism, like Orientalism, came into being in order to justify European colonialism. Not unexpectedly, then, Eurocentrism is rooted in the idea that the world is on an ever improving projectory and that this progress is due to the West's leadership. Eurocentrism thus celebrates democracy and claims it is indigenous to the West but trivializes or ignores failures in democracy caused by Western nations or within them, as illustrated by the lack of consensus in the United States that (allegedly) torturing and indefinitely detaining suspected terrorists in Guantanamo Bay is a human rights violation. One of the strategies that Eurocentrism uses to minimize its responsibility for such failures—police brutality in the United States, European governments' willful disregard for refugees fleeing Middle Eastern violence, anti-Semitism and Islamophobia, to name just a few—is to characterize them as anomalies, or minor glitches in an otherwise sound, humane system. To Shohat and Stam's list, we add the characteristic that Eurocentrism does not acknowledge how it benefits from such failures—for instance, refusing to admit that its current wealth and power are to a large extent attributable to colonialism and practices associated with it, such as slavery.

In addition to these general operations and traits, performances of Eurocentrism in specific spheres such as "the academy," institutions of learning and education, manifest other troubling features. For one thing, Eurocentrism rejects work by and on colonized peoples as irrelevant (Araújo and Maeso), which, despite some cosmetic changes to the canon in US schools since the 1980s, is evidenced by the erasure of so-called minorities and non-Europeans from the curriculum. Rarely, for example, are students in composition courses instructed to imagine a diverse audience for their essays, and the white, heterosexual, middle-class male is still the default citizen, client, customer, patient, or subject regardless of the discipline, with the exception of ethnic/multicultural studies, women's, gender, and sexuality studies. Worse yet, recent attempts to Christianize the public school curriculum by teaching creationism as science and to erase the history of slavery from textbooks by referring to slaves as "workers" and the transatlantic slave trade as "Atlantic triangular trade" have gained ground in some US states during the 2010s.

Furthermore, Eurocentrism fetishizes science (72), not merely privileging it but stipulating that it is *the* (singular) way of knowing the world, which constitutes intellectual totalitarianism and is, argues Jasbir Puar following Michel Foucault, a regulatory practice of constant monitoring, assessment, and control: "Through scientific observation, classification and taxonomy, the production of data, detail, and description, leading to the micromanagement of information and bodies" (25). Esoteric, obfuscating theorization is also a mark of Eurocentrism, Rey Chow implies in *The Protestant Ethnic and the Spirit of Capitalism* when he complains that it constructs Europeans as subjects and Others as objects (2–3). He further suggests that both these means of apprehension—scientific method and systematically abstruse explanations of the world—profit a specifically European consciousness or sense of self, presumably at a cost to the non-European Other: "The increasing objectification of the world . . . [is] part of an ongoing imperialist agenda for transforming the world into observable and hence manageable units, and the intensification of abstract theoretical processes, likewise, must be seen as inseparable from the historical conditions that repeatedly return the material benefits of such processes to European subjectivities" (3).

Unveiling Desire strives to resist such Eurocentrism, but as we conclude this book, we are more aware than ever of how all-encompassing it can be. Paradoxically, our attempts to project the voices of writers and scholars into the West where their words and works typically are excluded from Western curricula remind us of the difficulties involved in this task, even unto mundane decisions involved in preparing the manuscript—whether to provide a footnote explaining a concept likely to be unfamiliar to a US reader or to adhere to the "Eastern" convention of referring to a historical or literary figure by first name rather than surname. These considerations pale in comparison to the philosophical and ideological issues that have challenged us. For instance, we are aware that at this juncture in the evolution of literary and critical theories, concerns are emerging about the paradigms that we have employed to discuss Eastern literary, filmic, and cultural production. For example, Puar contends that the practice of looking at contingencies is now so common "that attending to the specificity of others has ironically become a universalizing project" (203). Second, chapters in *Unveiling Desire* examine and often celebrate women's transgressiveness, yet we are conscious that this might reinforce notions of freedom and individuality as superior to communalistic subjectivities, an error that we eschew because it is, well, so Eurocentric, for the ability to transgress hinges on a sense of self as autonomous, individuated and agentized. Likewise, resistance to regulatory gender norms, a maneuver that the chapters in *Unveiling Desire* examine as well as enact, might actually reinforce these controls, according to Puar: "Transgression (which is one step ahead of resistance, which has now become a normative act) relies on a normative notion of deviance, always defined in relation to normativity, often universalizing. Thus deviance, despite its claims to freedom and individuality, is ironically cohered to and by regulatory regimes . . . through, not despite, any claims to transgression" (22–23). Perhaps. But we are also conscious that both the historical and the fictional characters that chapters in *Unveiling Desire* investigate would not be known to us today if not for their transgressions and resistance, which justifies our project even as we acknowledge its risks. Furthermore, as transnational feminists with not a small degree of class consciousness, we are aware that Puar's critique of contingency-focused analysis assumes that it routinely operates outside the confines of literary and critical theory, the most elite of the scholarly discourses, and is a widespread, habitual praxis. However, this is not yet the case in less rarefied academic discourses, for classroom praxis, public conversation, and applied scholarship continue to resist such specificity, sometimes because of the pressures of institutionalization and often because access to this information continues to be limited in the United States, which itself justifies *Unveiling Desire*'s interest in excavating the local and contingent. Finally, we remain convinced that we must name oppression in order to end it—and continue to develop our own critical consciousness as we invite others to join us in this ongoing, sometimes painful, often exhilarating praxis of "being-in-community."

WORKS CITED

Araújo, Marta, and Sylvia Maeso. "Eurocentrism, Political Struggles and the Entrenched Will-to-Ignorance: An Introduction." *Eurocentrism, Racism, and Knowledge: Debates on History and*

Power in Europe and the Americas, edited by Marta Araújo and Sylvia Maeso, Palgrave Macmillan, 2015, pp. 1–22.

Chow, Rey. *The Protestant Ethnic and the Spirit of Capitalism*. Columbia UP, 2002.

Puar, Jasbir K. *Terrorist Assemblages: Homonationalism in Queer Times*. Duke UP, 2007.

Shohat, Ella, and Robert Stam. *Unthinking Eurocentrism: Multiculturalism and the Media*. Routledge, 2014.

CONTRIBUTORS

FIRDOUS AZIM is the chair of the Department of English and Humanities at BRAC University in Dhaka, Bangladesh. She obtained her PhD at the University of Sussex, UK, in 1989 and is also a member of Naripokkho, a women's activist organization in Bangladesh. A Fulbright fellow, Azim has published in the field of postcolonialism and on feminist issues. Her books include *The Novel's Imperial Past: Subjectivity and Sexuality in the Fictional Writings of Charlotte Bronte* (University of Sussex, 1989), *The Colonial Rise of the Novel* (Routledge, 1993), and *Infinite Variety: Women in Society and Literature* (UP Limited, Dhaka, 1996). She is a contributing editor for *Feminist Review* and also edited *Complex Terrains: Islam, Culture and Women in Asia* (Routledge, March 2013) and has coedited several books, including *Infinite Variety: Women in Society and Literature* (UP Limited, 1994) and *Other Englishes: Essays on Commonwealth Writing* (UP Limited, 1991).

LAVINIA BENEDETTI obtained her doctorate at Tsinghua University of Beijing and she is currently a researcher of Chinese language and literature at the University of Catania where she teaches Chinese. Her area of interest is Chinese court-case literature (*gong'an xiaoshuo*). Her forthcoming book is about the history of court-case literature in premodern China.

LOUIS BETTY is an assistant professor of French at the University of Wisconsin at Whitewater. His book *Without God: Michel Houellebecq and Materialist Horror* was published by Penn State Press in 2016. He has published numerous peer-reviewed articles on Michel Houellebecq and was UW-System Fellow at the Institute for Research in the Humanities at UW–Madison in fall 2014. His PhD (2011) is from Vanderbilt University.

CHANDRANI BISWAS is an associate professor in the Department of English at St. Xavier's University, Kolkata, India, and chaired the department from 2009 to 2013. She is the author of the monograph *Women and War: A Study of the Novels of Emecheta, Ekwensi and Amadi* (Books Plus, 1998). Biswas completed her doctoral degree at Jadavpur University and published numerous peer-reviewed articles on women in African literature and in South Asian culture.

RADHA CHAKRAVARTY is a critic, translator, and an associate professor of English Literature at Gargi College, University of Delhi. She has coedited *The Essential Tagore* (Harvard and Visva Bharati), an anthology of Rabindranath Tagore's works that was nominated for Book of the Year 2011 by Martha Nussbaum. She is the author of *Feminism and Contemporary Women Writers* (Routledge, 2008) and *Novelist Tagore: Modernity and Gender in Selected Texts* (Routledge, 2013) and editor of *Shades of Difference: Selected Writings of Rabindranath Tagore* (Social Science Press). Her translations of Tagore include *Gora, Chokher Bali, Boyhood Days, Farewell Song: Shesher Kabita,* and *The Land of Cards: Stories, Poems and Plays for Children.* Other works in translation are Bankim Chandra Chatterjee's *Kapalkundala* and Mahasweta Devi's *In the Name of the Mother, Vermillion Clouds: Stories by Bengali Women,* and *Crossings: Stories from Bangladesh and India.* She edited *Bodymaps: Stories by South Asian Women* and coedited *Writing Feminism: South Asian Voices and Writing Freedom: South Asian Voices.* She was nominated for the Crossword Translation Award in 2004.

KUHU SHARMA CHANANA is an associate professor of English literature at the University of Delhi. She has written three books: *D. H. Lawrence* and the *Poetic Novel, An Evening Rainbow: Queer Writings in Bhasha Literatures* (Queer Ink, 2015), and *LGBTQ Culture in Modern Indian Literature* (D. K. Printworld). She has published various peer-reviewed articles on facets of feminism and alternative sexuality and edited a special issue of *Indian Literature* dealing with same-sex love fiction. She is also a recipient of the Charles Wallace Trust Fellowship (Edinburgh University).

DEVALEENA DAS is a lecturer in gender and women's studies and a research fellow at the Institute for Research in the Humanities, University of Wisconsin–Madison. Prior to joining UW–Madison, Das was an assistant professor of English at Jesus and Mary College, University of Delhi. She earned her PhD from the Department of English, University of Calcutta. In 2009, she received an Endowment Foreign Travel Fellowship for her research to work at University of Queensland, Brisbane. Her current monograph, *Body Parts and Bodily Integrity,* focuses on representations of female body parts in feminist arts across culture and race. She has published peer-reviewed articles on transnational feminism in leading journals, and her books include *Critical Study of Nathaniel Hawthorne's* The Scarlet Letter (Atlantic Press, 2014), *Critical Essays on Alice Walker's* Color Purple (Pencraft International, 2014), and *Claiming Space: Australian Women's Writing* (Palgrave Macmillan, forthcoming, 2017).

NAINA DEY is an associate professor of English at University of Calcutta. She is a critic, translator, reviewer, and creative writer, and her works have appeared in newspapers, books, and academic peer-reviewed journals. Her book, *Real and Imagined Women: The Feminist Fiction of Virginia Woolf and Fay Weldon,* was published by Calcutta UP in 2011, and she has edited critical anthologies on Shakespeare's *Macbeth,* Christopher Marlowe's *Edward the Second,* and Virginia Woolf's *A Room of One's Own.*

NAWAL EL-SAADAWI is an Egyptian feminist writer, activist, physician, and psychiatrist. Some of her popular books on the subject of women in Islam are *Woman at Point Zero, God Dies by the Nile, A Daughter of Isis, Zeina, Two Women in One, The Fall of the Imam, Memoirs of a Woman Doctor,* and *The Hidden Face of*

Eve. She is the founder and president of the Arab Women's Solidarity Association and cofounder of the Arab Association for Human Rights and has been awarded honorary degrees on three continents. She is the founder of the Health Education Association and the Egyptian Women Writers Association and served as chief editor for *Health Magazine* in Cairo and editor for *Medical Association Magazine*.

AMRIT GANGAR is an Indian film scholar, historian, critic, curator, and writer living in Mumbai, Maharashtra. He is involved in establishing India's first film museum, the National Museum of Indian Cinema. Working in cinema for more than three decades, Gangar is responsible for developing a new theoretical concept, "Cinema of Prayoga," which aims to replace and expand the generally accepted Euro-American-centric term of "experimental film," and has been lecturing on it in various venues in and outside India.

PARAMITA HALDER is the chair of the Department of English at Gurudas Mahavidyalay. Her area of specialization is partition literature and gender studies. She earned her PhD from Kalyani University, India. She has published several peer-reviewed essays in international journals.

FEROZA JUSSAWALLA is a professor of English at the University of New Mexico in Albuquerque, New Mexico. She is the editor of *Conversations with V. S. Naipaul* (UP of Mississippi, 1997) and *Emerging South Asian Women Writers Essays and Interviews* (Peter Lang, 2015) and coeditor of *Interviews with Writers of the Post-Colonial World* (UP of Mississippi, 1992). She is also the author of a collection of poems entitled *Chiffon Saris* (Writers Workshop, 2003).

HAFIZA NILOFAR KHAN is a recipient of the East West Center scholarship and the PEO International Peace scholarship. She earned her PhD at the University of Southern Mississippi in 2008 and specializes in postcolonial literature, South Asian literature, and women's studies. She has served as the chair of the Department of English and Modern Languages at Independent University, Bangladesh.

TOMOKO KURIBAYASHI is a professor of English at the University of Wisconsin–Stevens Point. She earned her master's degree and PhD from the Universities of Tokyo, Alberta, and Minnesota and has taught courses in literature, composition, and women's studies in Minnesota, Vermont, and Wisconsin for the last twenty years. She specializes in contemporary fiction, mainly by women and minority writers from the United States, Canada, and Great Britain, and has coedited a collection of articles on women writers entitled *Creating Safe Space: Violence and Women's Writing* (SUNY P, 1998). She has also researched twentieth-century Japanese women writers and has edited a collection of articles on the subject, *The Outsider Within: Ten Essays on Modern Japanese Women Writers* (UPA, 2002). She is currently researching works by contemporary Canadian writers Margaret Atwood and Alice Munro.

MEENAKSHI MALHOTRA is an associate professor of English Literature at Hansraj College, University of Delhi, India. She has published peer-reviewed articles on gender and literary theory. Her PhD is from Jawharlal Nehru University, and she specializes in nineteenth- and twentieth-century women's autobiography. Additionally, Malhotra has been actively involved in framing and writing course material for the master's degrees in gender studies at Indira Gandhi National Open University and Ambedkar University.

COLETTE MORROW is an associate professor of English at Purdue University Northwest (formerly Purdue University Calumet). She is the former president of the National Women's Studies Association and a Senior Fulbright Scholar, and she has worked to develop women's and gender studies in universities in Eastern Europe and South Asia. She earned her PhD in English at Texas Christian University and has served on the board of *Feminist Formations* (formerly the *NWSA Journal*). She coedited (with Sue Rosser) *Feminist Formations'* retrospective book series, which includes her coedited book (with Terri Ann Fredrick) *Getting in Is Not Enough: Women in the Global Workplace* (Johns Hopkins UP, 2012).

INDEX

CPSIA information can be obtained
at www.ICGtesting.com
Printed in the USA
LVOW07s0332031217
558378LV00005B/16/P

9 780813 587844